Martha's
SEWING ROOM
Series 400

Martha's Attic

Program Guide For Public TV Series-400

by Martha Campbell Pullen, Ph.D.

May God Bless You

Martha Pullen

Book Team

Book Design: *Ann Le Roy*
Contributing Sewing Designers: *Kathy Brower, Charlotte Gallaher, Kathy McMakin,*
Claudia Newton, Sue Pennington, Gail Settle and Margaret Taylor
Construction Consultant and Editor: *Kathy McMakin*
Illustrated By: *Kris Broom, Kathy Brower, Tina McEwen and Angela Pullen*
Other Sewing Contributors: *Louise Baird, Dody Baker, Elda Bratager,*
Westa Chandler, Childern's Corner, Suzanne Crocker, Kathy Ghorashi, Kathy
Harrison, Marie Hendon, Mary Penton, Susie Price, Esther Randall, Patty Smith,
Rhonda Smith, Mary Soltice, Laura Jenkins Thompson, Aritta York, Susan York
Photography: *Jack Cooper Photography, Huntsville, Alabama*
Photo Stylists: *Claudia Newton, Margaret Taylor*

Printed By
The C.J. Krehbiel Company
Cincinnati, Ohio

Published And Distributed By
Martha Pullen Company, Inc.

518 Madison Street
Huntsville, Alabama 35801-4286

Phone 205-533-9586
Fax 205-533-9630

Library of Congress Catalog Card Number 96-920960

ISBN 1-878048-06-6

Dedication

To Mark Edward Pullen and his family; Sherry Ann Green, Morgan Ross and Bradley

God has blessed me in my lifetime with more than I ever imagined possible. One of those greatest blessings is my son, Mark Edward Pullen. When I married Joe, I got two wonderful sons and didn't even have to gain fifty pounds to get them. Mark and Jeff were in the fifth and fourth grades when Joe and I married in 1974. I loved them at first sight and I love them even more today. Since the last book was dedicated to Jeff, I'll make this one about Mark.

Mark was born the great communicator. Always having a way with words and influence, he is a great listener as well as talker. He knows how to ask questions and show compassion and concern for other people. I remember when he was a little boy he loved National Geographic magazines. With this early love of science it certainly seems appropriate that he continued this love into the study of dentistry. He loved animals from gerbils to guinea pigs to dogs.

Mark's love of literature was evident at an early age also. In the house on Cliffmanor, Mark had quite a collection of model airplanes and cars. His manual dexterity was evident from an early age since he could put together the most complicated of model figures. I was in complete amazement at his ability to figure out these boxes of pieces and get them together.

Mark always loved chocolate Coca Cola cake for his birthday; he still does. Sherry Ann was so sweet the first year they were married to call me for my recipe for "Mark's special cake."

After finishing his senior year at Huntsville High School, Mark went to Birmingham Southern College to study pre-dentistry. He pledged Sigma Alpha Episolon and thoroughly loved both college and his fraternity. His grades were excellent and he was accepted to The University of Alabama Dental School on his first application.

When Mark was a senior at Birmingham Southern, he met Sherry Ann Green who was also a student there. Mark had always had lots of girlfriends but never one that he liked for very long. All of a sudden, we were hearing about this beautiful girl with the green eyes that captivated him. He began to go on the weekends to Gadsden and we began to hear about her wonderful family. Telling us about her mother's cooking was a regular event. We fell in love with Sherry Ann when we first met her and completely understood his settling down to one girl. Sherry Ann was only eighteen when she met Mark and he was the final guy that she ever dated.

They married during her senior year at Birmingham Southern and his senior year in dental school. It was a very exciting day when Mark graduated from dental school. Becoming the third generation Pullen to practice dentistry in Huntsville was something that the whole family had dreamed about. We only wish that Pop Pullen could have lived to see that graduation ceremony. When Mark began to practice dentistry with him, Joe said, "This is the most exciting part of my dental career. Having Mark with me makes dentistry better than it ever has been. Mark is the great communicator and his practice has grown very, very quickly. Everybody loves Dr. Mark, even the little children."

Choosing to be a full time Mom and wife is Sherry Ann's chosen occupation and she does a wonderful job of both. Our first granddaughter is Morgan Ross Pullen and what a doll baby she is. She can speak full sentences at age three and she loves to paint and color. She loves to play kitchen and dolls. What a little girl she is! Loving her story books is another favorite activity. She also enjoys going to Pioneers (Skippers) with her grandmother since her Nannie is one of the teachers.

Two years later, Amanda Bradley Pullen was born. She is a little laughing girl and smiles all the time. She also loves books and playing with her big sister. She looks exactly like Mark and Morgan Ross looks exactly like Sherry Ann; they are both gorgeous. Is that spoken like a true grandmother? They love their smocked and French dresses and their Nannie loves making them or having them made for them.

Sherry Ann's mother Sherry is an excellent seamstress; however, Sherry Ann had never sewn until Morgan Ross was born. She began to smock and French sew and her work is perfection quality. I was so thrilled over her first Heirloom Party Dress which she completed after only one class with Dody Baker.

Sherry Ann is a member of the Junior League of Huntsville, the Gothic Guild, and the Constitution Village Society. She has volunteered at the Huntsville Botanical Gardens and she and Mark teach a middle school group of kids at First United Methodist Church. Called Mission Possible, this Bible study group is involved in service projects as part of their study at church. A former ballerina, she goes to the health club daily and keeps fit as a fiddle and trim as a pencil. She keeps a perfect house and entertains beautifully. I really don't know how she does all that she does and takes care of two babies at the same time.

Mark is an usher, a teacher and member of the planning committee at First United Methodist Church. He is a member of the Optimist Club of Huntsville, the Red Elephant Club and the Quarterback Club. He also enjoys the health club and works out on a regular basis. It thrills me so much to hear Mark and Sherry Ann talk about their work with the church and about their dependence on the Lord.

It is so exciting to have Mark, Sherry Ann, Morgan Ross and Bradley living in Huntsville. Joe and I talk a lot about the blessing of having three of our grown children and their families living in our same town. Almost every day, Joe tells me how much he enjoys working with Mark and about how proud he is of his excellent dentistry. Since the patients love him so much, that thrills Joe also. I love having my two little girls run in my office to tell me some important news. I love their little art projects which they share often with Nannie. Beyond wonderful would be my description on my being able to attend their grandparents events at the church. I love for them to come in my kitchen and look in the candy drawer to find a little goodie. Please don't tell their dentist grandfather and father that Nannie keeps a candy drawer.

It was a fortunate day for me when Mark Pullen became my son. He is precious to me and I love him very much. Marrying the beautiful Sherry Ann and having Morgan Ross and Bradley are his best accomplishments! I thank him for his love and support for me throughout his lifetime and he has brought me such joy. He is smart, gentle, funny, supportive and kind. This book is dedicated with much love to my son, Mark and his family, Sherry Ann, Morgan Ross and Bradley. ▨

Acknowledgments

"Blessed are the men whose strength is in thee, in whose heart are the highways to Zion." Psalms 84:5

I love the Psalms. Knowing that God is faithful is the most important thing in my life. Walking with God in the good times is easy. Knowing that God is faithful during my bad times is comforting. I love that story, Footprints, about God's carrying one through the bad times. There have been so many times in my life that God simply picked me up and carried me through because I wasn't able to do it myself. Isn't it wonderful that God is willing and able to carry us through each day, the good and the bad? He gives me the means to walk down the paths, but I must do the walking. I must obey God in all that I do and always give Him the praise and glory. This business belongs to God and it is He that has picked up the pieces time after time and shown us the next direction. I thank Him and praise Him for everything in my life.

Developing a television series for public television has been a dream of mine for many years, and without the help of God, my family, friends and staff, it would never have happened. I am forever grateful to the following people:

My mother and father, Anna Ruth Dicus Campbell and the late Paul Jones Campbell were my first and greatest teachers. Their example of living a Godly, decent, and hard-working life certainly formed my attitude toward life and what should and could be accomplished. I love them and I thank them.

My children, Camp and Charisse, John and Suzanne, Mark and Sherry Ann, Jeff and Angela and Joanna have always loved me and believed in me. I love them all, and I am so proud of them.

My grandchildren have to be the most beautiful, the smartest, the cutest, and the most creative in the world! Isn't that spoken like a true grandmother? To Campbell, Morgan Ross, Sarah Joy, Rebekah, Marshall and Bradley—I love you dearly, and I thank you for coming into my life bringing such pure joy!

My sisters and brothers-Mary, Dottie, Cliff, and Robin-and their families are beautiful individuals whom I love very much. Brothers and sisters are gifts from God who grow more precious with every year.

The University of Alabama has been a real cornerstone in my educational life. My first degree was awarded from this institution in 1965. In 1972, the College of Education offered me enough money for an assistantship making it possible for me to return to my alma mater to attend graduate school full time. I received my Ph.D. in 1977. To have "my" university as my partner in this television series demonstrates that once more, this great institution was there to help me achieve my goals. I am grateful for all that the University of Alabama means to me and my family.

Tom Rieland, Director, Center for Public Television, Alabama Public Television at the University of Alabama, returned my call very quickly when I contacted several states about the possibility of filming a public television series about sewing! Without his vision, this series and this book would not have been possible. Tom, you certainly started this dream on the track of possibilities.

Dwight Cameron, Program Director, University of Alabama Center For Public Television, was there to hear my ideas when we first visited Tuscaloosa with two suitcases full of clothing, quilts, and projects. Dwight is unshakable and very creative. Dwight, thanks for believing in me and in creative sewing.

Mike Letcher, Production Manager, University of Alabama, Center For Public Television, has been uplifting and helpful in the meticulous planning of this series. He carefully explained the necessity of sitting down and planning every minute of 26 shows two months before filming.

Bill Teague of the University of Alabama Theatre Department has worked long and hard building the wonderful set which houses *Martha's Sewing Room*. I love the stairs which lead to Martha's Attic. I've been talking about Martha's Attic all these years; now I even have one on my television show.

Dawn Leach and Vince Pruitt, graphics designers with the University of Alabama Center for Public Television, have captured the essence of *Martha's Sewing Room* with their graphics to introduce and close each show and to divide the sections of the show. Their research into the "feel" of heirloom sewing is greatly appreciated.

I am appreciative to the Southern Educational Communications Association (SECA) for choosing to air *Martha's Sewing Room* on their satellite. I am especially grateful to the SECA President, Skip Hinton and to the SECA Program Director, Chuck McConnell. Because of Chuck's advice to me a couple of years ago, I believe my performance on this television series is much better than it would have been if he hadn't taken the time to give me an honest evaluation.

Judy Stone and Henry Bonner of Alabama Public Television have offered nothing but encouragement about *Martha's Sewing Room*. They have done everything possible to share the joy of *Martha's Sewing Room* with other television networks. APT was the first television network in the U.S. to air the series and I thank them for being great partners.

I want to thank every television station throughout the whole country which has run *Martha's Sewing Room*. The program directors make decisions concerning which shows will air and which ones do not. We are grateful for every program director who chose us!

My business could not be a reality without the talents of many people. I have dedicated staff who has helped me produce this show and write this book. I love them and I appreciate them.

Kathy Pearce, Toni Duggar, Lakanjala Campbell, Angie Daniel, Amy Duggar, Camp Crocker and Leighann Simmons have kept the business running while others worked on this book!

Camp Crocker, my son who is in business with me, dreamed of this television show first. He believed that we could do it and insisted that we begin the process several years ago when I didn't think it could possibly happen. I thank him for his vision for not only this television show but for many other creative endeavors in this business.

Patti Smith has always been available to sew clothing for all of our publications. She works with great creativity, speed and enthusiasm even when we ask her to sew 40 things in two days.

Louise Baird creates such gorgeous things with a sewing machine. She always helps us sew and plan, never complaining about deadlines.

Seeley's Doll Company gave us permission to use their doll bodies for the pattern drafting section of this book. They have been wonderful to work with.

Tom Azuma made some of the gorgeous dolls which you see on *Martha's Sewing Room*. Of course, they have a Seeley's body!

Elda Bratager's doll clothing is absolutely fabulous. She designs, cuts, sews with the greatest of ease, it seems. She also made some of the dolls featured on this series.

The Bernina, Elna, Pfaff, Singer and Viking sewing machine companies have been with me from the beginning of *Sew Beautiful* magazine. They have invited me to teach at their national and international conventions, they have always advertised in the magazine, they have sent in hundreds of sewing machines for my schools here in Huntsville, they have sent educators to teach with us, they have planned for our traveling schools with their dealers over the world, and they have opened many doors for me. We appreciate their willingness to allow us to use their machines alternately on this television series. I consider this to be the ultimate in cooperation among companies. Each one of these companies is as wonderful as their machines, and I am very grateful not only to the corporate offices but also to the wonderful dealers around the world who have supported me and my business.

Susan York, Patti Smith, Rhonda Smith, Laura Jenkins Thompson, Kathy Ghorashi, Mary Soltice, Louise Baird, Dody Baker, Mary Penton, Gail Settle, Sue Pennington, The Children's Corner, Claudia Newton and Margaret Taylor loaned us garment after garment for our beautiful clothing for the introductory section of each show. Each of them have helped this endeavor in so many different ways.

My daughter, Joanna Pullen, modeled for the wedding show and was very patient during the fittings. She was the original inspiration for this whole business and she has been a vital part of all aspects.

Gail Settle designed and made pillows and crafts with such flair. Her work is so exciting and fresh.

Charlotte Gallaher has such creative ability. She made some of our boxes and crafts.

Aritta York has been one of the leaders in the world in smocking. Her baby music pillow and smocked design are precious.

Marie Hendon has helped us in so many aspects of our business for many years. Her sewing is wonderful.

Claudia Newton's work at a sewing machine is unbelievable. She's made clothing and pillows that take my breath away.

Louise Baird stitched the shadow applique squares and constructed the whole quilt. She has become a great little television star and demonstrates techniques like no one else can.

Margaret Boyles has been teaching with me for over 12 years. It is such a pleasure to have her demonstrate embroidery for the viewing audience.

Sue Pennington designed doll dresses, pillows, garments and "story boards" for the series. She stitched until all hours of the night helping us meet deadlines. I truly don't know what I would do in this business without her.

Suzanne Crocker stitched quilt squares with great mastery. She took Kathy Brower's designs and embellished them with love and beauty.

Jack Cooper's photography is professional and creative. He has such patience in working with little people.

Cynthia Handy-Quintella is much appreciated for the lovely illustrations on lace shaping.

Angela Pullen's drawings add life and magic to all of our books. Her illustrations have great depth, detail, and creativity. She always meets deadlines and never complains about the boxes of work that we send her.

Ann Le Roy's book design is creative and lends a professional touch to all of the sections. It is not an easy task to take hundreds of drawings and computer disks of information and create a book out of it. To have an element of style and beauty in addition to correctness of directions and pictures is quite a feat. It overwhelms me to think of all the decisions which she had to make concerning the layout of this book.

Margaret Taylor stitched the heirloom quilt, wrote directions on several sections, prepared items for the television show "how-to" portions and in general helped with everything. Margaret is always there with her talent in many different areas. I also think she is a great television teacher.

Kathy McMakin's pattern drafting, construction ideas, technical writing skills and designing/sewing ability make her invaluable to every aspect of this business. She literally helped with every part of this book from direction writing to sewing and serging. Her contributions to this television series program guide are vast. Now her talents include television teaching and she does a great job of it all.

Kris Broom's designing and drawing ability for the "how-to" sections absolutely amaze me. Not only are her illustrations gorgeous, she knows how to draw everything in the construction sequence by just looking at the craft.

Kathy Brower illustrated many of the "how-to" sections and wrote part of the directions including the entire silk ribbon section . I also think she is a wonderful "T.V. Star" when she teaches her silk ribbon segments.

There is one person to whom I am especially grateful. Next to God, he has been my faithful advisor, my financial partner, my idea person, and my mentor. My husband, Joe Ross Pullen, has always believed in me more than I believe in myself. He is a wonderful dentist and has been one of the worldwide pioneers in implant dentistry. He is a wonderful Christian husband and father, and God blessed me beyond my wildest imaginations the day that Joe asked me to marry him. He is my best friend and my partner; I love him, and I thank him.

A number of years ago, I gave this whole business to God. He took it, figured out what to do next, and has given the guidance for moving in the directions in which we are moving. All the credit and glory for any success that we have had in the sewing industry go to Him and Him alone. The path has not been nor is it now an easy one. I don't think He promised us an easy trip through life. He did promise to be with us always and I can testify that He has never failed me. ✼

Special Thanks To Our Underwriters

It is so exciting to have completed the 300 and 400 series of *Martha's Sewing Room!* Dreaming of producing a television series for PBS had been in my mind for many years. Having that dream come true is a blessing from God! Your response to this television series has been greatly appreciated and we are running on all or part of the public television stations in at least 44 states of this great United States of America! Many people helped this dream come true. Six of those "people" are actually companies who believed in this series enough to underwrite with great generosity! I thank them, and I believe in their products or I wouldn't have asked them to be the underwriters.

When you need notions please give consideration to calling Clotilde! Her catalogue is all inclusive for heirloom sewing and other types of sewing also! When you stitch with silk ribbon, wool thread or other types of decorative threads, please give consideration to choosing YLI brands! You won't be sorry! When you need to purchase a sewing machine cabinet, please look for the Parsons name! You will love the Martha Pullen cabinet! When you need scissors or rotary cutters, please look for the Fiskars name! You will love the quality and the price! When you need heirloom sewing supplies, please call Linda's Silver Needle! She has it all for heirloom sewing! When you are in the market for a new automobile, truck or van, please give consideration to buying a Ford! My family loves our Ford vehicles!

I have known Clotilde nearly as long as I have been in this business. Her catalogue will forever be a boost to the sewing industry and her enthusiasm is unending. She helped me spread the word about *Sew Beautiful* magazine to millions of people through her catalogue. She has sold thousands of books from us, and I have bought lots of notions from her. She even has an heirloom/Martha Pullen Suggests section in her catalogue! She has always been there for me for friendship and for business advice. She and Don even furnished the place for my son Camp and his bride Charisse to go for their honeymoon. Thanks Clotilde!

Esther and Dan Randall of YLI have been good friends for ever so long. My first trip to Utah was to teach for them in one of our traveling schools. I have enjoyed a long and exciting relationship with both them and their children, Nancy, Scott, Dana, and Esther. Esther Randall is responsible for reviving the art of silk ribbon embroidery and spreading it to the world. Esther and Dan have opened many doors for me in this sewing industry and they are truly close friends. Everyone has enjoyed the silk ribbon sections on *Martha's Sewing Room.* She is now importing the lovely New Zealand wools to bring back the art of wool embroidery. Thanks Esther and Dan!

Barbara Parsons Massey loves heirloom sewing and is a new shop owner in Arkansas. When I first told my school in February about the new television series, she came to me immediately and said, "Martha, who are your underwriters going to be?"

After I replied that I didn't know yet, she said, "Well, I want Parson's Cabinets to be one." I am so excited about the first Martha Pullen Designer Cabinet made by Parson's! It is everything I ever wanted in a sewing machine cabinet to go in my den! Thanks Barbara and Bud! And Jessie, too! (Jessie is their granddaughter who has traveled to Huntsville many times with her grandparents!)

My relationship with Fiskars Scissors company first came about when I purchased a pair of their "arthritis" scissors. After seeing the absolutely perfect quality of these lightweight scissors, I had to have several more pairs. I found out about the kindergarten scissors with the blunt point and I found my dream scissors for trimming fabric from behind laces! Another thing I enjoy about Fiskars is their reasonable price for the absolute best quality! I have enjoyed working with Kevin Phays and Sandra Cashman in telling them about our dreams and in sharing with them how completely sold I was on Fiskars.

Linda's Silver Needle has been one of the most dynamic mail order companies in the heirloom sewing industry! Linda has sold thousands of my books and offers quick service all over the United States. When I called Linda to see if she would like to underwrite the 300 and 400 series, she absolutely squealed and said, "I am so thrilled that you have called me. We love the series and would be honored to help bring it to our friends out across the United States." Linda Steffens is a true friend and conscientious supplier for loads of heirloom sewing supplies which are sometimes hard to find locally. Thanks, Linda!

To my friends at the Ford Motor Company in Detroit I must say thank you. I believe this is the first time that one of the largest companies in the world has chosen to fund a sewing show and I think that speaks to me in letting me know that Ford truly cares about women's interests and women. I can vouch for the fact that my immediate family has bought 3 Ford vehicles in the last two years and we have loved each one of them! Joe loves his big Ford truck (the biggest Ford makes) and says he would never drive another truck again because this one is so comfortable! Ford, thanks for believing in women who love to sew! Thanks for putting this woman's show as a top priority in your advertising plan!

To Clotilde, YLI, Parsons Cabinets, Fiskars, Linda's Silver Needle and Ford, I hope you love the programs as much as we do. Since your products are the very best, I know our viewers will be anxious to purchase them. I also know the readers and viewers who love *Sew Beautiful* magazine and *Martha's Sewing Room* will also appreciate your making this program possible, in part. Our readers and viewers tend to be very loyal individuals, and I feel assured that they will give your products every consideration. ✼

Table of Contents

Show Index

Foreword To This Program Guide

It is so wonderful to know that somewhere in 44 of the 50 states of this great USA our television series, *Martha's Sewing Room*, is appearing or has appeared. When we planned our 100 and 200 series, we didn't know exactly how people would react to our newest adventure. Thankfully, our series was received with glowing reports and we were well on our way to success.

In designing the 400 series of *Martha's Sewing Room*, we combed our resources for new and innovative techniques, designs and ideas to keep the excitement of the first three series traveling forward. Some of the world's top designers were brought together and the planning had begun. Developing the themes for 13 shows was the first task; that went easily and quickly. There are so many ideas for heirloom sewing that we never seem to run out. Our problem, which is a good one to have, is limiting our ideas to those which will fit in our 30 minute weekly program format. We wanted to make this series even better than the three which had preceded it. That is always our goal whether it is in magazine production, television production, or book production.

New and different techniques include straight and curved puffing, new silk ribbon embroidery techniques, beginning and picture smocking, ideas for weddings and babies, pleater usage, construction of the smocked yoke dress, antique themes, bow ideas, lingerie presentations, bonnets and sashes, lace and ribbon weaving, quilt construction and heirloom embroidery. Each show stands alone with all of its glorious projects, techniques and ideas. We have a standing joke at the planning sessions which happen throughout the year. Nothing is written in stone until the final projects are in and the evaluations are finished. We ask questions such as, "Is this pillow really beautiful and unique?" "Is this doll dress a 'killer' dress?" "Will our audience love, love, love this home decorating project?" "Is our craft really easy and exciting?" "Do we have enough variety on this show?" "Are our teaching boards easy to understand and have we planned our sections so that the audience will understand all techniques?" "Do we have beautiful antique clothing for the 'Martha's Attic' section of the show?" "Are the projects on this show so unique and beautiful that our audience will love to look at the show even if they don't sew?"

Several funny things have happened since the show began airing. We have a lot of men who watch the show and who don't ever intend to sew. Some of their comments are "I really enjoy watching all of the different projects and the teaching boards which show how to do them." A man at our church enjoys the show and very often tells me about one show in particular. A few weeks ago he said, "Martha, I have asked my wife for a new sewing machine for Christmas. Even though I have never sewn a stitch, I think I can after having watched your show for a year now." I wonder if she will get him his sewing machine!

In planning the pattern for this series, I wanted a lady's nightgown and a child's pattern for either a boy or a girl. My criteria for the gown was that it was comfortable to sleep in and that it had a perfect place for heirloom sewing and embellishment. I believe we have the perfect gown which will be fun and easy to decorate. I know the knickers outfit is perfect for many different occasions both dressy or casual. It looks so cute with needlework on the bib. Since knickers can be worn year round, your little one can have a summer version and a winter one also.

Margaret Taylor's traditional fabric quilt is an enchanting combination of using cotton quilting fabrics with heirloom laces and embroidery. She used the show themes to create a square for each show; the final quilt is fabulous and unique. Margaret Boyles once again has presented her stitching expertise with heirloom embroidery. Only Margaret can stitch so elegantly and masterfully. Since she is a wonderful teacher, I think your embroidery skills can skyrocket after few minutes with Margaret.

Kathy Brower's silk ribbon lessons are fun and easy to follow. With silk ribbon's being the hottest craze in this country, everybody loves learning how easy it is to stitch.

We have included new techniques as well as the old ones. Our books are complete in themselves and I would never refer you to another book for a technique which should have been included in this one. This book can stand alone as a French sewing encyclopedia. As usual, I think you will love the simplicity of our written and drawn directions. We really believe our instructions are easy to follow.

I love the crafts, the pillows, the patterns, the quilt, the techniques, the dolls clothes and the embroidery of this series. We have lovingly planned the whole series for your enjoyment and education. We are excited about the quality of this book and about the care which has gone into bringing you correctly sized patterns and explicit instructions on construction. We have bound the book in a hard cover because it lasts longer in your library. I hope that this book will be around 100 years from now long after I am gone. This type of sewing is permanently established with publications from us and others; that is part of my legacy on this earth. Women love to do heirloom sewing and 20 years ago it was almost impossible to get any information on this art. Today, we have lots of information and more is coming daily. These clothes and projects will be just as classic and beautiful 100 years from now as they are today. These projects will be in the antique stores tomorrow. These clothes will be the museum pieces for tomorrow. Heirlooms are forever and the memories formed from seeing them stitched will be etched on hearts throughout time. That is the glorious joy of heirloom sewing. Enjoy our series and this book which accompanies it. Please let us know how we can improve both our series and our books. Thank you for watching *Martha's Sewing Room* and for supporting public television so they can bring it to your home. Without your interest and enthusiasm, we couldn't bring *Martha's Sewing Room* into your home.

Introduction To Pillows

Browsing through decorator books is a passion of mine. I love to look at the glorious colors in the Victorian styled rooms. Picking out details which I think are beautiful is truly a hobby. Before Joe and I built out home, I tore out pages of things which I loved. I even made a scrapbook. I always worry about tearing up a magazine even when I know I am going to throw it away. Probably I should tear out every picture of a room that I believe to be especially pretty since I will certainly forget each detail.

Since dreaming is about the only decorating that I really get around to doing, it is fun to look at the accessories that I might recreate. It seems that almost every magazine with beautiful rooms has absolutely wonderfully creative pillows on the furniture. With Victoria Magazine's being one of my all time favorites, I love to look at the rooms found within. The pillows they use are fabulous; however, I don't think as fabulous as the ones found in this book. Of course when we sew we can have the most beautiful pillows of all at a fraction of the cost.

I love to look at expensive mail order catalogues. I haven't ordered one thing from any of them this year; however, I have noticed an abundance of spectacular pillows. Upon closer examination, I find that their pillows still aren't as pretty as the ones we have had our designers create for this book, *Martha's Attic*. Believe I am partial to our heirloom detailed pillows with their laces, ribbons, smocking, and embroidery. I think our methods are ones which will last throughout the centuries and which will one day be worthy of being placed in a museum. Our friends who sew can have one of those Architectural Digest beds with linens more beautiful than those in the expensive magazines. These pillows in this book are masterpieces and will be treasured by anyone who loves beautiful heirloom items. The magazines are full of Victorian treasures and our book has lots of those also.

In the expensive stores, a pillow sporting a $200 price tag isn't too unusual. My thinking is that if some of the pillows in this section were to be offered for sale, their prices would be much higher than $200. You can have the finest of the fine concerning designer pillows if you will just begin to flip these pages and begin to cut and sew. Perhaps you will need to learn a bit about ribbons and embroidery to complete all of the pillows. Remember, heirloom sewing is easy and fun and making these pillows is a great way to begin heirloom sewing.

For bedrooms or sun porches you will love the Loop Puffing, Netting Lace, Pleated Flower, or the Rose Pillow. For your living room or family room perhaps you might want to try the Blue Rose, Lace Piecing, or Woven Heart. For your new baby in your life, please make a Baby Pillow with smocking on the front and a music box to play pretty tunes in the back. The Neck Roll will be perfect for your bedroom or as a gift for someone else's bedroom. As a matter of fact, any of these pillows would make the perfect gift for many people on your list. Please don't forget that teenage girls who have a flowery bedroom will love heirloom pillows long after they refuse to wear smocking or French sewing. Joanna always loved her beautiful pillows which she piled very high on her bed each day. She always looked forward to receiving a gift of a beautiful pillow for her bed. From her collection of cross stitched pillows which Miss Judy made her each birthday from her first birthday through her fifth, to the French pillows that Suzanne made her for Christmas for several years, she loves her pillows. We have quite a collection of beautiful pillows on our bed and on the guest room bed. Our bedroom is pink and green and the guest bedroom is teal blue, pink and green. These heirloom pillows really do fit in almost any bedroom scheme except for a very contemporary one. Enjoy your heirloom sewing on a quick and easy project such as one of these pillows. ✄

Loops Of Puffing Pillow

Using either a damask napkin or damask fabric one can make this pillow which is a treasure house of ideas and heirloom techniques. This white on white pillow features curved puffing made the easy way with a gathering foot on a sewing machine. The curved puffing is in a loop and has lace insertion shaped around the curves of puffing. Gathered cluny lace is stitched on the outside edges to form a perfect finish to this unusual fabric. Although these laces are zigzagged to the damask, one might use the wing needle entredeux stitches for attaching the laces also. The lining of the pillow is blue as well as the back of the pillow. The pillow shows a little blue peeking out from behind the laces after the damask has been cut away. Shadowing another color from behind lace shaping is pretty and enables one to use the color of the bedroom even if the pillow is white or ecru.

Materials Needed

❧ 1 piece of white damask, 15¹/₂" square
❧ ¹/₂ yd. of light blue broadcloth
❧ ¹/₄ yd. of white Nelona
❧ 2¹/₂ yds. of ⁵/₈" wide lace insertion
❧ 3¹/₂ yds. of 1¹/₂" wide tatted edging or lace edging
❧ 1 pillow form, 14" square, or make your own
❧ puffing loop template, found on pattern pull-out

I. Creating the Pillow Top

1. Trace the loop template onto the white damask.

2. Cut three strips of the white Nelona, each 2¹/₂" x 44". Seam the strips together at the selvage edges to form one long strip.

3. Create puffing from the Nelona strip using a ¹/₂" seam allowance on each side of the strip. Shape the puffing and lace insertion over the loop template of the pillow top (refer to "Shaped Puffing" on page 234). Stitch in place as stated in the puffing directions. Trim the fabric from behind the lace and puffing loop.

4. Cut two 15¹/₂" squares from the blue broadcloth. One piece will be the pillow top lining and one piece will be the pillow back.

5. Place one square of broadcloth behind the decorated pillow top. Pin together and treat as one layer of fabric.

II. Finishing the Pillow

1. Place the completed pillow top/lining over the 15¹/₂" square broadcloth pillow back, with right sides together and raw edges even. Stitch the two pieces together, using a ¹/₂" seam. Leave an opening on one side for stuffing (**fig. 1**).

2. Trim the seams and clip the corners (**fig. 1**). Turn the pillow right side out and press the edges. Turn under the seam allowances at the opening (**fig. 2**).

Loops of Puffing Pillow

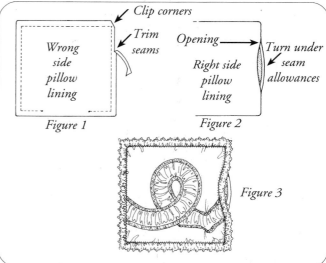

Figure 1

Figure 2

Figure 3

3. Gather the edging lace to fit the pillow. If tatting is used, run a machine gathering stitch in the edge of the tatting and gather to fit the pillow.

4. With right sides up, butt the gathered lace to the edges of the pillow.

5. Use a small zigzag to attach the edging to the pillow. At the opening attach the edging to the pillow front only (**fig. 3**).

6. Place the form inside the pillow. Stitch the opening closed by hand, or press the form out of the way and close with a small zigzag. ❧

Rose Pillow

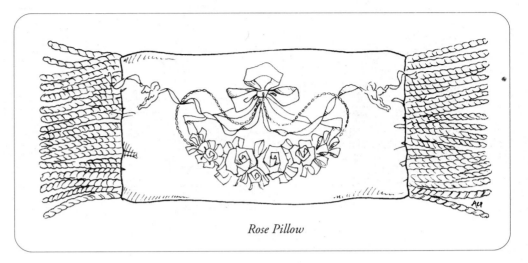

Rose Pillow

Almost breathtaking is this pillow's description. Pink silk dupioni makes the rectangular pillow; écru silk fringe finishes each end. Ecru satin folded roses make a cascade across the middle of the pillow. Ecru wired satin ribbon is used for the large bow on the top. Gold ribbons are stitched in cascades connecting the top bow and the bottom roses. Two little gold cherubs are stitched on either side of the gold ribbon and appear as if they are holding the ribbon. Another gold and organdy ribbon is intertwined throughout the folded roses and some gold fringe is peeking out from behind these gorgeous roses. Pearls are stitched almost in a heart shape from the top ribbon to the bottom roses. This designer's dream pillow would be beautiful for any room of the house by simply using that room's colors. To give the gift of a lifetime, consider making a pillow like this!

Materials Needed

- ❧ ³/₈ yd. silk dupioni
- ❧ ³/₄ yd. of bullion fringe, 3" to 6" wide
- ❧ 2 large roses, 2 smaller roses, 1 rose bud
- ❧ 2 brass cupids
- ❧ 1 yd. wired edge satin ribbon, 1" wide
- ❧ 1 yd. gold edged sheer ribbon, ¹/₂" wide
- ❧ 1 yd. gold mesh wired edge "ribbon", ³/₈" wide
- ❧ 2¹/₂ yds. of small gold cord (Balger #16 braided cord)
- ❧ ³/₄ yd. of craft pearls on a string
- ❧ 1 yd. of ¹/₈" wide satin ribbon (for tying rings on)
- ❧ polyfill to stuff the pillow, or make a pillow form 12" x 21"
- ❧ hot glue gun
- ❧ fabric glue

I. Constructing the Pillow

1. Cut two pieces of silk dupioni, each 13" x 22".

2. Stitch fringe along the short ends of one piece of silk, with the edges even and the fringe toward the middle of the pillow (**fig.** 1).

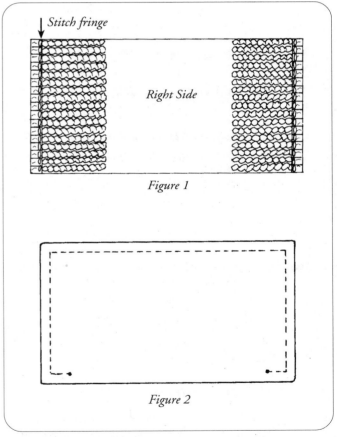

Stitch fringe

Right Side

Figure 1

Figure 2

3. Stitch the two pieces of silk together, right sides together. Be sure not to catch the ends of the fringe in the seam. Leave an opening on one side, by stitching only 1" past the corners (**fig.** 2).

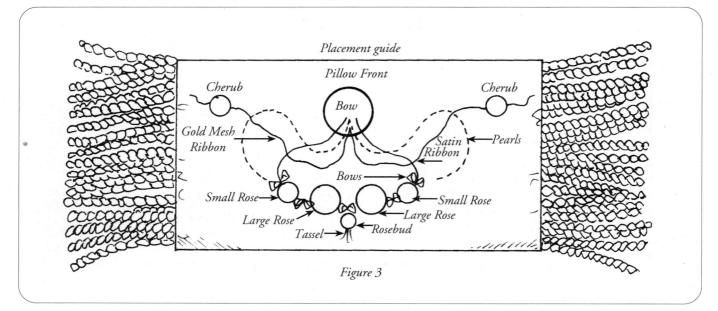

Figure 3

4. Trim the seams and clip the corners; turn the pillow right side out.

5. Stuff the pillow and sew the opening closed by hand.

II. Decorating the Pillow Top

Refer to figure 3 to arrange roses, ribbons, pearls, etc.

1. Make the roses according to the instructions given on page 151. Arrange the roses on the pillow top. Stitch in place or glue in place with the glue gun.

2. Cut the sheer ribbon into four pieces, each 6" long. Tie the gold cord around the centers of the sheer ribbon pieces to form bow shapes. Use the remaining sheer ribbon to make a fifth bow; make an extra loop in the gold cord and leave longer tails.

3. Tuck the five bows in among the roses and glue with the glue gun or fabric glue. The bow with the longer tails will go around the rose bud, with the cut ends tucked under and glued in place.

4. Make a bow with long tails from the 1" wide wired edge satin ribbon. Make long cascading tails from the ³/₈" gold mesh. Arrange and glue in place.

5. Use fabric glue to attach the pearls and cupids.

6. Loop the remaining gold cord to make a small tassel. Cut a small piece of the cord to tie around the top of the tassel. Attach the tassel under the edge of the rose bud. ▨

Baby Pillow

Using cotton netting and French laces, this pillow is delicate and full of heirloom sewing tricks. The white netting pillowcase has a pink pillow underneath which peeks through very sweetly on both the front and the back. White French insertion of a round thread pattern is used around the pillow and is mitered at the corners. This same insertion is featured running vertically with machine embroidery between the two strips of insertion. A tied bow of French insertion is found on the front with a fancy tail loop on the bottom tail. The initials APM have been stitched in by machine to indicate the baby's initials. A double netting ruffle finishes the outside of the pillow and a pink cotton pillow has been inserted. You could use any color of the baby's nursery to insert for the pillow. This pillow doesn't have to be a baby pillow because it would be just as pretty for an adult's bedroom or sun porch collection.

Baby Pillow

Materials Needed

- ⅝ yd. of cotton netting
- ¼ yd. of pink Nelona
- 3 yds. of ⅝" wide lace insertion
- rayon embroidery thread
- ¼ yd. of water soluble stabilizer (WSS)
- polyfill to stuff the pillow, or make a pillow form 8" x 13"
- bow template found on the pull-out section

I. Creating the Pillow Top

1. Cut two strips of the netting, 5" by the width of the netting, for the ruffle. From the remaining netting, cut two rectangles for the pillow, 9" x 14½".

2. Place one rectangle of netting over a piece of WSS. Stitch a piece of lace insertion 2¼" from each short side of the netting rectangle.

3. Miter lace insertion around the outer edge of the rectangle, with the outer edge of the lace ½" from the cut edge (**fig. 1**).

4. Place a decorative stitch between the two side pieces of lace (**fig. 2**).

5. Trace the bow onto the netting. Shape the insertion along the template lines. Stitch in place with a small zigzag (refer to "Tied Bows" on page 196).

6. Add machine-monogramed initials between the bow tails (**fig. 3**).

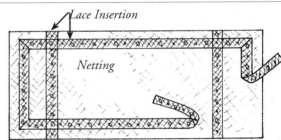

Lace Insertion

Netting

Figure 1

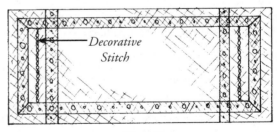

Decorative Stitch

Figure 2

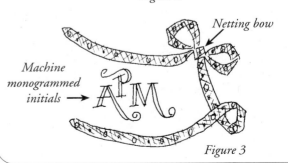

Netting bow

Machine monogrammed initials

Figure 3

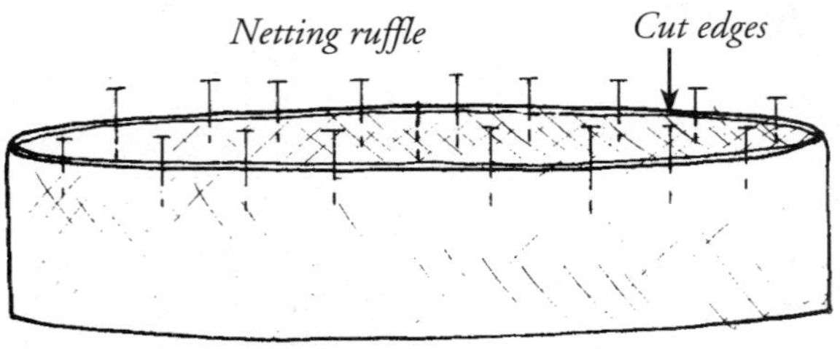

Figure 4

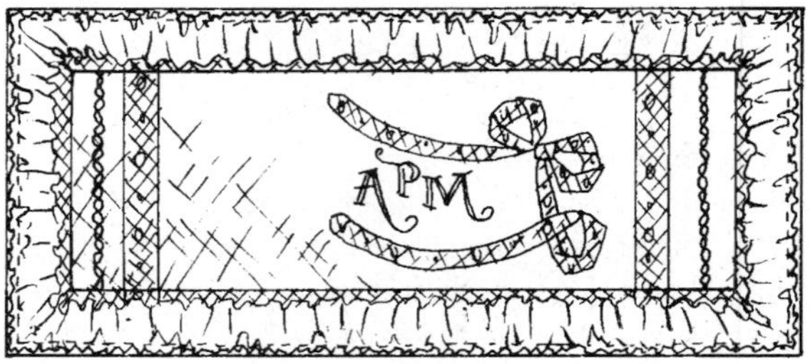

Figure 5

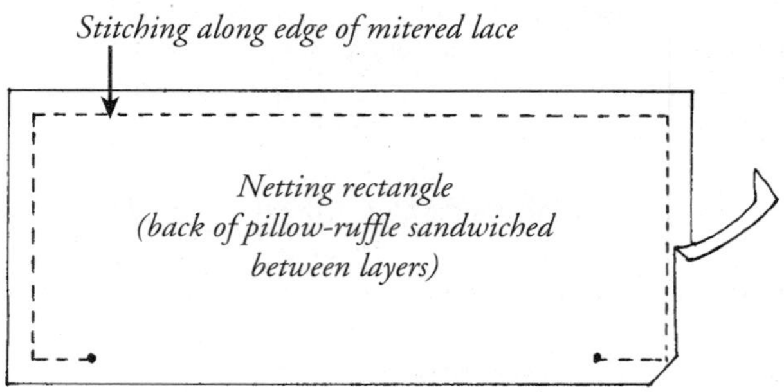

Figure 6

II. Ruffles

1. Sew the ends of the netting strips together to make a circle. Fold the cut edges of the strip together and press. The strip is now $2^1/_2$" wide. Pin the edges together and treat them as one layer (**fig. 4**).
2. Run two gathering rows along the raw edge of the ruffle, $^1/_4$" and $^1/_2$" from the edge. Gather the ruffle to fit the outer edge of the pillow.
3. Place the edge of the ruffle to the outer edge of the pillow top, with the ruffle toward the middle of the pillow. The $^1/_2$" gathering thread of the ruffle will fall along the edge of the mitered lace. Pin the ruffle in place and baste (**fig. 5**).

III. Finishing the Pillow

1. Place the second netting rectangle over the pillow top, with the ruffle sandwiched between the two layers. Pin the raw edges together and then stitch with a $^1/_2$" seam (the seam will be along the edge of the mitered lace). Leave an opening on one edge by stitching only 1" from the corners (**fig. 6**).
2. Trim the seams and clip the corners (**fig. 6**). Turn the pillow right side out.
3. Cut two rectangles from the Nelona, 9" x $14^1/_2$". These will make the inner pillow. Place the two rectangles together and stitch with a $^1/_2$" seam. Leave an opening for stuffing.
4. Turn the lining right side out and press.
5. Stuff the pillow lining with the polyfill. Stitch the opening closed by hand or machine.
6. Insert the stuffed pillow into the netting top. Stitch the opening closed by hand. ⁂

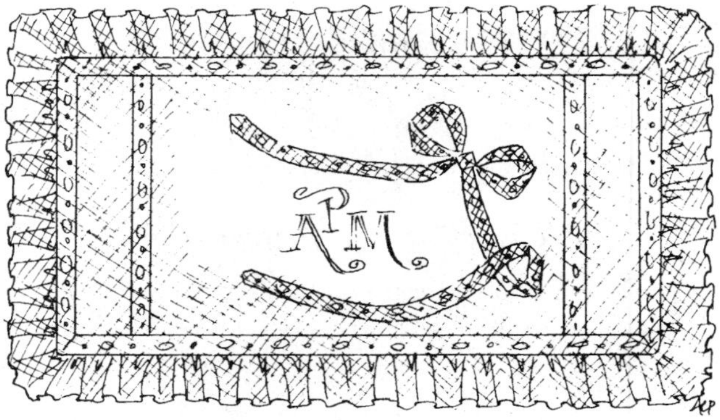

Ribbon And Smocking Pillow

Creativity abounds in this pillow. There are so many fabulous ribbons available in your fabric store, you have only to pick your favorite ribbons and begin to design a pillow just like this. The center strip is smocked with a geometric smocking pattern in shades of rose and teal taken from the purchased ribbon. Two rows of the ribbon are attached on either side of the smocking. Next, stitched on white silk dupioni is a pink zigzag scallop followed by another strip of the purchased ribbon. Once again stitched on white dupioni is a machine decorative pattern stitched in gold metallic thread. Another border of the ribbon is next. At the bottom of the pillow is another border of the purchased ribbon. A beautiful upholstery braid is found on the outside of the pillow; the colors are rose, white and beige.

Ribbon And Smocking Pillow

Materials Needed

- ³/₄ yd. of white silk dupioni
- 4 yds. of 1¹/₂ embroidered ribbon
- 1³/₄ yds. of twisted rope-type drapery piping
- decorative thread to match the ribbon
- 3 colors of DMC floss, two that are a light and dark shade of the same color, and one contrasting color (DMC 224 Light Rose, DMC 223 Dark Rose, DMC 3811 Teal).
- 14" square pillow form, or make your own
- smocking graph and written instructions found 260

I. The Smocked Strip

1. Tear a strip of the silk dupioni 3" wide across the width of the fabric. Pleat 8 rows on a smocking pleater, with the first row ¹/₄" from the edge.

2. Remove the pleating threads from ¹/₂" at each end of the strip, creating seam allowances.

3. Pull up the pleats and tie the threads off to 11¹/₂", pleat to pleat; steam and block the strip. Let the strip dry completely before smocking (**fig. 1**).

4. Smock the pleated strip, using the graph and written instructions found on page 260.

5. Re-block the strip if needed; do not remove the pleating threads until after the strip is attached to the pillow top.

II. Constructing the Pillow Top

1. Cut a 15" square of the silk dupioni; this will be the pillow front. Cut the ribbon into eight 15" strips.

2. Pin ribbon strips along the sides of the pillow ¹/₂" from the cut edges, creating a ribbon border (**fig. 2**).

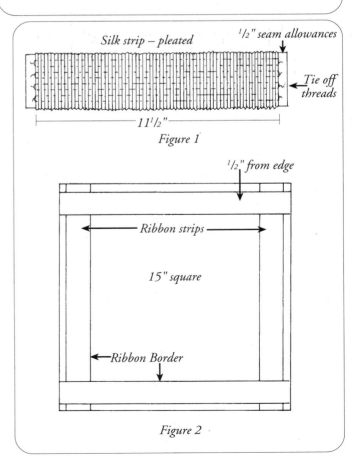

Silk strip – pleated

¹/₂" seam allowances

Tie off threads

11¹/₂"

Figure 1

¹/₂" from edge

Ribbon strips

15" square

Ribbon Border

Figure 2

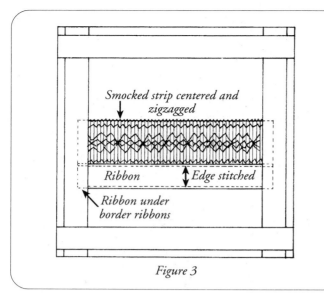

Smocked strip centered and zigzagged

Ribbon   Edge stitched

Ribbon under border ribbons

Figure 3

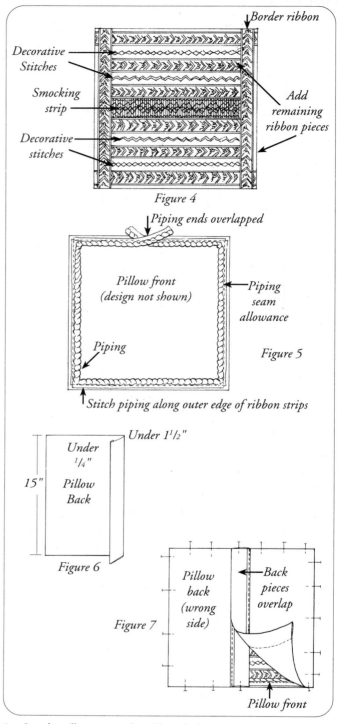

Border ribbon

Decorative Stitches

Smocking strip

Decorative stitches

Add remaining ribbon pieces

Figure 4

Piping ends overlapped

Pillow front (design not shown)

Piping seam allowance

Piping

Figure 5

Stitch piping along outer edge of ribbon strips

Under 1½"

Under ¼"

15"

Pillow Back

Figure 6

Pillow back (wrong side)

Back pieces overlap

Pillow front

Figure 7

3. Fold the pillow top in half and crease the fold. Place the smocked strip over the center crease. The ends of the smocked strip should fall under the side ribbons. Pin in place (**fig 3**).

4. Baste the smocked strip to the pillow top, just above the first smocked row and just below the last smocked row. Be sure that the smocked strip is straight. Zigzag along the cut edges of the smocked strip to help keep the edges flat. Trim away any excess fabric along the edges of the smocked strip outside the zigzags.

5. Overlap each long edge of the smocked strip with a piece of the 1½" ribbon, letting the edge of the ribbon cover the basted seam next to the smocked rows. Edge-stitch each of the ribbon pieces in place along both edges. Place the ends of the ribbon under the border ribbons (**fig. 3**).

6. Place the remaining pieces of ribbon between the border ribbon and the ribbon next to the smocked strip. Place the ends of the ribbon under the border ribbon. Edge-stitch in place (**fig. 4**).

7. If desired, work decorative stitches with decorative threads in the remaining fabric areas. Stabilizer may be needed for this decorative work (**fig. 4**).

8. Stitch the border ribbons in place along the edges.

9. Place the piping around the edge of the pillow top with the seam allowance toward the edge and the piping toward the middle of the pillow. Clip the seam allowance at the corners to let the piping lie flat. Overlap the ends of the piping and let the cut edges extend into the seam allowance. Use a zipper foot to stitch the piping to the pillow along the outer edge of the ribbon strips (**fig. 5**).

III. Constructing the Pillow

1. To make the pillow back, cut two pieces of silk dupioni, each 15" x 11".

2. Along one 15" edge of one silk piece, press under ¼", then press another 1½". Stitch the folded edge in place. Repeat for the other piece of silk (**fig. 6**).

3. Lay the pillow top on the table with the right side up. Place one piece of the pillow back over the pillow front, with right sides together and raw edges even. A little over one half of the pillow top will be covered. Place the other back piece so that the hemmed edges of the back pieces overlap each other. Pin all of the edges (**fig. 7**).

4. Stitch around the pillow, being sure to stitch close to the piping.

5. Turn the pillow to the right side through the back overlap and insert the pillow form. ▨

Pleated Flower Pillow

Who says that the pleating machine is only for smocking? Here is a new use for a cute pillow. The peach pillow has circles of netting, and two circles of pleated white batiste which has been unhemmed so that it fringes on the edges. The center of the flower is made with fringy braid in a beautiful shade of peach and a loopy braid in the same shade. The pleated outside ruffle has been pleated with the Perfect Pleater and it finishes the pleating concepts of this pillow. The fabric strip which has been pleated has the pleating rows left in near the bottom, this holds the pleats and keeps the look intact.

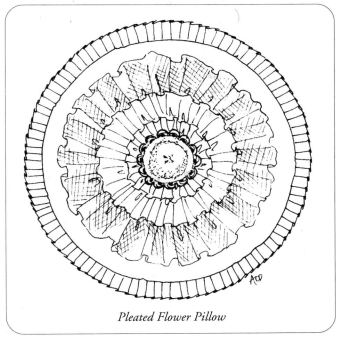

Pleated Flower Pillow

Materials Needed

- ¾ yd. of colored Nelona (Swiss batiste)
- ¼ yd. of white Nelona
- ⅛ yd. of loopy rayon drapery fringe
- ¼ yd. of cotton drapery fringe
- 2 large covered buttons, 1" to 1½" wide
- batting, 15" x 30"
- polyfill to stuff a 14" pillow, or a 14" round pillow form
- ¼ yd. of cotton netting
- fabric glue, or hot glue gun

I. Making the Pillow Ruffle

1. For the pillow ruffle, cut four strips of Nelona, 2½" by the width of the fabric.

2. Stitch the strips together to make one long strip.

3. Fold and press the strip in half along the length (**fig. 1**).

4. Pleat the strip, using Clotilde's Perfect Pleater, or by measuring and pressing overlapping pleats. Let the pleats cool completely before moving them (**fig. 2**).

5. Open the ends of the strip and sew together to make a circle, then refold and press the seam.

II. Constructing the Pillow

1. Cut two 14" circles of the colored Nelona, and of the batting. Fold the Nelona circles in quarters and mark the centers. Place one Nelona circle on top of one batting circle; this will be the pillow top.

2. Pin the ruffle to the right side of the pillow top, with the raw edges even and the folded edge of the ruffle toward the center of the pillow top. Adjust the fullness of the ruffle evenly around the pillow edge. Baste the ruffle in place (**fig. 3**).

3. Place the other batting and Nelona circles together to make the pillow back.

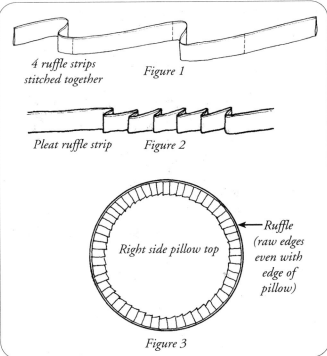

4 ruffle strips stitched together Figure 1

Pleat ruffle strip Figure 2

Right side pillow top ←Ruffle (raw edges even with edge of pillow)

Figure 3

4. Pin the pillow back and front with right sides together. Use a ½" seam allowance to stitch the front and back together, leaving an opening for turning.

5. Turn the pillow right side out and stuff with polyfill. Stitch the opening closed by hand.

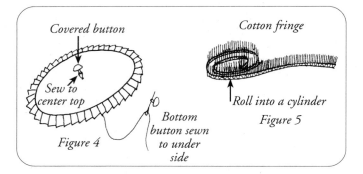

Figure 4

Covered button
Sew to center top
Bottom button sewn to under side

Cotton fringe
Roll into a cylinder
Figure 5

6. Cover the buttons with colored Nelona. Attach the buttons to the centers of the pillow front and back. Stitch all the way through the pillow by hand with a long needle and strong thread, attaching both buttons at the same time (**fig. 4**).

III. Making the Pleated Flower Pieces

1. Begin at one end and roll the cotton fringe into a cylinder; glue the end in place (**fig. 5**).

2. Roll the rayon fringe around the cotton fringe cylinder, with the loops of the rayon fringe in the same direction as the fringed edge of the cotton. Glue the rayon fringe in place (**fig. 6**).

3. Tear a 5" by 45" wide strip of the white Nelona. The strip should be torn on both of the long edges.

4. Pleat the 5" strip of white Nelona with a smocking pleater, using eight whole-space rows. The first row will be ¼" from one torn edge of the fabric (**fig. 7**).

5. Cut a 5" strip across the width of the netting. Run two gathering rows ¼" and ½" from one edge of the netting strip (**fig. 8**).

IV. Assembling and Attaching the Pleated Flower

1. Pull the gathered edge of the netting into a tight circle. Tuck the gathered edge under the button on the pillow top and glue it in place, fanning the netting into a circle on top of the pillow (**fig. 9**).

2. Place the rolled fringe cylinder over the netting on top of the button and glue it in place (**fig. 10**).

3. Fold the pleated Nelona strip over itself between pleating rows 4 and 5 (**fig. 11**).

4. Pull up the gathers to make the folded edge of the pleated piece fit around the fringe cylinder. Let the edges fan out to make a circle on top of the netting. Glue the folded edge of the pleated piece around the cylinder with the shorter layer on top (**fig. 12**).

5. Remove the first and last pleating rows.

6. Glue the overlapped edges of the netting. Glue the overlapped edges of the pleated piece. Also glue at intervals around the edges of the netting and pleated circles to hold them in place on the pillow top. ❈

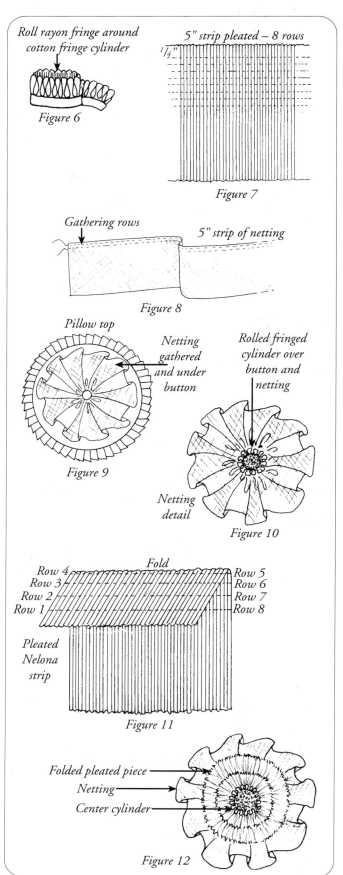

Roll rayon fringe around cotton fringe cylinder
Figure 6

5" strip pleated – 8 rows
¼"
Figure 7

Gathering rows
5" strip of netting
Figure 8

Pillow top
Netting gathered and under button
Rolled fringed cylinder over button and netting
Figure 9

Netting detail
Figure 10

Row 4   Fold   Row 5
Row 3   Row 6
Row 2   Row 7
Row 1   Row 8
Pleated Nelona strip
Figure 11

Folded pleated piece
Netting
Center cylinder
Figure 12

Lace Circle Pillow

Teal blue faille lined with teal blue lace makes the base of this pillow. Believe it or not this pillow is a large circle of fabric and lining finished on the edge with a beautiful teal braid. The circle is gathered up and tied with black elastic and then a piece of the edging braid is tied into a bow around the elastic. The pillow is then stuffed with polyfil and that is the extent of this pillow. It is precious when made in chintz and lined with a contrasting chintz. I first saw this type of pillow in a magazine, made much larger with two patterns of chintz- one flowered and one striped. A large grosgrain ribbon wrapped around the neck of the pillow. To be so cute, this pillow certainly is easy to make. I don't think you will find too many bedrooms with a pillow like this one.

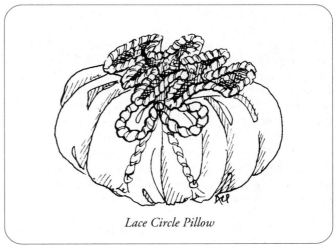

Lace Circle Pillow

Materials Needed

- 1 yd. of taffeta
- 1 yd. of all-over lace fabric
- 3 yds. of twisted drapery cord
- 8" of ¼" wide elastic
- polyfill to stuff the pillow

I. Constructing the Pillow

1. Cut a circle 28½" in diameter from each fabric piece.

2. Place the two circles with right sides together. Stitch the two circles together, using a ½" seam allowance. Leave an opening to turn through (**fig. 1**).

3. Turn the circle right side out and stitch the opening closed.

4. Place the cording around the finished edge of the pillow and use a small zigzag to edge-stitch the cording to the pillow. Overlap the ends. Zigzag over the raw edges (**fig. 2**).

II. Completing the Pillow

1. Lay the circle out flat, with the wrong (or inner) side up.

2. Place a handful of polyfill in the middle on top of the circle.

3. Pull up the edges of the circle around the polyfill to form a "bag" and tie with elastic, allowing the edges of the circle to flare (**fig. 3**).

4. Adjust the gathers evenly and tie the extra cording around the pillow to hide the elastic. See the finished pillow.

5. When you get tired of the pillow, you can reverse it to let the inside show. ✻

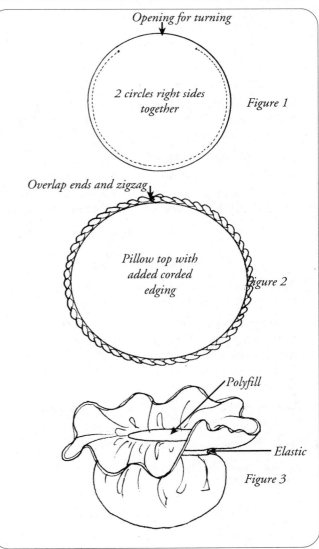

Opening for turning

2 circles right sides together

Figure 1

Overlap ends and zigzag

Pillow top with added corded edging

Figure 2

Polyfill

Elastic

Figure 3

Smocked Music Box Pillow

Playing "The Teddy Bear's Parade" the music box inside of the little pillow can keep baby entertained for a little while at least. I love this pillow with the adorable teddy bear smocked on the front holding an apple. The bear's shirt is robin's egg blue and the base fabric of this pillow is robin's egg blue gingham. The beading stitched on the front is Swiss and is threaded with blue ribbon. The outside ruffle is Swiss eyelet and it is gathered reasonably full. The pillow is stuffed with Polyfill and two buttonholes are worked on the back for the turn key of the music box to stick out. The pillow has a fold back closing in the back. Being so easy to make, this pillow can use any smocking design whatsoever as well as any music box appropriate for a baby. What an imaginative baby gift for that precious little one in your family!

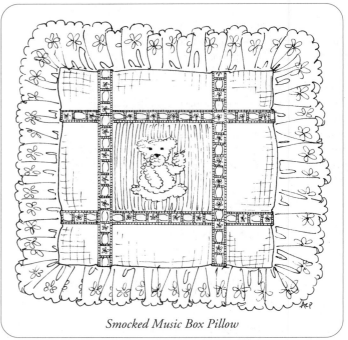

Smocked Music Box Pillow

Materials Needed

- ¼ yd. of ¼" gingham
- ¼ yd. of white broadcloth
- 1 yd. of ⅝" wide eyelet beading
- 1 yd. of ⅜" wide satin ribbon
- 1¼ yds. of 2½" wide eyelet edging
- DMC floss: DMC 738 light brown, DMC 437 medium brown, DMC 712 off-white, DMC 666 red, DMC 909 green, DMC 965 robin's egg, color to match gingham
- polyfill for stuffing an 8" pillow
- 1 key-wound craft music box
- The design is from Fancy Stitches, "Favorite Subject." Any smocking design can be used that will fit into the "window".

Special thanks to Aritta York for the pillow and pillow design.

I. The Smocked Inset

1. Tear a 3" x 10" strip of the broadcloth. Pleat 9 rows in the strip with a smocking pleater.

2. Remove pleats evenly from both ends until there are 40 pleats left. Note: More pleats may be used if a different smocking design is used. Pull up the pleating threads and tie off to 2", pleat to pleat. Trim the extra fabric away ½" from the last pleat on each side (**fig. 1**).

3. Steam and block the pleated piece. Let it dry completely before smocking.

4. Smock the inset, using the graph and written instructions.

5. Re-block the smocked piece if needed. Do not remove the pleating threads.

II. Making the Pillow Top

1. Cut an 8" gingham square from the center of the fabric. The selvage edges will be used for the pillow back.

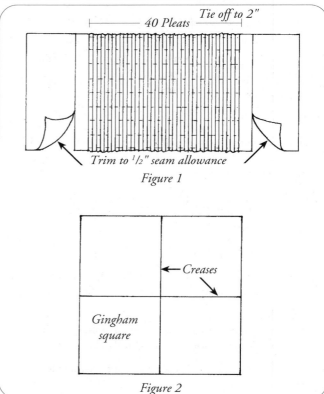

Figure 1

Figure 2

2. Fold the square in half, then in half again in the other direction, to divide it into four smaller squares. Press light creases along the fold lines (**fig. 2**).

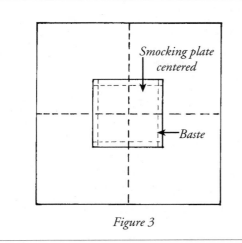

Figure 3

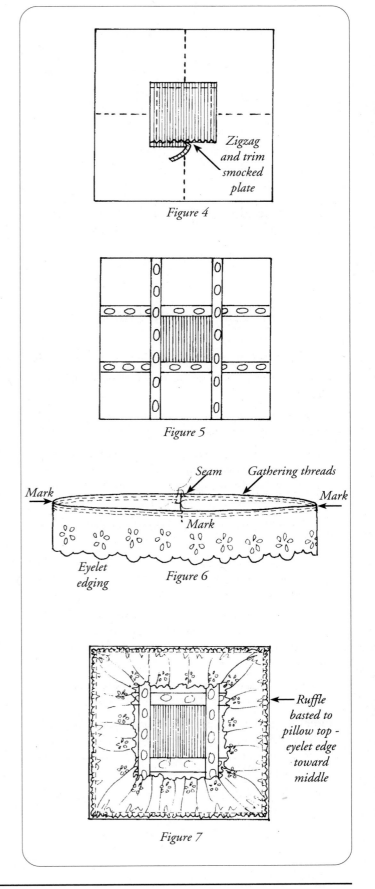

Figure 4

Figure 5

Figure 6

Figure 7

3. Place the smocked inset on top of the pillow top piece, with both pieces right side up. Position the smocked piece so that the center pleat is on the vertical crease and the middle smocking row is on the horizontal crease (**fig. 3**).

4. When the smocked piece is centered, pin and baste it in place. Baste close to the last pleat on each side, and between rows 1 and 2, and rows 8 and 9 (**fig. 3**).

5. Use a small zigzag to stitch close to the basted lines. Trim away any excess pleated fabric outside the zigzag (**fig. 4**).

6. Weave the ribbon through the beading. Cut the ribbon/beading into four 8" pieces.

7. Place one strip of the ribbon/beading across the top of the inset, covering the zigzag and basting stitches. The cut ends of the strip will be even with the edges of the pillow top (**fig. 5**).

8. Edge-stitch along both edges of the beading. Repeat steps 7 and 8 for the bottom and sides of the inset. You may want to use a zipper foot to stitch close to the pleats (**fig. 5**).

III. Constructing the Ruffle

1. Run two gathering rows along the raw edge of the eyelet edging, ¹/₄" and ¹/₂" from the edge.

2. Remove the gathering threads ¹/₂" at each end. Stitch the ends together with a ¹/₂" seam, right sides together, to form a circle.

3. Using the seam as one mark, divide and mark the eyelet into quarters (**fig. 6**).

4. Place the quarter marks at the creases and pin the ruffle to the pillow top, right sides together. The raw edges will be even and the eyelet edge will be toward the middle of the pillow. Pull up the gathers until the ruffle fits the pillow top. Pin and baste the ruffle in place (**fig. 7**).

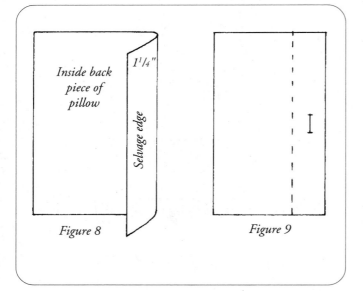

Figure 8

Figure 9

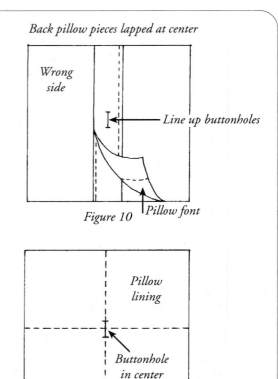

Back pillow pieces lapped at center

Wrong side

Line up buttonholes

Pillow font

Figure 10

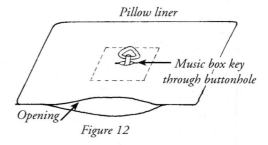

Pillow lining

Buttonhole in center

Figure 11

Pillow liner

Music box key through buttonhole

Opening

Figure 12

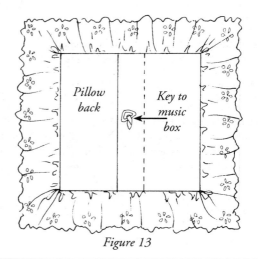

Pillow back

Key to music box

Figure 13

IV. Finishing the Pillow

1. Cut two pieces of the gingham, each 8" x 6½", with one 8" side of each rectangle on the selvage edge. These are the back pieces.

2. On each piece, turn the 8" selvage to the inside 1¼" and press (**fig. 8**).

3. In the center of each folded hem, work a 1" buttonhole, using a stabilizer under the buttonhole area (**fig. 9**).

4. Place the pillow top right side up. Lay one of the back pieces over the pillow top, right sides together and raw edges even, with the turned-under edge toward the center. The buttonhole should be over the center of the pillow top (**fig. 10**).

5. Place the remaining back piece over the pillow top, matching the buttonholes.

6. Stitch around the pillow edges with a ½" seam. Be sure that the eyelet ruffle is not caught in the seam. Turn the pillow to the right side.

7. Cut two 8" squares from the broadcloth for the pillow liner. Fold one square in quarters the same as for the pillow top and crease. Place stabilizer under the center and work a 1" buttonhole (**fig. 11**).

8. Place the two squares right sides together and stitch around the edges, leaving an opening. Turn the liner right side out.

9. Partly stuff the liner with polyfill, then insert the box into the liner. Place the key through the buttonhole. Add stuffing around the music box for padding. Finish stuffing the liner and stitch the opening closed (**fig. 12**).

10. Place the liner into the pillow and "button" the back over the key (**fig. 13**). ❈

Netting Lace Pillow

I first taught this pillow in Australia at one of my traveling Martha Pullen Schools of Art Fashion. The ladies there loved it and I hope you will also. The fabric is blue silk dupioni; the laces are a combination of French insertion and beading and English netting lace. The rectangular pillow has an inset in the center with a row of French insertion around the outside edges, and a row of beading inside that insertion. The center section is two pieces of English netting lace with the scallops meeting in the center to mace two ovals. The blue silk dupioni peeks through these laces. The pillow has a decoration around the edge of tubing which has been crushed and folded in several places and crushed and shaped on the corners to look a little like roses. There is piping around the pillow and it is stuffed with polyfil. This pillow is versatile enough to go into any room in your house by varying the fabric choice.

Netting Lace Pillow

Materials Needed

- ❧ 1 yd. of silk dupioni
- ❧ 1¼ yds. of ⅝" wide lace beading
- ❧ 1¼ yds. of ¾" wide lace insertion
- ❧ 2 yds. of ⅜" cording for piping
- ❧ ½ yd. of scalloped netting lace
- ❧ polyfill for stuffing, or make a 12" x 18" pillow form

I. Constructing the Pillow Top

1. Cut the silk according to the diagram (**fig. 1**).

2. Use one 12" x 18" silk rectangle for the top. Fold the rectangle in half in both directions, horizontal and vertical, and finger press the center creases (**fig. 2**).

3. Cut netting lace into two 7" pieces that are identical in pattern so that when they are placed across from each other a pattern is formed. Trim the width of each lace piece to 5".

4. Center the lace pieces on top of the 12" x 18" rectangle, with the scalloped edge toward the center. The center motif of the lace should be over the horizontal fabric crease, and the scalloped edges should meet along the vertical crease, with the lace designs matched (**fig. 3**).

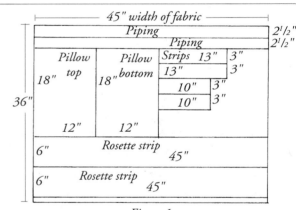

Figure 1

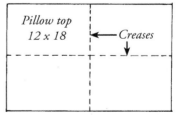

Figure 2

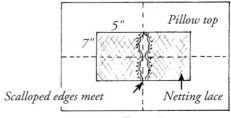

Figure 3

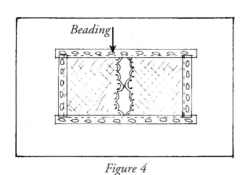

Figure 4

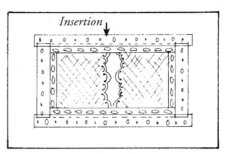

Figure 5

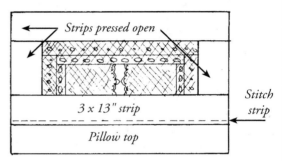

Figure 6

5. Once the lace pieces are positioned correctly, stitch along the scalloped edge of each piece.

6. Place a strip of beading lace across the 7" end of each piece of netting lace. The beading lace should overlap the netting by $^1/_8$" to $^1/_4$". If the edge of the netting shows through the holes in the beading, it is overlapped too far. Be sure to extend the beading a little past the edges of the netting at the top and bottom. Zigzag the beading in place along the overlapped edge. Repeat the procedure across the top and bottom edges of the netting lace (**fig. 4**).

7. Repeat step 6, using the lace insertion (**fig. 5**).

8. Place the 3" x 10" strips at each end of the lace rectangle, right sides together, so that a $^1/_4$" seam allowance on the outer fabric edge will overlap the lace heading of the outside edge of the lace insertion. Stitch the fabric in place and press the strips open. Repeat, using 3" X 13" strips across the top and bottom edges of the lace rectangle (**fig. 6**).

9. Trim the completed pillow top to 12" x 18".

II. Finishing the Pillow

1. Make and apply the piping as follows:

   a. Stitch the two $2^1/_2$" x 45" pieces together with a $^1/_4$" seam to make one long strip.

   b. Place the cording on the wrong side along the length of the fabric strip and wrap the fabric over the cording. The raw edges of the fabric should meet, wrong sides together. Use a zipper or cording foot to stitch through the layers of fabric, close to the cording (**fig. 7**).

   c. Place the piping to the right side around the outer edge of the pillow top, with the raw edges even and the piping toward the center. Clip the seam allowance at the corners to let the piping lie flat. The piping will be rounded as it turns the corners. As the two pieces meet, turn $^1/_4$" to the inside of one piping tube. Insert the end of the other tube inside so that no raw edges show (**fig. 8**).

   d. Pin and stitch close to the piping.

Wrap fabric over cording and stitch for piping

Figure 7

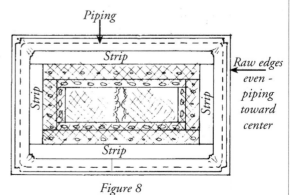

Figure 8

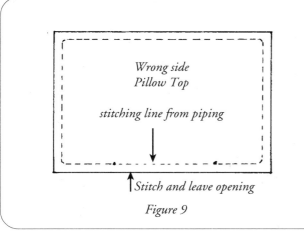

Wrong side
Pillow Top

stitching line from piping

↑ Stitch and leave opening

Figure 9

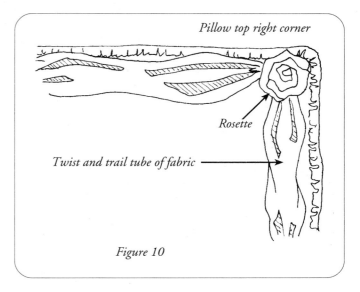

Pillow top right corner

Rosette

Twist and trail tube of fabric →

Figure 10

2. Place the pillow top over the 12" x 18" back piece, right sides together. Pin the two pieces together and stitch, covering the stitching line that applied the piping to the pillow top. Leave an opening along one side (**fig. 9**).

3. Turn the pillow to the right side. The corners will not be square, they will be slightly rounded.

4. Stuff the pillow, or make an inner pillow to insert. Stitch the opening closed.

5. Stitch the two 6" x 45" strips together at one short end to make one long strip; press the seam.

6. Fold the strip, right sides together, and stitch the long raw edges together. Turn the tube right side out and lightly press it with the long seam on one edge.

7. Place the seam of the tube at the top right corner of the pillow and pin. Curl the fabric tube to make a rosette; pin in place (**fig. 10**).

8. Continue twisting and trailing the tube around the pillow, curling to create rosettes at the corners. Pin. Any excess tubing can be trimmed away. The ends of the tube should be hidden in a rosette.

9. When the twists and rosettes are arranged attractively, tack the tube in place at the points where it is pinned. Tack the cut ends well. ✳

Floral Bouquet Pillow

Black, ecru, and gray striped pinwale corduroy is the background fabric for this pillow which would be wonderful in a den or a library. The pillow is large and measures 24 inches square. Black fringe and white braid are stitched to the outside of the pillow. Using a portion of a Battenburg placemat and pieces of embroidered motifs which are purchased by the yard, a bouquet is glued to the top of this pillow. Looking just as pretty in a summery, feminine chintz, this idea can be transferred to any type of pillow.

Materials Needed

- ¾ yd. of fabric
- 3 yds. of drapery fringe
- 3 yds. of decorative cord
- Battenburg motif shaped like a bowl
- assorted flower motifs cut from lace, or lace flower appliqués
- polyfill for stuffing a 24" pillow
- fabric glue

I. Making the Pillow Top

1. Cut two 24" squares from the fabric. One of these will be the top, the other will be the back.

2. Place the Battenburg "bowl" on the fabric and arrange the flower motifs above it like flowers in a vase. Glue the motifs in place.

II. Finishing the Pillow

1. Place the front and back pillow pieces with right sides together.

2. Stitch around the edges with a ½" seam allowance, leaving an opening to turn the pillow to the right side.

3. Turn the pillow right side out. Butt the fringe against the edges of the pillow and zigzag the fringe to the pillow. Stitch the fringe to the top layer across the opening. Overlap and zigzag the ends of the fringe (**fig. 1**).

4. Stitch the decorative cording over the fringe, next to the edge of the pillow (**fig. 2**).

5. Stuff the pillow with the polyfill. Stitch the opening closed. ▓

Floral Bouquet Pillow

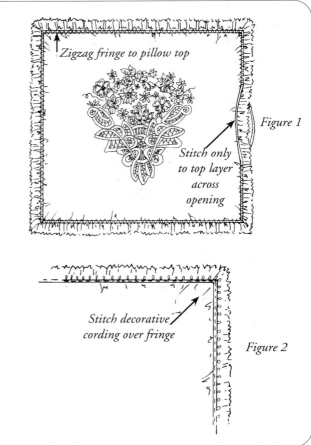

Zigzag fringe to pillow top

Figure 1

Stitch only to top layer across opening

Stitch decorative cording over fringe

Figure 2

Neck Roll Pillow

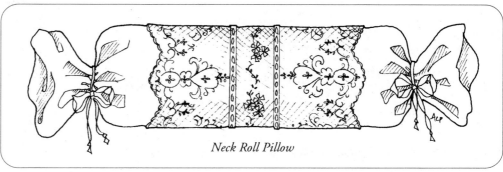

Neck Roll Pillow

Simple to make and very elegant to give is this pale powder blue satin neck roll pillow. English netting laces are zigzagged together in the center to make an outside sleeve to embellish the satin roll. Two pieces of wide ecru English netting are attached to a two inch wide piece of English netting insertion with two pieces of French beading. Pink ribbons are run through this beading. A casing in each end holds a piece of pink ribbon; after it is run through the casing, then it is tied around the casing on the outside. This is a magnificent bedroom pillow and would be a wonderful gift for a special lady in your life.

Materials Needed

- ❧ crib size quilt batting
- ❧ ⅝ yd. of bridal satin
- ❧ 1½ yds. of 6" wide netting lace edging
- ❧ ⅝ yd. of 1½" wide netting lace insertion
- ❧ 1¼ yds. of ½" wide lace beading
- ❧ 3 yds. of ¼" wide double-faced satin ribbon

I. Constructing the Neck Roll

1. Measure the batting in the package. If it measures about 18" long and 19" around, use as is. Take the roll out of the package and slip-stitch the loose edge to the roll (**fig. 1**).

2. If the roll of batting is not the right size, take it out of the package and refold until it measures 18" in width. Begin rolling at one short end and roll it firmly until it measures 19" around. Cut off any excess batting and slip-stitch the loose edge to the roll (**fig. 1**).

3. Cut a piece of satin 20" wide across the width of the fabric.

4. On each short end of the strip, fold and press ¼" to the wrong side (**fig. 2**).

5. Fold the fabric in half with the long edges meeting. Stitch the long edge with a ½" seam. Press the seam to one side.

6. Fold the ends of the tube to the wrong side 5½". Pin the ends in place.

7. Stitch along the ¼" folded edge, then stitch ½" away from the first stitching row to create a casing. If your machine has a free-arm, this is a great time to use it. Begin and end the stitching rows at the seam, and back-stitch over the seam for reinforcement (**fig. 3**).

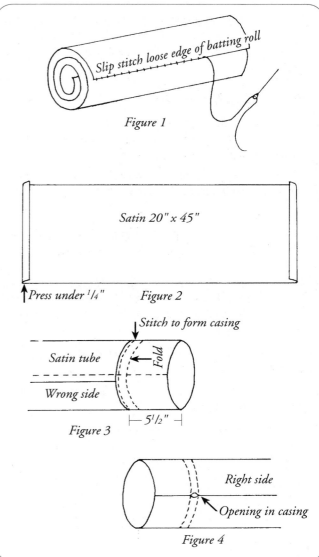

Slip stitch loose edge of batting roll

Figure 1

Satin 20" x 45"

↑ *Press under ¼"*   *Figure 2*

Stitch to form casing

Satin tube   *Fold*

Wrong side

├— 5½" —┤

Figure 3

Right side

Opening in casing

Figure 4

8. Turn the tube right side out. On the outside, carefully clip the threads to open the seam between the two rows of stitching. This opens up the casing (**fig. 4**).

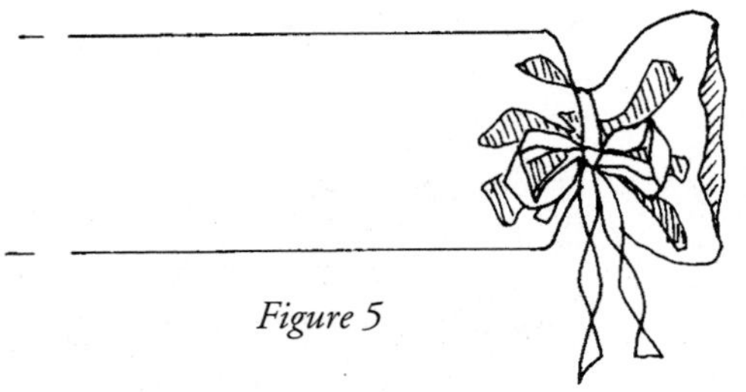

Figure 5

9. Cut two 27" lengths of satin ribbon. Run a ribbon through the casing at each end of the tube.
10. Slide the rolled up batting into the tube. Pull up the ribbons, wrap the ends around the gathers, and tie the streamers into bows at each end. Fluff out the ruffle that forms at each end of the pillow (**fig.** 5).

II. Making the Lace Sleeve

1. Fold the netting lace edging in half, meeting the short ends together. Slide the top layer until the design is a match to the bottom layer; pin the layers together (**fig.** 6).
2. Cut through both layers to create two 20" pieces of the lace; be sure that the lace is centered so that the 10" mark on the ruler rests over the center motif of the lace (**fig.** 6).
3. Cut a 20" length of the wide netting insertion; also cut two 20" lengths of the lace beading and two 21" lengths of the satin ribbon.
4. Place a beading strip along the long raw edge of each edging piece, letting the inside heading of the beading overlap the raw edge by 1/4". Stitch the beading to the edging (refer to "Extra-Stable Lace Finishing" on page 223).
5. Attach the beading strips to each long edge of the netting insertion, using the technique lace to lace.
6. Run a ribbon through each strip of beading and tack the ribbon ends to the beading.
7. Fold the lace section in half, right sides together and raw edges meeting. Stitch the raw edges in a 1/2" seam. Zigzag and trim the seam (**fig.** 7).
8. Turn the sleeve right side out and slip it over the pillow, matching the seams. ✱

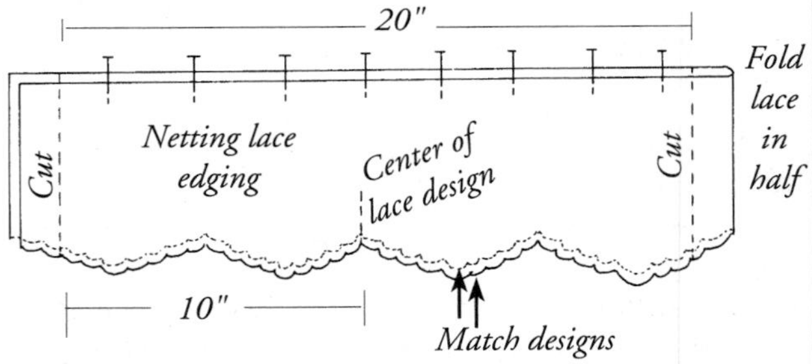

Figure 6

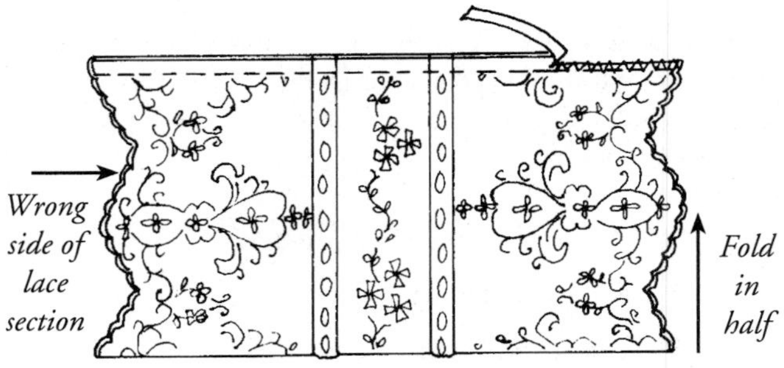

Figure 7

Blue Rose Pillow

Perhaps these are the most wonderful fabric roses that I have ever seen! They aren't too hard to make and the result is certainly worth your effort. This ecru water stained taffeta pillow has blue piping and a blue wrap across the top from corner to corner. In two shades of blue, one very pale and one medium, there are the most elegant scalloped roses! There are two medium blue roses and one pale blue. The back of the pillow is ecru also. What a gift this would be for anyone on your list! Made in a variety of fabrics and colors this tailored but sassy pillow could go in any room in your house.

Blue Rose

Materials Needed

- ¹/₂ yd. of cream moiré taffeta
- 1 yd. of medium blue moiré taffeta
- ¹/₄ yd. of light blue moiré taffeta
- 2 yds. of ³/₈" cording to make piping
- posterboard
- pillow form or 14" pillow form
- scallop templates found on the pull-out section

I. Constructing the Pillow

1. Cut two 15" squares from the cream taffeta, for the pillow front and back. Cut an 18" x 26" strip of the medium blue taffeta, for the pillow sash, with the 26" side on the straight grain of the fabric (**fig. 1**).

2. Fold the sash strip in half, right side together, and with the 26" edges meeting. Stitch the long edge with a ¹/₂" seam, press the seam open and turn the sash right side out (**fig. 2**).

3. Fold the sash in half with the short ends meeting. Mark the center fold with a crease. Open the sash out flat and run a sturdy gathering row along the center line crease (**fig. 3**).

4. Pull the gathers up tightly and stitch over the center to hold the gathers. Place the sash diagonally over the pillow top, with right sides up. Stitch across the gathers to hold the sash in place. Fan the ends of the sash out flat and pin the sash to the pillow top; baste the sash along the edges of the pillow top and trim the excess sash from the edges (**fig. 4**).

5. Make and apply the piping as follows:

   a. Cut and stitch two 2¹/₂" x 45" strips of the medium blue taffeta together with a ¹/₄" seam to make one long strip.

   b. Place the cording on the wrong side along the length of the fabric strip and wrap the fabric over the cording. The raw edges of the fabric should meet, wrong sides together. Use a zipper or cording foot to stitch through the layers of fabric, close to the cording (**fig. 5**).

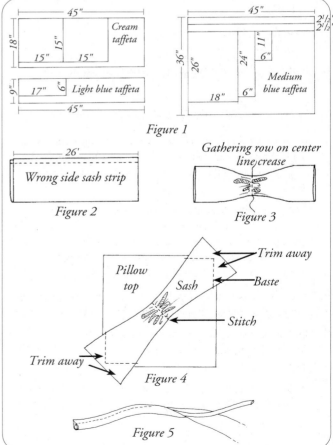

Figure 1

Figure 2

Figure 3

Figure 4

Figure 5

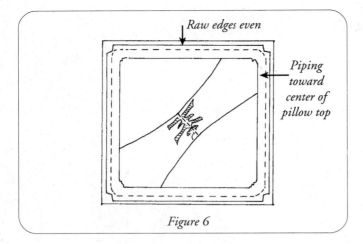

Figure 6

Figure 7

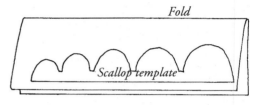

Figure 8

Figure 9

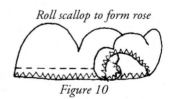

Figure 10

c. Place the piping to the right side around the outer edge of the pillow top, with the raw edges even and the piping toward the center. Clip the seam allowance at the corners to let the piping lie flat. The piping will be rounded as it turns the corners. As the two pieces meet turn ¹/₄" to the inside of one piping tube. Insert the end of the other tube inside (**fig. 6**).

d. Pin and stitch close to the piping.

6. Place the pillow top over the back piece, right sides together. Pin the two pieces together and stitch, covering the stitching line that applied the piping to the pillow top. Leave an opening along one side (**fig. 7**).

7. Turn the pillow to the right side. The corners will not be square, they will be slightly rounded.

8. Stuff the pillow, or make a pillow form to insert. Stitch the opening closed.

II. Making the Roses

1. From the medium blue taffeta, cut a 6" x 24" strip, and a strip 6" x 11". From the light blue taffeta, cut a 6" x 17" strip. Fold each strip in half along the length, right sides together and lightly press.

2. Trace the scallop templates onto posterboard; cut out the templates. Use the small and large templates for the medium blue roses, and use the medium template for the light blue rose. Place the templates over the fabric strips, with the scalloped edge toward the fold. Trace around the templates (**fig. 8**).

3. Stitch the scallops following the template lines, pivoting at the points. Trim the scallops, clip, turn right side out and press.

4. On the right side, run a sturdy gathering row ¹/₄" below the scallop pivot points. Serge or zigzag to finish the raw edge, ¹/₄" below the gathering row (**fig. 9**).

5. Pull up the gathers and roll the scallops to form roses, beginning at the small end. Stitch the bottom edge by hand to hold the rose shape (**fig. 10**).

6. Hand-stitch the roses in place over the center of the sash, with the light blue rose in the middle. ✳

Woven Heart Pillow

This ecru taffeta pillow has puffing around the sides and a woven heart surrounded by braid in the center. The braid is medium blue; the ribbon rosette and the ribbon through the beading is of the same shade of blue. There is an ecru tassel in the center of the ribbon rosette. The woven heart in the middle is woven of ecru lace insertion as well as bridal white. Ecru ribbon in addition to the blue ribbon is run through the pieces of lace insertion. A little music box is found inside the pillow; it plays "Bring In The Clowns." Ecru braid piping goes around the outside of the pillow. Sure to please anyone on your list, this pillow is easy to make and very stunning.

Materials Needed

- ¹/₂ yd. of cream taffeta
- ⁵/₈ yd. of ¹/₂" blue braid trim
- 1 yd. of cream twisted rope-type drapery piping
- 2 yds. of assorted lace insertions, ¹/₂" to ⁵/₈" wide
- 1 yd. of ³/₈" cream satin ribbon
- 4 yds. of ¹/₈" double-faced blue satin ribbon
- 1 small cream tassel
- 1 key-wound craft music box
- 7" square of lightweight fusible interfacing
- polyfill to stuff a 10" pillow, or a 10" round pillow form
- ¹/₃ yd. of white batiste (if you are not using a purchased pillow form)
- heart template found on the pull-out section

I. Weaving the Heart

1. Cut a 7" square of lightweight fusible interfacing. Trace the heart template onto the square.

2. Weave the lace and ribbons over the heart (refer to "Lace and Ribbon Weaving" on page 226). Alternate lace and ribbon, and alternate the two ribbon colors.

3. After the weaving is done, press and redraw the heart shape over the weaving. Stitch around the edges of the heart with a short straight stitch. Cut out the heart, close to the stitching, but do not cut the stitches (**fig. 1**).

II. Constructing the Pillow

1. Cut a 5¹/₂" strip of taffeta across the width of the fabric. Also cut two circles of taffeta, 11" in diameter.

2. Along one long edge of the taffeta, run two gathering rows, ¹/₂" and ¹/₄" from the edge. Along the other long edge, run 5 gathering rows ¹/₂" apart, with first row ¹/₄" from the edge. Stitch

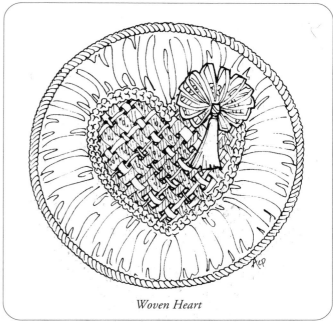

Woven Heart

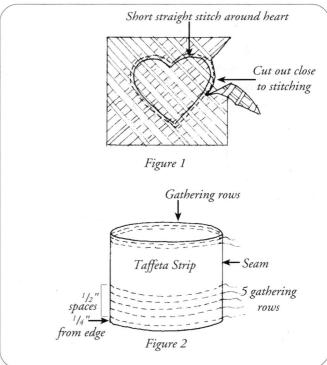

Short straight stitch around heart

Cut out close to stitching

Figure 1

Gathering rows

Taffeta Strip

Seam

5 gathering rows

¹/₂" spaces

¹/₄" from edge

Figure 2

the short ends of the strip together with a ¹/₄" seam, right sides together. Be sure that the gathering threads are not caught in the seam (**fig. 2**).

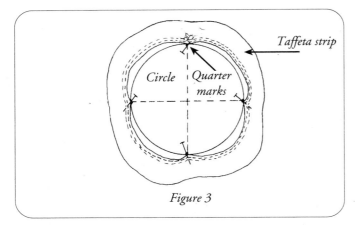

Figure 3

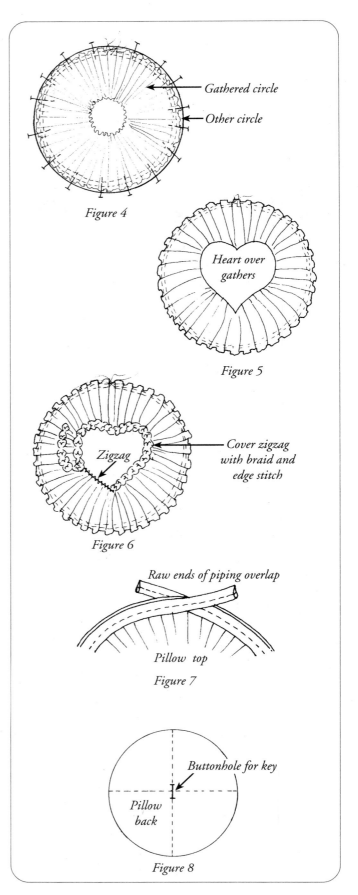

Figure 4

Figure 5

Figure 6

Figure 7

Figure 8

3. Mark the strip into quarters along both long edges. Fold one of the circles into quarters and mark the edges. Along the side of the strip with two gathering rows, pin the quarter marks of the strip to the quarter marks of the pillow (**fig. 3**).

4. Pull up the two gathering rows to make the strip fit the circle; pin but do not baste. Tie off the ends of the gathering threads. Pull up the five gathering rows on the inside edge to make the strip lie flat against the circle. The inner rows will be gathered tighter than the outer rows, allowing the gathers to fan out evenly from the center. Do not pull the gathers so tightly that the circle puckers (**fig. 4**).

5. Pin the heart over the gathers in the center of the circle; pin through only the heart and the gathered strip, the circle will not be caught. Remove the pins from the outer edge of the circle and remove the gathered strip with the heart from the circle (**fig. 5**).

6. Stitch the heart to the gathered strip with a small zigzag around the edges. Cover the zigzag with the braid, beginning and ending at the bottom point. Turn the raw end of the braid under. Stitch along both edges of the braid with a short straight stitch. Use a zipper foot, if needed. Trim the excess gathered fabric from behind the heart (**fig. 6**).

7. Replace the gathered section over the circle. Rearrange the gathers if necessary and pin the two layers together at the outer edges; baste the layers together and treat as one layer of fabric.

8. On the right side, place the piping around the outer edge of the pillow top, with the raw edges even; the piping will be toward the center of the pillow. Let the raw ends of the piping overlap and extend into the seam allowance. Baste the piping in place (**fig. 7**).

9. Fold the pillow back circle in quarters and mark the center point. Make a small buttonhole on the right side, in the center of the circle. The buttonhole must be large enough for the music box key (**fig. 8**).

10. Place the pillow front over the back, right sides together. Stitch with a $^1/_2$" seam, but leave a large opening on one side for inserting the pillow form. Turn the pillow right side out.

11. Make a loopy rosette from the remaining blue ribbon. Sew the rosette to the top right side of the heart. Sew the tassel over the rosette.

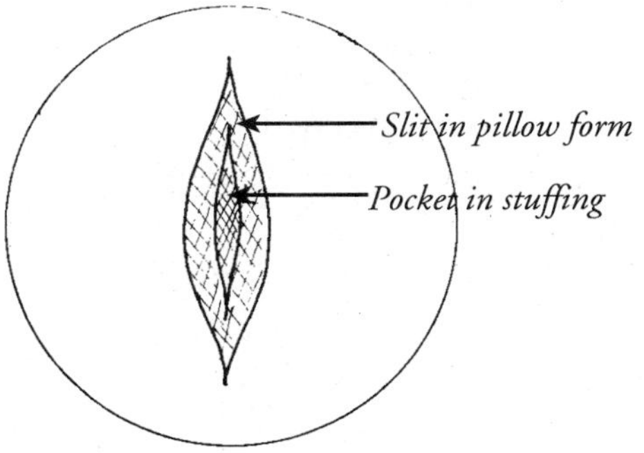

Figure 9

III. Inserting the Music Box

1. Use the white batiste and the polyfill to make a 10" round pillow form, or use a purchased form.
2. Cut a slit in the middle of the pillow form, large enough to insert the music box. Push the stuffing out of the way to form a pocket in the middle of the pillow (**fig. 9**).
3. Place the music box in the pocket and pull stuffing over it. There should be enough stuffing over the box to cushion it, but not enough to interfere with the winding key. Sew the slit closed, leaving an opening around the key stem (**fig. 10**).
4. Insert the pillow form into the pillow, placing the key through the buttonhole in the pillow back. Stitch the pillow opening closed. Also stitch the buttonhole closed, leaving a small opening around the key (**fig. 11**).

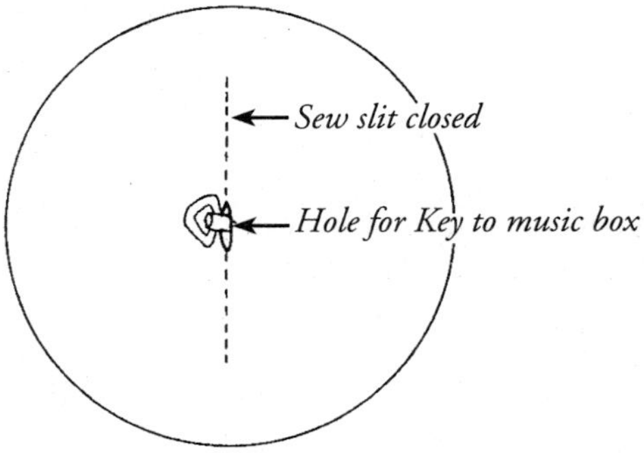

Figure 10

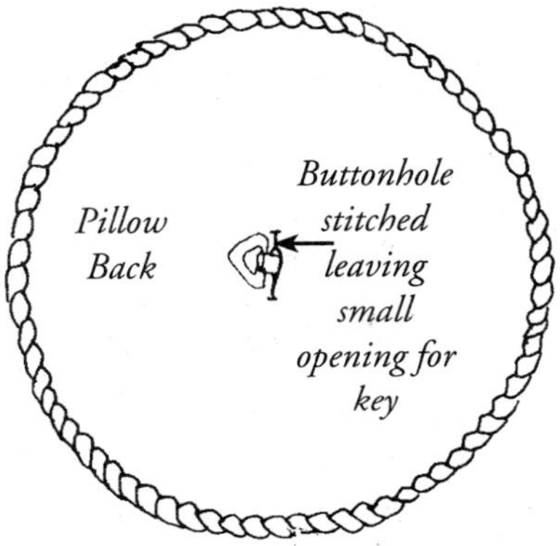

Figure 11

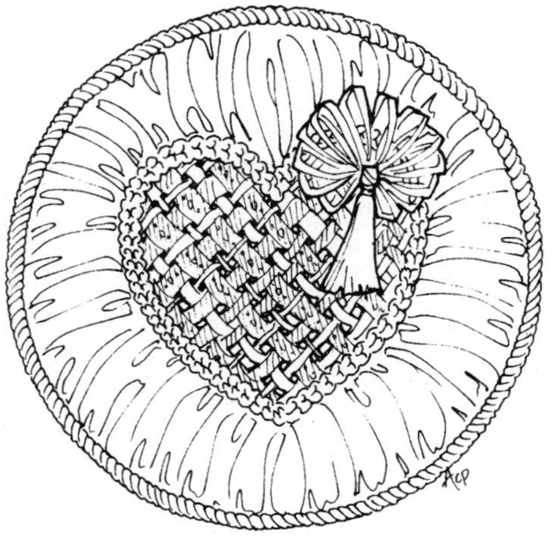

Lace Piecing Pillow

Green silk dupioni makes the perfect backdrop for this lace piecing pillow featuring ecru and bridal white laces with the forest green silk dupioni peeking through. Being square in shape the pillow measures seventeen inches square. The ecru lace design makes a square in the center and the side pieces make another square. The wide tubing is shaped around the edges in an interesting manner with a mitered fold in the corners. Self piping finishes the edges of the pillow and the center has a Swiss motif stitched down. It has been dyed bridal white. Using different fabrics, this pillow would be appropriate for any room in your house.

Materials Needed

- ❧ 1 yd. of silk dupioni

- ❧ 2¹/₂ yds. <u>each</u> of 5 different lace insertions (together the widths should equal about 3")

- ❧ 1 square lace medallion, approximately 2" wide

- ❧ 2¹/₂ yds. of ³/₈" cord for piping

- ❧ 16" square pillow form, self-made or purchased

I. Making the Pieced Lace

1. Stitch the 2¹/₂ yd. strips of lace together to make a band about 3" wide, using the lace to lace method found on page 167.

2. On pieces of wide paper, draw an 8" square and an 11¹/₂" square. Draw lines diagonally through the corners to serve as mitering lines (**fig. 1**).

3. Place the 11¹/₂" square on a lace shaping board. Shape the lace band into a square, mitering the corners with the fold-back method found on page 204. Pin the miters well, and lightly starch and press the lace dry. Remove the lace from the board.

4. Zigzag over the miter folds and trim the mitered lace away from behind the square.

5. Repeat steps 3 and 4 with the 8" square.

6. Place the small lace square diagonally over the large square. Pin and stitch the small square over the large square. Trim the lace from behind the small square (**fig. 2**).

II. Constructing the Pillow

1. Cut two 6" strips across the width of the silk dupioni. Also cut two 2" strips across the width of the fabric. Cut two 18" squares from the remaining silk.

2. Fold one of the silk squares in half vertically and horizontally. Finger press creases along the folded edges to divide the square into quarters. Open the square out flat.

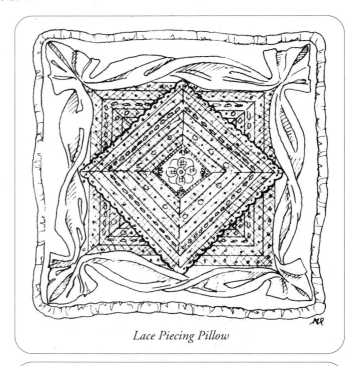

Lace Piecing Pillow

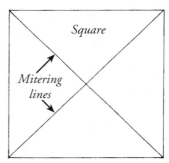

Figure 1

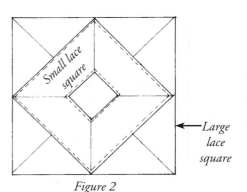

Figure 2

3. Place the pieced lace square over the quartered silk square, with the points of the small square lined up at the creases (**fig. 3**).

4. Pin the lace in place and use a straight stitch or tiny zigzag to attach the lace edges to the pillow top. Stitch the medallion in the middle of the pillow top.

5. Make and apply the piping as follows:

   a. Stitch the two 2" x 45" strips of the silk together with a $^1/_4$" seam to make one long strip.

   b. Place the cording on the wrong side along the length of the fabric strip and wrap the fabric over the cording. The raw edges of the fabric should meet, wrong sides together. Use a zipper or cording foot to stitch through the layers of fabric, close to the cording (**fig. 4**).

   c. Place the piping to the right side around the outer edge of the pillow top, with the raw edges even and the piping toward the center. Clip the seam allowance at the corners so the piping will lie flat. The piping will be rounded as it turns the corners. If you stretch it too tightly around the corners, it will pucker when you turn it right side out (**fig. 5**).

   d. Pin and stitch close to the piping.

6. Place the pillow top over the back piece, right sides together. Pin the two pieces together and stitch, covering the stitching line that applied the piping to the pillow top. Leave an opening along most of one side (**fig. 6**).

7. Turn the pillow to the right side. The corners will not be square, they will be slightly rounded.

8. Stuff the pillow, or make a pillow form to insert, and stitch the opening closed.

III. Adding the Fabric Trim

1. Stitch the two 6" strips together at the short ends to make a long strip. Fold the strip in half along the length, right sides together, and stitch the long edge with a $^1/_2$" seam. Turn the tube right side out and press so that the long seam is on one edge.

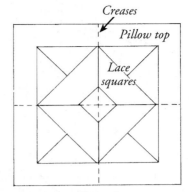

Figure 3

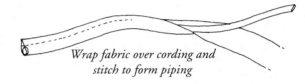

Wrap fabric over cording and stitch to form piping

Figure 4

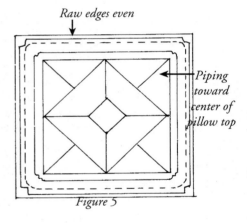

Figure 5

Figure 6

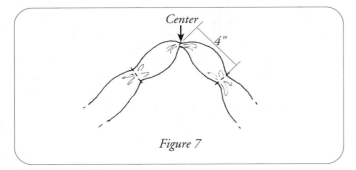

Center

4"

Figure 7

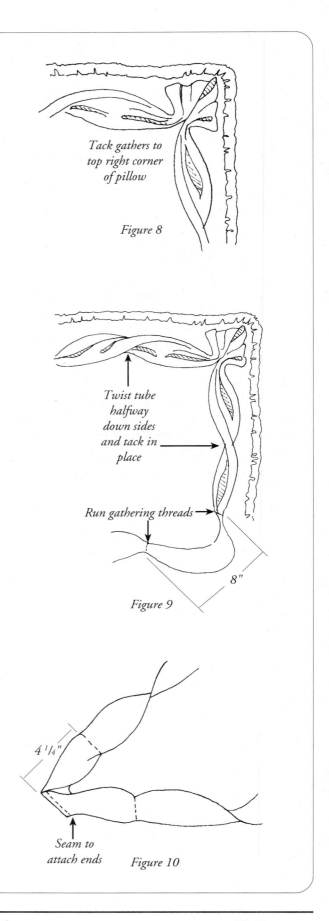

Tack gathers to
top right corner
of pillow

Figure 8

Twist tube
halfway
down sides
and tack in
place

Run gathering threads →

8"

Figure 9

4 1/4"

Seam to
attach ends

Figure 10

2. Place the short ends of the tube together and mark the center of
    the tube. Move out about 4" on each side of the center and run a
    gathering thread by hand across the tube. Pull the gathers up and
    tie off (**fig. 7**).

3. Make a loop and tack the gathers to the top right corner of the
    pillow (**fig. 8**).

4. Take the loose ends of the tube across the sides of the pillow, one
    to the left and one to the right, putting a loose twist halfway
    across the sides. Tack the twist in place (**fig. 9**).

5. When the tube reaches the corner of the lace, run gathers across
    the tube. Move out 8" from those gathers and run a second
    gathering thread (**fig. 9**).

6. Make the loop and tack the gathers in place (**see fig. 8**).

7. Repeat steps 4 and 5 for the top left corner. Put the loose twist in
    the ends as you move toward the last corner.

8. When you come to the bottom left corner, run gathering threads
    across each end of the tube as it reaches the corner. Move out
    4 1/4" from the gathers and zigzag or serge a 1/4" seam to attach the
    two ends of the tube. Be sure that the seam will be on the back
    side of the loop (**fig. 10**).

9. Fold and tack the gathers and the loop in place, hiding the seam
    behind the loop. ✖

Introduction to Doll Dresses

Visions of heirloom party dress still dance in my mind upon my remembering the very first French sewn dress that I ever saw. It was an ecru netting high yoke dress with miles of antique laces stitched in bands around the skirt. Puffing strips ran vertically in the high yoke and horizontally in the fancy band. I love high yoke dresses and Joanna had ten white ones made just like the doll dresses in this book before she ever had another color or style dress. Dolls love high yoke dresses just like little girls do. Ever classical, this style doll dress began its popularity long before the turn of the last century. Historically, high yokes have just always been there in one form or another. There are so many wonderful things one can do with a high yoke basic style and this section of fabulous doll dresses masterfully illustrates that fact. Enjoy your "big skirt" on this type of doll dress; enough room to really create is found on this style skirt. There are some spectacular doll dress variations for you in this series of *Martha's Sewing Room* and I give you permission to create many more using these patterns in this book and your own imagination. After all, that is the essence of heirloom sewing.

1. In this book, we have given general directions which you will use to construct all of the high yoke dresses. For each specific dress, we have written a section giving you all the specifics for that dress. The professional illustration of the finished dress as well as explicit diagrams for stitching each section will follow under the show number. On the directions for each doll dress you will find these words: *Please read through both the General Directions and the Specific Directions before starting the dress.* The general directions are found in the first part of this section; the specific directions are found on the pages with each specific dress. Usually the specific directions tell you how to embellish the bodice, the sleeves, the skirt or some other area of that specific dress. Then refer back to the general directions for the actual doll dress construction.

2. There are 12 beautiful doll dresses in this section, all a variation of the high yoke dress. The patterns and templates are included in the pattern section of this book. The fully illustrated, how to sew, directions follow in this section. We have designed a doll dress incorporating the main technique taught in the television show, *Martha's Sewing Room,* for the week.

3. We have used Seeley's composition bodies for cutting our patterns for the doll dresses. Each of these patterns fit 13 sizes of Seeley's bodies. We have chosen French, Modern and German Bodies for this book. The sizes range from FB12 to GB21 which is quite a size range. If you look under the section entitled Doll Dress Directions, you will find measurements for all of these bodies. To order Seeley's bodies, call 607-433-1240 or FAX 607-432-2042, or write Seeley's, 9 River St., Oneonta, NY 13820. These patterns fit many sizes of other types of doll bodies also.

4. Our porcelain doll makers have told us over and over how much they are enjoying the *Martha's Sewing Room* series and how much they enjoy having this many different doll patterns in 13 different sizes in one book! Thanks for your encouraging letters and calls! Please enjoy this new book with this precious high yoke doll dress pattern for all of the dolls in your life. I think you will love this section in the television program as well as in this book. Don't forget that you can call your local PBS station if you don't have *Martha's Sewing Room* in your area and request that they carry it!

5. These patterns fit not only Seeley's bodies, they fit many purchased "play with" dolls also. To make the gift of a life time, please choose your child's or grandchild's favorite doll and make her a wardrobe. The Christmas that Joanna was nineteen, her only request for a present was a new dress for her childhood doll, Mary. We used a pattern from this series to make a baby doll dress. There are several very popular "play with" dolls on the market which are about 18 inches tall. We have had many requests concerning which of these patterns fit those dolls. The answer is MB160 or FB17 fit best with just a few adjustments on the length. Of course the length you prefer is certainly your own decision; there are many cute lengths for doll's dresses as well as for children's.

6. You can use the ideas from any or all of these doll dresses to make garments for your child or grandchild. For children's dresses, I usually put 90 inches in the fullness of the skirt. The high yoke dress pattern for children is found in the 100 series guide called *Martha's Sewing Room* to go along with our very first television series. The sizes are girl's 3 months to 10 years in that book. It is very sweet to make matching doll and child dresses; that would make a lifetime memory. I know several mothers and grandmothers who make a matching doll dress for nearly every dress they make for their children. ✄

Doll Dress Directions

The Seeley body types and sizes given in the charts below, French, Modern and German, are the most popular composition child bodies. These charts will be referred to in each set of doll dress directions to create the proper lengths and/or widths for the size of the doll being dressed. The doll bodies are also divided into small, medium and large bodies. After determining the doll body style and size being used, refer to the measurements on the charts for that specific body size to create any one of these beautiful dresses. The general directions are given for the construction of the yoke dress. The doll dresses also have specific directions for the special details of each dress, listed by show number and dress name.

FB - French Child Bodies

MB - Modern Child Bodies

GB - German Child Bodies

Small Bodies Include: FB12, FB14, GB11, GB13

Medium Bodies Include: MB140, MB160, GB15, GB16

Large Bodies Include: FB17, FB19, MB190, MB21.5, GB21

Skirt Measurements

These measurements are the finished skirt measurements (length and width) including seam allowances and ruffles (if any). If a hem is desired, add 1" to 3" to these lengths for a hem allowance. The width given is the total width (front and back). Half this measurement will be the width of the front skirt piece and half will be the width for the back skirt piece. For example, if the chart has a finished width of 60, cut the front skirt to 30" wide and the back skirt piece to 30" wide.

FB12 $8^3/_8$" x 44"	MB140 $11^1/_8$" x 44"	GB11 $8^1/_2$" x 44"
FB14 $10^5/_8$" x 44"	MB160 $12^5/_8$" x 44"	GB13 $10^5/_8$" x 44"
FB17 $13^3/_8$" x 60"	MB190 $15^3/_8$" x 60"	GB15 $10^3/_4$" x 44"
FB19 $14^1/_4$" x 60"	MB21.5 $17^7/_8$" x 60"	GB16 $12^1/_4$" x 44"
		GB21 $17^1/_2$" x 60"

Neck Band Measurements (unfinished)

FB12 6"	MB140 $6^1/_2$"	GB11 5"
FB14 $6^3/_4$"	MB160 $7^1/_2$"	GB13 $6^1/_2$"
FB17 $7^1/_2$"	MB190 $7^1/_2$"	GB15 $6^3/_4$"
FB19 $7^3/_8$"	MB 21.5 $8^1/_2$"	GB16 $6^3/_4$"
		GB21 $8^1/_2$"

Sleeve Band Measurement (unfinished)

FB12 4"	MB140 $4^1/_2$"	GB11 $3^1/_2$"
FB14 $4^1/_2$"	MB160 $4^1/_2$"	GB13 4"
FB17 $5^1/_2$"	MB190 5"	GB15 $4^1/_2$"
FB19 $5^1/_2$"	MB 21.5 $5^1/_2$"	GB16 $4^1/_2$"
		GB21 $6^1/_2$"

Yoke Chart

(Length and width measurement for the yoke bodice created rectangle)

FB12 $3^1/_2$" x 6"	MB140 4" x 7"	GB11 3" x 5"
FB14 $3^1/_2$" x 6"	MB160 4" x 7"	GB13 $3^1/_2$" x 6"
FB17 4" x 8"	MB190 4" x $7^1/_2$"	GB15 4" x 6"
FB19 4" x 8"	MB21.5 5" x 9"	GB16 4" x 6"
		GB21 4" x 9"

General Directions

All pattern pieces are found in the pattern section of this book, pages 261- 277.

All dresses need the following pattern pieces: front yoke, back yoke, armhole guide and sleeve. These pattern pieces can be found in the pattern section, pages 261 - 277. The patterns for the bonnet, camisole, and petticoat can also be found in the pattern section. The pantalettes pattern can be found on the center pull-outs.

All seams are ¼". Overcast the seam allowance using a zigzag or serger.

I. Cutting

1. Refer to the specific directions for decorating the front yoke. Cut out the front yoke from decorated fabric or plain fabric.

2. Cut out two yoke backs from the selvage. Mark the placket fold lines along the backs.

3. Cut out two sleeves. Refer to the specific directions for decorating the sleeves.

4. The skirt will be cut out later. Finished measurements are given in the chart. Specific directions for each skirt are given under each dress title. Remember to cut the armhole from the sides of the skirt front and back.

5. If the dress has a collar, the collar will also be cut later. Refer to the specific dress title.

II. Construction of the Yokes and Skirt

1. Place the shoulders of the front yoke and back yoke, right sides together and stitch (**fig. 1**).

2. Finish the collar or ruffle, using the directions under each dress title.

3. Finish the neck of the dress, attaching the collar or using a simple neck finish (refer to Neck Finishes).

4. Cut front and back skirt pieces (refer to specific directions and the skirt chart for the length and width of the skirt pieces).

5. Place the armhole guide along the sides of the skirt. Cut armholes from the sides of both skirt pieces (**fig. 2**).

6. Cut a slit down the center back of the skirt for the back placket to the following measurement: small bodies = 3¹/₂", medium bodies = 4¹/₂", large bodies = 5¹/₂" (**fig. 2**).

7. Back Placket -

   a. Cut a strip of fabric from the selvage ³/₄" wide by twice the length given above, plus 1". For example, the small doll placket will be figured as follows: 2 x 3¹/₂ = 7" and 7 + 1 = 8". The strip would be cut ³/₄" by 8".

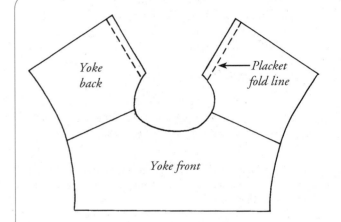

Figure 1

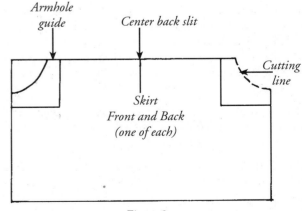

Figure 2

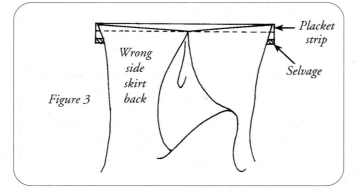

Figure 3

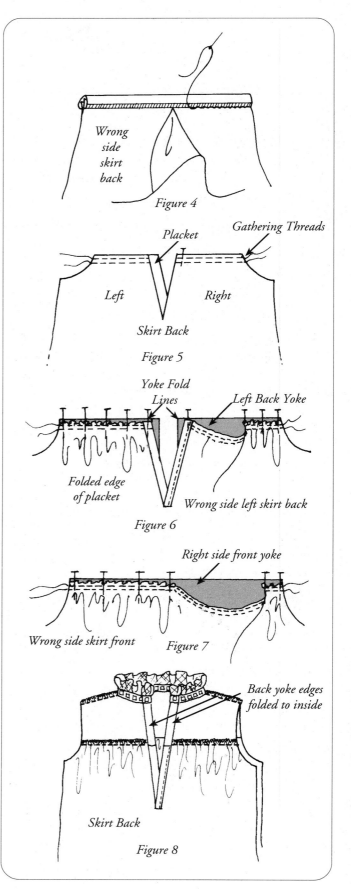

b. Pull the slit in the skirt apart to form a "V". Place the right side of the strip to the right side of the skirt slit. The stitching will be done from the wrong side with the skirt on top and the placket strip on the bottom. The placket strip will be straight and the skirt will form a "V" with the point of the "V" $^1/_4$" from the edge of the placket. Stitch, using a $^1/_4$" seam. As you stitch, you will just catch the tip (a few fibers) at the point of the "V" (**fig. 3**).

c. Press the seam toward the selvage edge of the placket strip. Turn the selvage edge to the inside of the dress, enclosing the seam allowance. Whip by hand or stitch in place by machine (**fig. 4**).

8. The back of the dress will lap right over left. Fold the right side of the placket to the inside of the skirt and pin. Leave the left back placket open (**fig. 5**).

9. Run two rows of gathering in the top edges of each skirt piece at $^1/_8$" and $^1/_4$" (**fig. 5**).

10. Open up the fold back on each side of the back yoke pieces (fold line is clearly marked).

11. Place the back yokes to the back skirt piece, right sides together. Pull up the gathered skirt backs to fit the back yokes. The placket edge will come to the fold line on the left back yoke. The folded edge of the placket will come to the fold line on the right back yoke. Stitch in place using a $^1/_4$" seam (**fig. 6**). Overcast with a zigzag.

12. Place the front skirt to the front yoke, right sides together. Pull up the gathers to make the skirt fit the yoke. Stitch using a $^1/_4$" seam (**fig. 7**). Overcast.

13. Pull the back yokes away from the skirt, folding the back yokes to the inside along the fold lines (**fig. 8**).

III. Constructing the Sleeves

1. Decorate the sleeve as desired (refer to specific directions for each dress).

2. Run gathering rows in the top and bottom of the sleeve at $^1/_8$" and $^1/_4$".

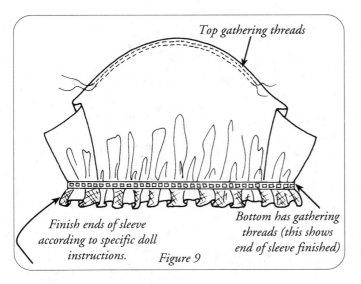

Top gathering threads

Finish ends of sleeve according to specific doll instructions.

Bottom has gathering threads (this shows end of sleeve finished)

Figure 9

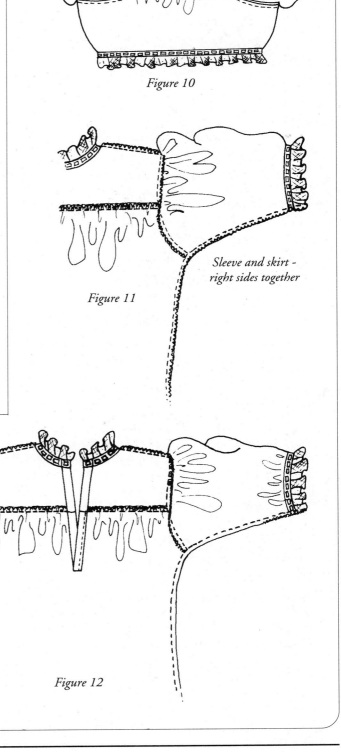

Figure 10

Figure 11

Sleeve and skirt - right sides together

Figure 12

3. Finish the ends of the sleeve using the trims and instructions for each specific dress (refer to Sleeve Finishes) (**fig. 9**).

4. Gather the top of the sleeve to fit the arm opening of the dress. Match the center of the sleeve with the shoulder seam of the dress. The gathers should fall $^3/_4$" to $1^1/_2$" on each side of the shoulder seam. The gathers of the sleeve should not extend past the bodice seam of the yoke. Pin the right side of the sleeve to the right side of the arm opening.

5. Stitch the sleeve to the dress using a $^1/_4$" seam (**fig. 10**). Overcast.

IV. Side Seams and Fancy Band

1. Stitch one side together by placing the sides of the sleeve and skirt right sides together. Stitch in place using a $^1/_4$" seam. Overcast (**fig. 11**).

Optional: If the dress has a fancy band, stitch this band to the bottom of the skirt, right sides together.

2. Place the other side of the dress with right sides together. Stitch in place, using a $^1/_4$" seam. Overcast (**fig. 12**).

A. Neck Finishes

a. Entredeux to Gathered Edging

1. Cut a strip of entredeux to the neck band measurement given in the chart for the specific doll body to be dressed.

2. Cut a piece of edging lace two times this length and gather to fit the entredeux strip.

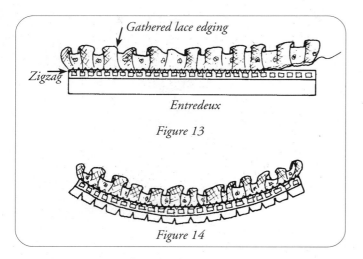

Gathered lace edging

Zigzag

Entredeux

Figure 13

Figure 14

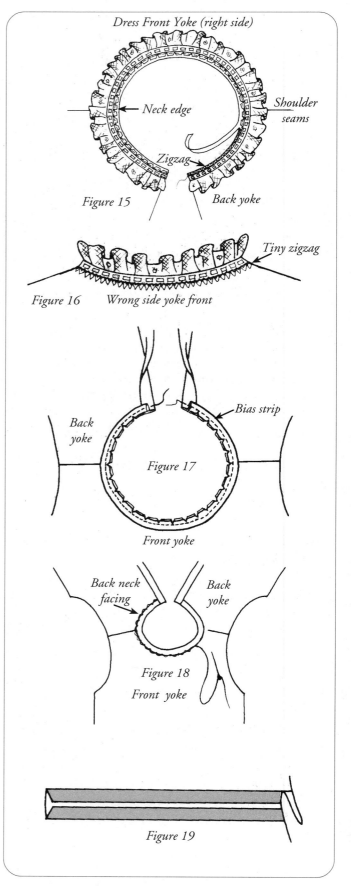

Dress Front Yoke (right side)

Neck edge

Shoulder seams

Zigzag

Figure 15

Back yoke

Tiny zigzag

Figure 16   Wrong side yoke front

Back yoke

Bias strip

Figure 17

Front yoke

Back neck facing

Back yoke

Figure 18

Front yoke

Figure 19

3. Trim away one side of the entredeux and attach the gathered edging lace to the trimmed entredeux using the technique "Entredeux to Gathered Lace" (**fig. 13**).

4. If the fabric edge remaining on the entredeux is not already $^1/_4$", trim to $^1/_4$". Clip this fabric so that it will curve along the neck edge of the dress (**fig. 14**). Place this strip to the neck (back plackets extended - not folded) of the dress, right sides together. Attach using the technique "Entredeux to Fabric" (**fig. 15**).

5. Using a tiny zigzag, tack the seam allowance to the dress. This stitching will keep the entredeux/gathered lace standing up at the neck (**fig. 16**).

b. Bias Neck Facing

1. Cut a bias strip 1" wide by the length of neck band measurement given in the neck band chart. Fold the bias strip in half along the length and press. Place the cut edges of the strip to the neck of the dress. Cut the ends of the strip off $^3/_8$" from each side of the back bodice edges.

2. Flip the back yoke edges to the outside along the fold lines. Place these folds under the bias strip. Stitch the bias strip to the neck edge using a $^1/_4$" seam. Trim the seam allowance to $^1/_8$". Clip the curves (**fig. 17**). Flip the bias strip and the back bodice edges to the inside of the bodice. Hand stitch the bias strip in place, finishing the neck edge (**fig. 18**).

c. Bias Neck Binding

1. Trim $^1/_4$" off the edge of the neck. Fold the back edges of the back bodice to the inside $^3/_8$". Press.

2. Measure around the neck with the back folds in place and add $^1/_2$" to this measurement. Cut a bias strip 1" wide by this measurement. Fold each long side of the bias strip to the inside $^1/_4$". Press in place (**fig 19**). Open out one side of the bias strip and stitch to

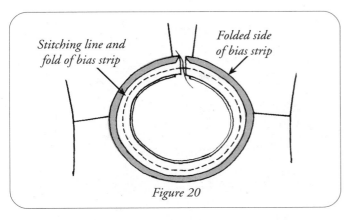

Figure 20

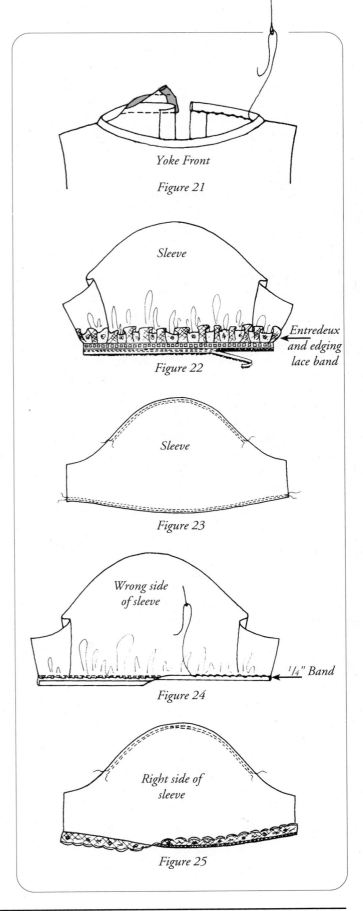

Yoke Front

Figure 21

Sleeve

Entredeux and edging lace band

Figure 22

Sleeve

Figure 23

Wrong side of sleeve

¹/₄" Band

Figure 24

Right side of sleeve

Figure 25

the neck using a ¹/₄" seam (stitch in the fold) (fig. **20**). The bias strip will extend ¹/₄" beyond the folded plackets of the back. Flip the bias up, away from the neck, fold the ends to the inside and pull the upper folded edge of the bias strip over the seam allowance (**fig. 21**). Press. Hand stitch or machine stitch in place.

B. Sleeve Bands and Ruffles

Refer to specific directions for decorating the sleeves.

a. Entredeux and Gathered Edging Lace

1. Cut two strips of entredeux to the measurement for the specific doll body given on the sleeve band chart. Cut two pieces of edging lace twice the length of the entredeux.

2. Gather the edging lace to fit the entredeux. Stitch together using the technique "Entredeux to Gathered Lace" (**refer to fig. 13**).

3. Gather the bottom of the sleeve to fit the entredeux/edging lace band. Stitch the band to the sleeve, right sides together, using the technique "Entredeux to Gathered Fabric" (**fig. 22**).

4. Refer to the General Directions III to attach the sleeve to the bodice (**refer to fig. 10**).

b. Bias Sleeve Bindings

1. Cut two bias strips of fabric 1" wide by the measurement given on the sleeve band chart for your specific doll body.

2. Gather the bottom of the sleeve to fit the bias band (**fig. 23**). Stitch the band to the sleeve, right sides together, using a ¹/₄" seam. Fold the lower edge of the band to the inside ¹/₄". Place the folded edge just over the seam line on the inside of the sleeve creating a ¹/₄" band. Hand stitch or machine stitch in place (**fig. 24**). This will finish the bottom of the sleeve.

c. Gathered Sleeve with Elastic and Lace

1. Stitch a strip of edging lace along the bottom of each sleeve using the technique "Lace to Fabric" (**fig. 25**).

2. Measuring from the finished edge of the wrong side of the sleeves, draw a line with a fabric marker at the following measurement: small dolls = 1", medium dolls = 1¹/₄", large dolls = 1¹/₂"(**fig. 26**).

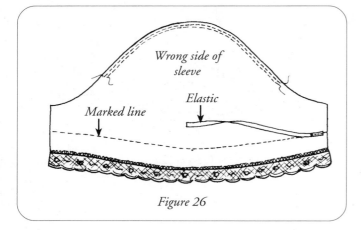

Figure 26

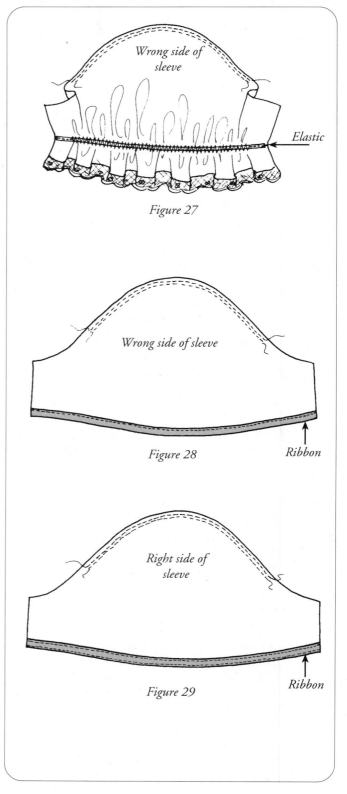

Figure 27

Figure 28

Figure 29

3. Start with two pieces of ¹/₈" elastic 1" longer than the measure-ment given on the sleeve band chart. The longer measurement will aid in attaching the elastic. Place a dot 1" from each end of the elastic.

4. Place one elastic piece on the drawn line of one sleeve with the dot ¹/₄" from the side edge of the sleeve. Stitch elastic in place with several tiny straight stitches (**fig. 26**). Continue stitching with a loose zigzag that encloses the elastic but does not catch the elastic. Pull the elastic until the second dot is ¹/₄" from the side edge. Tack in place with several tiny straight stitches (**fig. 27**). Trim elastic even with the sides of the sleeve. Repeat for other sleeve.

d. Gathered Sleeve with Elastic and Ribbon

1. Cut sleeves ¹/₂" longer for this technique.

2. Cut two pieces of ¹/₄" ribbon the length of the sleeve bottom.

3. Place the ribbon across the bottom edge of the sleeves on the wrong side. The ribbon can be stitched in place along the top edge of the ribbon or held in place with wash-away basting tape (**fig. 28**).

4. Flip the ribbon to the right side of the sleeve. Stitch along the top and bottom edges of the ribbon to hold in place (**fig. 29**).

5. Refer to steps 2 to 4 in section C above for attaching elastic to the sleeves. ✄

Puffing Doll Dress and French Slip

What an enchanted evening for any doll who is the lucky recipient of this netting and puffing high yoke doll dress. Puffing, about one inch wide, is secured by ecru lace insertion on the front yoke, the center sleeves and the fancy band. The bottom of the gathered puffed sleeve is finished with entredeux and gathered lace trim. Ecru silk ribbon has been beaded through the entredeux for an elegant sleeve. Entredeux and gathered lace edging finishes the top of the neckline. Entredeux is stitched all the way around the front yoke

and gathered lace edging has been added right below the entredeux. The skirt has an insertion, puffing, insertion fancy band finished by a gathered ruffle with flat lace edging on the bottom. The back is closed with Velcro™ fasteners. Three French slips were made in different colors to be worn under this dress; blue, peach, and pink to give just a hint of color and variety. This type of dress is just as elegant with an ecru slip underneath. Of course, this exact dress, made a little bigger, would be just as beautiful for a child as it is for a doll.

Show 1

Netting Dress

Puffing Doll Dress

Fabric Requirements

	Small Body	Medium Body	Large Body
Fabric - Netting	1 yd.	$1^{1}/_{4}$ yds.	$1^{3}/_{4}$ yds.
Lace Insertion ($^{1}/_{2}$")	$3^{1}/_{2}$ yds.	4 yds.	5 yds.
Entredeux	$1^{1}/_{2}$ yds.	$1^{3}/_{4}$ yds.	2 yds.
Edging Lace ($^{5}/_{8}$")	6 yds.	7 yds.	10 yds.
Silk Ribbon (7 mm)	1 yd.	1 yd.	$1^{1}/_{2}$ yds.

Other Notions: Lightweight sewing thread, and Velcro™, snaps or tiny buttons for back closure.

All Seams $^{1}/_{4}$" unless otherwise indicated.

Please read through both the General Directions and the Specific Directions before starting the dress. The General Directions can be found on page 39. These Specific Directions tell how each piece is embellished. The General Directions tell how the dress is constructed.

A. Embellishing the Yoke

1. Cut a strip of netting $2^{1}/_{4}$" wide for medium and large dolls and $1^{3}/_{4}$" wide for small dolls by two to two and one half times the length of the yoke measurement found on the chart on page 38.

2. Gather each side of the strip with a $^{1}/_{2}$" seam allowance to make a puffing strip. Gather to the required yoke length. Refer to the directions for making puffing found on page 178. Note: depending on the weight of the netting used, the entire puffing strip may not be needed. Simply cut off the unused part of the strip after it is attached to the yoke.

3. Cut two pieces of insertion lace to the length of the yoke found on the chart. Each piece of lace will be attached to each side of the puffing. Place the side of the lace over the gathering row(s) of the puffing. Stitch in place using a small, tight zigzag. Trim the seam allowance of the puffing close to the zigzag stitching (**fig. 1**).

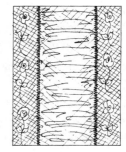

Figure 1

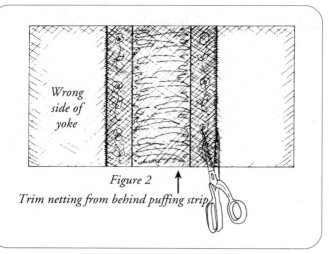

Figure 2

Wrong side of yoke

Trim netting from behind puffing strip

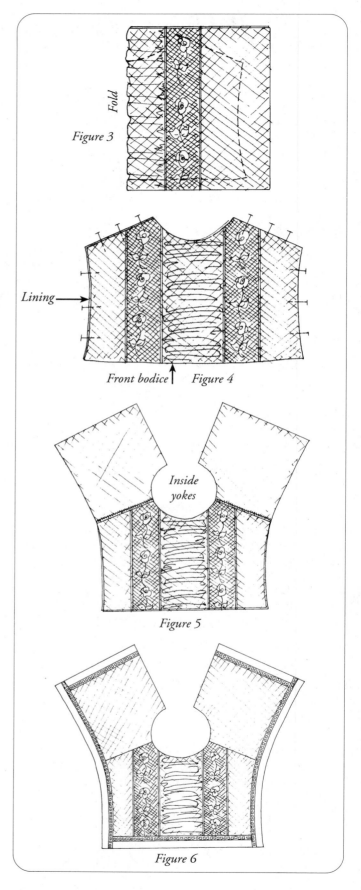

Fold

Figure 3

Lining →

Front bodice | Figure 4

Inside yokes

Figure 5

Figure 6

4. Cut two pieces of netting to the rectangular measurement on the yoke chart. Set one piece aside. Place the lace and puffing strip in the center of the other piece of netting. Zigzag in place along the outer edges of the lace insertion (**fig. 2**). Trim the netting away from the back of the puffing/lace strip. This completes the created fabric for the yoke.

5. Place the second piece of netting on the back side of the created fabric. Fold the two pieces in half along the center and cut out the yoke (**fig. 3**). Pin the two layers of the yoke together and treat as one layer of fabric (**fig. 4**).

B. Constructing the Yokes and Upper Skirt

1. Cut out two back yokes.

2. Place the front yoke to the back yokes at the shoulders and stitch together using a ¹/₄" seam. Overcast the seam allowance with a zigzag or serge (**fig. 5**).

3. Attach a piece of entredeux to the lower edge of the front yoke using the technique "Lace to Fabric" and a ¹/₄" seam. Press away from the yoke.

4. Attach pieces of entredeux to the lower edge of the back yokes using the technique "Entredeux to Fabric" and a ¹/₄" seam. Press away from the yoke.

5. Attach entredeux along the sides of the yoke using the technique "Entredeux to Fabric" and a ¹/₄" seam. Press away from the yoke (**fig. 6**).

6. Finish the neck of the yoke. Refer to the General Directions - A. Neck Finishes - a. Entredeux to Gathered Edging.

7. Cut the skirt pieces 4¹/₄" shorter than the length given on the chart.

8. Refer to the General Directions II - steps 4 - 13. Note: The gathered skirt pieces will be attached to the entredeux of the yoke using the technique "Gathered Fabric to Entredeux."

C. Embellishing the Sleeves

1. Cut out two sleeves from the netting. Measure the center of the sleeve from top to bottom. Create a lace/puffing/lace band twice this length using the same method for creating the band used in the yoke.

2. Cut the band in half and place along the center of each sleeve. Zigzag in place along the outer edge of the lace insertion pieces (**fig.** 7).

3. Refer to the General Directions - III for sleeve construction.

4. Refer to General Directions - B. Sleeve Bands and Ruffles - a. Entredeux and Gathered Edging Lace, to finish the ends of the sleeves.

5. Measure around the outer edges of the yoke along the entredeux. Cut a piece of edging lace two and one half times this measurement. Gather the edging lace to fit the outer edges of the yoke. Topstitch the edging lace to the entredeux using a small tight zigzag (**fig.** 8).

D. Side Seams and Fancy Band

1. Stitch one side seam/sleeve right sides together using a $1/4$" seam. Overcast (**fig.** 9).

2. Cut two pieces of lace 45" long for the small and medium dolls and 60" long for the large dolls.

3. Puffing Band - Cut three $2^{1}/_{4}$" netting strips 45" long for the small and medium dolls and 60" long (four 45" strips equal three 60" strips) for the large dolls. Attach the strips to form one long strip (do not sew in a circle.) Gather each side as before using a $1/2$" seam allowance on each side of the strip. Place the insertion lace pieces over the gathering row(s) and zigzag the lace in place on top of the puffing strip. This puffing lace band is made using the same method as the band for the yoke (refer to section A. Embellishing the Yoke - steps 2 and 3.)

4. Ruffle - Cut three netting strips 45" long for the small and medium dolls and 60" long (four 45" strips equal three 60" strips) for the large dolls by 3" for the large and medium dolls and $2^1/2$" for the small dolls. Attach the strips to form one long strip (do not sew in a circle). Place the edging lace on top of the ruffle strip with the scalloped edge of the lace to the bottom edge of the netting strip. Zigzag along the top edge of the lace edging with small tight zigzag. Trim away the excess netting close to the zigzag (**fig.** 10).

5. Gather the top of the ruffle strip using a $1/2$" seam allowance to fit the lace/puffing band. Place the band on top of the ruffle with the lower edge of the lace/puffing band over the gathering row(s) of the ruffle. Zigzag in place along the edge of the band. Trim the ruffle seam allowance close to the zigzag.

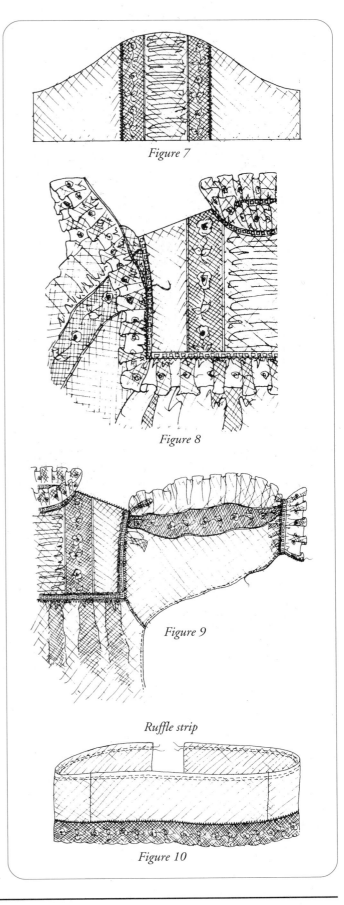

Figure 7

Figure 8

Figure 9

Ruffle strip

Figure 10

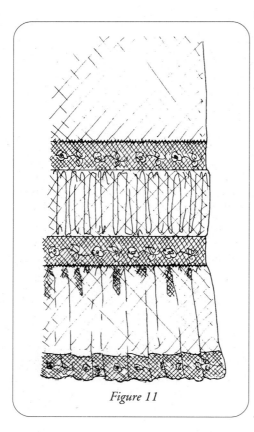

Figure 11

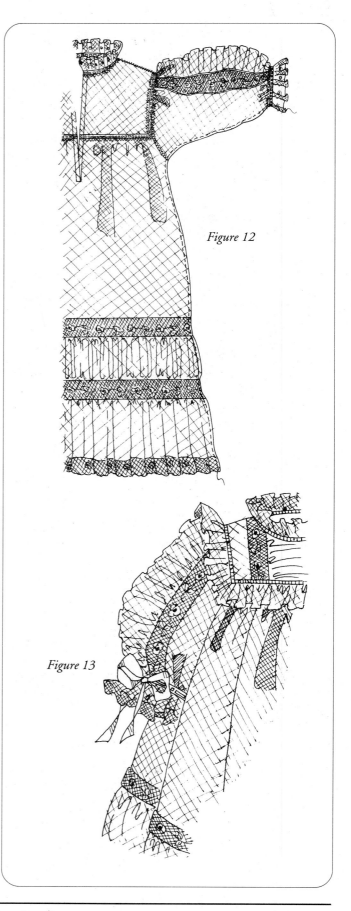

Figure 12

Figure 13

6. Attach the fancy band to the skirt by placing the band on top of the skirt with a ¹/₂" overlap. Zigzag in place along the upper edge of the band. Trim excess seam allowance close to the zigzag (**fig. 11**).

7. Place the second side of the dress right sides together and stitch from the end of the sleeve to the end of the ruffle (**fig. 12**).

8. Weave silk ribbon through the beading (under two bars, over two bars) at the sleeves. Tie into bows at the center of the sleeves (**fig. 13**).

9. Attach Velcro™, buttons and buttonholes or snaps to the back of the yokes to close the dress. ✖

French Slip

Fabric Requirements

	Small Body	Medium Body	Large Body
Edging Lace ($^1/_2$")	1 yd.	$1^1/_4$ yds.	$1^2/_3$ yds.
Fabric	$^1/_3$ yd.	$^1/_2$ yd.	$^2/_3$ yd.

I. Cutting the Slip

Cut out one yoke front from the fold. Cut out two yoke backs from the selvages. Refer to the skirt chart on page 38 for the length and width to cut the skirt. Cut two skirt pieces (one front and one back) using the measurements on the chart.

II. Constructing the Slip

1. Stitch the yokes of the slip right sides together at the shoulders using a $^1/_4$" seam. Overcast with a zigzag or serge (**fig. 1**).

2. Draw off the armholes on the skirt pieces using the armhole guide. Cut out the armholes (**fig. 2**).

3. Place a placket in the back skirt using the General Directions Section II. step 7 on page 39.

4. Continue construction using the General Directions Section II. step 8-13.

5. Finish the armholes and neck edge in the following manner: Stitch $^3/_8$" from the cut edge of the neck and armholes. Clip the curve to the stitching line (**fig. 3**). Press the seam allowance to the

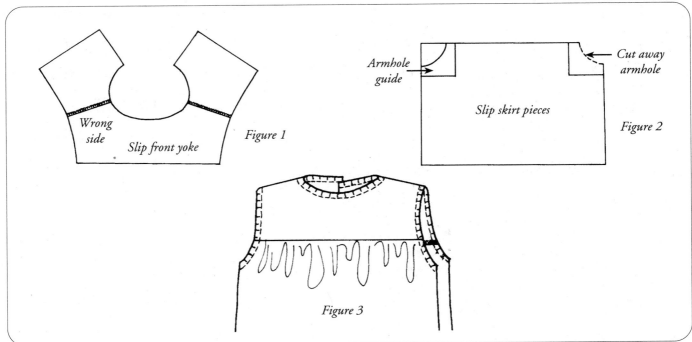

Wrong side

Slip front yoke

Figure 1

Armhole guide

Cut away armhole

Slip skirt pieces

Figure 2

Figure 3

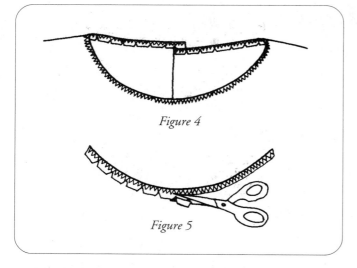

Figure 4

Figure 5

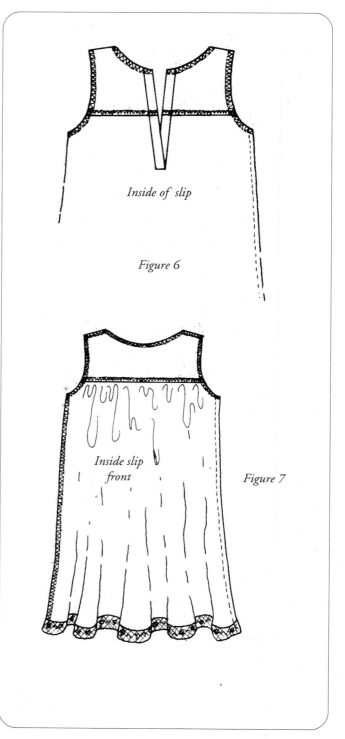

Inside of slip

Figure 6

Inside slip front

Figure 7

wrong side of the slip along the stitching line. From the right side, stitch over the folded edge using a small zigzag (**fig. 4**). Trim the excess fabric close to the stitching (**fig. 5**).

6. Fold the back yokes to the inside of the slip along the fold lines. Whip by hand to the seam line on the dress.

7. Place one side of the slip right sides together and stitch using a ¹/₄" seam (**fig. 6**). Overcast using a zigzag or serge.

8. Attach lace along the lower edge of the slip using the technique "Lace to Fabric."

9. Place the other side of the slip right sides together and stitch using a ¹/₄" seam. Overcast using a zigzag or serger (**fig. 7**).

10. Attach Velcro™, snaps or buttons and buttonholes along the folds of the back yokes to close the slip. ❈

Stitch Key for Doll Dress
Embroidery Templates (pages 54 and 90)
(Colors are given to be used for the Lace and Ribbon Weaving Template. The Ribbon Netting Diamond Template is worked all in ecru.)

Outline stitch - green floss

Spider Web Rose with - 4mm pale pink silk ribbon

Japanese Ribbon Stitch - 4mm green silk ribbon

Straight Stitch Flower with - 4mm blue silk ribbon
French Knot Center - 2mm light ecru silk ribbon

Lazy Daisy Petal - 4mm pale pink silk ribbon

French Knot - 2mm or 4mm silk ribbon

Show 2
Log Cabin Silk Dupioni Doll Dress

Combining ecru silk dupioni, white organdy, ecru, white and bridal white laces has to be yummy! The fabric of the dress is ecru silk dupioni. The white organdy high yoke is stitched with narrow double needle pintucks, and the neckline is finished with ecru entredeux and gathered lace edging. The sleeves have an inset of a log cabin square with ecru Swiss handloom, with a pink rose in the center, and outlined with ecru and white and bridal white laces. At the top and the bottom of this sleeve inset one can find vertically placed strips of the white organdy double needle pintucked. To inset this log cabin piece into the sleeve, ecru entredeux runs down each side of this piece. Ecru entredeux with gathered French lace edging finishes the bottom of this puffed sleeve. Pink silk ribbon runs through the entredeux and is tied in a perky bow. Pink silk ribbon also runs through the entredeux, which joins the organdy yokes to both the front and the back of the gathered skirt. The dress closes in the back with Velcro.

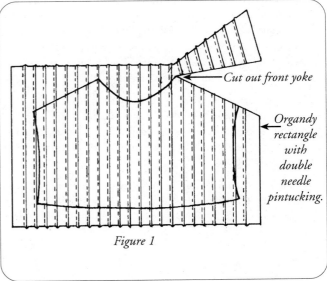

Log Cabin Silk Dupioni Doll Dress

Fabric Requirements

	Small Body	Medium Body	Large Body
Fabric	²/₃ yd.	1 yd.	1¹/₄ yds.
Organdy	¹/₄ yd.	¹/₄ yd.	¹/₄ yd.
Entredeux	1³/₄ yds.	2 yds.	2³/₄ yds.
Edging Lace (¹/₂") neck	¹/₂ yd.	¹/₂ yd.	²/₃ yd.
Edging Lace (1") sleeves	¹/₂ yd.	¹/₂ yd.	³/₄ yd.
Silk Ribbon (2 mm)	1¹/₂ yds.	1¹/₂ yds.	2 yds.
Motif*	2 (1" by 1")	2 (2" by 2")	2 (2" by 2")

Lace Insertion ¹/₄ yd. each of eight different laces for log cabin lace sleeves

Other Notions: Lightweight sewing thread, and Velcro™, snaps or tiny buttons for back closure.

*Rosebud embroidered insertion was used in this dress instead of motifs. This embroidered insertion was cut to the desired size with the rosebud in the center of the square.

All Seams ¹/₄" unless otherwise indicated.

Please read through both the General Directions and the Specific Directions before starting the dress. The General Directions can be found on page 39. These Specific Directions tell how each piece is embellished. The General Directions tell how the dress is constructed.

A. Embellishing the Yoke

1. Cut a rectangle of organdy twice the width of the yoke measurement given on the chart (page 38).

2. Using a double needle and a pintuck foot, start pintucking the fabric starting about ¹/₂" from the edge. Continue pintucking until there is enough pintucked fabric to cut out the yoke.

Cut out front yoke

Organdy rectangle with double needle pintucking.

Figure 1

3. Cut out the yoke front from the pintucked fabric (**fig. 1**).

— B. Constructing the Yokes and Skirt —

1. Cut out two back yokes from the dress fabric.

2. Place the front yoke to the back yokes, right sides together at the shoulders and stitch in place using a $1/4$" seam. Overcast the seam allowance with a zigzag or serge.

3. Attach a piece of entredeux to the lower edge of the front yoke using the technique "Entredeux to Fabric" and a $1/4$" seam. Press away from the yoke (**fig. 2**).

4. Attach pieces of entredeux to the lower edge of the back yokes using the technique "Entredeux to Fabric" and a $1/4$" seam. Press away from the yoke (**fig. 2**).

5. Finish the neck of the yoke. Refer to the General Directions - A. Neck Finishes - a. Entredeux to Gathered Edging.

6. Refer to the skirt chart on page 38. Cut two skirt pieces 2" longer for small dolls and 3" longer for medium and large dolls than the measurement given on the chart. This extra length is for the hem. Refer to the General Directions II - steps 4 - 13. **Note:** The gathered skirt pieces will be attached to the entredeux of the yoke using the technique "Gathered Fabric to Entredeux."

— C. Embellishing the Sleeves —

1. To create the log cabin design for the sleeves, start with the 2" by 2" motif. Using eight different pieces of lace and the directions for Log Cabin Lace found on page 227, create a motif about 3" square for small dolls and 4" square for medium and large dolls. Repeat for the second sleeve.

2. Cut two rectangles of organdy 5" by 8" for small dolls, 7 by 8" for medium dolls and 9" by 8" for large dolls. Pintuck the fabric parallel to the 5", 7" or 9" side. Begin 1/2" from the edge. Pintuck until the pintucked fabric measures about 5". Cut the pintucked fabric in half across the pintucks (**fig. 3**). Attach one pintucked piece to the top of each log cabin lace design using the technique "Lace to Fabric." Attach pintucking to the lower edge of each log cabin design. Press. Trim the sides of the pintucked fabric even with the log cabin design. This will give you two created panels, one for each sleeve (**fig. 4**).

3. Place entredeux to each side of the created strip using the technique "Entredeux to Fabric". Note: When a created strip consists of lace and fabric, and entredeux is to be attached to the strip always use the technique "Entredeux to Fabric" along the entire strip (**fig. 4**).

4. Cut four rectangles of fabric to the following measurements: small dolls 5" by 4", medium dolls 7" by $4^{1}/_{2}$", large dolls 9" by 5".

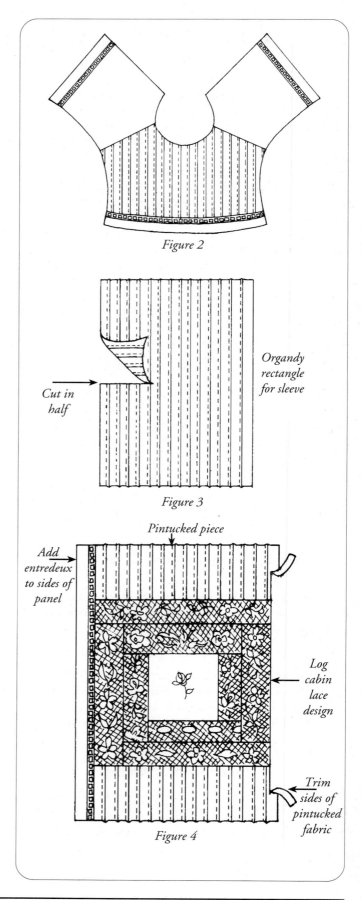

Figure 2

Cut in half

Organdy rectangle for sleeve

Figure 3

Add entredeux to sides of panel

Pintucked piece

Log cabin lace design

Trim sides of pintucked fabric

Figure 4

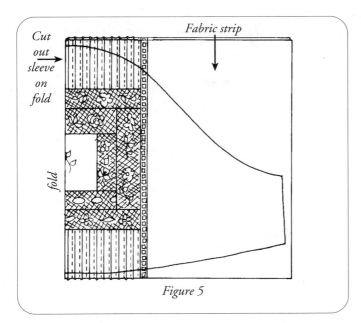

Figure 5

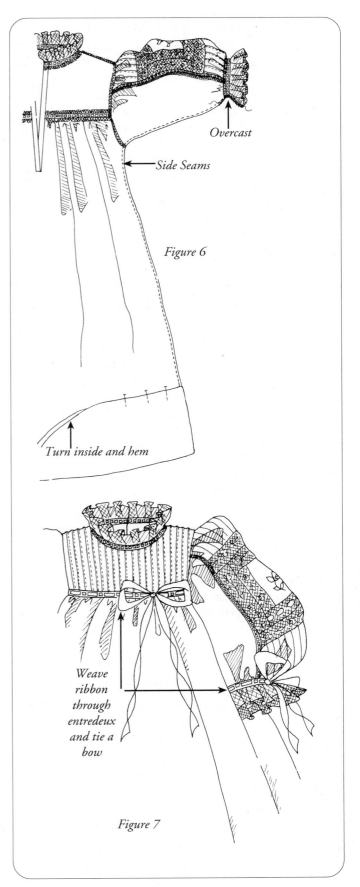

Figure 6

5. Attach the fabric strips to each side of the created strips, using the technique "Entredeux to Fabric." This creates two rectangles. Fold these pieces in half with the log cabin design in the center and cut out the sleeves (**fig. 5**). Run gathering rows in the top and bottom of the sleeve at $1/8$" and $1/4$".

6. Refer to General Directions - III. Constructing the Sleeves. To finish the ends of the sleeves refer to General Directions - B. Sleeve Bands and Ruffles - a. Entredeux and Gathered Edging Lace.

D. Side Seams

1. Stitch each side seam/sleeve together using a $1/4$" seam. Overcast (**fig. 6**).

2. Turn the bottom of the skirt to the inside $1/4$" and again $1^3/4$" for small dolls or $2^3/4$" for medium and large dolls. Hem in place by hand or machine hem (**fig. 6**).

3. Weave silk ribbon through the entredeux (under two bars, over two bars) at the sleeves. Tie into a bow at the center of each sleeve (**fig. 7**).

4. Cut two 12" pieces of silk ribbon. Tack one end of a ribbon to the sleeve seam at the end of the front yoke seam. Weave silk ribbon through the entredeux (under two bars, over two bars) at the front yoke. Tie into a bow at the right of center (**fig. 7**).

5. Attach Velcro™, buttons and buttonholes or snaps to the back of the yokes to close the dress. ❈

Figure 7

Ribbon And Netting Diamonds Dress

Details make the difference in making gorgeous doll clothes. Blue Nelona Swiss batiste is the fabric of the dress. Ecru French laces and ecru entredeux are used also. Ecru cotton netting is placed behind the flip-flopped diamonds made from ¼" blue polyester ribbon. The shadow diamonds go all the way around the dress. A sweet little ecru silk ribbon embroidery design is on the front yoke of the dress. A batiste ruffle finished with flat ecru French edging is found at the bottom of the dress; the back placket closes with Velcro. The traditional puffed sleeve has entredeux with gathered ecru lace edging at the bottom. Blue silk ribbon runs through the entredeux and ties in a pretty bow at the top.

Ribbon and Netting Diamonds Dress

Fabric Requirements

	Small Body	Medium Body	Large Body
Fabric - Batiste	³/₄ yd.	1 yd.	1¹/₈ yds.
Fabric - Netting	¹/₈ yd.	¹/₈ yd.	¹/₄ yd.
Entredeux	2 yds.	2 yds.	2¹/₂ yds.
Edging Lace (⁵/₈")	3 yds.	—	—
Edging Lace (1")	—	3 yds.	4¹/₂ yds.
Edging Lace (¹/₂")	¹/₂ yd.	¹/₂ yd.	¹/₂ yd.
Silk Ribbon (2 mm) YLI blue #9	1 yd.	1 yd.	1¹/₂ yds.

Other Notions: Lightweight sewing thread, and Velcro™, snaps or tiny buttons for back closure. YLI #12 Ecru silk ribbon for yoke embroidery.

All Seams ¹/₄" unless otherwise indicated.

Please read through both the General Directions and the Specific Directions before starting the dress. The General Directions can be found on page 39. These Specific Directions tell how each piece is embellished. The General Directions tell how the dress is constructed. The template for ribbon and netting diamonds can be found on page 55.

A. Constructing the Yokes, Upper Skirt and Sleeves

1. Cut out one front yoke on the fold. Cut out two back yokes on the selvages.

2. Place the front yoke to the back yokes at the shoulders, right sides together, and stitch together using a ¹/₄" seam. Overcast the seam allowance with a zigzag or serge. See General Directions II, figure 1.

3. Finish the neck of the yoke. Refer to the General Directions - A. Neck Finishes - a. Entredeux to Gathered Lace.

4. Cut the skirt pieces 2¹/₄" shorter than the length given on the chart for the large and medium dolls and 1³/₄" shorter for the small dolls.

5. Refer to the General Directions II - steps 4 - 13.

6. Cut two sleeves from the fabric.

7. Refer to the General Directions - III for sleeve construction.

8. Refer to General Directions - B. Sleeve Bands and Ruffles - a. Entredeux and Gathered Edging Lace, to finish the ends of the sleeves.

B. Side Seams and Decorating the Skirt

1. Stitch one side seam/sleeve right sides together using a ¹/₄" seam. Overcast. See General Directions IV., figure 11.

2. Trace the ribbon and netting diamond template starting at the stitched side seam, 1³/₄" from the bottom of the skirt for the large and medium dolls and 1" from the bottom for the small dolls.

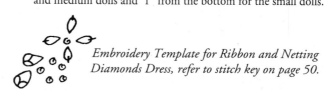

Embroidery Template for Ribbon and Netting Diamonds Dress, refer to stitch key on page 50.

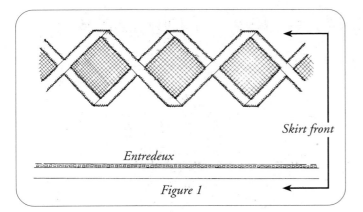

Skirt front

Entredeux

Figure 1

Ruffle

Gathering rows at ¹/₄" and ¹/₈"

Figure 2

Skirt

Figure 3

Figure 4

Dress back

Sleeve detail

Figure 5

Silk ribbon design

Figure 6

3. Using the directions found on page 229 for ribbon and netting diamonds, stitch the ribbon and netting in place (**fig. 1**).

4. Attach a strip of entredeux at the lower edge of the skirt using the technique "Entredeux to Fabric" (**fig. 1**).

4. Ruffle - Cut the following:

> Small dolls - two fabric strips 45" by 1³/₄"
>
> Medium dolls - two fabric strips 45" by 2¹/₄"
>
> Large dolls - three fabric strips 45" by 2¹/₄"

5. Stitch the strips together to form one long strip (do not sew in a circle).

6. Cut a piece of edging lace the length of the fabric strip. Attach this lace to the lower edge of the strip using the technique "Lace to Fabric" (**fig. 2**).

7. Gather the top of the ruffle strip to fit the skirt bottom using a ¹/₄" seam allowance (**fig. 2**).

8. Attach the ruffle to the skirt using the technique "Entredeux to Gathered Fabric" (**fig. 3**).

9. Place the second side of the dress right sides together and stitch from the end of the sleeve to the end of the ruffle (**fig. 4**).

10. Weave silk ribbon through the beading (under two bars, over two bars) at the sleeves. Tie into bows at the center of the sleeves (**fig. 5**).

11. Stitch silk ribbon embroidery on the left side of the yoke (**fig. 6**).

12. Attach Velcro™, buttons and buttonholes or snaps to the back of the yokes to close the dress. ✳

Template for Ribbon and Netting Diamonds Doll Dress

Sweet And Simple Doll Dress

Using variegated colored floss, this peach and ecru doll dress with geometric smocking is gorgeous. In between the geometric diamonds in the middle are flowerets each filled with a tiny crystal bead. The neckline is finished with ecru entredeux and gathered lace edging. The sleeves have ecru entredeux, insertion and gathered lace edging at the bottom. The fancy band at the bottom of the dress has entredeux, three strips of ecru insertion, entredeux and gathered lace edging at the bottom. Tiny peach silk ribbons are tied at the sides of the dress. The high yoke in the back has snaps for actual closing and two tiny pearl buttons stitched on to pretend that the dress closes with buttons rather than snaps. What an elegant smocked doll dress!

Fabric Requirements

	Small Body	Medium Body	Large Body
Fabric	³/₄ yd.	1 yd.	1¹/₂ yds.
Lace Insertion (³/₄")	1¹/₄ yds.	2 yds.	2¹/₂ yds.
Lace Insertion (¹/₂")	3 yds.	3¹/₂ yds.	4 yds.
Entredeux	3 yds.	4 yds.	4³/₄ yds.
Edging Lace (⁵/₈")	1 yd.	1 yd.	1 yd.
Edging Lace (1")	2¹/₂ yds.	3¹/₂ yds.	4 yds.
Silk Ribbon (7 mm)	1 yd.	1 yd.	1¹/₂ yds.

Smocking graph on page 254.

Other Notions: Lightweight sewing thread, and Velcro™, snaps or tiny buttons for back closure, embroidery floss (variegated peach and ecru or DMC 754 peach) 7mm peach YLI silk ribbon #5 and clear beads for smocking.

All Seams ¹/₄" unless otherwise indicated.

Please read through both the General Directions and the Specific Directions before starting the dress. The General Directions can be found on page 39. These Specific Directions tell how each piece is embellished. The General Directions tell how the dress is constructed.

A. Constructing the Yokes

1. Cut out one front yoke from the fold. Cut out two back yokes from the selvage.

2. Place the front yoke to the back yokes at the shoulders right sides together, and stitch in place using a ¹/₄" seam. Overcast the seam allowance with a zigzag or serge (see General Directions - fig. 1).

3. Finish the neck of the yoke with entredeux and ⁵/₈" edging lace. Refer to the General Directions - A. Neck Finishes - a. Entredeux to Gathered Lace.

B. Smocking the Skirt

Some of the skirts will need added width to accommodate smocking.

Sweet and Simple Doll Dress

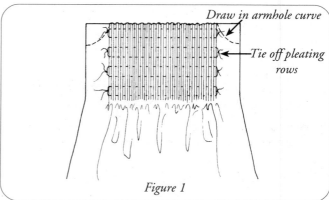

Draw in armhole curve

Tie off pleating rows

Figure 1

1. Cut the skirt pieces 2³/₄" shorter than the length given on the skirt chart (page 38) and to the following widths: small dolls — 22¹/₂" front and 22¹/₂" back, medium dolls — 28" front and 28" back, large dolls — 36" front and 36" back.

2. Pleat the front skirt piece with 7 rows for small dolls and 8 rows for medium and large dolls, with the first row of pleating ¹/₈" from the top edge of the skirt. Draw in the armhole curve. Pull out the pleating threads at and under the armhole. This smocking does not continue under the arm. Tie off the pleating rows to fit the lower edge of the yoke (**fig. 1**). Smock the skirt front using the graph and directions on page 254.

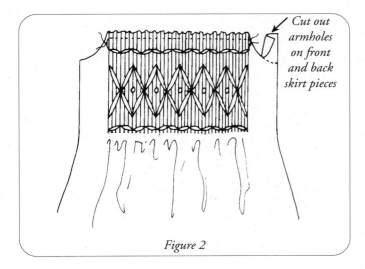

Cut out armholes on front and back skirt pieces

Figure 2

3. Cut out armholes on both the front and back skirt pieces (**fig. 2**).

4. Refer to the General Directions II - steps 6 - 13. Note: Use the top pleating thread as the gathering threads referred to in step 9.

C. Embellishing the Sleeves

1. Cut out two sleeves from the fabric.

2. Refer to the General Directions - III. Constructing the Sleeves.

3. Refer to the sleeve band chart (page 38). Cut two pieces of entredeux to the measurement on the chart. Cut two pieces of lace insertion ($^1/_2$" for small dolls and $^3/_4$" for medium and large dolls) to the entredeux measurement. Attach the lace to the entredeux using the technique "Lace to Entredeux" (**fig. 3**).

4. Cut two pieces of $^5/_8$" edging lace twice the length of the entredeux. Gather to fit the insertion lace and attach using the technique "Lace to Lace" (**fig. 3**).

5. Refer to General Directions - B. Sleeve Bands and Ruffles - a. Entredeux and Gathered Edging Lace - steps 3 and 4 to attach the sleeve band to the sleeve.

6. Attach the sleeves to the bodice (refer to the General Directions III. Constructing the Sleeves).

D. Side Seams and Fancy Band

1. Stitch one side seam/sleeve together using a $^1/_4$" seam. Overcast (**fig. 4**).

2. Fancy band - Cut two pieces of $^1/_2$" lace insertion, one piece of $^3/_4$" lace insertion, and two pieces of entredeux to the following measurements: Small dolls - 47", Medium dolls - 58", Large dolls - 74".

3. Attach the $^1/_2$" lace insertion to each side of the $^3/_4$" lace insertion using the technique "Lace to Lace". Attach entredeux to each side of the $^1/_2$" lace insertion using the technique "Lace to Entredeux". This creates the fancy band (**fig. 5**).

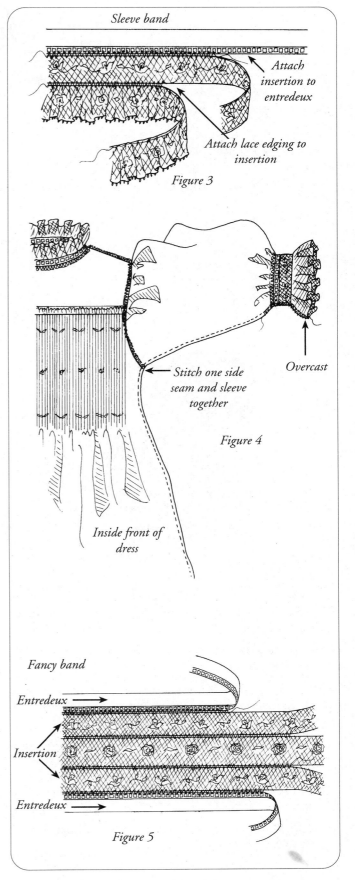

Sleeve band

Attach insertion to entredeux

Attach lace edging to insertion

Figure 3

Stitch one side seam and sleeve together

Overcast

Inside front of dress

Figure 4

Fancy band

Entredeux →

Insertion

Entredeux →

Figure 5

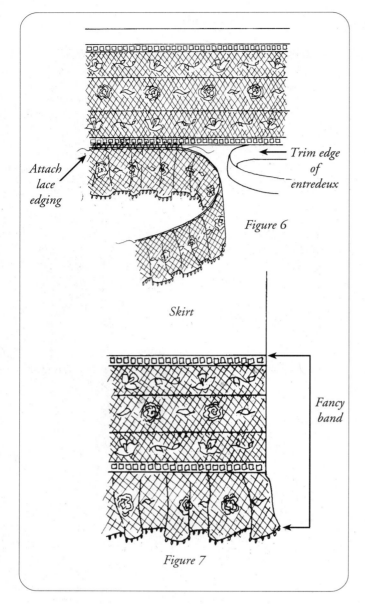

Attach lace edging

Trim edge of entredeux

Figure 6

Skirt

Fancy band

Figure 7

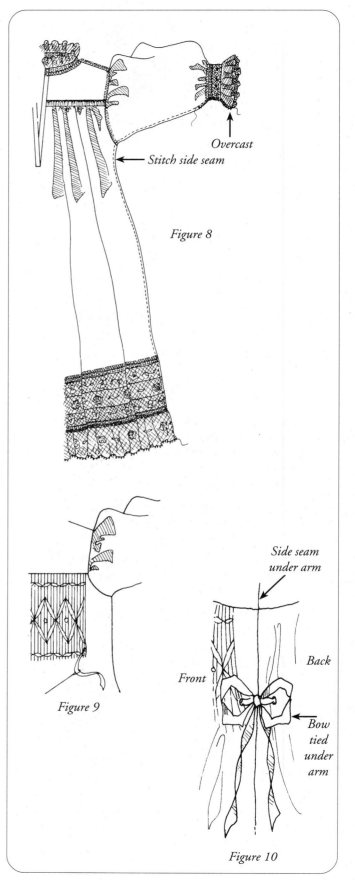

Overcast

Stitch side seam

Figure 8

Figure 9

Side seam under arm

Front

Back

Bow tied under arm

Figure 10

4. Gather the 1" lace edging to fit the entredeux of the created band and attach using the technique "Lace to Entredeux" (**fig. 6**).

5. Attach the fancy band/ruffle to the skirt using the technique "Entredeux to Fabric" (**fig. 7**).

6. Place the second side of the dress right sides together and stitch in place from the end of the sleeve to the end of the lace ruffle (**fig. 8**).

7. Side ties - Cut the silk ribbon into 4 equal pieces. Knot one end of each ribbon. Using a tapestry needle, place ribbons along the lower row of smocking on the skirt front (**fig. 9**). Place back ribbons 1" from the side seam, even with the front ribbon. Tie under the arms (**fig. 10**).

8. Attach Velcro™, buttons and buttonholes or snaps to the back of the yokes to close the dress. ✺

Printed Smocked Doll Dress

Printed calico is just the fabric for an old fashioned doll dress. The colors of dusty pink gold, ecru, dusty blue, burgundy and forest green are enhanced by the dusty pink smocking with dusty blue flowerets in the center of the diamonds. One quarter inch burgundy ribbon finishes the ruffle around the neck and the bottom of the sleeves. Elastic holds in the fullness of the puffed sleeve. The dress closes in the back with snaps. The sweetest tuck is stitched in right above the hemline of the dress. A tailored bias binding attaches the neckline ruffle to the dress.

Fabric Requirements

	Small Body	Medium Body	Large Body
Fabric	1 yd.	1¼ yds.	1½ yds.
Entredeux	¼ yd.	¼ yd.	¼ yd.
Edging Lace (⁵/₈")	1 yd.	1 yd.	1 yd.
Ribbon (¼")	1¼ yds.	1½ yds.	1¾ yds.

Smocking graph on page 255.

Other Notions: Lightweight sewing thread, and Velcro™, snaps or tiny buttons for back closure, ⅛" elastic for sleeves, embroidery floss (DMC 3687 rose and DMC 799 blue) for smocking.

All Seams ¼" unless otherwise indicated.

Please read through both the General Directions and the Specific Directions before starting the dress. The General Directions can be found on page 38. These Specific Directions tell how each piece is embellished. The General Directions tell how the dress is constructed.

A. Constructing the Yokes

1. Cut out one front yoke from the fold. Cut out two back yokes from the selvage.

2. Place the front yoke to the back yokes together at the shoulders, right sides together and stitch in place using a ¼" seam. Overcast the seam allowance with a zigzag or serge (refer to the General Directions - fig 1).

3. Cut a neck ruffle to the following measurements: Small dolls 1½" by 18", Medium dolls 2" by 22", Large dolls 2½" by 26". Finish one long side of the ruffle with ribbon by placing the ribbon along the edge of the wrong side of the ruffle. Stitch in place along the top of the ribbon or hold the ribbon in place with wash-away basting tape. Flip the ribbon to the right side, which will turn up a small hem in the ruffle. Stitch in place along the top and bottom edges of the ribbon (**fig. 1**).

4. Finish the short sides of the ruffle by turning the ruffle edge to the wrong side ⅛" and ⅛" again. Stitch in place (**fig. 2**).

5. Run two gathering rows in the top edge of the ruffle at ⅛" and ¼" (**fig. 2**).

Printed Smocked Doll Dress

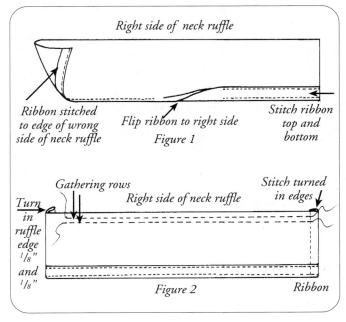

Right side of neck ruffle

Ribbon stitched to edge of wrong side of neck ruffle

Flip ribbon to right side
Figure 1

Stitch ribbon top and bottom

Gathering rows
Right side of neck ruffle

Stitch turned in edges

Turn in ruffle edge ⅛" and ⅛"

Figure 2

Ribbon

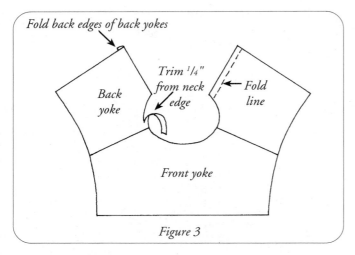

Fold back edges of back yokes

Trim ¼" from neck edge

Back yoke

Fold line

Front yoke

Figure 3

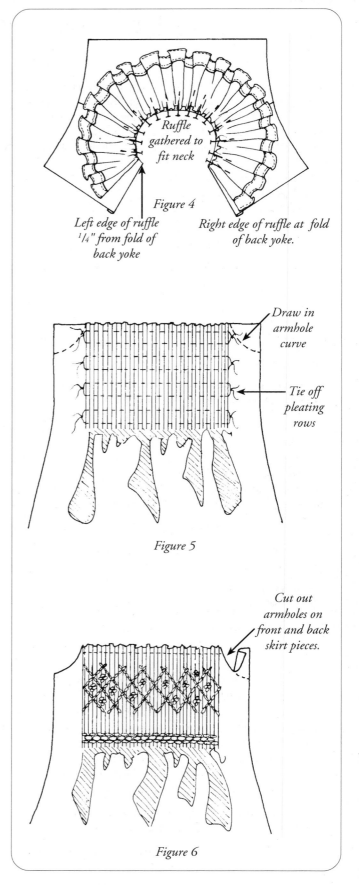

Ruffle gathered to fit neck

Figure 4

Left edge of ruffle ¼" from fold of back yoke

Right edge of ruffle at fold of back yoke.

Draw in armhole curve

Tie off pleating rows

Figure 5

Cut out armholes on front and back skirt pieces.

Figure 6

6. Trim ¼" from the neck edge to allow for the bias binding. Fold the back edges of the back yokes to the inside ⅜". Press (**fig. 3**).

7. Gather the ruffle to fit the neck of the yoke, allowing the right edge of the ruffle to meet the fold of the back and the left edge of the ruffle to fall ¼" from the fold. Pin in place (**fig. 4**).

8. Finish the neck of the yoke with a bias binding. Refer to the General Directions - A. Neck Finishes - c. Bias Neck Binding.

B. Smocking the Skirt

Some of the skirts will need added width to accommodate the smocking.

1. Cut the skirt pieces 2½" longer than the length given on the skirt chart (page 38) to allow for a hem and a tuck and to the following widths: small dolls — 22½" front and 22½" back, medium dolls — 28" front and 28" back, large dolls — 36" front and 36" back.

2. Pleat the front skirt piece with 6 rows for small dolls and 8 rows for medium and large dolls, with the first row of pleating ⅛" from the top edge of the skirt. Draw in the armhole curve. Pull out the pleating threads in line with the armhole. The smocking does not continue under the arm. Tie off the pleating rows to fit the lower edge of the yoke (**fig. 5**). Smock the skirt front using the graph and directions on page 255.

3. Cut out armholes on both the front and back skirt pieces (**fig. 6**).

4. Refer to the General Directions II - steps 6 - 13. Note: Use the top pleating thread as the gathering threads referred to in step 9.

C. Embellishing the Sleeves

1. Cut out two sleeves from the fabric.

2. Refer to the General Directions - III. Constructing the Sleeve and B. Sleeve Bands and Ruffles - d. Gathered Sleeve with Elastic and Ribbon

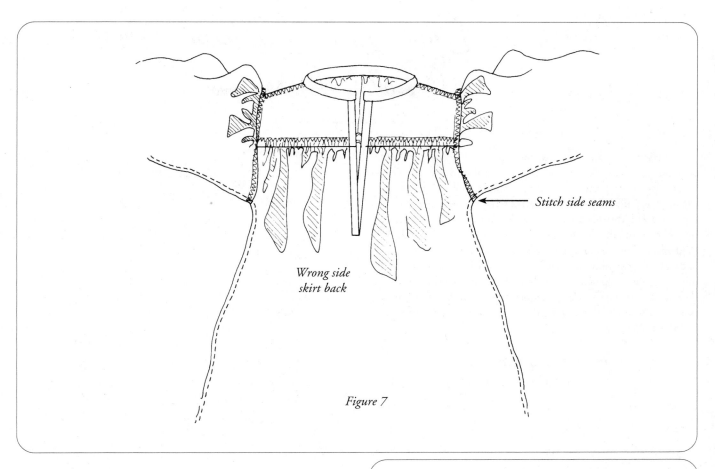

Stitch side seams

*Wrong side
skirt back*

Figure 7

D. Side Seams and Fancy Band

1. Place the sides of the dress together and stitch in place. Overcast
    (**fig.** 7).

2. Turn the lower edge of the dress to the inside $1/4$" and again $1^1/4$".
    Stitch in place. This stitching line will be hidden by the tuck
    (**fig.** 8).

3. Measure from the bottom of the dress $1^7/8$". Mark. Fold on the
    marked line. Stitch $1/2$" from the fold, creating a tuck (**fig.** 9).

4. Attach Velcro™, buttons and buttonholes or snaps to the back of
    the yokes to close the dress. ✽

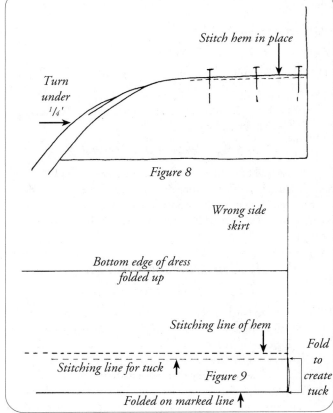

Stitch hem in place

*Turn
under
$1/4$'*

Figure 8

*Wrong side
skirt*

*Bottom edge of dress
folded up*

Stitching line of hem

*Fold
to
create
tuck*

Stitching line for tuck ↑   *Figure 9*

Folded on marked line ↑

Robin's Egg Blue Heirloom Party Doll Dress

A classic heirloom party dress in robin's egg blue Swiss Nelona is the ultimate for any size doll. The yoke is embellished with three strips of ecru lace insertion and the neckline is entredeux plus gathered lace edging. The puffed sleeve has ecru lace insertion down the center and is finished with entredeux and gathered lace insertion. Robin's egg blue silk ribbon is run through the entredeux and the bow is tied at the center front. The gorgeous fancy band has two rows of entredeux on both sides filled with two rows of ecru lace insertion. An embroidered robin's egg blue strip decorated with machine stitching is in between the two rows of entredeux/lace treatments. A narrow Swiss batiste ruffle has flat insertion in ecru for the bottom of the dress. The back is closed with Velcro.

Fabric Requirements

	Small Body	Medium Body	Large Body
Fabric - Batiste	3/4 yd.	1 yd.	1 1/8 yds.
Entredeux	6 yds.	6 yds.	8 yds.
Insertion Lace (1/2")	6 yds.	—	—
Insertion Lace (5/8")	—	6 yds.	8 yds.
Edging Lace (5/8")	—	3 1/2 yds.	5 yds.
Edging Lace (1/2")	3 1/2 yds.	—	—
Silk Ribbon (2 mm)	1/2 yd.	1/2 yd.	3/4 yd.

Other Notions: YLI color #131 for robin's egg blue, lightweight sewing thread, and Velcro™, snaps or tiny buttons for back closure, silk ribbon for sleeves.

All Seams 1/4" unless otherwise indicated.

Please read through both the General Directions and the Specific Directions before starting the dress. The General Directions can be found on page 39. These Specific Directions tell how each piece is embellished. The General Directions tell how the dress is constructed.

A. Constructing the Yokes, Upper Skirt and Sleeves

1. Cut out a rectangle of fabric to the measurement on the front yoke chart (page 38). Trace the front yoke pattern on this rectangle. Using the technique for extra stable lace (page 223), place one strip of lace in the center of the traced yoke. Place lace strips on either side of the center lace starting at the neck of the dress. Stitch in place using the same technique. Stay stitch just inside the traced line of the yoke. Cut out one front yoke (**fig. 1**).

Robin's Egg Blue Heirloom Party Doll Dress

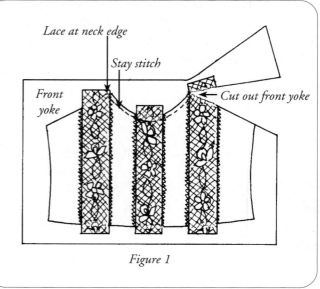

Figure 1

Labels in Figure 1: *Lace at neck edge*, *Stay stitch*, *Front yoke*, *Cut out front yoke*

2. Cut out two back yokes from the selvage.

3. Place the front yoke to the back yokes at the shoulders right sides together, and stitch in place using a $^1/_4$" seam. Overcast the seam allowance with a zigzag or serge. See General Directions II, figure 1.

3. Finish the neck of the yoke. Refer to the General Directions - A. Neck Finishes - a. Entredeux to Gathered Lace.

4. Cut the skirt pieces $4^1/_4$" shorter for small dolls, 5" shorter for medium and $5^1/_2$" for large dolls than the length given on the chart.

5. Refer to the General Directions II - steps 4 - 13.

6. Cut two sleeves from the fabric. Place a strip of insertion lace down the center of the sleeve using the extra stable lace technique (**fig. 2**).

7. Refer to the General Directions - III for sleeve construction.

8. Refer to General Directions - B. Sleeve Bands and Ruffles - a. Entredeux and Gathered Edging Lace, to finish the ends of the sleeves.

— *B. Side Seams, Fancy Band and Ruffle* —

1. Stitch one side seam/sleeve together using a $^1/_4$" seam. Overcast. Refer to General Directions IV., figure 11.

2. Fancy Band - cut the following:

   Small dolls - 4 pieces of $^1/_2$" insertion lace 46" long, 4 pieces of entredeux 46" long, one strip of fabric $1^1/_2$" by 45".

   Medium dolls - 4 pieces of 5/8" insertion lace 46" long, 4 pieces of entredeux 46" long, one strip of fabric $1^3/_4$" by 45".

   Large dolls - 4 pieces of $^5/_8$" insertion lace 61" long, 4 pieces of entredeux 61" long, two strips of fabric $1^3/_4$" by $30^1/_2$" (stitch the two fabric strips together to create one long piece of fabric $1^3/_4$" by 60").

3. Attach two of the lace strips together using the technique "Lace to Lace" (**fig. 3**). Repeat for the other two pieces of lace. Now there are two bands of two laces each.

4. Attach entredeux on each side of the two lace bands, using the technique "Lace to Entredeux" (**fig. 3**).

5. Decorate the center of the fabric strip with a machine decorative stitch. Note: stabilizer may be needed for the decorative stitch (**fig. 4**).

6. Attach the lace/entredeux bands to each side of the decorated fabric strip using a $^1/_4$" seam allowance and the technique "Entredeux to Fabric". This completes the fancy band (**fig. 4**).

7. Ruffle - Cut the following:

   Small dolls - two fabric strips 45" by $1^1/_4$"

   Medium dolls - two fabric strips 45" by $1^1/_4$"

   Large dolls - three fabric strips 45" by $1^3/_4$"

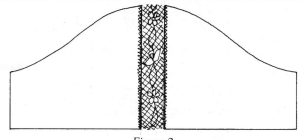

Figure 2

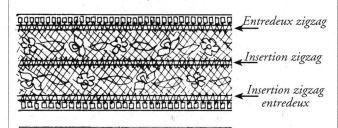

Entredeux zigzag

Insertion zigzag

Insertion zigzag entredeux

Figure 3

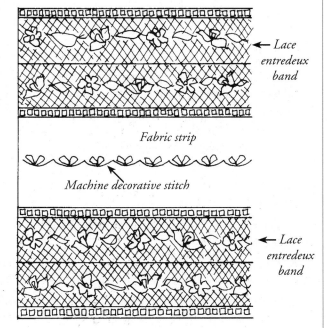

← Lace entredeux band

Fabric strip

Machine decorative stitch

← Lace entredeux band

Figure 4

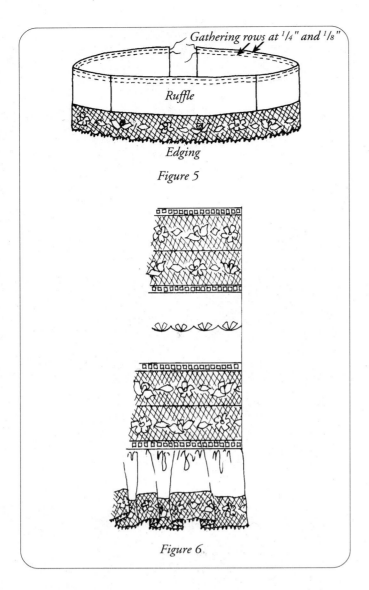

Gathering rows at ¼" and ⅛"

Ruffle

Edging

Figure 5

Figure 6

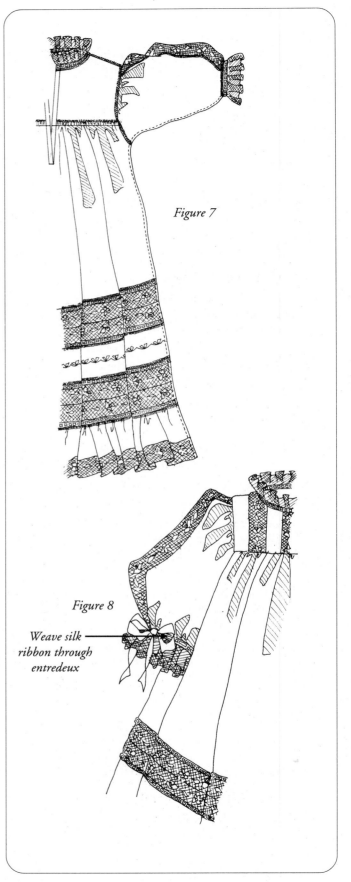

Figure 7

Figure 8

Weave silk ribbon through entredeux

8. Stitch the strips together to form one long strip (do not sew in a circle).

9. Cut a piece of edging lace the length of the fabric strip. Attach this lace to the lower edge of the strip using the technique lace to fabric (**fig. 5**).

10. Gather the top of the ruffle strip to fit the skirt bottom using a ¼" seam allowance (**fig. 5**).

11. Attach the ruffle to the skirt using the technique "Entredeux to Gathered Fabric" (**fig. 6**).

12. Place the second side of the dress right sides together and stitch in place from the end of the sleeve to the end of the ruffle (**fig. 7**).

13. Weave silk ribbon through the entredeux (under two bars, over two bars) at the sleeves. Tie into bows at the center of the sleeves (**fig. 8**).

14. Attach Velcro™, buttons and buttonholes or snaps to the back of the yokes to close the dress. ✳

White Piqué Classic Appliqué Dress

The details are so pretty on this white piqué classic summer dress. Blue rickrack is stitched where the front and back high yokes join the skirt. Blue and white $1/32$ nd gingham finds the bottom of the puffed sleeve and makes a hem on the bottom. Blue rickrack is stitched on where the piqué and blue and white fabric joins the bottom of the dress. Three sailboats embellish the bottom of the skirt. Two orange fish swim in the water. The sailboat bottom is yellow, the two sails are blue and teal green, the flag is hot pink. The colors in this dress are so refreshing and this idea would be precious on a child's garment also. The back closes with snaps. A bias binding of white piqué finishes the top of the dress.

Fabric Requirements

	Small Body	Medium Body	Large Body
Fabric - Pique	$1/2$ yd.	$2/3$ yd.	1 yd.
Fabric - Gingham	$1/4$ yd.	$1/4$ yd.	$1/4$ yd.

Medium Rickrack

Boat pattern on page 66.

Other Notions: Lightweight sewing thread, and Velcro™, snaps or tiny buttons for back closure, small fabric pieces of yellow, teal, light blue, dark pink and orange for appliqué.

All Seams $1/4$" unless otherwise indicated.

Please read through both the General Directions and the Specific Directions before starting the dress. The General Directions can be found on page 39. These Specific Directions tell how each piece is embellished. The General Directions tell how the dress is constructed. The template for appliqué can be found on page 66.

A. Constructing the Yokes, Upper Skirt and Sleeves

1. Cut out one front yoke on the fold. Cut out two back yokes on the selvage.

2. Place the front yoke to the back yokes at the shoulders right sides together, and stitch in place using a $1/4$" seam. Overcast the seam allowance with a zigzag or serge. See General Directions II, figure 1.

3. Finish the neck of the yoke. Refer to the General Directions - A. Neck Finishes - b. Bias Neck Facing.

4. Cut the skirt pieces $3/4$" shorter for the small and medium dolls and $1 1/4$" shorter for the large dolls than the length given on the chart.

5. Appliqué three boats $1 1/4$" from the lower edge of the skirt front. The boats are about 2" apart. Refer to the appliqué directions found on page 211. The boat appliqué template can be found on page 66.

6. Refer to the General Directions II - steps 5 - 13.

7. Stitch rickrack over the seams of the yokes to the skirt (**fig 1**).

White Piqué Classic Appliqué Dress

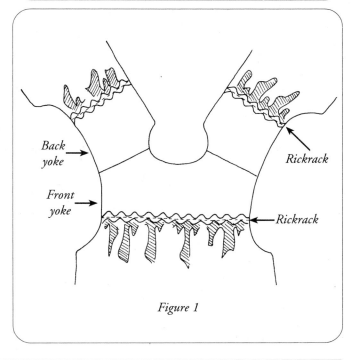

Back yoke

Front yoke

Rickrack

Rickrack

Figure 1

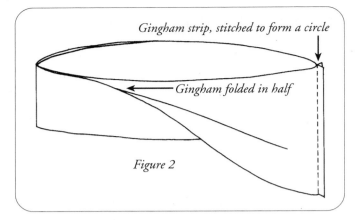

Gingham strip, stitched to form a circle

Gingham folded in half

Figure 2

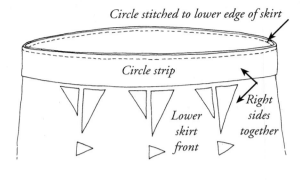

Circle stitched to lower edge of skirt

Circle strip

Lower skirt front

Right sides together

Figure 3

8. Cut two sleeves from the fabric.

9. Refer to General Directions - III. Constructing the Sleeves and B. Sleeve Bands and Ruffles - b. Bias Sleeve Binding. Note: This binding is cut from gingham fabric.

B. Side Seams and Skirt Hem

1. Stitch the seam/sleeve together using a $^1/_4$" seam. Overcast. Repeat for other side.

2. Cut a gingham strip $2^1/_2$" by 45" for the small and medium dolls and two strips $3^1/_2$" by 30" for the large dolls.

3. Stitch the strip(s) together to form a circle. This circle needs to be the same circumference as the skirt (**fig. 2**).

4. Fold the gingham circle in half, with the cut edges of the circle together. Treat the two layers of fabric as one layer (**fig. 2**).

5. Stitch the circle to the lower edge of the skirt using a $^1/_4$" seam (**fig. 3**). Overcast.

6. Place rickrack over the skirt/band seam and stitch in place (**fig. 4**).

7. Attach Velcro™, buttons and buttonholes or snaps to the back of the yokes to close the dress. �֎

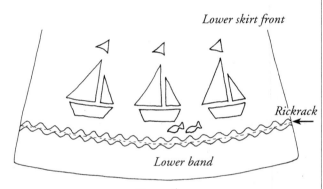

Lower skirt front

Rickrack

Lower band

Figure 4

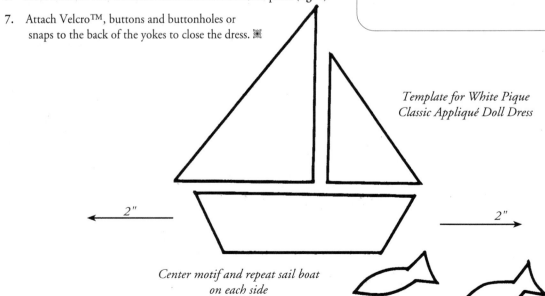

Template for White Pique Classic Appliqué Doll Dress

2"   2"

Center motif and repeat sail boat on each side

Smocked Bow Doll Dress

A pretty picture smocked blue bow with a green trellis/pink rosebud trim is the central feature on this white broadcloth smocked dress. The neckline is finished with entredeux and gathered lace with blue embroidery floss being run through the white entredeux. The sleeves have elastic and there is a blue bow tied and stitched down with a sweet white pearl right in the middle. Flat white French lace edging is on the bottom of the sleeve. The colors for smocking are blue, green and pink. The back is closed with snaps with a button stitched on top of the snaps to look as if it were buttoned rather than snapped. What a precious doll dress for you to practice your picture smocking.

Fabric Requirements

	Small Body	Medium Body	Large Body
Fabric	1 yd.	1¹/₄ yds.	1¹/₂ yds.
Entredeux	¹/₄ yd.	¹/₄ yd.	¹/₄ yd.
Edging Lace (⁵/₈")	1 yd.	1 yd.	1 yd.
Ribbon (¹/₄")	¹/₂ yd.	¹/₂ yd.	¹/₂ yd.

Smocking Design on page 256

Other Notions: Lightweight sewing thread, and Velcro™, snaps or tiny buttons for back closure, embroidery floss for smocking (DMC 827 blue, DMC 995 green and DMC 819 pink), two small pearls.

All Seams ¹/₄" unless otherwise indicated.

Please read through both the General Directions and the Specific Directions before starting the dress. The General Directions can be found on page 39. These Specific Directions tell how each piece is embellished. The General Directions tell how the dress is constructed.

A. Constructing the Yokes

1. Cut out one front yoke from the fold. Cut out two back yokes from the selvage.

2. Place the front yoke to the back yokes at the shoulders right sides together, and stitch in place using a ¹/₄" seam. Overcast the seam allowance with a zigzag or serge (refer to the General Directions - fig. 1).

3. Finish the neck of the yoke with entredeux and ⁵/₈" edging lace. Refer to the General Directions - A. Neck Finishes - a. Entredeux to Gathered Lace.

B. Smocking the Skirt

Some of the skirts will need added width to accommodate the smocking.

1. Cut the skirt pieces 2" longer for small dolls, 2¹/₂" longer for medium dolls, and 3" longer for large dolls than the length given on the skirt chart (page 38) and to the following widths: small dolls — 22¹/₂" front and 22¹/₂" back, medium dolls — 28" front and 28" back, large dolls — 36" front and 36" back.

Smocked Bow Doll Dress

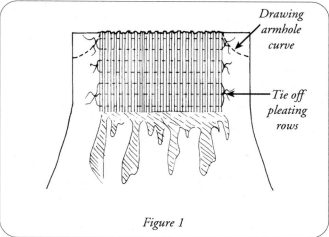

Drawing armhole curve

Tie off pleating rows

Figure 1

2. Pleat the front skirt piece with 7 rows, with the first row of pleating ¹/₈" from the top edge of the skirt. Draw in the armhole curve. Pull out the pleating threads even with the armhole. The smocking does not continue under the arm. Tie off the pleating rows to fit the lower edge of the yoke (**fig. 1**). Smock the skirt front using the graph and directions on page 256.

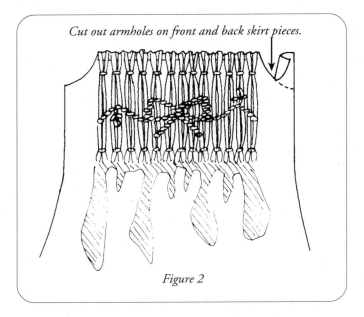

Cut out armholes on front and back skirt pieces.

Figure 2

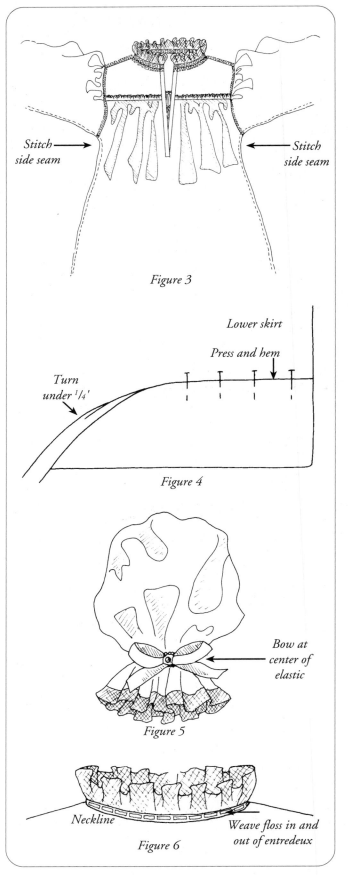

Stitch side seam

Stitch side seam

Figure 3

Lower skirt

Press and hem

Turn under ¹/₄'

Figure 4

Bow at center of elastic

Figure 5

Neckline

Weave floss in and out of entredeux

Figure 6

3. Cut out armholes on both the front and back skirt pieces (**fig. 2**).

4. Refer to the General Directions II - steps 6 - 13. Note: Use the top pleating thread as the gathering threads referred to in step 9.

C. Sleeves

1. Cut out two sleeves from the fabric.

2. Refer to the General Directions - III Constructing the Sleeve with B. Sleeves Bands and Ruffles - c. Gathered Sleeve with Elastic and Lace.

D. Side Seams and Fancy Band

1. Stitch the side seams together using a ¹/₄" seam. Overcast (**fig. 3**).

2. Turn the bottom of the skirt to the inside of the dress ¹/₄" and again 1³/₄" for small dolls, 2¹/₄" for medium dolls and 2³/₄" for large dolls. Press and hem in place by hand or machine hem (**fig. 4**).

3. Tie small bows from the ribbon and tack in place at the center of the sleeve elastic. If desired, stitch a pearl in the center of the bow (**fig. 5**).

4. Weave floss in and out of the entredeux holes at the neck of the dress (**fig. 6**).

5. Attach Velcro™, buttons and buttonholes or snaps to the back of the yokes to closed the dress. ▨

Antique Netting Doll Dress

We called this the ecru antique netting dress because of the style which resembles doll clothing of the turn of the century. The ecru Swiss batiste lining is built into this dress because the whole garment is lined. The over fabric is Swiss cotton netting. The bodice has ecru beading stitched horizontally where the high yoke joins the skirt on both the front and the back; ecru silk ribbon is run through this beading and tied into two bows on either side on both the front and the back of the dress. Gathered ecru French edging is stitched on at the bottom of this beading on both the front and back of the dress. Ecru netting and French edging ruffles travel over the sleeve to make a little shoulder ruffle. The puffed sleeves have a piece of ecru French insertion stitched right down the middle and the fullness is gathered onto ecru entredeux and gathered French edging. The back is closed with snaps; however, three tiny buttons are stitched on to make it look as if the dress were buttoned rather than snapped. The fancy band on the bottom of the netting overskirt of the dress consists of a row of ecru insertion, beading, ecru insertion and flat ecru edging. The Swiss batiste underskirt is finished at the bottom with ecru entredeux, one row of insertion and one row of edging, all stitched on flat without fullness. The center top of this dress yoke has a tiny pink and green silk rosebud stitched down. What a magnificent doll dress!

Fabric Requirements

	Small Body	Medium Body	Large Body
Fabric	$^1/_2$ yd.	$^2/_3$ yd.	1 yd.
Netting	$^1/_2$ yd.	$^2/_3$ yd.	1 yd.
Entredeux	2 yds.	2 yds.	$2^1/_2$ yds.
Lace Insertion ($^1/_2$")	$4^1/_4$ yds.	$4^1/_4$ yds.	6 yds.
Lace Beading ($^1/_2$")	2 yds.	2 yds.	$2^1/_4$ yds.
Edging Lace ($^5/_8$")	5 yds.	5 yds.	6 yds.
Silk Ribbon (4mm) YLI ecru # 12	4 yds.	$4^1/_2$ yds.	5 yds.

Other Notions: Lightweight sewing thread, and Velcro™, snaps or tiny buttons for back closure, small rosette for the neck.

All Seams $^1/_4$" unless otherwise indicated.

Please read through both the General Directions and the Specific Directions before starting the dress. The General Directions can be found on page 39. These Specific Directions tell how each piece is embellished. The General Directions tell how the dress is constructed.

A. Embellishing the Yoke

1. Cut one front yoke and two back yokes from netting and from fabric.

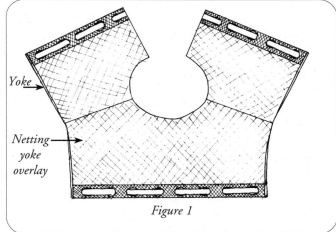

Figure 1

2. Place the netting yokes on top of the fabric yokes and treat as one layer of fabric. Stitch front yoke to back yokes at the shoulders, right sides together (**fig. 1**).

3. Stitch a strip of lace beading $^1/_4$" from the lower edges of the front and back yokes. Run ribbon through the beading (**fig. 1**).

4. Finish the neck of the yoke. Refer to the General Directions - A. Neck Finishes - a. Entredeux to Gathered Lace.

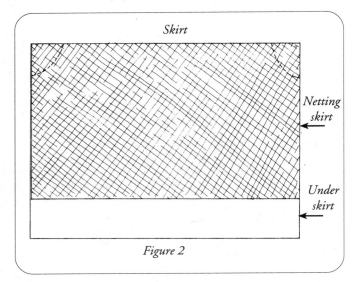

Figure 2

Skirt

Netting skirt

Under skirt

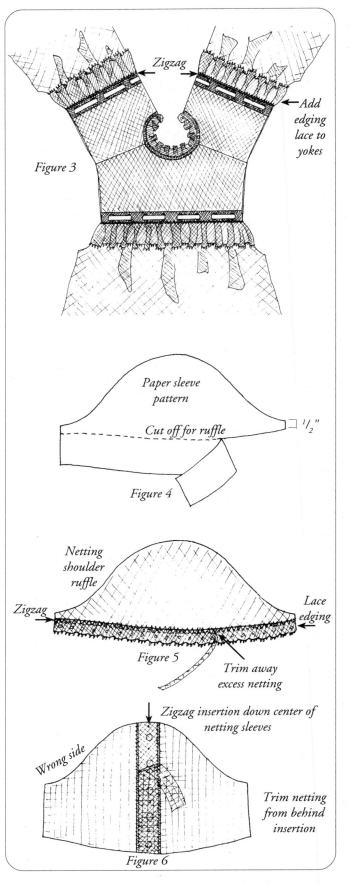

Figure 3

Zigzag

Add edging lace to yokes

Paper sleeve pattern

Cut off for ruffle

□ ¹/₂"

Figure 4

Netting shoulder ruffle

Zigzag

Lace edging

Figure 5

Trim away excess netting

Zigzag insertion down center of netting sleeves

Wrong side

Trim netting from behind insertion

Figure 6

B. Upper Skirt and Sleeves

1. Cut two skirt pieces from netting 1³/₄" shorter than the measurement on the skirt chart found on page 38.

2. Cut two skirt pieces from the fabric 1" shorter than the measurement on the skirt chart found on page 38.

3. Place the netting skirt pieces over the fabric skirt pieces. Each netting/fabric skirt piece will be treated as one layer of fabric (**fig. 2**).

4. Refer to the General Directions II - steps 4 - 13.

5. Cut a piece of edging lace twice the length of the lower edge of the front yoke (where the yoke meets the skirt). Gather the lace and top stitch in place with a zigzag to the skirt/yoke seam. Repeat for the two back yokes (**fig. 3**).

6. Shoulder ruffle - trace the sleeve pattern on a piece of paper. Cut off the sleeve so that ¹/₂" of the underarm seam remains. This is the shoulder ruffle pattern. Cut two shoulder ruffles from netting (**fig. 4**).

7. Place lace edging along the bottom edge of the shoulder ruffle allowing the lace to overlap the netting ¹/₄". Zigzag in place along the upper edge of the lace. Trim away excess netting (**fig. 5**).

8. Cut two sleeves from netting and two from fabric. Place a piece of insertion lace down the center of each netting sleeve. Zigzag in place along the outer edges of the lace. Trim the netting away from behind (**fig. 6**).

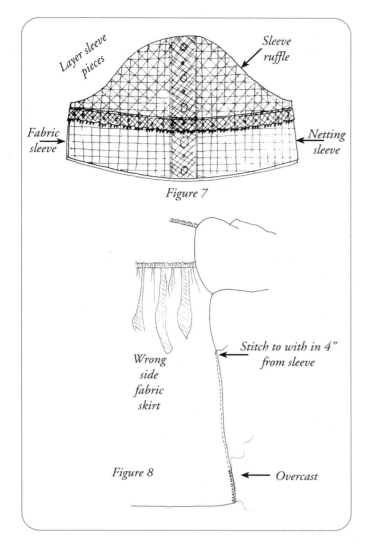

Figure 7

Figure 8

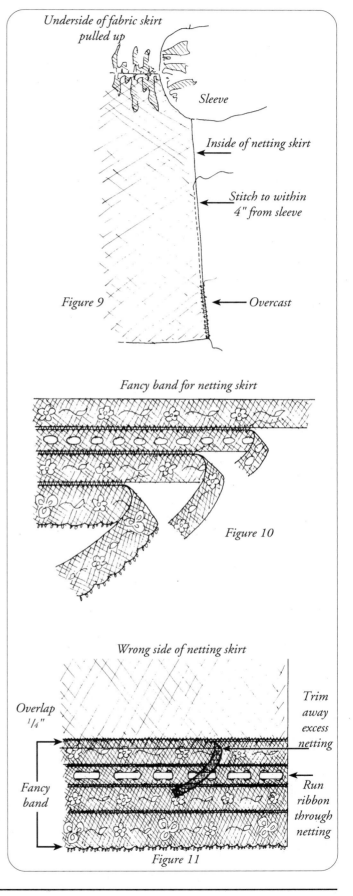

Figure 9

Figure 10

Figure 11

9. Place the netting sleeve on top of the fabric sleeve. Place the sleeve ruffle on top of the netting sleeve. Treat all layers as one (**fig. 7**).

10. Refer to General Directions - III. Constructing the Sleeves. To finish the ends of the sleeves refer to General Directions - B. Sleeve Bands and Ruffles - a. Entredeux and Gathered Edging Lace.

C. Side Seams and Fancy Band

1. Place one side of the fabric skirt together and stitch from the bottom stopping 4" from the sleeve seam (**fig. 8**). Overcast. Repeat for the netting skirt piece (**fig. 9**).

2. Fancy band for netting skirt - Cut the following pieces to 46" for small and medium dolls and 61" for large dolls: two pieces of lace insertion, one strip of edging lace and one strip of beading. Attach lace insertion to either side of the beading using the technique "Lace to Lace". Attach edging lace to one side of the insertions using the technique "Lace to Lace" (**fig. 10**). Place the fancy band to the netting skirt overlapping ¹/₄". Zigzag in place and trim away the excess netting. Run ribbon through the beading (**fig. 11**).

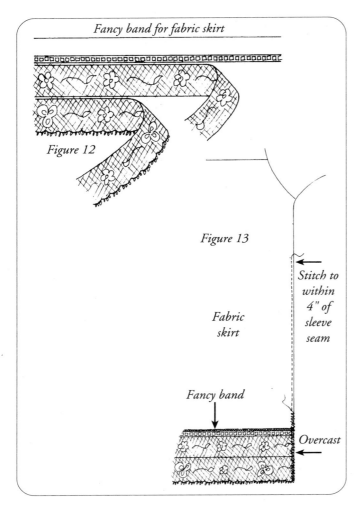

Fancy band for fabric skirt

Figure 12

Figure 13

Fabric skirt

Fancy band

Stitch to within 4" of sleeve seam

Overcast

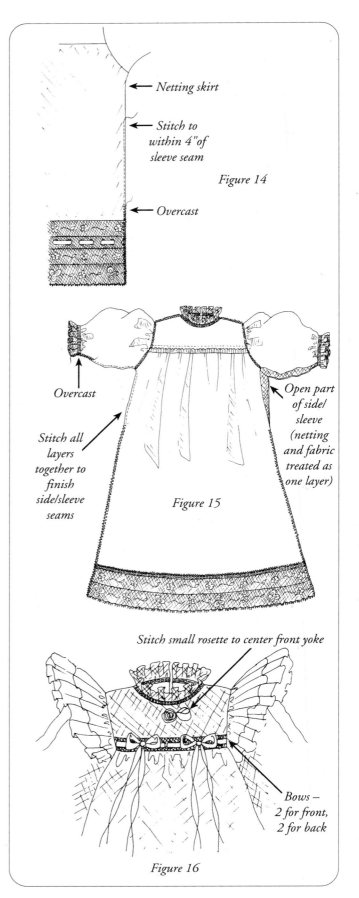

Netting skirt

Stitch to within 4" of sleeve seam

Figure 14

Overcast

Overcast

Stitch all layers together to finish side/sleeve seams

Open part of side/ sleeve (netting and fabric treated as one layer)

Figure 15

Stitch small rosette to center front yoke

Bows — 2 for front, 2 for back

Figure 16

3. Fancy band for fabric skirt - Cut the following pieces to 46" for small and medium dolls and 61" for large dolls: one piece of lace insertion, one strip of edging lace and one strip of entredeux. Attach edging lace to one side of the lace insertion using the technique "Lace to Lace". Attach entredeux to the other side of the insertion lace using the technique "Lace to Entredeux" (**fig. 12**). Place the fancy band to the fabric skirt using the technique "Entredeux to Fabric."

4. Place the other side of the fabric skirt together and stitch from the bottom, stopping 4" from the sleeve seam. Overcast (**fig. 13**). Repeat for the netting skirt piece (**fig. 14**).

5. To complete the dress place the open part of the side/sleeves together and stitch, treating the netting and fabric as one layer of fabric. Overcast (**fig. 15**).

6. Attach Velcro™, buttons and buttonholes or snaps to the back of the yokes to close the dress.

7. Divide the remaining ribbon into four pieces. Tie into four bows (two for the front and two for the back) and attach to the beading at the yoke (**fig. 16**).

8. Stitch a small purchased rosette to the center front at the neck (**fig. 16**). ▨

Ruched Trim Doll Dress

This peach Nelona Swiss batiste dress has the most wonderful detailing! Two colors of peach ribbons are used for the magnificent ribbon trims. The high yoke is ecru Swiss cotton netting with $^1/_{16}$ th ribbon stitched down in a spoke fashion. The neckline is finished with ecru entredeux and gathered ecru lace trim. The back of the dress closes with Velcro. A peach ribbon rosette is pinned to the yoke on one side. Ruched dark peach ribbon travels around the neckline where the yoke joins the dress and over the shoulders. On the puffed sleeve are two shades of peach ribbon; a narrow ribbon stitched down on either side of the wider ribbon. The bottom of the sleeve is finished with ecru entredeux and gathered ecru French edging. The skirt has a piece of ecru Swiss entredeux stitched between the double hem and the top of the skirt. This is a dress which any doll would be proud to wear!

Roched Trim Doll Dress

Fabric Requirements

	Small Body	Medium Body	Large Body
Fabric	$^2/_3$ yd.	1 yd.	$1^1/_4$ yds.
Netting	$^1/_4$ yd.	$^1/_4$ yd.	$^1/_4$ yd.
Entredeux	2 yds.	2 yds.	$2^2/_3$ yds.
Edging Lace ($^1/_2$") neck	$^1/_2$ yd.	$^1/_2$ yd.	$^2/_3$ yd.
Edging Lace (1") sleeves	$^1/_2$ yd.	$^1/_2$ yd.	$^3/_4$ yd.
Ribbon ($^1/_8$")	4 yds.	$4^1/_2$ yds.	5 yds.
Ribbon ($^3/_8$")	2 yds.	2 yds.	3 yds.

Other Notions: Lightweight sewing thread, and Velcro™, snaps or tiny buttons for back closure, Water Soluble Stabilizer, adhesive tape and paper for pattern adaptation.

All Seams $^1/_4$" unless otherwise indicated.

Please read through both the General Directions and the Specific Directions before starting the dress. The General Directions can be found on page 39. These Specific Directions tell how each piece is embellished. The General Directions tell how the dress is constructed.

A. Embellishing the Yoke

1. This yoke will need to be constructed without shoulder seams. To create a pattern without shoulder seams simply trace the front yoke and back yoke on a piece of paper. Cut out. Draw the $^1/_4$" seams at the shoulder of each pattern piece. Overlap the $^1/_4$" seam lines and tape in place. This is the "new" pattern piece without shoulder seams. Transfer fold lines along the back edges of the yoke, the "cut on fold" symbol at the center front and the old shoulder seam markings (**fig. 1**).

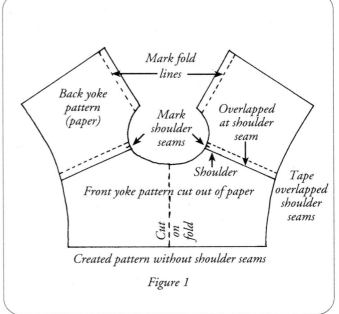

Created pattern without shoulder seams

Figure 1

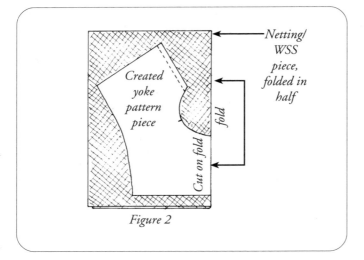

Figure 2

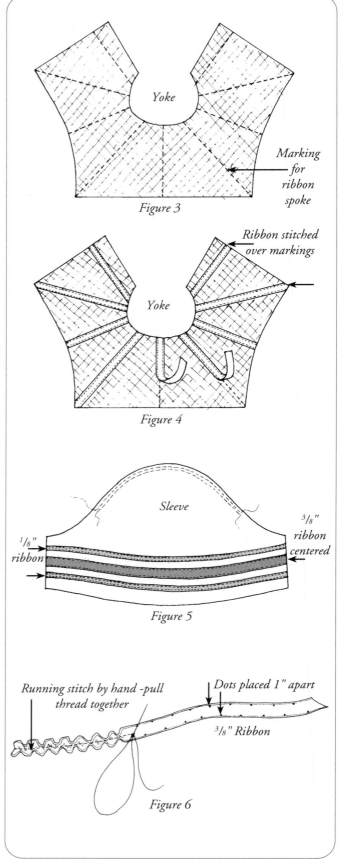

Figure 3

Figure 4

Figure 5

Figure 6

2. Water soluble stabilizer will be used to stabilize the netting. Cut a piece of water soluble stabilizer 9" by 9" and a piece of netting 9" by 9". Press (medium heat) the netting to the water soluble stabilizer. Fold the netting/WSS in half and cut the "new" pattern from the netting/WSS (**fig. 2**).

3. Ribbon placement - Using a water soluble pen draw 5 lines: center front, old shoulders seams and ¹/₂" from the fold lines of the backs. Add four more lines from the neck to each outer corner of the yoke. This completes the lines for the ribbon spokes on the small dolls. Add more spoke lines as desired for medium and large dolls (**fig. 3**).

4. Place ribbon on top of the lines and stitch in place along each edge of the ribbon (**fig. 4**).

5. Finish the neck of the yoke. Refer to the General Directions - A. Neck Finishes - a. Entredeux to Gathered Lace.

B. Upper Skirt and Sleeve Embellishment

1. Refer to the skirt chart on page 38. Cut two skirt pieces 2" shorter than the measurement given on the chart. Refer to the General Directions II - steps 4 - 13.

2. Cut two sleeves. Draw a line across the sleeves, centered from underarm to underarm. Center the ³/₈" ribbon along the line and stitch in place along each edge of the ribbon. Stitch a piece of ¹/₈" ribbon ¹/₄" from each side of the larger ribbon (**fig. 5**).

3. Refer to General Directions - III. Constructing the Sleeves. To finish the ends of the sleeves refer to General Directions - B. Sleeve Bands and Ruffles - a. Entredeux and Gathered Edging Lace.

4. Ruched yoke trim - Ruching can be made using one of the two methods: Method I - Using the ³/₈" ribbon, place dots 1" apart along one edge of the ribbon. Repeat for the other edge with dots 1" apart placed in between the upper dots. Using a hand needle and a doubled thread, join the dots in a zigzag with running stitches. Pull the thread to gather (the gathering thread will form a straight line), creating ruching (**fig. 6**). Also see page 154.

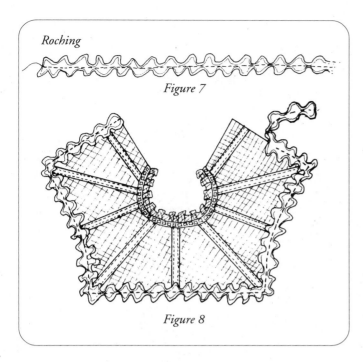

Roching

Figure 7

Figure 8

Method II - Using ³/₈" ribbon, the three step zigzag stitch built in to most machines and a loosened tension - set the stitch to zigzag across the ribbon simulating the running stitches of Method I. Pull the thread to gather (the gathering thread will form a straight line), creating ruching (**fig. 7**).

5. Stitch the ruching to the yoke seam by hand or machine along the gathering row (**fig. 8**).

C. Side Seams and Fancy Band

1. Stitch one seam/sleeve together using a ¹/₄" seam. Overcast. See General Directions IV., figure 11.

2. Attach a strip of entredeux around the bottom of the dress using the technique "Entredeux to Fabric" (**fig. 9**).

3. Stitch the second side/sleeve together using a ¹/₄" seam. Overcast (**fig. 10**).

4. Cut a fabric strip 5" by 45" for the small and medium dolls and two strips 5" by 30" for the large dolls.

5. Stitch the strip(s) together to form a circle. This circle needs to be the same circumference as the skirt (**fig. 11**).

6. Fold the fabric circle in half, with the cut edges of the circle together. Treat the two layers of fabric as one layer (**fig. 11**).

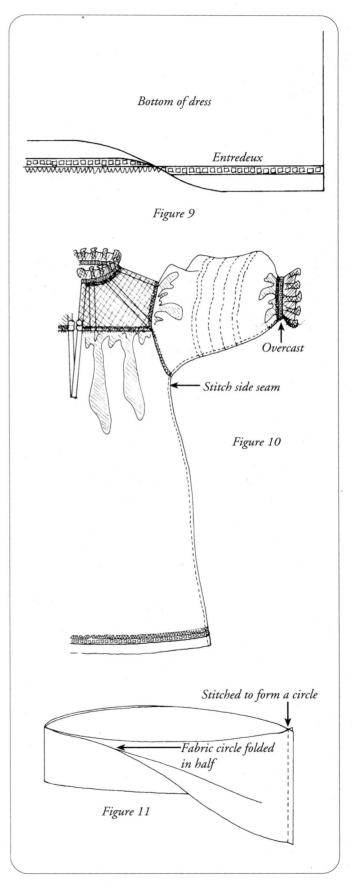

Bottom of dress

Entredeux

Figure 9

Overcast

Stitch side seam

Figure 10

Stitched to form a circle

Fabric circle folded in half

Figure 11

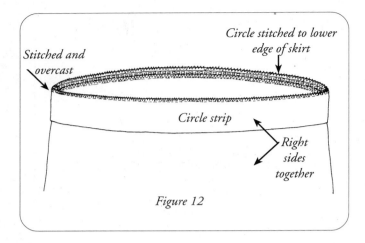

Figure 12

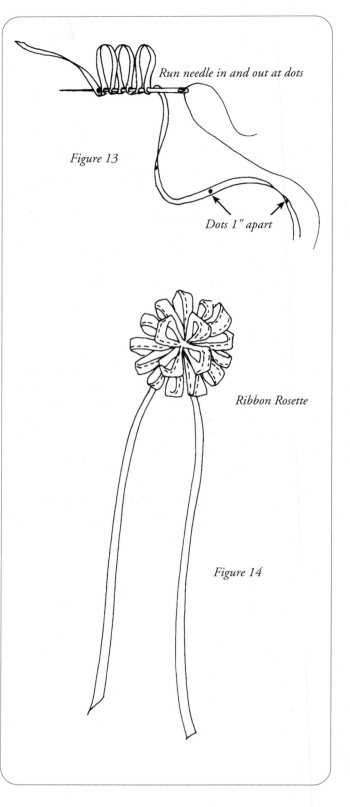

Figure 13

Ribbon Rosette

Figure 14

7. Stitch the circle to the lower edge of the skirt using a ¹/₄" seam and the technique "Entredeux to Fabric" (**fig. 12**).

8. Attach Velcro™, buttons and buttonholes or snaps to the back of the yokes to close the dress.

D. Ribbon Rosette

1. Cut one piece of ¹/₈" ribbon to 40". Starting 5" from the end mark every 1" across the ribbon until 5" from the other end (**fig. 13**).

2. Using a hand sewing needle and doubled thread, pick up each of the dots, creating loops. Hold all the loops on the needle.

3. When all dots have been picked up, stitch the beginning loop to the ending loop, creating a ribbon rosette (**fig. 14**).

4. Hand stitch in place along the front yoke. ✳

Doll Camisole, Pantalettes and Petticoat

Dolls must have lovely lingerie to go under their beautiful clothing! Here are three beautiful and easy to make doll undergarments. All are ecru, made of Swiss Nelona batiste, and have pink silk ribbon for trim. The petticoat features a gathered waistline with three double needle pintucks at the bottom of the batiste portion. The bottom of the petticoat has ecru entredeux, ecru French insertion and ecru French edging stitched on flat. Pink silk ribbon is run through the entredeux and tied into a bow on the side. The camisole has ecru entredeux and French edging on the top neckline. The armholes have slightly gathered narrow ecru edging around them also. The bottom is finished with ecru entredeux and straight ecru French edging. The back is finished with snaps and buttons stitched above the snaps to make the back look as if it were buttoned. The very easy-to-make pantalettes have three double needle pintucks near the bottom of each leg and the legs are finished with ecru entredeux, ecru insertion and ecru edging. Pink silk ribbon is run through the entredeux and tied in the center front of each leg. The top is gathered with elastic run through a casing.

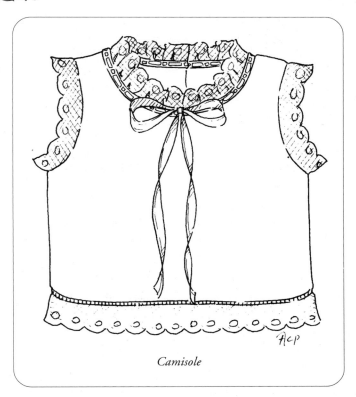

Camisole

Camisole

Fabric Requirements

	Small Body	Medium Body	Large Body
Edging Lace (1/2")	1 yd.	1 1/4 yds.	1 1/2 yds.
Entredeux	3/4 yd.	1 yd.	1 yd.
Fabric	1/4 yd.	1/4 yd.	1/4 yd.
Silk Ribbon (2mm)	1 yd.	1 yd.	1 yd.

Other Notions: Lightweight sewing thread and snaps, Velcro® or tiny buttons

Cutting and Constructing the Camisole

1. Cut one camisole front on the fold, and two camisole backs on the selvage.

2. Place the front camisole to the back camisole pieces at the shoulders right sides together. Stitch the shoulders together using a 1/4" seam. Overcast using a zigzag or serger (**fig. 1**).

3. Stay stitch around each armhole 1/8" from the fabric edge (**fig. 1**). Zigzag over the stay stitch line, enclosing the edge of the fabric (**fig. 1**).

4. Topstitch (straight stitch) a piece of edging lace over the finished edge of the armhole (**fig. 2**).

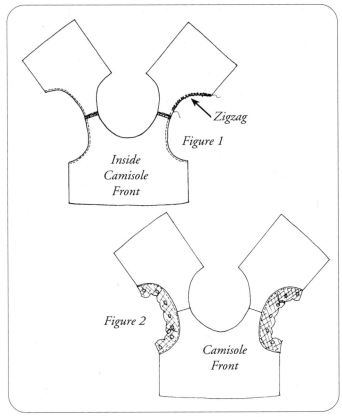

Zigzag

Figure 1

Inside Camisole Front

Figure 2

Camisole Front

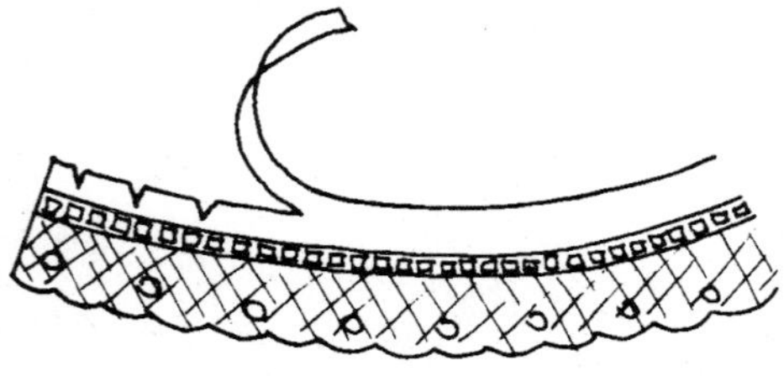

Figure 3

5. Measure around the neck opening and add 1/2" to this measurement. Cut a piece of entredeux and a piece of edging lace to this measurement.
6. Attach the edging to the entredeux using the technique "Lace to Entredeux." If the remaining seam allowance of the entredeux is not 1/4", trim to 1/4" and clip to curve (**fig. 3**).
7. Attach the entredeux/lace band to the neck edge of the camisole using the technique "Entredeux to Fabric" (**fig. 4**).
8. Place the sides of the camisole right sides together, and stitch using a 1/4" seam. Overcast using a zigzag or serge (**fig. 5**).
9. Measure across the bottom of the camisole and add 1/2" to this measurement. Cut a piece of entredeux and edging lace to this measurement.
10. Attach entredeux to the edging lace using the technique "Entredeux to Lace" (**fig. 6**).
11. Attach the entredeux/lace band to the bottom of the camisole using the technique "Entredeux to Fabric" (**fig. 7**).
12. Cut the piece of silk ribbon in half. Starting at the back edge of the camisole weave (over two bars and under two bars) the ribbon through the entredeux ending with a long tail at the center front. Tack the ribbon in place along the back edge of the camisole. Tie a small bow at the center front (**fig.** 7).
13. Fold the back edges of the camisole to the inside and press (**fig.** 7).
14. Close with Velcro®, snaps or buttons and buttonholes. ✱

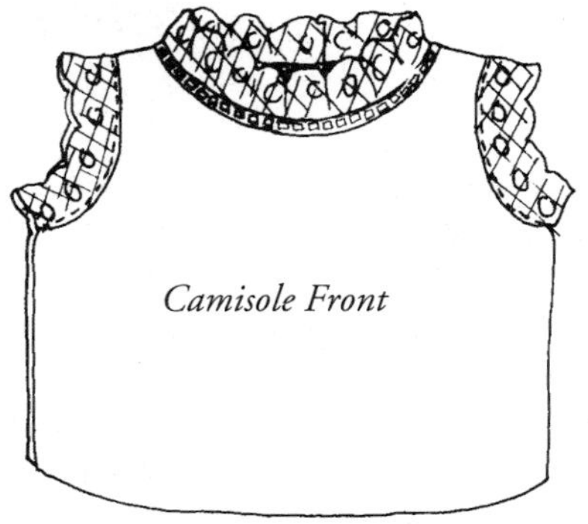

Figure 4

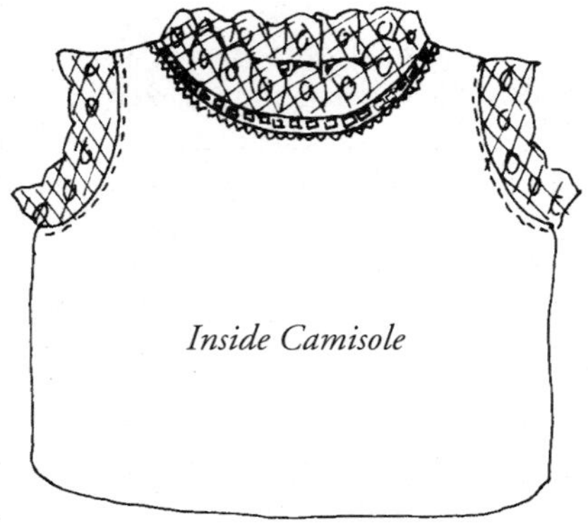

Figure 5

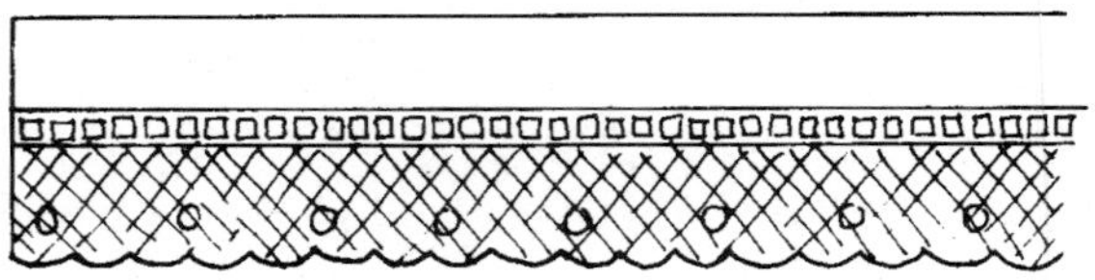

Figure 6

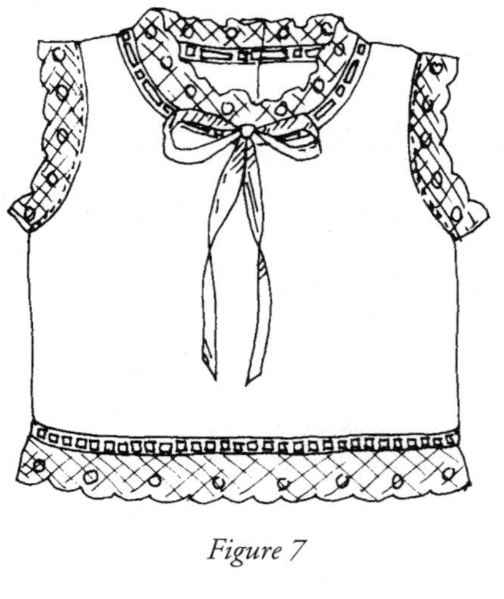

Figure 7

Pantalettes

Fabric Requirements

	Small Body	Medium Body	Large Body
Edging Lace ($^1/_2$")	$^1/_2$ yd.	$^1/_2$ yd.	$^1/_2$ yd.
Lace Insertion ($^1/_2$")	$^1/_2$ yd.	$^1/_2$ yd.	$^1/_2$ yd.
Entredeux	$^1/_2$ yd.	$^1/_2$ yd.	$^1/_2$ yd.
Fabric	$^1/_3$ yd.	$^3/_8$ yd.	$^1/_2$ yd.
Elastic ($^1/_4$")	$^1/_4$ yd.	$^1/_4$ yd.	$^3/_8$ yd.
Silk Ribbon (2mm)	1 yd.	1 yd.	1 yd.

Note: There will be enough fabric to make the pantalettes and the camisole using the fabric requirements above.

Other Notions: Lightweight sewing thread (two spools), double needle (size 1.6/70 or 2.0/80)

All Seams are $^1/_4$" unless otherwise indicated.

I. Cutting the Pantalettes

Cut two pantalettes from the pattern found in the pull-out sections.

Note: These patterns have a 1" entredeux/lace strip along the bottom of the legs. If this embellishment is not being used and a $^1/_4$" hem is required, add 1" to the lower edge of the pattern piece.

II. Embellishing the Pantalettes

1. Attach the lace insertion to the edging lace using the technique "Lace to Lace" (**fig. 1**).

2. Attach entredeux to the lace insertion using the technique "Lace to Entredeux" (**fig. 1**).

3. If the remaining fabric edge of the entredeux is not already $^1/_4$", trim to $^1/_4$".

4. Cut the entredeux/lace strip in half and attach to the lower edge of each pantalette piece, right sides together, using the technique "Entredeux to Flat Fabric" (**fig. 2**).

Pantalettes

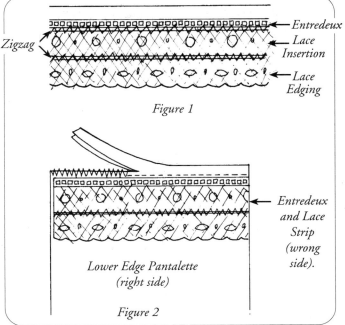

Figure 1

Entredeux

Lace Insertion

Lace Edging

Zigzag

Lower Edge Pantalette (right side)

Entredeux and Lace Strip (wrong side).

Figure 2

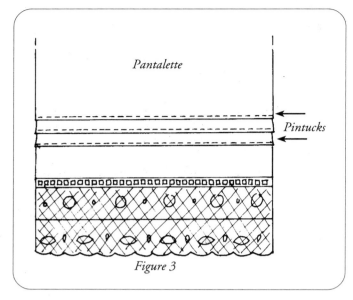

Figure 3

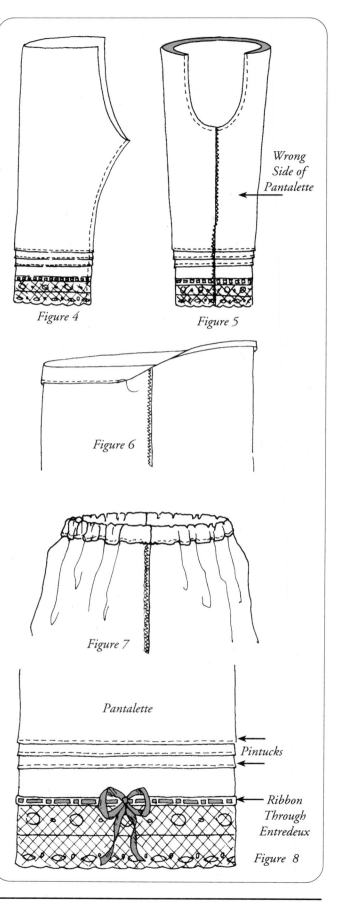

Figure 4

Figure 5

Figure 6

Figure 7

Pantalette

Pintucks →

Ribbon Through Entredeux

Figure 8

5. Using a double needle and two spools of thread, place three double needle pintucks above the entredeux. Refer to double needle pintuck instructions found on page 181. These pintucks are $1/4$" apart and start $5/8$" above the entredeux (**fig. 3**).

III. Constructing the Pantalettes

1. Place the leg portion of the each pantalette piece right sides together. Stitch, using a $1/4$" seam. Overcast or serge (**fig. 4**).

2. Turn one pantalette right side out. Place this pantalette inside the other. The two pantalettes are now right sides together. Match the U shape (crotch) of the two pieces, front to front and back to back. Stitch along the U (**fig. 5**). Overcast with a zigzag or serge. Turn to the right side.

3. Fold the top of the pantalettes to the inside $1/8$" and $3/8$" again. Press. Stitch along the lower fold to form a casing leaving an opening about $1/2$" (**fig. 6**).

4. Cut one piece of elastic to the following measurement:

FB12	6"	MB140	$8^1/2$"	GB11	$5^1/2$"
FB14	7"	MB160	$9^1/2$"	GB13	$6^1/2$"
FB17	10"	MB190	$10^1/2$"	GB15	$7^3/4$"
FB19	10"	MB21.5	$11^1/2$"	GB16	8"
				GB21	10"

5. Insert the elastic into the casing. Overlap the elastic $3/8$" and stitch securely in place. Hand stitch the casing closed (**fig. 7**).

6. Cut the piece of silk ribbon in half. Weave silk ribbon through the holes of the entredeux, starting and stopping in the center front of each leg. Tie the tails of ribbon in a small bow. Trim the tails of the bow. Place a fabric sealant at the ends of the ties to keep the ribbon from raveling (**fig. 8**). ▨

Petticoat

Fabric Requirements

	Small Body	Medium Body	Large Body
Edging Lace ($1/2$")	1 yd.	1 yd.	$1^1/4$ yds.
Lace Insertion ($1/2$")	1 yd.	1 yd.	$1^1/4$ yds.
Entredeux	1 yd.	1 yd.	$1^1/4$ yds.
Fabric	$1/4$ yd.	$1/3$ yd.	$1/2$ yd.
Elastic ($1/4$")	$1/4$ yd.	$1/4$ yd.	$3/8$ yd.
Silk Ribbon (2mm)	$1^1/2$ yds.	$1^1/2$ yds.	$1^3/4$ yds.

Other Notions: Lightweight sewing thread (two spools), double needle (size 1.6/70 or 2.0/80)

All Seams are $1/4$" unless otherwise indicated.

I. Cutting the Petticoat

Cut a fabric rectangle to the length below by 35" wide for the small and medium bodies and 40" wide for the large bodies:

FB12	7"	MB140	$8^3/4$"	GB11	7"
FB14	8"	MB160	10"	GB13	$8^1/2$"
FB17	11"	MB190	$11^1/2$"	GB15	$8^3/4$"
FB19	12"	MB21.5	14"	GB16	10"
				GB21	13"

II. Embellishing the Petticoat

1. Attach the lace insertion to the edging lace using the technique "Lace to Lace" (**fig. 1**).

2. Attach entredeux to the lace insertion using the technique "Lace to Entredeux" (**fig. 2**).

3. If the remaining fabric edge of the entredeux is not already $1/4$", trim to $1/4$" (**fig. 2**).

4. Attach the entredeux/lace strip to the lower edge of the fabric rectangle, right sides together, using the technique "Entredeux to Flat Fabric" (**fig. 3**).

Petticoat

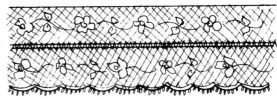

Figure 1

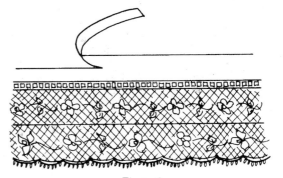

Figure 2

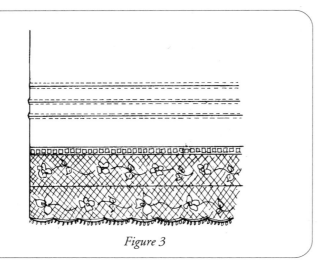

Figure 3

5. Using a double needle and two spools of thread, place three double needle pintucks above the entredeux. Refer to double needle pintuck instructions found on page 181. These pintucks are $^1/_4$" apart and start $^5/_8$" above the entredeux (**fig. 3**).

III. Constructing the Petticoat

1. Place the back edges of the rectangle right sides together, matching the laces and entredeux. Stitch, using a $^1/_4$" seam. Overcast with a zigzag or serge (**fig. 4**).

2. Fold the top of the petticoat to the inside $^1/_8$" and $^3/_8$" again. Press. Stitch along the lower fold to form a casing, leaving an opening about $^1/_2$" (**fig. 5**).

3. Cut one piece of elastic to the following measurement:

FB12	6"	MB140	8$^1/_2$"	GB11	5$^1/_2$"
FB14	7"	MB160	9$^1/_2$"	GB13	6$^1/_2$"
FB17	10"	MB190	10$^1/_2$"	GB15	7$^3/_4$"
FB19	10"	MB21.5	11$^1/_2$"	GB16	8"
				GB21	10"

4. Insert the elastic into the casing. Overlap the elastic $^3/_8$" and stitch securely in place (**fig. 6**). Hand stitch the casing closed (**fig. 7**).

5. Weave silk ribbon through the holes of the entredeux (over two bars and under two bars), starting and stopping in the desired position for the bow(s). Tie the tails of ribbon in a small bow. Trim the tails of the bow. Place a fabric sealant at the ends of the ties to keep the ribbon from raveling (**fig. 8**). ✠

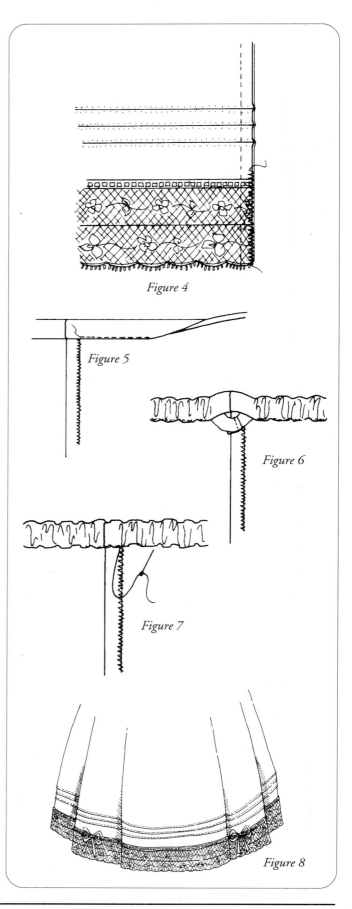

Figure 4

Figure 5

Figure 6

Figure 7

Figure 8

Doll Bonnets

Some people say that a doll's hat absolutely makes the dress. This basic bonnet has a fancy band across the head, and a horseshoe shaped back of the bonnet. The bottom of all of these bonnets has entredeux plus gathered lace edging. The high brim is lined on all of the bonnets and the back is as pretty as the front. All of the bonnets have gathered lace trim around the brim of the bonnet. All have a ribbon rosette of some kind with ribbons to tie the bonnet under the doll's chin. Some of the brim trims are netting over pink batiste, insertion and entredeux over ecru batiste, insertions and beading stitched together over blue batiste, Swiss handlooms, entredeux and lace over white batiste, ecru laces and beading over blue batiste, and pintucked fabrics, ecru entredeux and ecru laces over ecru batiste. Many of the brims also have silk ribbon rosettes stitched on at various places. Many of the brims have ribbons run through the beading; some of the crowns have ribbons run through beading also. Some of the crowns are simply plain fabric, others have laces and other trims stitched together before the crown was cut out.

The bonnet pattern is sized to fit the doll's head - not necessarily the body size. Measure your doll from bottom ear tip, over the crown to the other ear tip. Compare this measurement to the crown pattern piece to decide on the proper size to fit your doll. The fabric and lace requirements are given for the basic bonnet pictured. The other bonnets shown are variations of the basic bonnet. The rectangular measurements given below can be used to create any number of designs. Let your imagination fly!

Doll Bonnets

Fabric Requirements

	8/9"	10/11"	12/13"	14/15"
Fabric	¼ yd.	¼ yd.	¼ yd.	¼ yd.
Interfacing	¼ yd.	¼ yd.	¼ yd.	¼ yd.
Lace Insertion (5/8")	3 yds.	4 yds.	4 yds.	5 yds.
Entredeux	2 yds.	2 yds.	2 yds.	2¼ yds.
Edging Lace (⁵/₈")	2 yds.	2¼ yds.	2½ yds.	3 yds.
Silk Ribbon (7mm)	2 yds.	2 yds.	2 yds.	2 yds.

Notions: Lightweight sewing thread, small purchased roses, and embroidery floss or 2mm silk ribbon to thread through the holes of the entredeux.

Chart for Rectangle Sizes:	Crown horizontal design	Brim vertical design
8/9 (XS)	4" by 10"	7" by 7"
10/11(S)	4½" by 10½"	8" by 8"
12/13 (M)	5" by 11"	8½" by 8½"
14/15 (L)	5½ by 12"	9" by 9"

Bonnet Pattern Pieces (crown, back and brim) can be found on pages 276 and 277.

Beginning French sewing directions can be found on page 167.

I. Brim

1. Create a square of lace and entredeux for the brim piece starting with 3 pieces of lace insertion and 2 pieces of entredeux cut to the following measurement: XS=7", S=8", M=8-1/2", L=9".

2. Attach the three pieces of lace together using the technique "Lace to Lace." Attach entredeux to each side of the created lace strip using the technique "Lace to Entredeux." Continue attaching lace

pieces and/or entredeux pieces to each side of the center strip until the width (XS=7", S=8", M=8¹/₂", L=9") is reached, repeating the (three lace strips, one entredeux strip) design as width permits. Starch and press. Cut out the brim, centering the pattern on the created lace fabric (**fig. 1**).

3. Cut two brims from plain fabric (lining and back) and one brim piece from interfacing.

4. Trim the outer edge of the brim interfacing ¹/₄" to eliminate bulk. If the interfacing is fusible, fuse to one fabric brim. This will be the back of the brim.

5. Pin the lace brim to the brim lining, wrong sides together. Treat as one layer of fabric (**fig. 2**).

6. Cut one piece of lace edging to the following measurement: XS=40", S=40", M=50", L=50". Mark the center of the edging. Match the center of the lace with the center of the fabric brim back. Gather the edging to fit just inside the ¹/₄" seam line of the outer edge. Baste in place (**fig. 3**).

7. Place the lace brim piece to the fabric back brim right sides together. The edging lace will be between the layers. Pin together and stitch along the basting line made in step 6 (**fig. 4**).

8. Trim the seam to ¹/₈" and zigzag the remaining seam allowance.

9. Turn to the right side. Remove any visible basting stitches. Pin the lower raw edges together and baste through all layers. Set aside (**fig. 5**).

II. Crown

1. Create a rectangle for the crown by cutting 3 pieces of lace insertion and 2 pieces of entredeux to the following measurement: XS=10", S=10¹/₂", M=11", L=12".

2. Attach the three pieces of lace together using the technique "Lace to Lace." Attach entredeux to each side of the created lace strip using the technique "Lace to Entredeux" (**fig. 6**).

3. Cut two fabric strips to the following measurement: XS=2" by 10", S=2" by10¹/₂", M=2¹/₂" by 11", L=2¹/₂" by 12".

4. Attach the fabric strips to each side of the entredeux/lace panel using the technique "Fabric to Entredeux" (**fig. 6**). If desired, ribbon can be woven through the entredeux at this time. Fold the created rectangle in half with the short ends together. Cut the crown from the fold.

5. Cut one crown from the fabric to be used for the lining.

6. Run a basting stitch ¹/₄" along the **back** edge of the lace crown piece. Repeat for the lining.

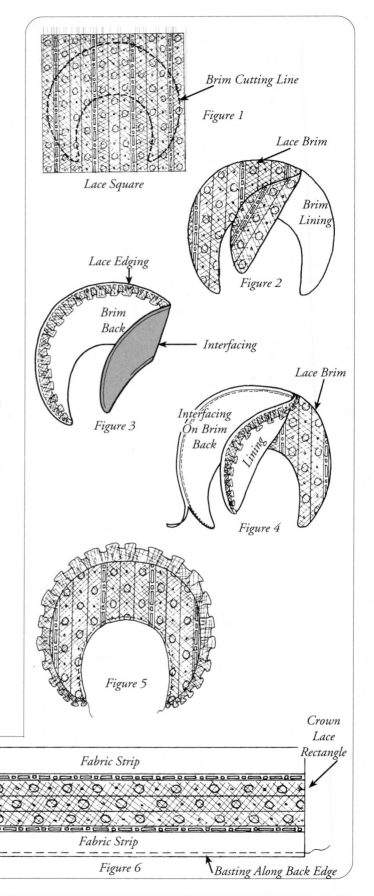

Figure 1

Brim Cutting Line

Lace Square

Lace Brim

Brim Lining

Figure 2

Lace Edging

Brim Back

Interfacing

Figure 3

Lace Brim

Interfacing On Brim Back

Lining

Figure 4

Figure 5

Crown Lace Rectangle

Fabric Strip

Fabric Strip

Figure 6

Basting Along Back Edge

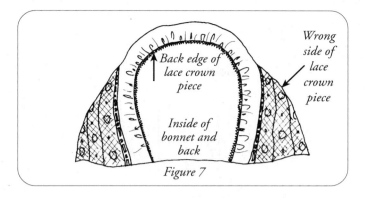

Back edge of lace crown piece

Inside of bonnet and back

Wrong side of lace crown piece

Figure 7

III. Bonnet Construction

1. Cut two back bonnet pieces. One piece will be used for the lining.

2. Pin the back edge of the lace crown piece to the bonnet back, right sides together matching centers. Use the basting row run in step 6 of section II, to ease in place. Stitch, using a ¼" seam. Trim to ⅛" and overcast the seam allowance, using a zigzag (**fig. 7**).

3. Repeat steps 1 and 2 for the crown lining and bonnet back lining.

4. Mark the center of the brim and the center of the lace crown front and crown front lining.

5. The brim will be placed between the lace crown and crown lining as follows: Pin the right side of the crown lining to the lace side of the brim, allowing the crown edge to extend ¼" beyond the lace edging of the brim (**fig. 8**). Place the right side of the lace crown to the brim back allowing the crown edge to extend ¼" beyond the lace edging of the brim. Stitch along the front edge, using a ¼" seam. Trim to ⅛" and overcast the remaining seam allowance, using a zigzag. Remove any visual basting stitches (**fig. 9**). Flip the crown and crown lining to the right side. Baste the unfinished edges together (**fig. 10**).

6. Measure around the bottom, unfinished edge of the bonnet. Add 1" to this measurement. Cut a piece of entredeux to this measurement. Cut a piece of edging lace twice this measurement. Gather the edging to fit the entredeux and attach, using the technique "Entredeux to Gathered Lace" (**fig. 11**).

7. Center the entredeux/gathered lace to the unfinished edge of the bonnet. The ½" tabs of the entredeux/gathered lace will extend beyond the edge of the bonnet. Stitch the entredeux to the bonnet with a ¼" seam, right sides together. Trim the seam to

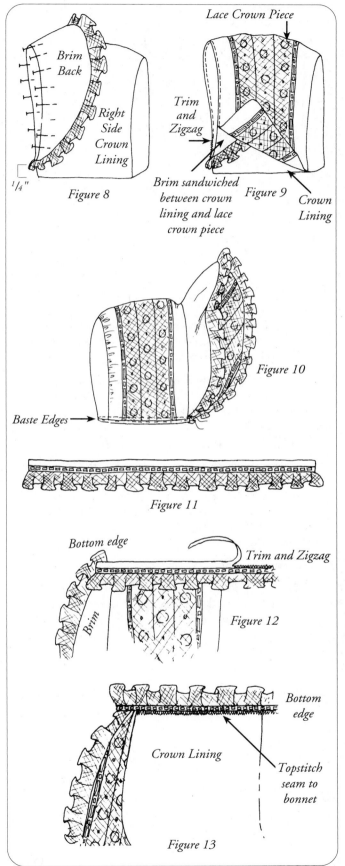

Brim Back

Right Side Crown Lining

¼"

Figure 8

Lace Crown Piece

Trim and Zigzag

Brim sandwiched between crown lining and lace crown piece

Figure 9

Crown Lining

Baste Edges

Figure 10

Figure 11

Bottom edge

Trim and Zigzag

Brim

Figure 12

Bottom edge

Crown Lining

Topstitch seam to bonnet

Figure 13

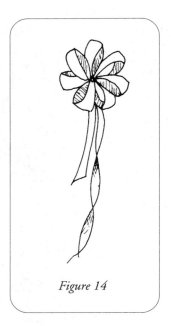

Figure 14

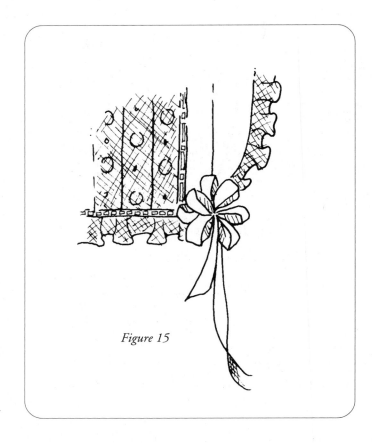

Figure 15

¹/₈" and overcast the remaining seam allowance with a zigzag (**fig. 12**). Press the seam allowance toward the bonnet and top stitch in place with a zigzag (**fig. 13**).

8. Fold and roll up the entredeux/gathered lace tabs along the right side of the bonnet close to the edge of the brim lace. Stitch in place by hand. The ribbon bows will cover the raw edges.

IV. Ties, Bows and Embellishment

1. Cut 2 pieces of ribbon 36" long. Starting 1¹/₂" from one end of the ribbon, dot every 1¹/₂", having a total of 8 dots. With a hand sewing needle and a doubled, knotted thread pick up each dot creating 7 loops. Take several small stitches on the back of the rosette to hold all the loops in place. Repeat for the second piece of ribbon (**fig. 14**).

2. Place the bows at the corners of the bonnet and secure with several hand stitches (**fig. 15**).

3. Optional: Place several small purchased roses on the brim and crown of the bonnet. ✖

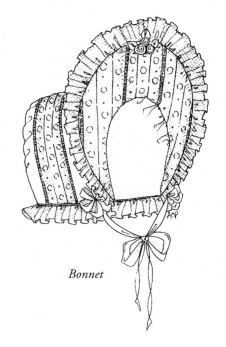

Bonnet

Woven Insets Ribbon Doll Dress

This has to be one of the most beautiful doll dresses that I have ever seen. It is an artist's dream with its use of pink, blue, ecru and green ribbon woven insets on the skirt and the sleeves and the silk ribbon embroidery on the center front of the high front yoke. The basic dress is ecru Swiss Nelona batiste; ecru entredeux attaches the front and back skirts to the high yokes. Ecru entredeux with gathered ecru lace trim finishes the neckline; a pretty silk ribbon arch of flowers and leaves finishes the front yoke. The sleeves have a woven ribbon panel down the middle. The panel consist of three pieces of ecru French lace insertion woven with two different widths of ecru, green, pink and blue silk ribbons. This panel is attached on either side with ecru entredeux and another piece of ecru French insertion lace. The puffed sleeve is gathered at the bottom with entredeux, ecru insertion and gathered ecru edging. A pink silk ribbon runs through the sleeve entredeux and ties in a bow on the top. The skirts feature ecru French insertion running vertically from the yokes to the fancy band. In between every other panel is another piece of the same ribbon woven panel as is found in the center of the sleeve. The bottom of the dress is finished with entredeux, straight insertion lace and straight edging. The back of the dress is closed with Velcro™.

Woven Insets Ribbon Doll Dress

Fabric Requirements:

	Small Body	Medium Body	Large Body
Fabric	$^2/_3$ yd.	1 yd.	$1^1/_4$ yds.
Entredeux	5 yds.	5 yds.	6 yds.
Edging Lace ($^5/_8$")	$2^1/_2$ yds.	$2^1/_2$ yds.	3 yds.
Lace Insertion ($^5/_8$")	$8^1/_2$ yds.	9 yds.	10 yds.
Lace Insertion ($^3/_8$")	$1^1/_2$ yds.	$1^1/_2$ yds.	$2^1/_4$ yds.
Silk Ribbon*	3 yds./color	3 yds./color	3 yds./color

Colors - pink #007 (4mm), light blue # 009 (4mm), light green #18 (4mm), pale yellow #156 (4mm), dark ecru #12 (2mm). These ribbons will be used for weaving and for the embroidery on the yoke.

Silk Ribbon-pink (4mm)	4 yds.	4 yds.	4 yds.

2 yds. will be used for weaving, 1yd. for the bows on the sleeves and 1 yd. for the embroidery on the yoke.

Other Notions: Lightweight sewing thread, and Velcro™, snaps or tiny buttons for back closure, and $^1/_4$ yd. So Sheer™ (a very lightweight fusible knit interfacing).

All Seams $^1/_4$" unless otherwise indicated.

Please read through both the General Directions and the Specific Directions before starting the dress. The General Directions can be found on page 39. These Specific Directions tell how each piece is embellished. The General Directions tell how the dress is constructed. The embroidery design for the yoke can be found on page 90.

A. Constructing the Front and Back Yokes

1. Cut one front yoke from the fold and two back yokes from the selvage.

2. Place the front yoke to the back yoke, right sides together, at the shoulders and stitch in place using a $^1/_4$" seam. Overcast the seam allowances. (See the general directions figure 1.)

3. Finish the neck of the yoke. Refer to the General Directions - A. Neck Finishes - a. Entredeux to Gathered Lace.

4. Attach a piece of entredeux to the lower edge of the front yoke using the technique "Lace to Fabric" and a $^1/_4$" seam. Press away from the yoke.

5. Attach pieces of entredeux to the lower edge of the back yokes using the technique "Lace to Fabric" and a $^1/_4$" seam. Press away from the yoke.

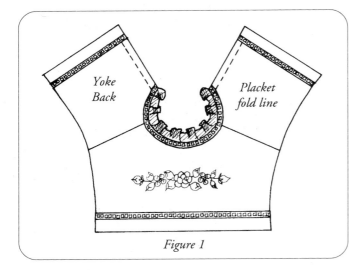

Figure 1

6. Work the silk ribbon design in the center of the front yoke (**fig. 1**).

B. Lace and Ribbon Weaving

1. Cut two pieces of So Sheer™ fusible interfacing 3" wide by the following length: small dolls 18$\frac{1}{2}$", medium dolls 23", large dolls 25$\frac{1}{2}$".

2. Overlap the two pieces $\frac{1}{2}$" and stitch in place creating one long piece (**fig. 2**).

3. Cut three pieces of $\frac{5}{8}$" lace to the following measurements: small dolls 36", medium dolls 45", large dolls 50".

4. Place the fusible interfacing, fusible side up, on the ironing board. Center the three strips of lace on top of the interfacing with the edges touching but not overlapping. Pin the laces in place at the top of each strip. Place a piece of wash away basting tape $\frac{1}{8}$" away from the outer lace pieces. The paper backing of the wash away basting tape will be removed as the sticky surface is needed (**fig. 2**).

5. Cut strips of silk ribbon into 2$\frac{1}{2}$" pieces. Start weaving in the following order (right to left): blue, light ecru, green, pink, dark ecru, blue, light ecru, green, and pink. As the pieces are woven, use the sticky tape on each side of the lace to hold the ribbon in place. Continue working until the strip is complete (**fig. 2**).

6. Lay a press cloth on the woven ribbon and lace. Press lightly to secure ribbon and lace. Turn up-side-down and press on the interfacing side to make sure all pieces are fused.

7. Attach entredeux to **one long side** of the woven piece. The stitching line for the entredeux should be right above the insertion lace (**fig. 3**).

8. Cut six pieces from the woven strip to the following measurement: small dolls 3$\frac{1}{2}$", medium dolls 4", large dolls 5". These pieces will be used in the skirt (**fig. 3**).

9. On the remaining woven strip attach entredeux to the other side of the strip. This strip will be used later in the sleeves (**fig. 4**).

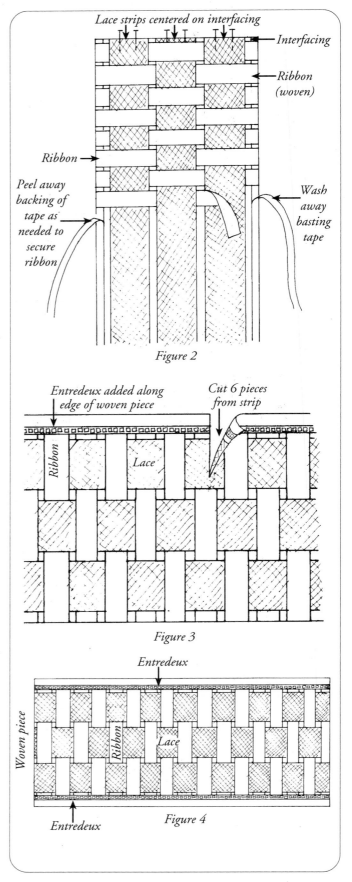

Figure 2

Figure 3

Figure 4

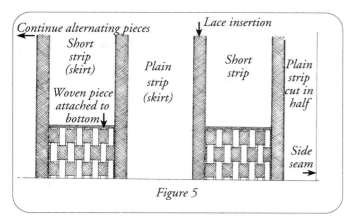

Figure 5

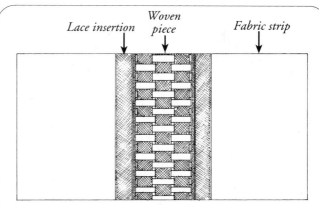

Figure 6

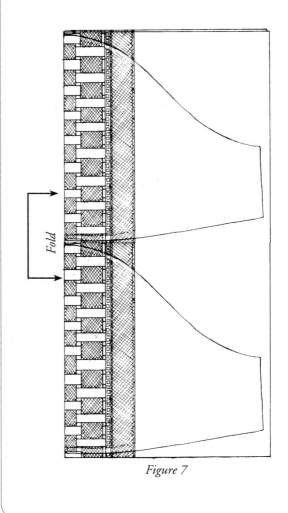

Fold

Figure 7

C. Constructing the Skirt

1. This skirt will be constructed from strips of fabric.

   Long strips - Cut 6 fabric strips 3½" wide for small dolls, 4" wide for medium dolls, 5" wide for large dolls with the length of the strips cut ¾" shorter than the skirt measurement given on the chart. These will be called the plain pieces.

   Short strips - Cut 6 fabric strips 3½" wide for small dolls, 4" wide for medium dolls, 5" wide for large dolls with the length of the strips cut 2¾" shorter than the skirt measurement given on the chart.

2. Attach a woven piece to the end of each short strip using the technique "Entredeux to Fabric." Press. These strips will be called the woven pieces. Now the woven strip and the plain strips should be the same length. Three plain strips and three woven strips will be used for the front skirt and the same will be used for the back skirt.

3. Alternate the skirt strips beginning in the middle with a woven piece. Place lace on each side of the strip using the extra stable lace technique found on page 223. Attach a plain strip on each side of the woven strip using the same technique. Attach lace strips on either side of the plain strips. Attach woven strips to each side of these plain strips in the same manner. Attach lace strips on either side of the woven strips (**fig. 5**).

4. Cut one plain strip in half (same length, half the width) and attach these half strips to the lace on either side of the woven strips. This completes the front skirt panel. Repeat strip construction for back skirt panel (**fig. 5**).

5. Refer to the General Directions II - steps 4 - 13. **Note:** The gathered skirt pieces will be attached to the entredeux of the yoke using the technique "Gathered Fabric to Entredeux."

D. Embellishing The Sleeves

1. Attach lace insertion pieces to each side of the woven sleeve piece using the technique "Lace to Entredeux" (**fig. 6**).

2. Cut two fabric strips to the length of the woven strip and to the following measurements: small dolls 4", medium dolls 6", large dolls 7".

3. Attach the fabric strips to each side of the woven piece using the technique "Lace to Fabric" (**fig. 6**). Press and cut out two sleeves from this created fabric (**fig. 7**).

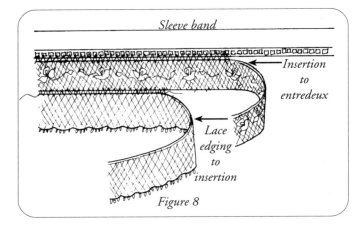

Sleeve band

Insertion to entredeux

Lace edging to insertion

Figure 8

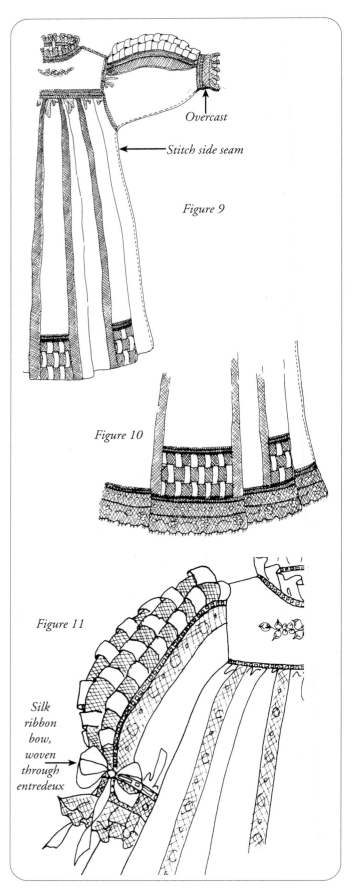

Overcast

Stitch side seam

Figure 9

Figure 10

Figure 11

Silk ribbon bow, woven through entredeux

4. Refer to the sleeve band chart (page 38). Cut two pieces of entredeux to the measurement on the chart. Cut two pieces of ³/₈" lace insertion to the entredeux measurement. Attach the lace to the entredeux using the technique "Lace to Entredeux" (**fig. 8**).

5. Cut two pieces of edging lace twice the length of the entredeux. Gather to fit the insertion lace and attach using the technique "Lace to Lace" (**fig. 8**).

6. Refer to General Directions - III. Constructing the Sleeves. To finish the ends of the sleeve refer to B. Sleeve Bands and Ruffles - a. Entredeux and Gathered Edging Lace - steps 3 & 4 - to attach the sleeve band to the sleeve.

E. Side Seams and Fancy Band

1. Stitch one side seam/sleeve together using a ¹/₄" seam. Overcast (**fig. 9**).

2. Fancy band - Cut a piece of entredeux, a piece of ³/₈" insertion lace and a piece of edging lace to the following measurement: 46" for small dolls, 46" for medium dolls and 61" for large dolls.

3. Attach the insertion lace to the entredeux using the technique "Lace to Entredeux." Attach edging lace to the insertion lace using the technique "Lace to Lace" (see fig. 8).

4. Attach the band to the lower edge of the skirt using the technique "Entredeux to Fabric" (**fig. 10**).

5. Stitch the second side of the dress together using a ¹/₄" seam. Overcast (**fig. 10**).

6. Weave silk ribbon through the beading (under two bars, over two bars) at the sleeves. Tie into a bows at the center of the sleeves (**fig. 11**).

7. Attach Velcro™, buttons and buttonholes or snaps to the back of the yokes to close the dress. ✶

Embroidery Template for Woven Insets Ribbon Doll Dress, refer to sitch key on page 50.

Introduction to Crafts

Who doesn't love to make craft items, especially elegant ones? This section of *Martha's Sewing Room* television series is designed to present just that - elegant crafts. Some of the crafts for this series are detailed and take a little time to complete. Some are terribly easy, involving hot glue gun and minimal skills and time. We have the most wonderful selection for your individual choices.

I think you will love the five baby bonnets in this section. We have even included a boy bonnet. Any of these choices will be sure to please your lucky baby. We have gathered up lots of elegant sash ideas to make that extra special dress even more special. Let your fancy be the only guide to finishing your sashes. For the special women on your list, make each of them a covered mirror in colors to match her bedroom. She will be pleased as punch. I love the flower girl's petal basket for her to carry in the wedding. If a wedding isn't in your little girl's plans, then make one for her to carry to church. It is so special and appropriate for either occasion.

The netting angel is really a masterpiece and would be lovely for many different gift occasions. There is even a little poem about guarding the baby's life which you might stitch in with this gift. Making a covered footstool called a tuffet is easy and very unusual. This tiny little footstool can be made in any type of upholstery fabric to match a variety of interiors. Once again for your home is this pleated lamp shade to go on a purchased lamp. With fringe on the bottom, you will be sure to please several people on your gift list. A beautiful tissue box cover will be used in the bedroom or bath to make the ordinary utility tissues appear like a decorator accessory. As long as we are making home decorating items, how about a light switch cover for a child? This one is a little train traveling on a green felt base. In the home decorating world, taffeta bows to go above a picture frame are all the vogue. You can make yours at a fraction of the cost of the expensive stores.

Do you have antique goodies such as collars? Frame them as we have done on this show. Add a little silk ribbon embroidery or purchased silk ribbon trims and you have finished, taking something out of the bottom of the drawer and putting it up for all to enjoy. In the 1950's we always kept our lingerie in bags in the dresser drawer. Since I travel so much, I still enjoy lingerie bags to keep my lingerie separated in my suitcase. I think you will enjoy ours in this book; it is very pretty. Decorating a purchased hat is so much fun and easy to do. You can have a one of a kind hat for very little money. Weaving picture frames is certainly not a new idea. I first saw something similar to this in England about ten years ago. This solves the problem of having a picture frame to match the colors of your room. It is easy to make. Crazy patch is so much fun to do. Using scraps in your favorite colors, you can make our collar to go with any sweater in your wardrobe.

I hope you have lots of fun making the crafts in this section. None are really too hard and all will be treasured gifts. We show you in living color how to make each of these crafts on our weekly television show. Please join us on *Martha's Sewing Room* on your local PBS station or via our videos which are available from us. ✖

Covered Mirror

Using articles purchased from a craft supply store, we have created a very elegant covered mirror for you to recreate. Green water stained taffeta is the fabric used for covering the frame. Gathered taffeta makes a puffing effect around the outside edge on the back. The back covered piece has taffeta, tatting and a Swiss motif in the center. Green braid is glued around the outside edge, the inside edge and the mirror portion of the mirror. This would be such a beautiful gift for any woman on your list and if you are redecorating your bathroom, you might want to make one of these for yourself in your chosen colors.

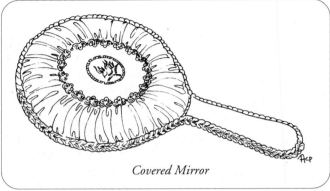

Covered Mirror

Supplies

* 1 plywood hand mirror form (you may have one cut at a craft store)
* batting to cover the front and back of the mirror form
* $^1/_2$ yd. of moiré
* 1 round mirror to fit the plywood shape
* $1^1/_4$ yds. of braid (to match moiré)
* $^1/_2$ yd. of tatting
* lace motif for center decoration
* 1 posterboard circle, the same size as the mirror
* glue or hot glue gun

Directions

1. Cut two pieces of batting, each a little larger than the plywood mirror form. Glue the two pieces of batting to the front and back of the plywood and trim the excess from around the edges.

2. Cut a strip of the moiré, $1^3/_4$" wide, across the width of the fabric. Run gathering rows on each side of the strip to create puffing. (Refer to "Puffing Techniques" found on page 178).

3. Cover the handle with moiré, front and back, letting the raw edges meet on the edges of the handle.

4. Arrange the puffing into a circle so that the edge of the puffing extends over the edge of the plywood form (this will be the front of the mirror). Turn the gathered edge under where the puffing meets the edge of the form. Glue around the edges and the center gathers (**fig. 1**).

5. Cover one side of the posterboard circle with batting. Trim away the excess batting. Cover the circle with moiré and wrap the edges of the moiré to the back of the circle. Glue the edges of the moiré in place.

6. Glue the covered circle to the plywood form so that it covers the raw edges of the puffing. Glue tatting around the edges of the circle. Glue a lace motif in the center of the circle (**fig. 2**).

7. Cover the other side of the mirror form with moiré, letting the edges overlap the sides of the plywood as before; you will need to

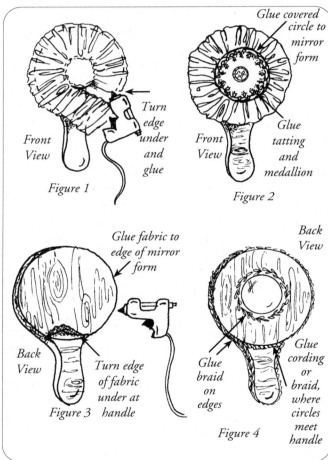

Turn edge under and glue

Front View

Figure 1

Glue covered circle to mirror form

Front View

Glue tatting and medallion

Figure 2

Glue fabric to edge of mirror form

Back View

Turn edge of fabric under at handle

Figure 3

Back View

Glue braid on edges

Glue cording or braid, where circles meet handle

Figure 4

turn under the edge of the fabric where the top meets the handle. Glue the fabric in place (**fig. 3**).

8. Glue the mirror in the center. Glue braid around the edges of the mirror (**fig. 4**).

9. Glue a piece of small cording or braid where the circles of fabric meet the handle. Glue braid around the edge of the mirror form to cover the edges of the fabric (**fig. 4**). ✄

Flower Basket

For your little flower girl in the wedding, make this flower petal basket for her to carry down the aisle just filled with rose petals. This triangular shaped basket is made of batiste and it is trimmed with wide gathered white French edging. There is a French lace galloon running down both the front and the back of the purse. French gallooning is stitched over the top openings. Beautiful satin ribbon bows with lots of streamers finish the top edges. A piece of white French lace gallooning is folded in half for the handle for this basket. This would be the perfect present to present to your flower girl because she could use it as a purse to carry to Sunday School or as a wall hanging in her bedroom. Special handmade presents like this add so much to a wedding to remember. As a matter of fact, making a basket like this would be a lovely bridesmaid's present also because it is a lovely little container to fill with silk flowers and put on the wall of her bedroom or dressing room.

Supplies

* ³/₈ yd. of fabric

* 1³/₄ yds. of galloon lace (scallops on both sides)

* ³/₈ yd. of thin batting or heavy interfacing

* 1¹/₂ yds. of 3" edging

* 5 yds. of ¹/₈" satin ribbon

* 2 small lace motifs and a few pearl-type beads

* hot glue gun or fabric glue

* pattern found on pattern pull-out

Directions

1. Cut four basket pieces from fabric and two from the batting/interfacing; sandwich each piece of batting/interfacing between two of the fabric pieces. These form the front and back of the basket. Pin or baste the layers together to hold them in place while you work on the basket.

2. Fold the basket pieces in half, with the fold from top to bottom. Make a light crease. Stitch a piece of the galloon lace down the center front and the center back (**fig. 1**).

3. Fold a piece of the galloon lace over the raw edge at the top of the front and back pieces to form a border on the outside and a facing on the inside. Stitch the lace in place (**fig. 2**).

4. Gather the lace edging and pin it to one of the basket pieces, right sides together, with the gathered edge of the lace pinned on the ¹/₄" seam line. The outer edge of the lace can be pinned to the basket piece to keep it away from the seam area (**fig. 3**).

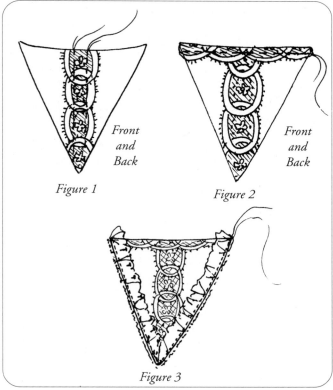

Front and Back

Figure 1

Front and Back

Figure 2

Figure 3

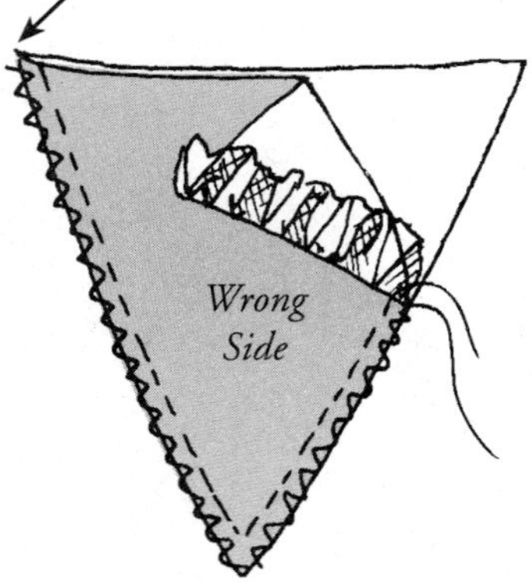
Seam together finish edge.
Wrong Side

Figure 4

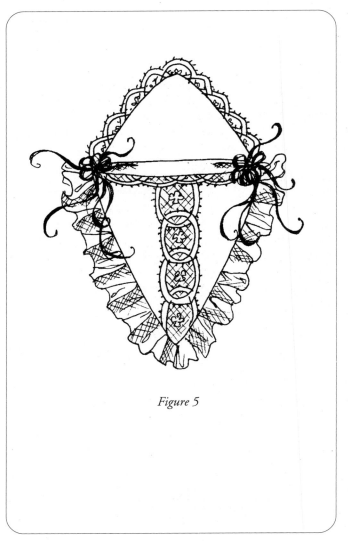

5. Place the front and the back basket pieces with right sides together. Sew around the sides and bottom point with a 1/4" seam. Finish the seam with a zigzag and trim, or use a serger **(fig. 4)**.

6. Turn the basket right side out. Make a handle from 18" of the galloon; fold the galloon in half along the length and stitch the layers together. Place the ends of the handle inside the basket top edge at the side seams and stitch in place **(fig. 5)**.

7. Cut the ribbon in half. Make a loopy bow from each half to stitch on the basket at the points where the handle is sewn; you may cut extra tails to stream down the sides if desired. You may also choose to glue a small lace medallion and beads over the center of each bow (see finished drawing). ⌘

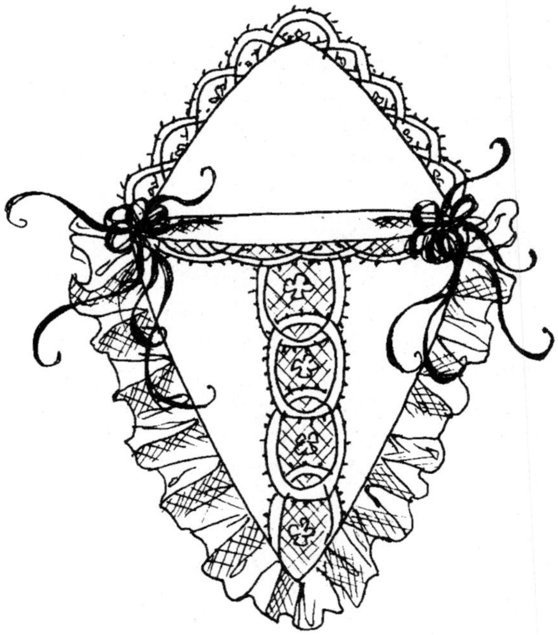

Figure 5

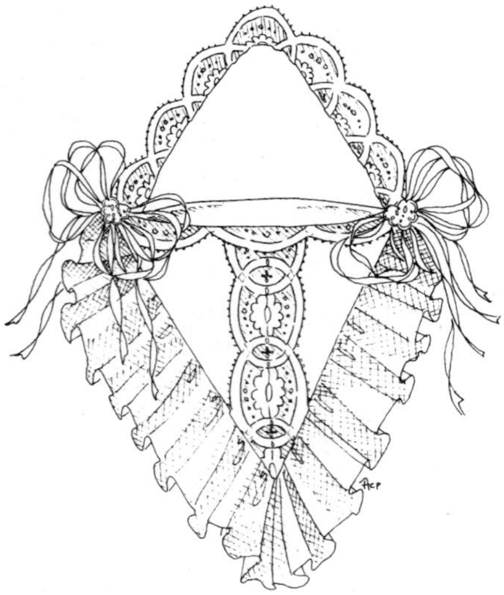

Netting Angel

This little guardian netting angel is the perfect gift for that new baby in your life. There is the sweetest little poem which has been transferred to wide ecru satin ribbon at the photocopy store. The poem reads, "Guard this little baby, please, Dear angels up above, May her days be filled with laughter, And her life be filled with love." Using ecru nylon tulle and ecru French lace edging, this little angel has tied arms and a head covered with gold hair and a gold halo. Her wings in the back are shaped like a heart with tulle in the center and satin ribbon going around the outside edge of the heart. She would be beautiful hanging on a baby's wall or on a piece of furniture. This would be a keepsake which could travel with a little girl into adulthood.

Supplies

- ❋ 1 yd. of netting
- ❋ 7 yds. of lace edging, 1¹/₂" wide
- ❋ 26" of 1" wide wired ribbon
- ❋ 12" of gold lace, ³/₄" to 1" wide
- ❋ 12" of gold wired cord for the halo
- ❋ 6" square piece of peach or ecru batiste
- ❋ small piece of fiberfill or cotton balls
- ❋ 6" piece of a small wooden dowel or skewer
- ❋ gold wire flower hair, or doll hair
- ❋ 12" piece of ¹/₄" satin ribbon
- ❋ fabric glue or hot glue gun
- ❋ 1 rubber band, or 8" of clear elastic
- ❋ washable marking pen
- ❋ pattern for wings and head found on pattern pull-out

Directions

1. Cut a 6" strip across the width of the netting. Cut two 28¹/₂" x 28¹/₂" squares of the netting.

2. Stitch lace edging around the edges of each square of netting, mitering the corners (refer to "Shaping Lace Diamonds" on pg. 191 for mitering instructions) (**fig.1**).

3. Use the head pattern piece to trace a circle on the batiste. Do not cut out the circle. Stitch a gathering row on the line (**fig. 2**).

4. Pull the gathers until a pocket forms. Stuff fiberfill into the pocket. Insert the dowel into the fiberfill. Continue drawing up the gathers until a tight circle is formed around the dowel and tie the threads. Trim away the large corners of the batiste. This will become the head (**fig. 3**).

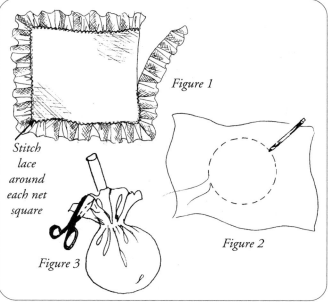

Stitch lace around each net square

Figure 1

Figure 2

Figure 3

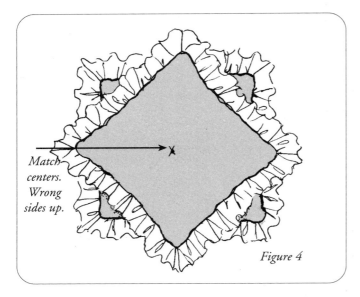

Figure 4

5. Find and mark the center of each netting square. Lay one square over the other, wrong sides up, with the centers matched; let the squares be offset so that the points of one square are between the points of the other square (**fig. 4**).

6. Put the stuffed head in the center of the squares, with the dowel sticking up. Gather the netting around the head and secure it around the dowel with clear elastic or a rubber band (**fig. 5**).

7. Cut a piece of netting 25" by 6". Mark the center and tie a very loose knot 1" from each side of center. This forms the shoulders and arms. Tie tighter knots in each end to form the hands. Trim off the loose ends (**fig. 6**).

8. Tie a scrap of the netting around the neck, with the ends in the back. Before making the second loop of the tie, place the center of the shoulder piece on top of the tie and finish tying so that the shoulders are attached to the back of the neck (**fig. 7**).

9. Tie a piece of ribbon around the neck to make a bow in front. Cut a small piece of the ribbon to make a hanging loop and glue it to the back of the neck.

10. Place a piece of netting over the wing pattern, on a shaping board. Shape the 1" wired ribbon over the outline, and pin it in place. Stitch the ribbon to the netting around the inside edge only. Trim away the excess netting (**fig. 8**).

11. Glue the wings on the back, adjusting as necessary (**fig. 9**).

12. Glue gold hair to the top of the head. Glue a band of gold lace around the bottom of the hair. Make a circle of the wired gold cord and glue it in place for a halo (**fig. 10**).

13. You may glue the hands together in front, or glue the hands to a small card with the following poem written on it:

Guard this little baby, please
Dear angels up above.
May her days be filled with laughter
And her life be filled with love. ✄

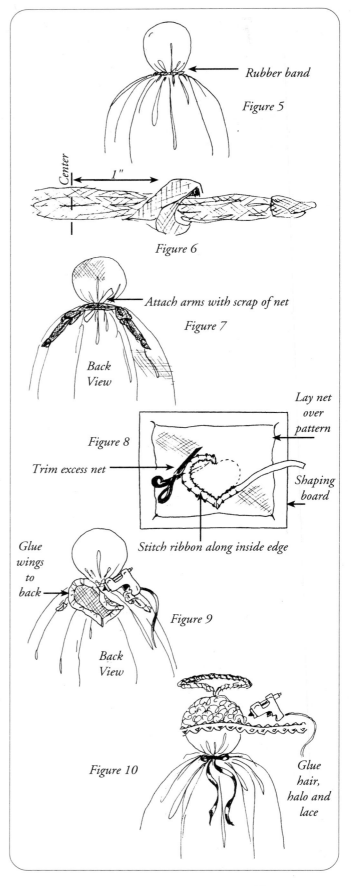

Rubber band

Figure 5

Center
1"

Figure 6

Attach arms with scrap of net

Figure 7

Back View

Lay net over pattern

Figure 8

Trim excess net

Shaping board

Stitch ribbon along inside edge

Glue wings to back

Figure 9

Back View

Figure 10

Glue hair, halo and lace

Covered Tuffet

Making a pretty stool for your feet is quite a creative craft for this show. Covered in red silk dupioni, this stool is trimmed with black braid and black fringe. The gathered center section has a covered button for the center surrounded by black braid. The double ruffle is gathered around the outside edge to finish this little stool. You can use a stool from the craft store or use this method to recover a stool that you already have and aren't using. This is a sweet present for yourself or for someone you love.

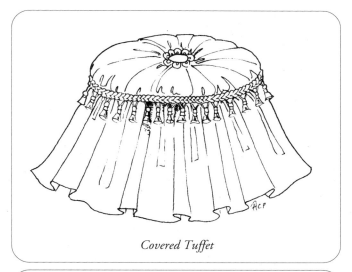

Covered Tuffet

Supplies

* 1 small wooden stool
* 1³/₈ yd. of fabric
* 1 yd. of tassel trim
* 6" of braid
* 1 large button to cover, 1¹/₂" to 2"
* batting to cover stool with 4 layers
* glue or hot glue gun
* staple gun
* 1 rubber band

Directions

1. Cut a strip of fabric 12" wide across the width of the fabric. Gather one long side of the fabric into your hand and wrap a rubber band around it to hold the gathers in place (**fig. 1**).

2. Cut four layers of the batting large enough to cover the top and wrap around the sides of the stool. Stack all of the layers on a table top.

3. Fan the gathered fabric over the batting with the right side of the fabric up, adjusting the gathers as evenly as possible. Cover the button. Sew it to the center of the fabric. This will cover the center of the gathers (**fig. 2**).

4. Glue, with a glue gun, the batting/fabric layer to the top of the stool, with the button in the center of the stool. Arrange the gathers evenly and pull the fabric/batting to the underside of the stool. Use a staple gun to fasten the fabric/batting to the stool. Glue the overlapped edges of the fabric together (**fig. 3**).

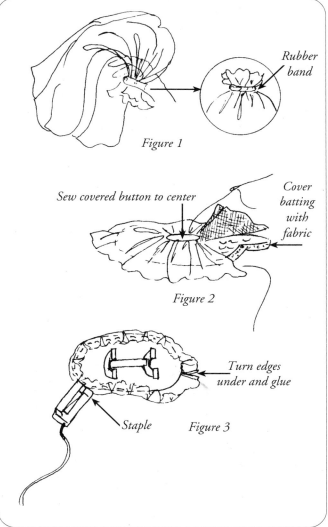

Rubber band

Figure 1

Sew covered button to center

Cover batting with fabric

Figure 2

Turn edges under and glue

Staple

Figure 3

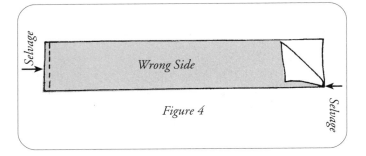

Figure 4

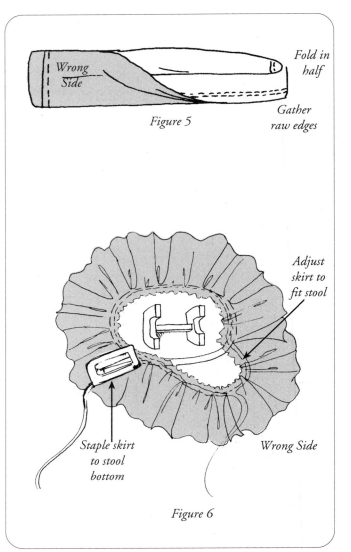

Figure 5

Figure 6

5. Cut two fabric strips the width of the fabric by the distance from the top of the stool to the floor, doubled plus 2". This stool measured 7"to the floor, doubled equals 14", plus 2" equals 16". Stitch the two strips, right sides together along the short edges to make a circle. This will be the skirt for the tuffet (**fig. 4**).

6. Fold the fabric in half with wrong sides together and raw edges meeting. Run two rows of gathering threads along the raw edge through both layers. Gather the skirt to fit the stool (**fig. 5**).

7. Turn the stool upside down on the table. Slide the skirt down over the stool with the hem (folded edge) flared out around the stool and the gathered edge closest to the edge of the stool. Readjust gathers to fit around the edge of the stool. Gather as evenly as possible. Use a staple gun to attach the gathered edge of the skirt around the edge of the stool (**fig. 6**).

8. Turn the stool right side up. Glue the tassel braid around the edge of the stool. Glue the braid around the button in the center top.▨

Pleated Lamp Shade

Making home decorating items is easy and fun. Covering this lamp shade is a wonderful gift idea for yourself or for a friend. Using a purchased lamp and shade, choose fabric to match or blend with the room for which this lamp is being made. Fringe the bottom of the fabric if desired and pleat the fabric. Our lamp is trimmed at both the top and the bottom with matching braid which is glued on. This is truly a very simple gift for you to make. You could also use this idea and cover a larger lamp. In some of my turn of the century magazines, covering lampshades was considered quite the vogue. Some women even embroidered lamp covers which simply hung on top of the lamps. This is an easy craft and one I think you will have fun doing.

Supplies for Lampshade Shown

- ❧ Lampshade (Height 5^1/$_2$", Top 10", Bottom 20")
- ❧ Fabric 13" by 60"
- ❧ Braid 1 yd.

How to determine requirements for other shade sizes -

1. Take three measurements from the lampshade:

    a. Height

    b. Length around the top

    c. Length around the bottom

2. Fabric requirement: length of fabric = 2 x height of strip + 2"

    width of fabric = 3 x bottom measurement (Several strips can be sewn together to achieve this width.)

3. Braid requirement = Top measurement + bottom measurement + 6"

Additional requirements

- ❧ hot glue gun
- ❧ washable marking pen
- ❧ Clotilde's Perfect Pleater

Directions

1. Seam the strips together at the selvage edges to form one long strip, if necessary. Press the seams to one side.

2. Fold the fabric strip in half, wrong sides together, with the long edges meeting. Press. Draw and stitch along a line 1" from the cut edge (**fig. 1**).

3. Pleat the fabric with Clotilde's Perfect Pleater, or make ^{1}/$_2$" knife pleats; pleat until you have a pleated strip as long as the top edge measurement of the shade, plus 2" for overlapping. Press and steam the pleats. Let the fabric cool completely (**fig. 2**).

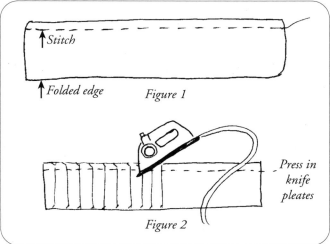

↑ *Stitch*

↑ *Folded edge*   *Figure 1*

Press in knife pleats

Figure 2

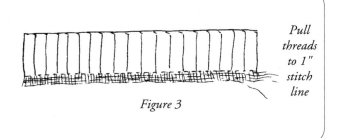

Pull
threads
to 1"
stitch
line

Figure 3

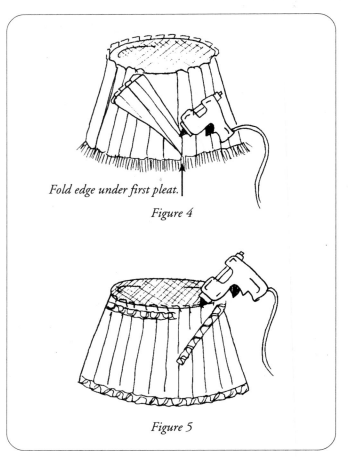

Fold edge under first pleat.

Figure 4

4. Stitch a line ¼" from the folded edge across the top of the pleats. Pull the threads out of the fabric beginning at the bottom edge and continuing to the 1" stitching line (**fig. 3**).

5. Place the pleated fabric on the shade with the folded edge slightly above the edge of the shade. One side edge of the fabric should be lined up with the seam in the shade. Wrap the fabric around the top edge of the shade and glue it in place. Fold the ending fabric edge under at the beginning pleat. Cut off any excess fabric (**fig. 4**).

6. Fan the pleats to fit around the bottom edge of the shade. Glue in place, overlapping the same pleat as before.

7. Glue the braided trim around the top and bottom edges of the shade, covering the stitching lines (**fig. 5**). ▩

Figure 5

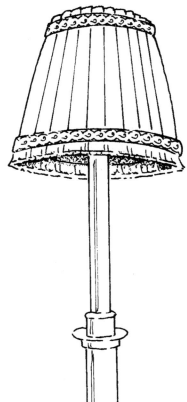

Tissue Box Cover

Selling for a lot of money in speciality shops, tissue box covers are a lovely addition to a bedroom or bath. This particular one is white. Your choices of fabrics for the top are unlimited; however, a placemat of cutwork is a wonderful and easy one to use. The decorator fabric leaves an opening in the top of the box cover and there is a little "overcoat" which fits over the tissue box on the bottom. Two perky bows are tied at both sides of the opening. Having a lovely cover like this to fit over a plain tissue box is really a lovely way to hide one of life's necessities.

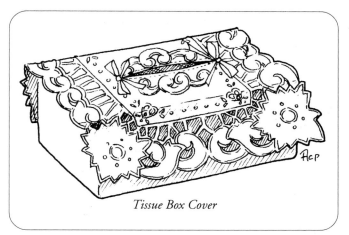

Tissue Box Cover

Supplies

✻ 1 cutwork placemat, 11" x 16", for the top

✻ ¹/₃ yd. of fabric for the sides

✻ 12" of ³/₈" elastic

✻ ¹/₂ yd. of ¹/₄" double-faced satin ribbon

✻ washable marking pen

✻ Pattern found on pull-out section

Note: The supplies and instructions given here are for a standard size tissue box; you will have to adjust the measurements and supplies to fit a different size box. All seams are ¹/₄" unless otherwise specified.

Directions

1. From the fabric, cut the following pieces (**fig. 1**).

   ✻ 2 strips, 10" long x 2³/₄" wide (cut from the opposite edges of the fabric so that each piece has a 10" selvage).

   ✻ 1 strip, 28³/₄" long by 6" wide

2. Pin the two 10" strips wrong sides together, with selvage edges matching. At each end, sew the selvage edges together 3", leaving a 4" slit unsewn in the middle. Press the seam open. The seam will be on the right side but will be hidden during construction (**fig. 2**).

3. Fold the placemat with the two short edges meeting each other. Cut the placemat in half along the fold, making two pieces 11" x 8"(**fig. 3**). Cut away a 2" by 1" rectangle at the upper sides (**fig. 4**).

4. Clip ¹/₂" into the placemat at the newly cut corner. Refer to figure 4 and the pattern for placement. Press all edges of the extension to the right side ¹/₂". Press the extension to the right side creating a crease (fold line) (**fig. 5**).

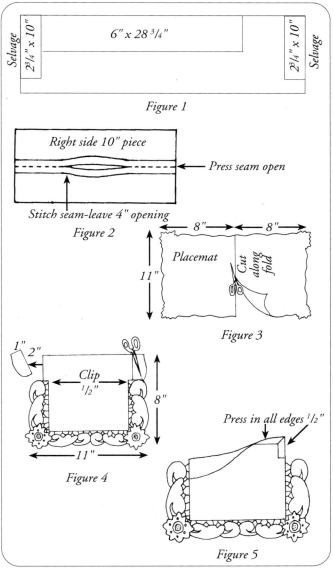

Figure 1

Right side 10" piece

Press seam open

Stitch seam-leave 4" opening

Figure 2

Placemat

Cut along fold

Figure 3

Clip ¹/₂"

Figure 4

Press in all edges ¹/₂"

Figure 5

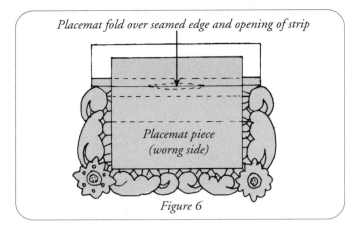

Placemat fold over seamed edge and opening of strip

Placemat piece (worng side)

Figure 6

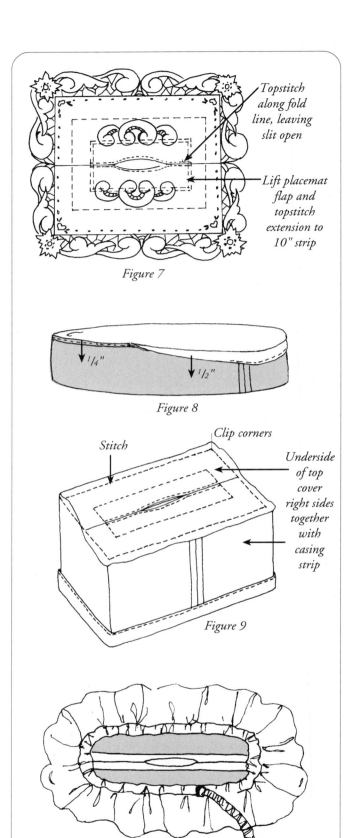

Topstitch along fold line, leaving slit open

Lift placemat flap and topstitch extension to 10" strip

Figure 7

Figure 8

Stitch

Clip corners

Underside of top cover right sides together with casing strip

Figure 9

Figure 10

5. Open the extension out flat at the fold line, with the ¹/₂" hems still turned under. With right sides together, place one of the placemat extensions on top of the 10" strip that was sewn earlier. Match the fold line of the placemat piece with the seamed edge and opening of the strip. Repeat for the other side (**fig. 6**).

6. Fold the placemat pieces to expose the slit. Top stitch the 10" piece to the placemat along the fold line. Be sure that the slit is left open (**fig. 7**). Lift the placemat flap and topstitch the extension piece to the 10" strip. This completes the top of the cover.

7. With right sides together, join the short ends of the 28³/₄" strip. Make a casing for the elastic on one edge by turning ¹/₄" and ¹/₂" again to the inside and pressing. Stitch the casing in place, leaving an opening to insert the elastic, but do not insert the elastic yet (**fig. 8**).

8. With right sides together, sew the under strips of the top cover to the raw edge of the casing strip. Clip corners where necessary and turn the cover right side out (**fig. 9**).

9. Cut the ribbon in half and make two bows; tack the bows at each end of the slit (see finished drawing). Run the elastic through the casing and adjust to fit. Stitch the ends of the elastic together and close the opening in the casing (**fig. 10**). ▨

Light Switch Cover

What little boy wouldn't love a light switch cover with green felt grass and a little wooden train? By covering a purchased light switch with felt, you have the base for this train. Glue the train on and put it up in someone's room. Then, wait for the squeals of delight when your little one discovers that he or she has a new light switch. This project takes almost no time and costs very little money; those two combined make happy thoughts!

Supplies

* 1 standard plastic light switch cover
* 4" x 6" piece of green felt
* 1 miniature wooden decorative train
* awl or ice pick
* glue or hot glue gun

Directions

1. Glue the felt over the light switch cover, wrapping the edges of the felt to the back. Glue in place. Carefully cut an "X" across the hole in the center for the switch. Glue the raw edges to the inside edge of the hole (**fig. 1**).

2. Glue the train to the cover, making sure that it does not cover the center hole, or screw holes. Carefully punch holes for the screws, using an awl or ice pick. ✠

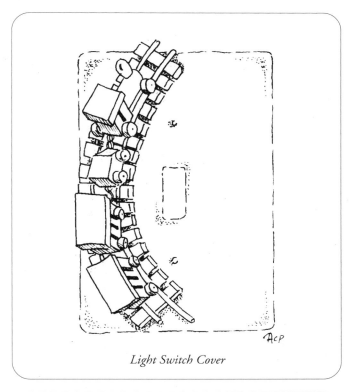

Light Switch Cover

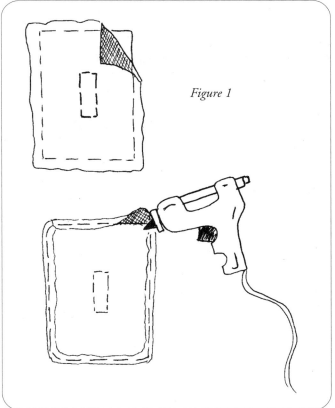

Figure 1

Picture Frame Bow

When we recorated our upstairs bedrooms several years ago, our decorator used many types of bows. One of them was used above oil paintings as well as framed prints. I thought these bows added magic to the paintings and to the room in general since our decor was very romantic and somewhat Victorian. They are so easy to make that we loved sharing them with you on this television show. To purchase them, they are very expensive! Folding the water stained taffeta into the bow, simply wrap a tie around the bow. After you attach your tails, you have a decorator touch for a fraction of the cost. These would be great wedding gifts, Mother's Day gifts or Christmas gifts for someone who loves decorating her home.

Supplies

✤ 1 yd. of fabric

✤ 1 curtain ring

✤ washable marking pen

Directions

1. Cut the following pieces of fabric (**fig. 1**).

    2 pieces 35” x 6$\frac{1}{2}$”

    1 piece 10” x 20”

    1 piece 10” x 18”

    1 piece 3 $\frac{1}{2}$” x 6”

2. Use the two 35” long strips to make the streamers. Sew the short ends of the strips together to make one long strip. Press the seam open. Fold the strip in half lengthwise, right sides together. Pin the two long raw edges together (**fig. 2**).

3. Make a mark on the long raw edge 2” from the short side. Also make a mark on the folded edge $\frac{1}{2}$” from the short side. Draw a line to connect the two marks (**fig. 3**).

4. Stitch the long edges with a $\frac{1}{2}$” seam, pivoting and stitching on the drawn line, leaving an opening in the middle of the seam (where the two pieces are sewn together)(**fig. 4**).

5. Trim the corners and turn the streamer through the opening. Press.

6. To make the large bow loop, use the 10” x 20” piece of fabric. Fold the piece in half lengthwise, with the long edges meeting. Stitch along the raw edges, pivoting at the corners and leaving an opening in the middle of the long side as for the streamers. Trim the corners, turn and press.

Picture Frame
Bow

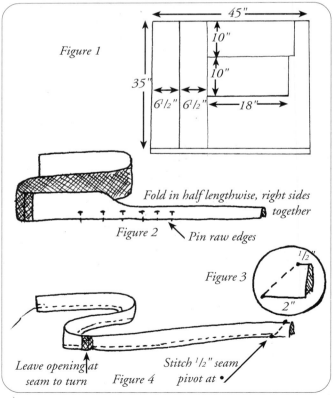

Figure 1

Fold in half lengthwise, right sides together

Figure 2 — Pin raw edges

Figure 3

Leave opening at seam to turn

Figure 4

Stitch $\frac{1}{2}$ seam pivot at •

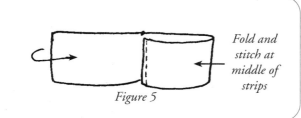

Fold and stitch at middle of strips

Figure 5

7. To make the small bow loop, use the 10" x 18" piece of fabric and follow the instructions in Step 6.

8. Once both loop pieces are sewn, shape the bows. Fold the ends to the middle of the strips, and stitch (**fig. 5**).

9. Place the small bow on top of the large bow and gather the center slightly. Place the bow over the center of the streamer piece (**fig. 6**).

10. Bow knot - Sew the long edges of the 6" by 3$^1/_2$" piece together, and turn. Press.

11. Wrap the knot around the bow and streamer; overlap the ends in back and whip by hand. Sew the curtain ring on the back of the knot (**fig. 7**). ✼

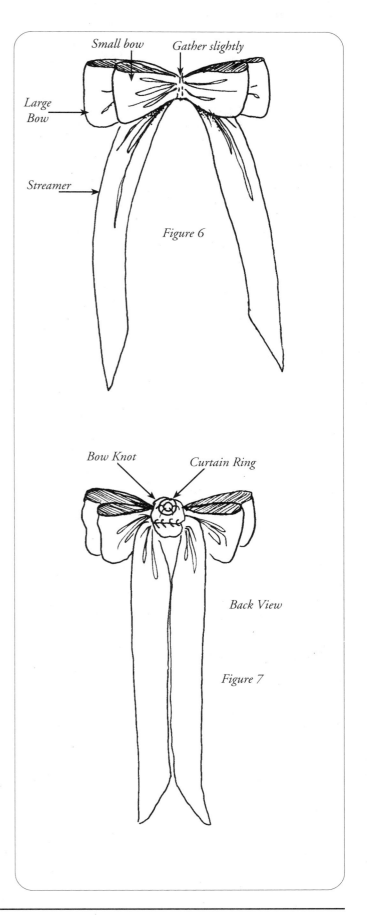

Small bow *Gather slightly*

Large Bow

Streamer

Figure 6

Bow Knot *Curtain Ring*

Back View

Figure 7

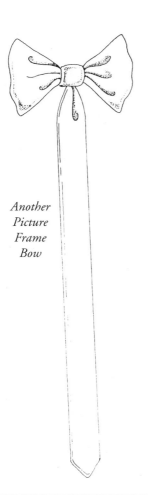

Another Picture Frame Bow

Framed Antique Collar

Joe, my husband, has said for a number of years now, "Martha, you have an unnatural atraction to antique clothing." Sometimes it is hard to explain how nearly every closet in our house is filled with my white treasures. Actually there is an unused shower in my sewing room which we have installed two hanging rods over so I can have more hang up space for my collection. Now, the point of my telling you that is to share with you that you can use these antique pieces for home decorating items. Your treasures can come out of the drawers and go onto your walls and keep you from purchasing expensive pictures for your walls. Anyway, you can tell your husband that. Using a little antique collar with a sweet bow in the front, we glued it to a mat which has been covered in pink faille fabric. A little purchased silk rosebud trim was glued at the top of the collar to add a little color. This is a really simple way to make a pretty picture. By the way, I also hang my little antique dresses in the bedrooms on the walls instead of paintings. I have no money left over for decorating my walls after I purchase my antique clothing. In all seriousness, I love little dresses hung on pretty satin hangers for paintings.

Framed Antique Collar

Supplies

* 1 self-stick mounting board OR cardboard cut to fit your frame
* antique collar
* fabric for the background
* picture frame
* clear nylon thread
* fabric glue or glue gun
* optional trims: lace scraps, ribbons, flowers, buttons or charms

Directions

1. Attach the collar to the background by basting or gluing. If the piece is in good shape, basting is preferable, so that it could be removed later if you wish; soft, clear nylon thread works well.

2. If there are stains or tears in the collar, they can be covered with ribbon, old lace, or other trim. Sew or glue in place. If desired, embellish the collar with buttons, fabric flowers, etc. All sewing must be done before the background is mounted on the board. Some gluing may be done after mounting to the board.

3. After the collar is fastened to the background and the sewn embellishments are complete, stretch the background smoothly over the mounting board. Pull the edges to the back in a miter. Glue or tape the corners and edges in place (**fig. 1**).

4. Secure the mounted collar into the frame. ✻

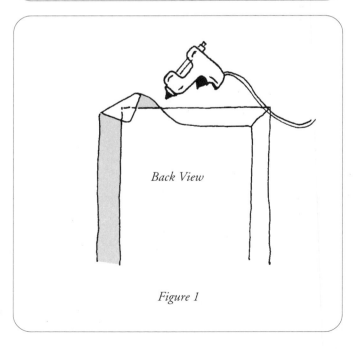

Back View

Figure 1

Lingerie Keeper

Pale blue silk dupioni is featured as the outside fabric for this crazy patched lingerie bag. The inside oval features several Swiss embroideries as well as pink and blue silk dupioni strips crazy patched together by using machine decorative stitches in blue thread. This is the perfect place to use those wonderful machine embroidery stitches on your sewing machine. Scallops stitched in pale blue encircle the center oval. White bows tie this case together at the sides. Inside, the case has two loose pockets; on one side there is another pocket. On the other side there are two pockets with a strip of Swiss insertion dividing them. The inside of this case is silk batiste in the same pale blue shade of the silk dupioni. This would be such a nice traveling lingerie case or it would be wonderful to keep hoisery in all the time in your dresser drawer. When I was growing up, lots of ladies kept their lingerie in separate bags in their dresser drawers. This beautiful bag reminds me of one that my Aunt Chris had in her lingerie drawer.

Lingerie Keeper

Supplies

- ❋ silk dupioni, 27" x 14"
- ❋ fusible batting, 27" x 14"
- ❋ fabric and lace scraps for crazy patch
- ❋ 1yd. of 45" or wider - lining fabric
- ❋ 4 yds. of ¼" double-faced satin ribbon
- ❋ 5" x 8" scrap of muslin or batiste for crazypatch backing
- ❋ water-soluble stabilizer (WSS), 5" x 8"
- ❋ decorative thread
- ❋ washable marking pen
- ❋ oval template found on pattern pull-out

Note: All seams are ¼" unless otherwise specified.

Directions

1. Trace the oval shape onto the muslin or batiste. Cover the oval with crazy patch (refer to "Basic Crazy Patch Technique" on page 221). When the crazy patch is finished and embellished with stitches, re-draw the oval, making sure the crazy patch fills the entire oval shape. <u>Do not</u> cut out the oval.

2. Place the piece of WSS over the oval shape. Straight stitch along the oval outline. Cut out the oval leaving a ¼" seam allowance, clip the curves (**fig. 1**).

3. Cut a slit across the long direction of the WSS, leaving about 1" uncut at each end. Turn the oval through the slit, so that the WSS makes a lining on the back side of the oval. Press the edges from the right side. Lay the oval aside (**fig. 2**).

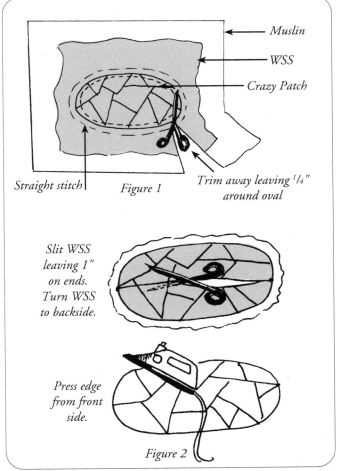

Muslin

WSS

Crazy Patch

Straight stitch

Figure 1

Trim away leaving ¼" around oval

Slit WSS leaving 1" on ends. Turn WSS to backside.

Press edge from front side.

Figure 2

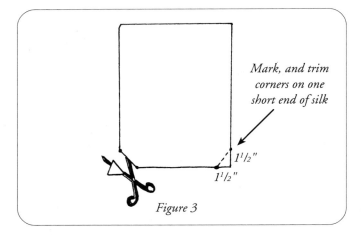

Mark, and trim corners on one short end of silk

1½"

1½"

Figure 3

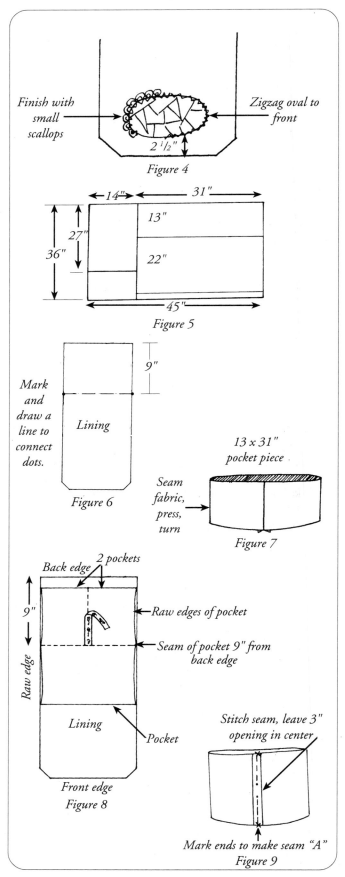

Finish with small scallops

Zigzag oval to front

2½"

Figure 4

←14"→ ←—— 31" ——→

13"

27"

36"

22"

←———— 45" ————→

Figure 5

9"

Mark and draw a line to connect dots.

Lining

Figure 6

13 x 31" pocket piece

Seam fabric, press, turn

Figure 7

Back edge   *2 pockets*

Raw edges of pocket

9"

Seam of pocket 9" from back edge

Raw edge

Lining

Pocket

Front edge

Figure 8

Stitch seam, leave 3" opening in center

Mark ends to make seam "A"

Figure 9

4. Fuse the rectangle of silk dupioni to the batting. Trim the edges to neaten if necessary.

5. Choose one short end to be the front edge; the long edges will be the sides. At each front corner, make two dots. Each dot will be 1½" away from the point of the corner. Draw a line to connect the two dots. Cut on the lines to shape the front edge (**fig. 3**).

6. Center the oval on the front, 2½" from the edge; pin the oval in place. Attach the oval to the front with a zigzag or decorative machine stitch. Stitch small scallops around the outer edge of the oval for decoration (**fig. 4**).

7. Cut the lining and pockets according to the diagram (**fig. 5**).

8. Lay the bag piece over the lining piece and trim the lining to fit the bag. Make a dot on each lining side edge 9" from the square short end (the back edge). Draw a line to connect the two dots (**fig. 6**).

9. Fold the 13" x 31" pocket piece right sides together, with the two short ends meeting. Stitch, then press the seam open. Turn the pocket right side out and press, with the seam in the center (**fig. 7**).

10. Pin and stitch the pocket to the right side of the lining; the seam of the pocket will face down and should be placed on the line 9" from the back edge. The raw edges of the pocket will be even with the side edges. This will create two pockets. Stitch down the middle of one pocket to form two smaller pockets. The stitched line can be covered with trim or machine decorative stitches (**fig. 8**).

11. Pin the lining to the bag with right sides together. Stitch around all edges, leaving an opening in the back edge for turning. Clip the corners and turn the bag right side out; press.

12. Whip the opening closed. Top stitch ³/₈" from the edges.

13. Sew the short ends of the 22" x 31" pocket piece, with right sides together, but leave a 3" opening in the middle of the seam. Press the seam open. Use a washable pen to make a small "X" at the end of each seam. This will become seam A (**fig. 9**).

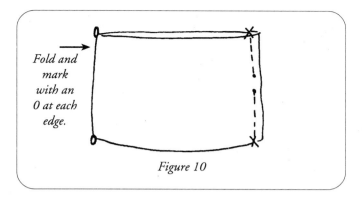

Fold and mark with an 0 at each edge.

Figure 10

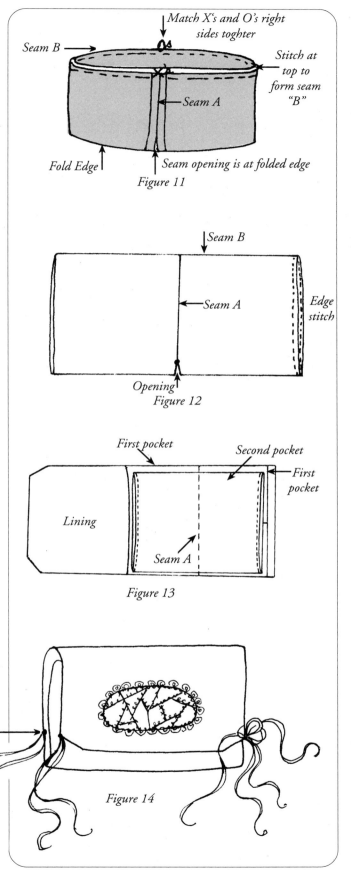

Match X's and O's right sides toghter

Seam B

Stitch at top to form seam "B"

Seam A

Fold Edge

Seam opening is at folded edge

Figure 11

Seam B

Seam A

Edge stitch

Opening

Figure 12

First pocket

Second pocket

First pocket

Lining

Seam A

Figure 13

Mark points for ties; sew ties in place

Figure 14

14. Fold the pocket piece with the seam along one edge. Mark a small "O" on the raw edge at each end of the other fold (**fig. 10**).

15. With right sides together, match the two long edges together so that the two ends of seam A are now matched together (the "X's" meet). Match the two "O's" together. Pin the long edges together to form a circular seam, which will be seam B. Stitch the seam and press it to one side (**fig. 11**).

16. Turn the tube right side out through the 3" opening left in seam A. Press the tube so that seam B lies along one edge. Seam A will run down the center of the pocket. Edge-stitch the folds at each end of the tube (**fig. 12**).

17. Match seam A to the pocket seam that was stitched across the lining. Stitch the new pocket to the bag along seam A (**fig. 13**).

18. Cut four ribbon ties, each 36" long. Stitch the middle of one ribbon piece to one front corner, on the right side. Repeat for the other front corner. Fold the back flap of the bag over along the pocket stitching line. Fold the front flap over the back flap so that the front edge is about 1" from the folded back edge. Make dots on the back side edges that match the points where the front ties are sewn. Open the bag out flat and sew the back ties in place (**fig. 14**).

19. Fold the bag again and tie it closed with double ribbon bows. ✄

Victorian Garden Hat

Joanna, my mother and I were invited to a Mad Hatter's Party last Christmas. Hats were required. I began to reminisce about the "days of old" when we wore hats and gloves to every occasion. It seems that hats are back in vogue in a big way if displays in the stores are any sure indication. This hat is easy to make and has a piece of antique ecru French lace insertion glued around the crown. Silk ribbon stitched and pulled up is found on top of the French insertion. Silk roses have been glued down and a variegated ribbon is tied at the base of the roses. A perky hat pin is found in the crown.

Victorian Garden Hat

Supplies

- ✽ 1 straw hat
- ✽ 2" - 3" wide lace to fit around the crown of the hat
- ✽ 2" wide wired ribbon, twice as long as the lace
- ✽ 5 or 6 silk roses and buds, some with leaves
- ✽ 1¼ yd. of 1" wide wired ribbon
- ✽ 1 hat pin
- ✽ glue or hot glue gun
- ✽ wire cutters

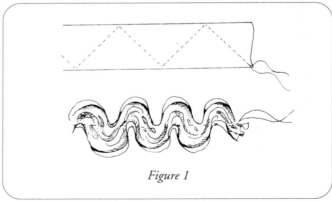

Figure 1

Directions

1. Measure around the crown of the hat at the brim to determine how much lace to buy. Wrap the lace around the crown, about 1" above the brim. Glue in place, overlapping the ends.

2. Cut a piece of 2" wide wired ribbon that is approximately twice as long as the lace used. Mark the top of the ribbon with dots 3" apart. Mark the lower edge of the ribbon with dots 3" apart alternating from the top set of dots. Stitch by hand or machine, gathering stitches from top dot to bottom dot, repeat for all dots. Pull the gathering thread to create ruching (**fig. 1**). Glue the ruched ribbon around the bottom edge of the lace band, overlapping the ends.

3. Use wire cutters to remove the long stems from the roses and arrange them on the brim against the crown, covering the ends of the lace and ribbon. Glue the flowers and leaves in place.

4. Use the 1" wide wired ribbon to make a loopy bow. Glue the bow to the hat. Place a hat pin above and behind the flowers. ✽

Woven Picture Frame

Shades of peach grosgrain ribbons are inverwoven with shades of ecru ribbon. One strip of ribbon is white with gold woven into a pattern. This picture frame is a purchased acrylic base with a space for the picture to be slipped in between the acrylic layers. The ribbons are woven on top of the acrylic frame and gold braid is glued around the rectangle for the picture and around the outside of the frame. These colors are especially pretty when using an antique picture such as the one shown in our color photograph.

Supplies

* 1 clear acrylic picture frame
* lightweight fusible interfacing slightly larger than the frame
* assorted ribbons and/or lace to weave
* braid or trim to go around the frame and the picture opening
* glue
* tape
* washable marking pen

Directions

1. Cut the interfacing at least 1" larger than the frame on all sides. Trace the outline of the frame onto the interfacing. Also trace the outline for the picture opening you will be using (**fig. 1**).

2. Place the interfacing on a pinning board with the fusible side up; pin or tape in place.

3. Weave ribbon to completely cover the frame area (refer to "Lace and Ribbon Weaving" on page 226).

4. After the ribbon has been woven and pressed as directed, stitch along the outlines for the frame and the picture opening. Trim away the excess interfacing and ribbon from the outer edge and the opening, leaving only the frame (**fig. 2**).

5. Apply glue to the back of the woven ribbon "frame" and glue it to the front of the plexiglas frame. Glue braid or trim over the raw edges of the frame and opening. ✺

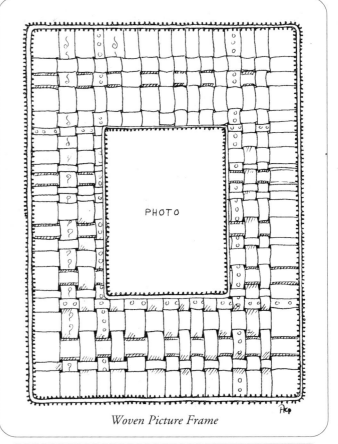

PHOTO

Woven Picture Frame

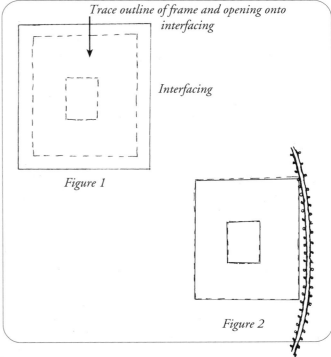

Trace outline of frame and opening onto interfacing

Interfacing

Figure 1

Figure 2

Quilted Collar

Crazy patch is so much fun to do and so creative. This crazy patch collar uses moirés, silk dupioni's, old tie fabrics, and satins. Using old ties in a crazy patch garment really makes it possible to remember a special man in one's life. The outside of this collar is an ecru Battenburg placemat. In the center front of the collar there are several buttons attached. Burgundy silk ribbon cascading is attached by purchased silk ribbon roses in gold, pink, blue and white. A little tatting and braid are stitched around several of the shapes and an antique Swiss rose motif is stitched down also. The collar ties in the back with a burgundy bow.

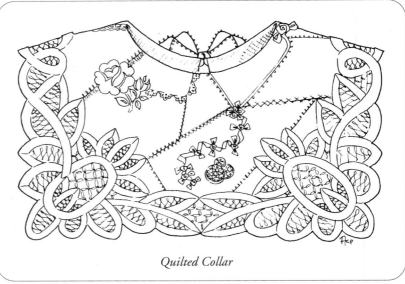

Quilted Collar

Supplies

- ❋ square collar pattern found on page 270-271
- ❋ 1 Battenburg- trimmed placemat, 14" x 20"
- ❋ 1 yd. of ³/₈" double-faced satin ribbon
- ❋ ⁵/₈ yd. of muslin
- ❋ ⁵/₈ yd. of lining
- ❋ fabrics for crazy patch
- ❋ decorative threads
- ❋ embellishments: buttons, charms, ribbons, flowers, lace, etc.
- ❋ washable marking pen

Directions

1. Trace the collar on the muslin. Stay-stitch around the collar outline, then cut out the collar, ¹/₄" from the stitching.

2. Cut the Battenburg lace from the placemat (**fig 1**). Place the Batternburg lace along the edge of the collar outline, cutting as needed for desired placement. Trace around the inner edge of the lace with a washable pen (**fig. 2**).

4. Remove the lace from the collar. Cover the collar with crazy patch, extending a little past the edges and covering the lines for the lace placement (refer to "Basic Crazy Patch Technique" on page 221). You may use fusible film to secure the patches, but

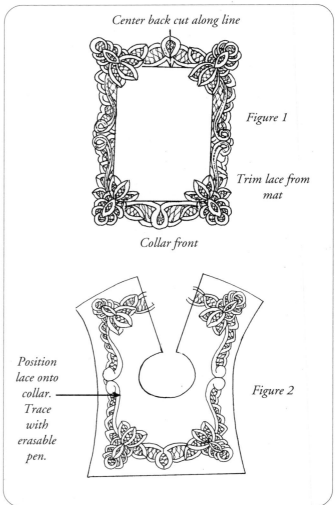

Center back cut along line

Figure 1

Trim lace from mat

Collar front

Position lace onto collar. Trace with erasable pen.

Figure 2

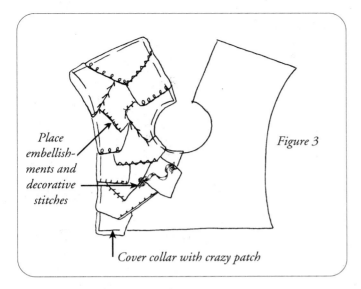

Place embellishments and decorative stitches

Cover collar with crazy patch

Figure 3

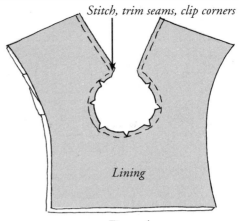

Stitch, trim seams, clip corners

Lining

Figure 4

you must be sure that the edges are fused well. Embellish the collar with flat trims and decorative stitches, running the embellishments all the way to the edges of the patchwork (**fig. 3**).

5. Cut a collar piece from the lining fabric. Place the collar on top of the lining, right sides together. Straight stitch the collar to the lining along the center back edges and the neckline edge. Trim the seams and clip the curves (**fig. 4**).

6. Turn the lining to the inside of the collar and press. Baste the raw edges together (**fig. 5**).

7. Replace the Battenburg lace and pin it in place; let the lace extend ¹/₄" past the back edges. Stitch the lace in place with a straight stitch, through the collar and lining.

8. Trim the fabric away from under the lace, close to the stitching. After the trimming is done, turn under the ¹/₄" extensions at the center back edges. Zigzag over the straight-stitched edges of the lace, to cover the raw edges of fabric underneath (**fig. 6**).

9. Cut the ribbon in half and stitch one piece to each back neck edge for ties. Add buttons, charms, and flowers to the collar, sewing through both layers. ✠

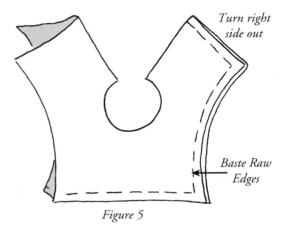

Turn right side out

Baste Raw Edges

Figure 5

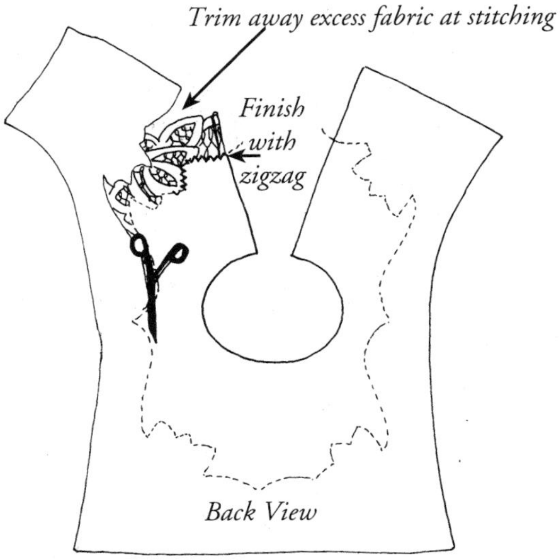

Trim away excess fabric at stitching

Finish with zigzag

Back View

Figure 6

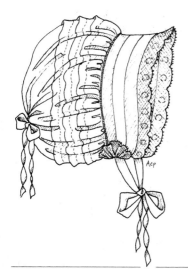

Bonnets

Pouf Bonnets

The front bands of the bonnets will be made from decorative ribbon or lace, lined or unlined. The body of the bonnet is made of fabric, decorated with tucks or lace shapes. The following chart lists three sizes with the length to cut the front band, finished length of the front band, and the back rectangle sizes for the lace shaped bonnet as well as the tucked bonnet. The finished front band lengths are measured from ear to ear across the top of the head.

Pouf Bonnet Chart

Size	Front Band		Cut Rectangle Sizes	
	Cut Size	Finished Length	Lace-shaped Bonnet	Tucked Bonnet
3-6 months	11" x 1" to 1¹/₂	10"	6" x 36"	9" x 36"
6-12 months	12" x 1¹/₂" to 2"	11"	6¹/₂" x 40"	9¹/₂" x 40"
12-18 months	13" x 2"	12"	6³/₄" x 45"	9³/₄" x 45"

You will also need 1³/₄ yds. of ³/₈" wide double-faced satin ribbon for each bonnet.

General Instructions for Pouf Bonnet

Note: See the specific instructions for each bonnet for a list of other supplies.

I. Front Bands

Refer to specific instructions for each bonnet to construct the front band.

II. Bonnet Decoration

Refer to specific instructions for each bonnet to make the lace-shapes or tucks.

III. Construction

Note: The drawings in this section will show a plain front band and a plain rectangle for the bonnet, rather than including any specific decorations. Drawings for each specific bonnet are included in the specific instructions for that bonnet.

1. After the front band is made and the back rectangle is finished, trim the front band to the length given in pouf bonnet chart. Trim any uneven edges on the rectangle.

2. Run two gathering rows across the front edge of the created rectangle, ¹/₈" and ¹/₄" from the edge (**fig. 1**).

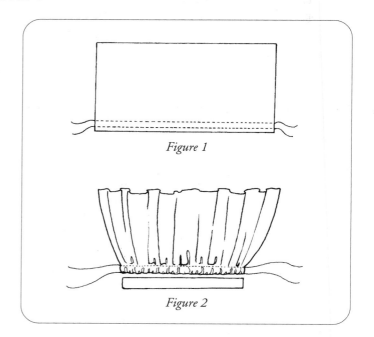

Figure 1

Figure 2

3. Gather the front edge of the rectangle to fit the long edge of the front band. Attach the gathered edge to the entredeux of the band using the technique given in specific directions. Press (**fig. 2**).

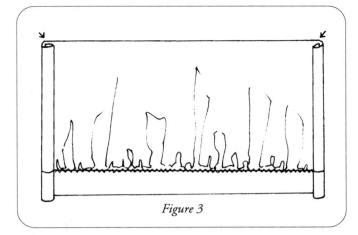

Figure 3

4. Fold ¹/₄" to the wrong side along the short ends of the bonnet, then fold ¹/₄" again. Press and stitch in place (**fig. 3**).

5. To form the back casing of the bonnet, fold ¹/₄" to the wrong side along the long unfinished edge, then fold ¹/₂" to the wrong side, to create a ¹/₂" casing. Press and stitch along the inner edge of the fold (**fig. 4**).

6. Make a ³/₈" to ¹/₂" pleat in the bottom edge of the front band. Cut two 18" pieces of the ribbon. Attach ribbon ties over the pleat. Lace medallions can be placed over the pleats, or the end of the ribbon ties can be hidden in the fold of the pleat (see specific instructions for each bonnet) (**fig. 5**).

7. Thread 27" of ³/₈" double-faced satin ribbon through the back casing, adjust the gathers and tie to fit the child (**fig. 6**). ✠

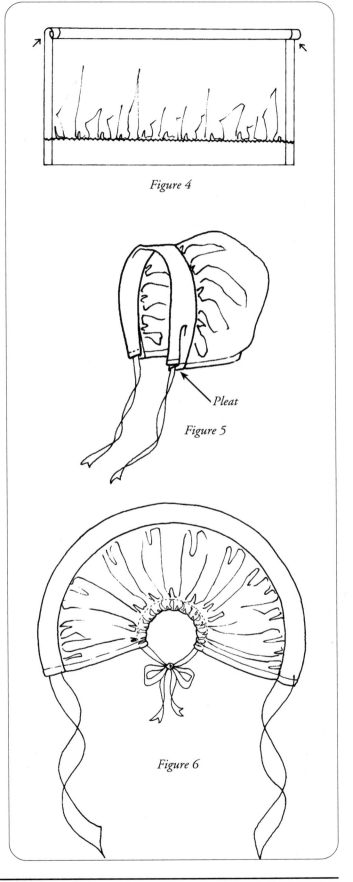

Figure 4

Pleat

Figure 5

Figure 6

Tucked Bonnet

Supplies

- ❧ ³/₈ yd. ribbon(2" wide)
- ❧ ³/₈ yd. of entredeux
- ❧ ⁵/₈ yd. of ⁵/₈" wide lace edging
- ❧ ¹/₃ yd. fabric

Specific Instructions

1. Stitch the flat lace edging to one long edge of the ribbon (refer to "Ribbon to Lace Insertion" on page 169).

2. Trim one side of the entredeux and attach to the other long edge of the ribbon using the technique "Lace to Entredeux." Do not trim the second side of the entredeux.

3. Tucks - there will be three ¹/₂" tucks, spaced ¹/₄" apart.

   a. Mark three lines, 1³/₄" apart, across the length of the rectangle, with the first line being 2" from one long edge (this will become the front edge of the bonnet) (**fig. 1**).

   b. With wrong side together, fold and press along the lines to form three creases.

   c. Shorten the stitch length slightly and stitch the tucks ¹/₂" from each fold. After all three tucks are sewn, press the tucks toward the back edge of the bonnet (**fig. 2**).

4. Cut the left-over lace edging into two pieces; pull the gathering threads to make each lace piece into a small circle. Whip the ends of the lace together by hand, and fold the circles in half. They will be tacked on top of the ribbon ties (**fig. 3 and fig. 4**).

5. Refer to the general directions to finish the bonnet. ❈

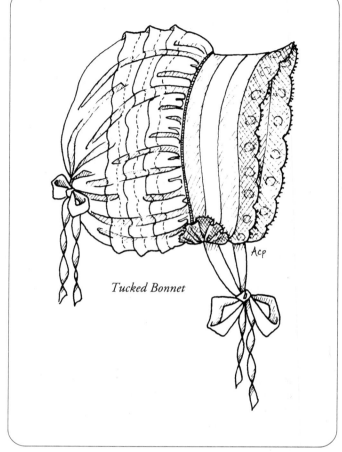

Tucked Bonnet

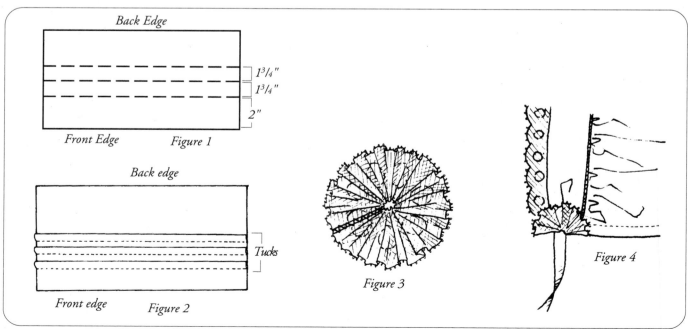

Back Edge

1³/₄"
1³/₄"
2"

Front Edge   Figure 1

Back edge

Tucks

Front edge   Figure 2

Figure 3

Figure 4

Lace-shapes Bonnet

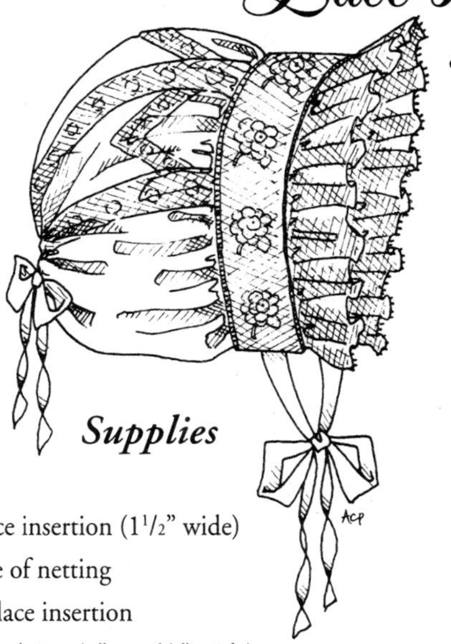

Supplies

- 1/3 yd. fabric
- 1 1/2 yds. of lace insertion (1 1/2" wide)
- 15" x 6" piece of netting
- 3/4 yd. of 5/8" lace insertion
- 3/4 yd. of lace edging (1" to 1 1/4" wide)
- 3/4 yd. of entredeux
- Lace shaping template on page 275.

1. Cut a piece of the wide insertion the length of the front band given in the pouf bonnet chart. Place the insertion lace over a strip of fabric the length and width of the lace. This will act as a lining for the front band. Baste in place 1/8" from each edge **(fig. 1)**.
2. Cut the entredeux into two pieces. Attach the entredeux to the long sides of the "lined" lace front band using the technique "Lace to Fabric." Trim the fabric edge of the entredeux from one side only **(fig. 2)**.
3. Gather the lace edging to fit the front band. Attach the lace edging to the trimmed side of the entredeux on the front band using the technique "Gathered Lace to Entredeux." This completes the front band.
4. Cut a rectangle of fabric to the size given in the pouf bonnet chart. Trace the lace shaping template in the center of the fabric **(fig. 3)**.
5. Shape 5/8" lace along template lines #1. Pin in place. Place 1 1/2" lace insertion along template lines #2. Zigzag the laces to the fabric where indicated **(fig. 4)**. Note: The laces are not zigzagged to the fabric along the inside part of the pointed lace pieces.
6. Trim fabric from behind laces. The area under the pointed lace pieces will be removed. Place a piece or pieces of netting under the open area of the pointed lace. Pin laces pieces on the netting. Zigzag the lace to the netting in the areas under the pointed lace **(fig. 5)**. Trim netting from behind the lace. This completes the bonnet rectangle.
7. Refer to the general directions in section II to finish the bonnet. Let the ends of the ribbon ties be hidden in the folds of the pleats on the front band **(fig. 6)**.

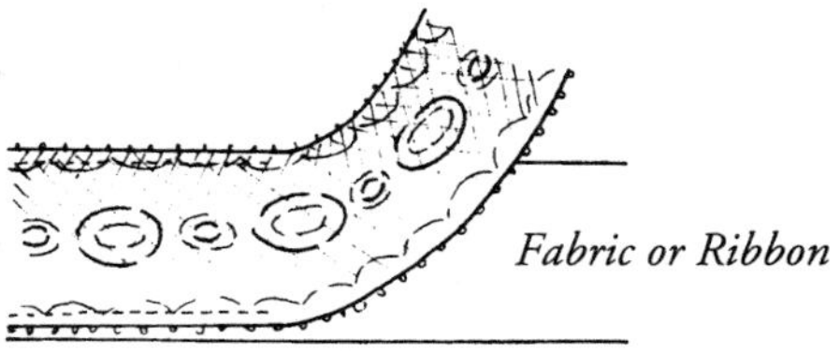

Figure 1

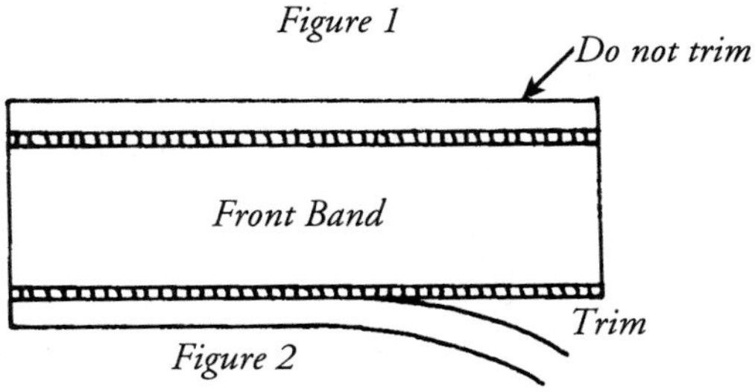

Figure 2

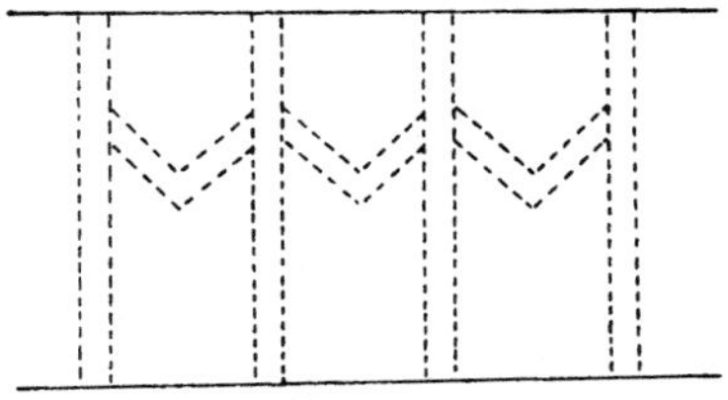
Figure 3

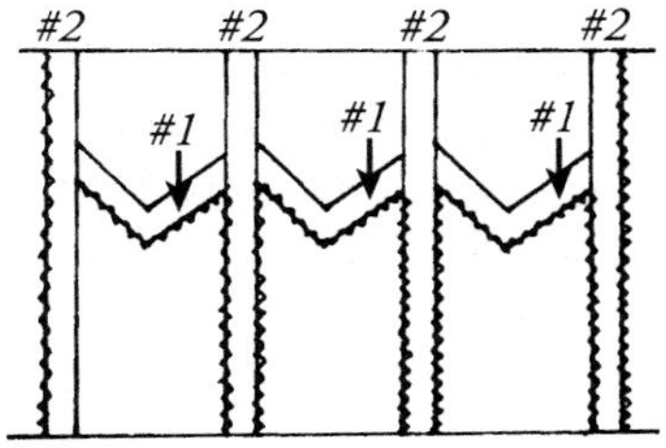

Figure 4

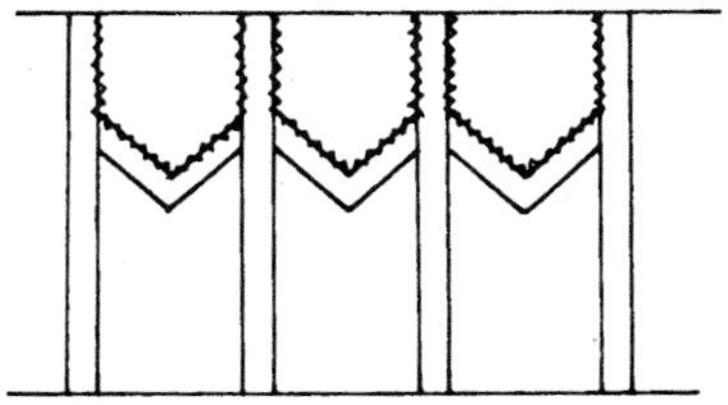
Figure 5

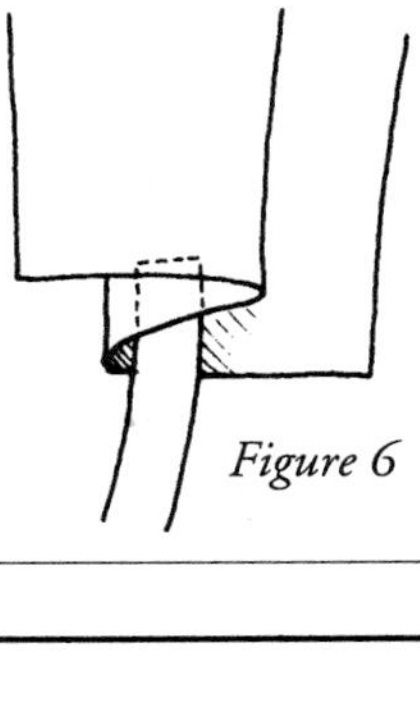
Figure 6

French Bonnets

Each bonnet will be cut from a rectangle of lace or fabric, with the length of the rectangle forming the front edge of the bonnet. Instructions for creating the rectangles are given in the Specific Instructions for each bonnet. The following chart shows finished rectangle sizes.

French Bonnet Chart

Size	Rectangle size	Gather Curve To
Preemie/doll	13" x 7½"	7½"
0 - 6 months	13½" x 8"	8"
6 - 12 months	14" x 9"	8½"
12 - 18 months	15" x 10"	9"

See Specific Instructions for bonnet supplies.

General Instructions for French Bonnet

I. Front Bands

Refer to specific instructions for each bonnet to embellish/construct the rectangle and cut out the bonnet.

II. Construction

Note: The drawings in this section will show a plain bonnet. Drawings for each specific bonnet are included in the specific instructions for that bonnet.

1. After the rectangle is completed and the bonnet is cut out, run 2 gathering rows along the curved edge at ⅛" and ¼" (**fig. 1**).

2. Cut a piece of entredeux that is the length of the "gather curve to" measurement on the chart. (These measurements are guides; a more accurate measurement can be made by measuring the child, from ear to ear across the back of the neck.)

3. Trim one side of the entredeux and attach flat narrow edging to the trimmed edge. Let the lace extend ½" beyond the ends of the entredeux.

4. Pull up the gathering threads on the curved edge of the bonnet to make the bonnet fit the entredeux/lace band. Attach the bonnet to the entredeux using the technique "Entredeux to Gathered Fabric" (**fig. 2**).

5. Fold the ½" lace extension diagonally to the inside and stitch in place. Trim away the excess lace (**fig. 2**).

6. Cut the ribbon for the ties in half. Make two or three loops in one end of each ribbon piece. Attach the looped end of the ribbon ties to the bottom edge of the front band (**fig. 3**). ✳

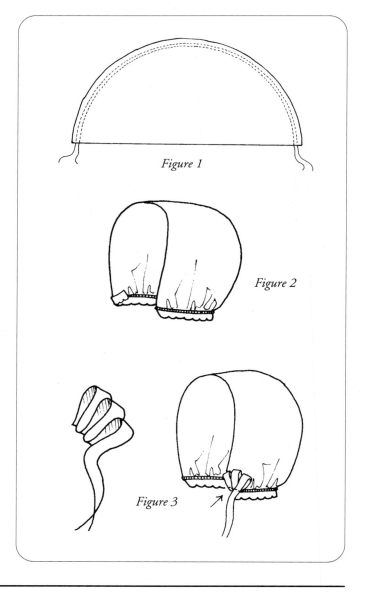

Figure 1

Figure 2

Figure 3

English Netting Lace Bonnet

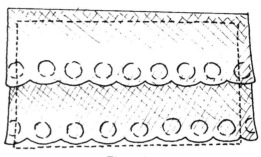

Figure 1

Supplies

❈ ¹/₂ yd. netting lace 7" to 11" wide

❈ ¹/₃ yd. lace edging (¹/₂" to ⁵/₈" wide)

❈ ¹/₃ yd. entredeux

❈ 1¹/₂ yds. double faced satin ribbon (³/₈")

❈ Bonnet Pattern on page 274.

Center

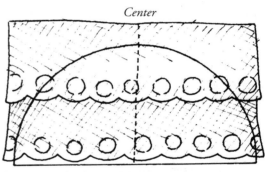

Figure 2

1. The embroidered edge of the lace will form the front edge of the bonnet. If the lace is not wide enough to form the rectangle, add lace or netting to the unfinished edge of the lace (this will be the back of the bonnet) (**fig. 1**). If lace will be used to add extra width, purchase additonal lace.

2. Place the embroidered edge of the lace along the front edge of the pattern piece. If the lace has a definite pattern, make sure that the design is centered (**fig. 2**).

3. Cut along the curved edge of the pattern piece.

4. Construct the bonnet using the French bonnet general directions. ❈

Hemstitched Bonnet

Supplies

* ✿ ³⁄₈ yd. linen

* ✿ 1¹⁄₂ yd. of ³⁄₈" double-faced satin ribbon

* ✿ decorative machine embroidery thread (for the hemstitching)

* ✿ stabilizer (if necessary)

* ✿ wing needle

* ✿ Bonnet pattern on page 274.

This bonnet is made of handkerchief linen, but other fabric may be used if it will allow holes to form when you stitch it with one of your machine's built-in hemstitches. A wing needle is used to work the hemstitching.

1. Refer to the rectangle sizes given in the French bonnet chart, and cut a rectangle of fabric 2" wider than the measurement on the chart (**fig. 1**).

2. Fold and press the extra 2" to the wrong side, creating a rectangle the same measurements as those on the chart. Starch the fabric and press it dry (**fig. 2**).

3. Make the first row of hemstitching about ¹⁄₂" from the folded edge on the right side, stitching through both layers of fabric. Use stabilizer if needed (**fig. 3**).

4. Stitch rows to make a band about 1¹⁄₄" to 1¹⁄₂" wide.

5. Trim away the excess fabric from the wrong side. If stabilizer was used, carefully remove it now.

6. Place the folded/hemstitched edge of the fabric along the front edge line of the pattern and cut out the bonnet.

7. Construct the bonnet using the French bonnet general directions. If desired, weave embroidery floss, several strands of thread or tiny ribbon through the entredeux. ✖

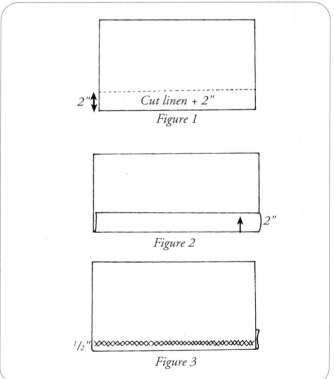

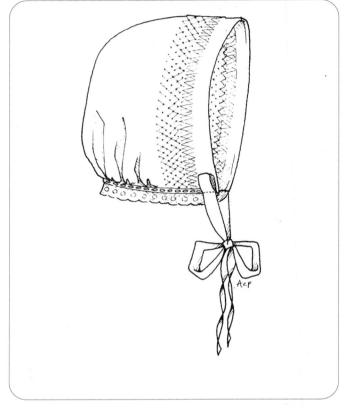

Cut linen + 2"

2"

Figure 1

2"

Figure 2

¹⁄₂"

Figure 3

Lace and Ribbon Weaving Bonnet

Supplies

- ✤ ¹/₂ yd. of ⁵/₈" to ³/₄" wide lace edging (for the bonnet front edge)
- ✤ 1¹/₂ yds. of ⁵/₈" double-faced satin ribbon (for ties)
- ✤ ¹/₃ yd. entredeux
- ✤ ¹/₃ yd. ⁵/₈" edging lace
- ✤ Bonnet pattern on page 274.

Additional Lace and Ribbon Requirements

Size	³/₄" Lace Insertion	³/₈" Ribbon
Preemie/doll	4¹/₄ yds.	1¹/₂ yds.
0 - 6 months	4¹/₂ yds.	1⁵/₈ yds.
6 - 12 months	5¹/₃ yds.	1⁵/₈ yds.
12 - 18 months	6¹/₂ yds.	1³/₄ yds.

1. The lace strips will run from the front of the bonnet to the back (across the width of the rectangle).

2. Cut the lace into pieces as long as the width of the desired rectangle. Mark a dot 2" from one end of each piece of lace (**fig. 1**).

3. Stitch the lace pieces together into a rectangle. Stop the stitching at the dots, leaving the front 2" of each seam unsewn (**fig. 2**).

4. Cut the ³/₈" ribbon into 4 pieces. Weave ribbon over and under the loose lace ends (refer to "Lace and Ribbon Weaving" found on page 226). Weave enough ribbon strips to make a band about 1¹/₂" wide. Pin the ends of the ribbon and lace to form a rectangle (**fig. 3**).

5. Topstitch the flat lace edging along the edge of the last piece of woven ribbon. Trim away the loose ends of the lace under the edging. This completes the front band (**fig. 4**).

6. Place the edging along the front edge line of the bonnet pattern. Cut out the bonnet and construct using the French bonnet general directions. ✺

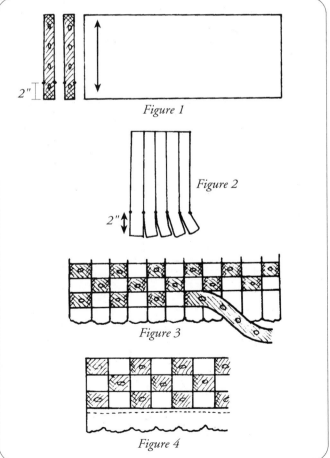

Figure 1

Figure 2

Figure 3

Figure 4

Introduction To Nightgowns

Choosing patterns to go along with our series is always so much fun. For this *Martha's Attic* TV series, I wanted to choose an adult pattern to go along with our adorable knickers for either a little boy or little girl. I love comfortable night wear. I simply won't wear anything uncomfortable to sleep in. I also adore pretty nightgowns. Using these two criteria – pretty and comfortable – I chose this nightgown style

and had it cut sizes 6-24. I love the yoke because it can have needlework or a little overbib with all of your fancy stitches. Practicing your heirloom sewing on a little piece is always fun before you begin the dress of the century. With this nightgown, you can "do a little piece" and use it as the bib over a terribly comfortable and easy to make nightgown. ▨

Lady's Nightgown Directions

Sizing

XS = 6 - 8; S = 10 - 12; M = 14 - 16; L = 18 - 20; XL = 22 - 24

Approximate finished back lengths (all sizes):

short	mid-length	long
36"	44"	51"

These lengths are only approximate; your best length can be determined by using your personal back length measurement and adjusting the skirt cut length accordingly. Adding length may require extra fabric.

Fabric Requirements for All Gowns

	Short Length	Medium Length	Long Length
All Sizes	2 ¹/₂ yds.	3 yds.	3¹/₂ yds.

(Add ¹/₄" yd. to gown fabric for Looped Puffing Gown.)

Additional Fabric Requirement for Pointed Yoke Overlay

(Shadow Embroidered Gown Only)

All Sizes   ¹/₂ yd. (white or ecru, suitable for shadow embroidery); buy ¹/₂ yd. less of gown fabric

Lace and Other Supplies

Refer to specific directions under each gown title.

All pattern pieces, templates and embroidery designs are found on the pattern pull-out.

All edges finished with lace have a ¹/₄" seam allowance (armhole, neckline, and hem). All other seams (shoulders, yokes to skirts, and sides) are ¹/₂", trimmed to ¹/₄" and overcast using a serger or zigzag. French seams can be used.

General Sewing Directions

I. Cutting Directions

Refer to specific directions under each gown title for cutting yokes, overlays and puffing strips. Dimensions for the skirt rectangles are given below:

Skirt Chart

Size	Width		Length		
	smocked	other than smocked	short	mid-length	long
XS	45"	26"	28"	36"	43"
S	45"	27¹/₂"	28"	36"	43"
M	45"	30"	28"	36"	43"
L	45"	31"	28"	36"	43"
XL	45"	32"	28"	36"	43"

II. Skirts

A. Shaping the Skirt Pieces

After the skirt rectangles have been cut and the fronts decorated according to the specific directions for each gown, you are ready to shape the skirt pieces.

1. Fold the skirt pieces in half, with the fold running from top to bottom (**fig. 1**).

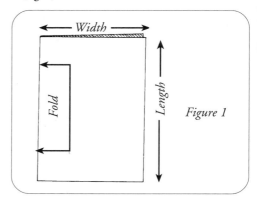

Figure 1

2. Place the skirt top template for your gown size at the top edge of
    the piece, with the foldline on the fold and the armhole curve on
    the cut edges; cut along the top curve and the armhole curve
    (**fig. 2**).

3. Place the skirt bottom template at the bottom edge of the piece,
    with the side seam on the cut edges; cut the bottom curve,
    extending a straight line from the edge of the template to the fold
    (**fig. 2**).

B. Finishing the Skirt Bottoms

Finish the bottom edges of the skirt pieces with gathered or flat
lace edging (the side seams <u>are not</u> sewn yet).

1. For gathered lace edging, measure the bottom edge of one skirt
    piece; cut two pieces of the edging that are $1^1/_2$ times the bottom
    edge measurement. Gather each piece of lace edging to fit the
    bottom edges of the gown front and back. Place more gathers
    around the curves so that the lace will not flip up or turn under.
    Attach the lace to the bottom of each piece using the technique
    for extra-stable lace finishing found on page 223 (**fig. 3**).

2. For flat lace edging, pin the straight edge of the lace $1/_4$" from the
    bottom edge of one skirt piece, pulling the top thread of the
    heading to shape the lace around the curves. Repeat for the other
    skirt. After the lace is pinned to each skirt piece, attach the lace
    using the technique for extra-stable lace finishing found on page
    223 (**fig. 4**).

III. Yokes to Skirts

After the yokes have been made according to the directions for
each individual gown, you are ready to attach the yokes to the skirt
pieces.

A. Lined Yokes

(Woven Ribbon Bodice and Smocked Gowns)

1. The decorated front yoke piece should be basted to the yoke
    lining piece all the way around the edges and treated as one piece
    of fabric. The yoke back is a single layer of fabric.

2. Run two rows of gathering ($1/_4$" and just inside the $1/_2$" seam line)
    across the top edges of the front and back skirt pieces (**fig. 5**).

3. Mark the centers of the yoke bottoms and skirt tops. With right
    sides together, match the center marks . Gather the skirts to fit
    the yokes. Pin in place (**fig. 6**).

4. Stitch, using a $1/_2$" seam allowance. Trim and overcast the seam
    allowance. Press the seam toward the yoke.

B. Yokes with Overlays

(Loops of Puffing and Shadow Embroidery Gowns)

1. You should have two single layer yoke pieces and a completed
    overlay piece.

2. Run two rows of gathering ($1/_4$" and just inside the $1/_2$" seam line)
    across the top edges of the front and back skirt pieces (**see fig. 5**).

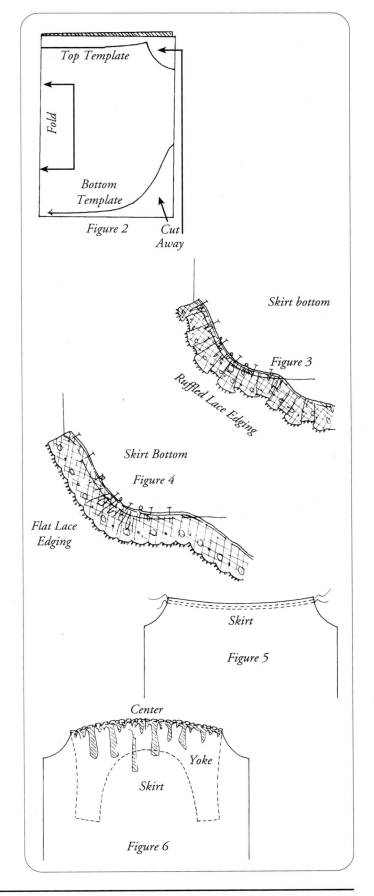

Top Template

Fold

Bottom
Template

Figure 2   Cut
             Away

Skirt bottom

Figure 3

Ruffled Lace Edging

Skirt Bottom

Figure 4

Flat Lace
Edging

Skirt

Figure 5

Center

Yoke

Skirt

Figure 6

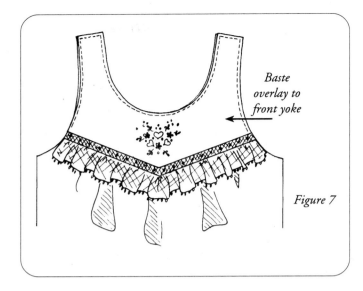

Baste overlay to front yoke

Figure 7

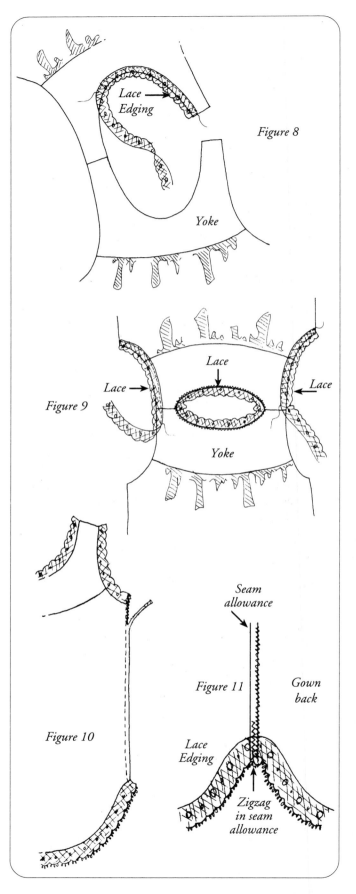

Lace Edging

Figure 8

Yoke

Lace

Lace

Lace

Figure 9

Yoke

Seam allowance

Figure 11

Gown back

Figure 10

Lace Edging

Zigzag in seam allowance

3. Mark the centers of the yoke bottoms and skirt tops. With right sides together, match the center marks . Gather the skirts to fit the yokes. Pin in place (**see fig. 6**).

4. Stitch, using a ¹⁄₂" seam allowance. Trim and overcast the seam allowance. Press the seam toward the yoke.

5. Place the overlay on top of the gown front, matching the neck, shoulder and armhole edges. Pin together and baste along the matched edges (**fig. 7**). Treat as one layer of fabric.

IV. Finishing the Gown

A. Neck and Armholes

1. With right sides together, stitch one shoulder seam. Trim and overcast the seam allowance. Press the seam toward the back.

2. Attach lace edging to the neck edge using the technique for extra-stable lace finishing found on page 223 (**fig. 8**).

3. Stitch the remaining shoulder seam. Trim and overcast the seam allowance. Press the seam to the back.

4. Attach lace edging to the armholes using the technique for extra-stable lace finishing found on page 223 (**fig. 9**).

B. Side Seams and Finishing

1. With right sides together, stitch the side seams. Trim and overcast the seam allowance (**fig. 10**).

2. Press the side seams toward the gown back.

3. To reinforce the seam along the lace at the hem, underarms, neck edge and shoulder seam, press the seam allowance flat and zigzag the seam allowance to the gown (**fig. 11**). �

Specific Directions for Lady's Gowns

Before You Begin This Section

In this section you will see references such as III-B or II-C. These are used to refer you back to the previous section, "Lady's Nightgown Directions." The sections are for armhole, neck and hem finishes, as well as skirt shaping and general construction of the gowns.

Show 1

Blue Nelona Puffing Nightgown

Practicing your puffing skills is perfectly wonderful when you end up with a blue Nelona Swiss batiste gown like this one. For the overbib, there is a row of curved puffing with white French insertion at the top and the bottom. Entredeux and gathered lace edging finishes the overbib. Narrow white French edging finishes the neckline and the armholes of this gown. I almost called this large loop on the skirt the "ballerina loop." It is so graceful. The loop is of puffing and it is surrounded on both sides by white lace insertion which curves on both outside ends. White slightly gathered French edging finishes the front and back hemline of this gown. Making this gown for a trousseau or for a grandmother would be equally as appropriate. Don't forget how comfortable this gown is!

Gown Supplies

In addition to the fabric yardages listed under general directions, you will also need the following supplies:

✿ 3 yds. of ³/₈" lace edging (for neck and armholes)
✿ 6 yds. of ⁵/₈" lace insertion (for overlay and shaping around puffing)
✿ 5¹/₂ yds. of 1¹/₄" edging (for skirt bottom and overlay)
✿ ³/₄ yd. entredeux
✿ Loop template found on the pull-out section

A. Skirt Directions

1. Cut two skirt rectangles to the measurements given on the skirt chart found on page 122. Also cut seven strips 2" x 45" for making puffing. The remaining fabric will be used later for the yokes.

2. Fold one skirt piece in half with the fold running from top to bottom; mark the center front with a crease or line. Trace the loop template on the skirt piece, with the bottom edge of the loop 6" from the skirt bottom. Make sure the loop is centered over the fold (**fig. 1**).

Looped Puffing Gown

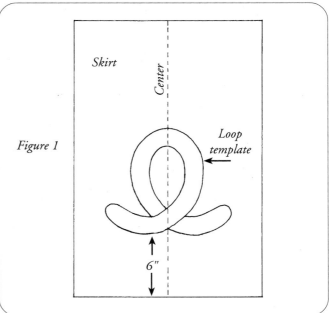

Figure 1

Skirt

Center

Loop template

6"

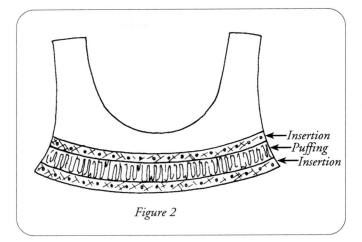

Figure 2

Figure 3

Figure 4

Lace Edging

Trim entredeux seam allowance

Figure 5

3. Stitch the ends of the puffing strips together to form one long strip. Gather each side of the puffing strip ¹/₂" from the edges. Shape the puffing and ⁵/₈" lace insertion on the skirt using the directions for shaped puffing found on page 234. You should have at least 18" of the puffing strip left over to use on the yoke overlay; if you don't have this much, re-adjust the gathers or cut more strips.

4. Shape the skirt pieces (refer to General Directions, section II-A) and finish the skirt bottoms (refer to General Directions, section II-B.2).

B. Yoke Overlay Directions

1. Cut three yoke pieces (one will be the overlay).

2. Shape puffing across the bottom edge of one yoke piece using the directions for shaped puffing found on page 234. The lower gathering line of the puffing strip should fall 1" from the cut edge of the yoke. Shape ⁵/₈" lace insertion to both edges of the puffing. Zigzag along both edges of the top piece of insertion and along the top edge of the lower insertion. Trim away the fabric behind the lace and puffing (**fig. 2**).

3. Trim away the seam allowance on one side of the entredeux. Clip the other seam allowance of the entredeux so that it can be shaped into a curve (**fig. 3**).

4. Pin the bottom edge of the yoke piece to a lace board, and shape the entredeux to fit the curve of the lace insertion. Pin the entredeux in place and lightly steam it to help set the curve (**fig. 4**).

5. Stitch the entredeux to the lace insertion using the technique "Entredeux to Lace."

6. Trim away the remaining seam allowance of the entredeux. Cut a piece of 1¹/₄" edging lace , twice as long as the width of the bottom edge of the yoke overlay. Gather the lace edging and attach it to the entredeux using the technique "Entredeux to Lace" (**fig. 5**).

7. Attach the yokes and overlay to the skirt pieces (refer to General Directions, section III-B).

C. Finishing the Gown

Refer to General Directions, section IV to finish construction of the gown. ✳

Shadow Work Bow/Smocked Nightgown

What could be more wonderful to sleep in than silk batiste? Choosing a beautiful bridal white fabric, we shadow embroidered lovely bows on the yoke; a little smocking in the same colors as the bows is featured right under the front yoke. The embroidery thread is in variegated colors of vintage blue, dusty lavender and dusty green. Variegated embroidery floss is available from Margaret Boyles, 400 Wedgeway, Atlanta, GA 30350. The variegation is so slight that you can almost miss that it is several different colors, not just one. The front yoke is lined; ecru lace edging finishes the neckline and the armholes. An ecru French edging is also stitched around the front and back hemline of the gown. This would be a wonderful gown for yourself or for a gift.

Gown Supplies

In addition to the fabric yardages listed under general directions, you will also need the following supplies:

❧ 3 yds. of ³/₈" lace edging (for neck and armholes)

❧ 4¹/₄ yds. of ³/₄" lace edging (for skirt bottom)

❧ Over-dyed variegated pastel floss or DMC 504 green floss for smocking and shadow embroidery

❧ Yoke shadow embroidered bows template found on the pattern pull-out and smocking graph found on page 254.

A. Skirt Directions

1. Cut two skirt rectangles 45" wide by the measurements given on the skirt chart found on page 122.

2. Shape the skirt pieces (refer to General Directions, section II-A) and finish the skirt bottoms (refer to General Directions, section II-B.2).

3. Pleat and smock the skirt front. The smocking plate can be found on page 254 . Smocking directions can be found on page 254.

B. Yoke Directions

1. Cut two yoke pieces. Draw a third yoke piece onto a rectangle of fabric, but do not cut out (**fig. 1**).

2. Trace the bow embroidery design onto the drawn yoke, making sure that the design is centered (**fig. 1**).

3. Embroider the bows using one strand of floss. The directions for shadow embroidery can be found on page 230.

4. Press the embroidered piece and cut out the yoke. Place the yoke, with right side up, on top of a second yoke piece, which will be the lining. Baste the two layers of fabric together on all edges and treat as one piece of fabric (**fig. 2**).

5. Attach the yokes to the skirts (refer to General Directions, section III-A).

C. Finishing the Gown

Refer to General Directions, section IV to finish construction of the gown. ❧

Smocked Nightgown

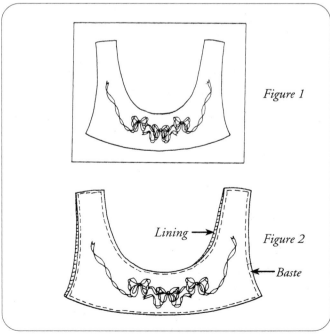

Figure 1

Lining

Figure 2

Baste

Pink Hearts and Dreams Nightgown

Frothy, gorgeous and original is this pink Nelona Swiss batiste nightgown. Trimmed with white French laces and shadow work embroidery by hand this gown is easy to make and sweet. The shadow work embroidery on the overbib of white Nelona has pink bows, pink hearts, green leaves, white pearls and pale pink lazy daisy flowers. This embroidery design would be beautiful other places as well as on this nightgown. The overbib is trimmed at the bottom with white lace insertion and gathered lace edging. Traveling down the front of this gown is a sweet panel consisting of two strips of white French insertion with mitered pieces at four and one half inch intervals. One and one fourth inch wide white French edging is slightly gathered and attached all the way around the front and back hemlines of the gown. Absolutely luscious would be my description of this gown; however, I mustn't forget that it is also comfortable!

Gown Supplies

In addition to the fabric yardages listed under general directions, you will also need the following supplies:

❀ 3 yds. of $3/4$" lace edging (for neck and armholes)

❀ $5/8$" lace insertion in the following amounts:

　　short gown $3^1/2$ yds.

　　medium gown $4^1/4$ yds.

　　long gown 5 yds.

❀ $7^1/2$ yds. of $1^1/4$" lace edging (for overlay and skirt bottom)

❀ 1 pkg. Mill Hill antique glass beads #03021, or small "pearl" beads

❀ DMC floss:
　　957 bow and satin dots, 911 leaves and stems, 600 hearts, 963 lazy daisy flowers

❀ lace and embroidery templates found on the pull-out section

A. Skirt Directions

1. Cut two skirt rectangles to the measurements given on the skirt chart found on page 122. Lay one piece aside, this piece will be the skirt back.

2. The remaining rectangle will be the skirt front. Draw two lines on the skirt front 2" from each side of center (**fig. 1**). Trace the lace shaping template along the center front of the skirt with the template even with the top edge of the skirt. Trace the first and second lace 'V's on the fabric (**fig. 2**). Move the template down until the first lace shape outline is over the second drawn lace

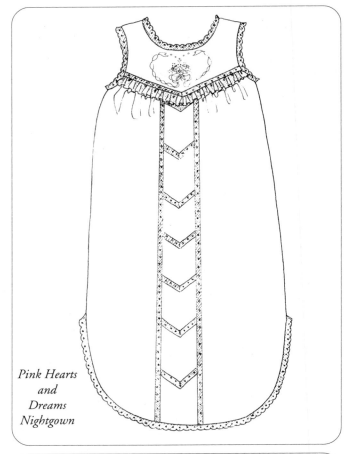

Pink Hearts and Dreams Nightgown

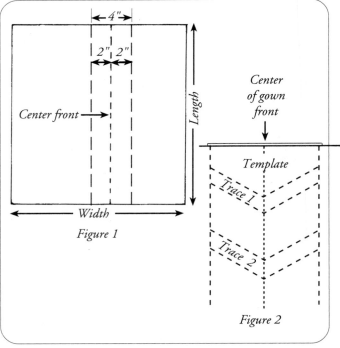

Figure 1

Figure 2

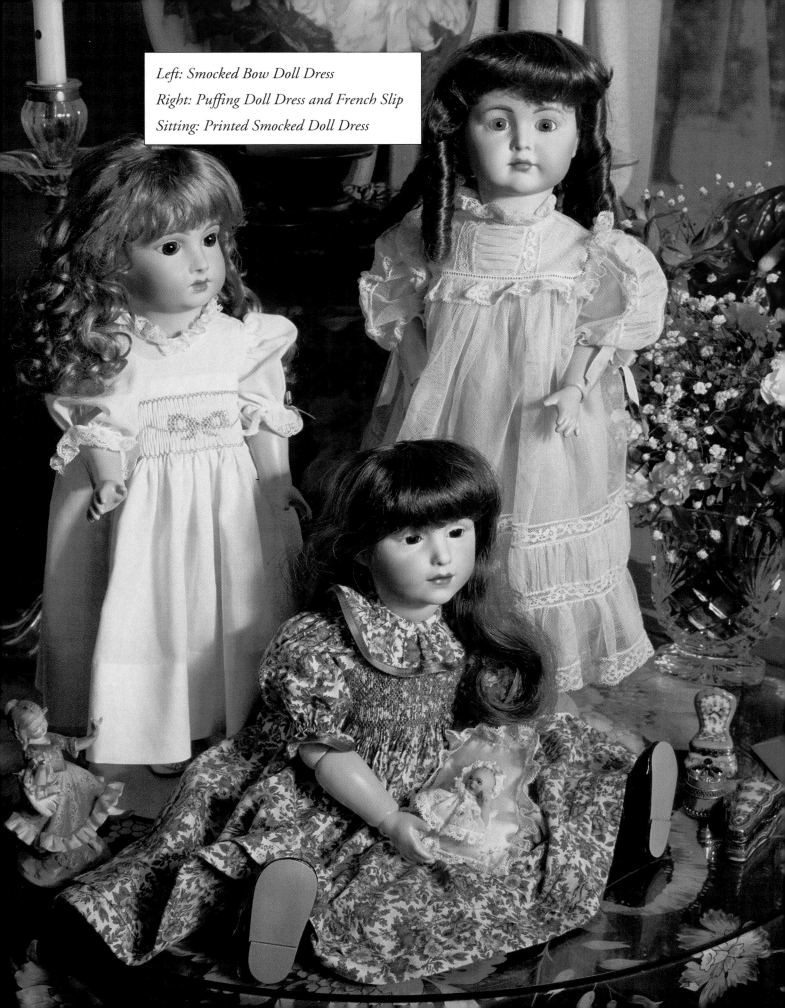

Left: Smocked Bow Doll Dress
Right: Puffing Doll Dress and French Slip
Sitting: Printed Smocked Doll Dress

Left: Woven Insets Ribbon Doll Dress

Right: Log Cabin Silk Dupioni Doll Dress

Left: Pleated Flower Pillow

Right: Ruched Trim Doll Dress

Left: Floral Bouquet Pillow

Right: Sweet And Simple Doll Dress

Left: Robin's Egg Blue Heirloom Party Doll Dress

Right: Smocked Music Box Pillow

Left: Woven Ribbon Bib Knickers

Right: White Pique Classic Appliqué Doll Dress

Top Right: Quilted Collar

Left: Ribbon And Netting Diamonds
  Doll Dress

Right: Pleated Lamp Shade

Front: Lingerie Keeper

Left: Doll Bonnet

Right: Antique Netting Doll Dress with Matching Doll Bonnet

Above:
  Starting from the left;
  Doll Bonnet,
  Doll Petticoat,
  Doll Camisole,
  Doll Pantalettes

Right: Lace Piecing Pillow

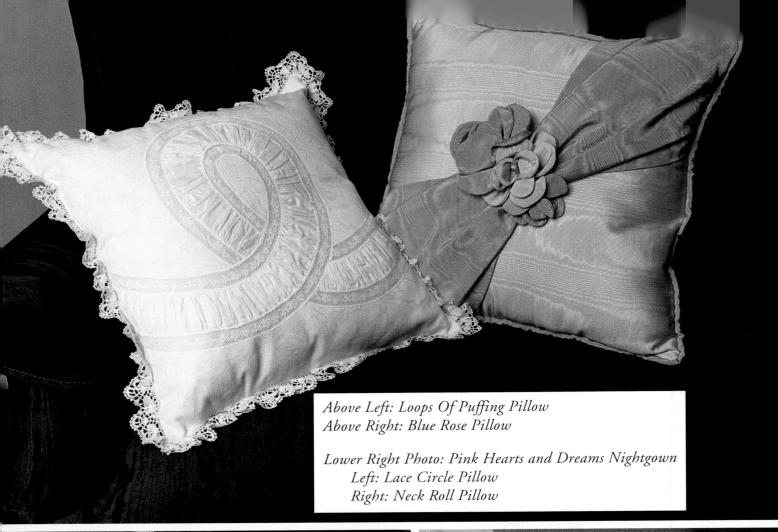

Above Left: Loops Of Puffing Pillow
Above Right: Blue Rose Pillow

Lower Right Photo: Pink Hearts and Dreams Nightgown
Left: Lace Circle Pillow
Right: Neck Roll Pillow

Below: Ribbon And Smocking Pillow

Above: Left Rose Pillow

Middle: Woven Heart Pillow

Right: Netting Lace Pillow

Left: Blue Nelona Puffing Nightgown

Middle: Baby Pillow

Right Back: Silk Ribbon Weaving Nightgown

Right Front: Shadow Work Bow Nightgown

Baby Bonnets starting from the Left: Tucked Bonnet, Lace and Ribbon Weaving Bonnet, Lace -Shapes Bonnet and Hemstitched Bonnet

Below Sash Tails starting from the Left: Pink Nelona Heart with Netting Center, Lilac Nelona Sash with Elongated Lace Diamond, Blue Nelona Flip-Flop Ribbon Bow Sash, White Fancy Band Sash, Ecru Silk Sash Bow with Organdy Inserts, Peach and Ecru Loop Insert Sash, Robin's Blue Nelona Pintucks and Curved Lace Sash, Ecru Fancy Band Sash

Left: English Netting Lace Bonnet, and Two Doll Bonnets

Woven Picture Frame

Above: Victorian Garden Hat

Left: Picture Frame Bow

Right: Framed Antique Collar With Picture Frame Bow

Above: Flower Basket

Below Left: Covered Mirror

Below Right: Tissue Box Cover

Guard this little baby, please,
Dear angels up above.
May her days be filled with laughter
And her life be filled with love.

Above:
Netting
Angel

Left:
Covered
Tuffet

Margaret's Quilt

1

5

9

2

6

10

3

7

11

4

8

12

Martha's Sewing Room

P.B.S. T.V. Program Video Series 400

Filmed and produced by The University of Alabama Center For Public Television

$29.95

For Each Video-American VHS Format*
(postage paid)

Video 400-A contains 5 (26 min.) shows: Video 400-B
and Video 400-C each contain 4 (26 min.) shows

Video 400-A

401 Lace and Puffing Loops: Martha Pullen demonstrates the easy technique of lace and puffing loops. This technique is shown on a nightgown, doll dress and a quilt square. Also, an elegant covered mirror and a ribbon cabbage rose; vintage clothing.

402 Wedding Show: Here comes the bride - Martha Pullen tells how easy it is to embellish a wedding dress and veil. Step-by-step instructions on log cabin lace are shown and incorporated in a doll dress. Rose pillow; flower girl basket; quilt square of wedding roses; and vintage clothing.

403 Ribbon and Netting Diamonds: Ribbon and netting diamonds are "sew" easy when Martha Pullen shows how. This interesting technique is demonstrated on a doll dress, quilt square and a baby gown. A pillow, netting angel and silk ribbon fly stitch are also shown; vintage clothing.

404 Beginning Smocking: Martha Pullen shows easy smocking methods for cables, outlines, stems and waves. Smocking is also shown on a nightgown, pillow, doll dress and a quilt square; vintage clothing.

405 Pleater: Pleating fabric for smocking is fun, quick and easy - no more picking up dots to smock. Host Martha Pullen pleats an insert, yoke dress and a bishop dress. A pleated flower pillow, lamp shade, doll dress and a quilt square all are embellished with pleating. Silk ribbon embroidery - Herringbone stitch and vintage clothing.

Video 400-B

406 Smocked Yoke Dress: Constructing a smocked yoke dress is easy when Martha Pullen is at the sewing machine. Also demonstrated: tissue box cover, two doll dresses and a quilt square; vintage clothing.

407 Picture Smocking: Trains, tigers, boats and hearts can be smocked using the simple stacking technique of picture smocking. The technique is shown on a doll dress, quilt square and a music box pillow. A light switch cover and a concertina rose are also made; vintage clothing.

408 Bow Show: Host Martha Pullen explains how to embellish skirts, blouses and a quilt square with fabric bows and handkerchief bows. Netting lace pillow; picture frame bow hangers; and vintage clothing.

409 Themes from Antique Clothing: Airplane lace, set of three tucks and draw string necklines are explained by host Martha Pullen. These antique techniques are demonstrated in a quilt square and a doll dress. Floral bouquet pillow; framed antique collar; silk ribbon embroidery - rouching; and vintage clothing.

Video 400-C

410 Lingerie Show: Martha Pullen shows the easy steps of constructing a French nightgown with extra stable lace finishing. Martha also explains the how-to's of a lingerie bag quilt square, heirloom neck roll pillow, lingerie for dolls and a lingerie keeper; vintage clothing.

411 Fancy Bonnets and Sashes: Host Martha Pullen shows how to make two precious baby bonnets, several French doll bonnets, sash embellishments, a Victorian garden hat and a rose pillow. Silk ribbon weaving and vintage clothing are also shown.

412 Lace and Ribbon Weaving: Lace and ribbon weaving on a doll dress, picture frame, woven heart pillow, bonnets and knickers are easy when Martha Pullen tells how. Martha also visits her attic to show a wonderful antique garment.

413 Quilt Construction and Heirloom Embroidery: Host Martha Pullen gives the secrets of putting together an heirloom quilt. Hand embroidery stitches - satin stitch, French knots, and feather stitch are also featured; how to make crazy patch quilted collar and a lace piecing pillow; vintage clothing.

400 Series Videos

A set of three videos is available for the 100, 200, 300 series, also.

American VHS Format does not work on all foreign video systems.

VIDEO ORDER FORM

Check		Quantity	Price
☐	Video 400-A		29.95
☐	Video 400-B		29.95
☐	Video 400-C		29.95
☐	Video 300-A		29.95
☐	Video 300-B		29.95
☐	Video 300-C		29.95
☐	Video 200-D		29.95
☐	Video 200-E		29.95
☐	Video 200-F		29.95
☐	Video 100-A		29.95
☐	Video 100-B		29.95
☐	Video 100-C		29.95

TOTAL AMOUNT $_____

(Alabama Residents add 8% tax.)

please call for Canadian or Foreign Shipping charges

Name _____

Address _____

City/State/Zip _____

Daytime Phone # _____

Credit Card # _____ Exp. Date _____

☐ MasterCard ☐ Visa ☐ American Express ☐ Discover

Mail order to: *Martha Pullen Co.*
518 Madison Street • Huntsville, AL 35801
Phone: 1-800-547-4176 or 1-205-533-9586 or Fax: 205-533-9630

Linda's Silver Needle

1-800-SMOCK-IT!®

Let us bring our charming specialty sewing shop right to your mailbox! Call 1-800-766-2548 for a complimentary copy of our latest newsletter filled with wonderful fabric swatches and all the latest in specialty sewing supplies!

Visiting the Chicagoland area? We'd *love* to meet you in person! Stop in to see us at our lovely retail store in Naperville's historic Fifth Avenue Station Mall!

The Comfortable Edge!

Reach over the edge and grasp the comfort of Softouch! Fiskars proudly introduces the Softouch family– Softouch Craft Snip, Blunt-Tip, Micro-Tip and Multi-Purpose Scissors. These tools go hand-in-hand meeting your everyday cutting needs. Complemented by oversized cushion-grip handles, an easy-action spring gently re-opens blades after each cut and reduces fatigue. Ideal for left or right hand, the superior comfort and ease of use will take you over the edge.

FISKARS

Innovative Products For Creative People
Fiskars Inc. P.O. Box 8027, Wausau, WI 54402

SC4856

HAVE YOU DRIVEN
A FORD LATELY?

shape, and draw the next shape. Keep moving the template and tracing the shapes, making the last shape 2" - 4" from the bottom edge of the strip (**fig. 3**).

3. Use the ⅝" lace insertion to make the mitered lace s"v's". The lace "v's" should stop on the vertical drawn lines. Refer to the directions for mitering lace (page 191). Use the directions for extra stable lace finishes found on page 223 to attach the lace "V's"(**fig. 4**).

4. Center ⅝" insertion along the drawn vertical lines. Use the directions for extra stable lace finishes found on page 223 to attach the lace (**fig. 5**).

5. Shape the skirt pieces (refer to General Directions, section II-A) and finish the skirt bottoms (refer to General Directions, section II-B.1).

—— *B. Yoke Overlay Directions* ——

1. Cut two yokes from the gown fabric. Draw the pointed yoke overlay on a rectangle of white or ecru fabric, but don't cut it out (**fig. 6**).

2. Trace the embroidery template onto the yoke overlay, making sure that the design is centered (**fig. 6**).

3. Work the shadow embroidery using one strand of DMC floss. The directions for shadow embroidery can be found on page 230. Attach the beads with floss to match their color.

4. After the embroidery is finished, press the overlay from the wrong side, and cut out.

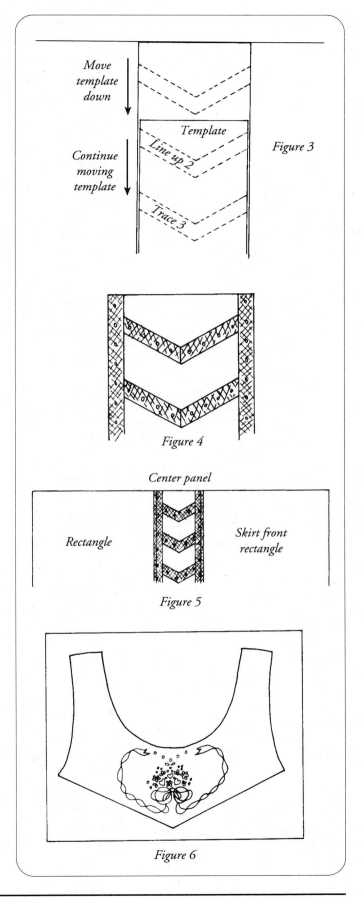

Figure 3

Figure 4

Center panel

Rectangle

Skirt front rectangle

Figure 5

Figure 6

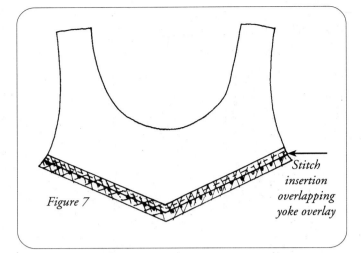

Figure 7

Stitch insertion overlapping yoke overlay

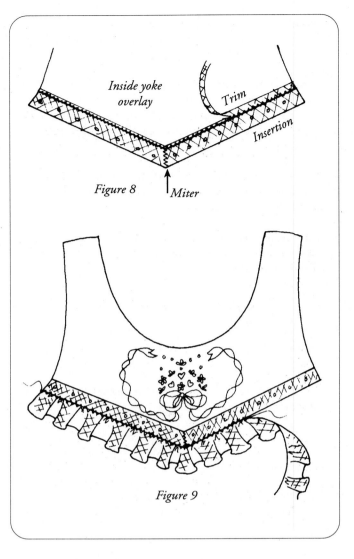

Inside yoke overlay

Trim

Insertion

Figure 8

Miter

Figure 9

5. Place the overlay on a lace board, right side up. Pin and miter ⁵/₈" lace insertion along the bottom edge of the overlay using the mitering technique found on page 223. Stitch in place along the upper edge of the lace using the technique for extra-stable lace finishes found on page 223 (**fig. 7**). After the fabric is trimmed away behind the lace, stitch the miter (**fig. 8**).

6. Cut a piece of 1¹/₄" lace edging that is 1¹/₂ times the length of the mitered insertion. Slightly gather the edging and attach it to the insertion using the technique "Lace to Lace" (**fig. 9**).

7. Attach the yokes and overlay to the skirt pieces (refer to General Directions, section III-B)

C. Finishing the Gown

Refer to General Directions, section IV to finish construction of the gown. ✄

Silk Ribbon Weaving Nightgown

Silk ribbon weaving, machine stitched featherstitch, lace weaving, and embroidered hearts all blend together to create such an unusual nightgown yoke. The fabric is ecru Nelona Swiss batiste. Dusty blue silk ribbons one and one fourth inches wide are woven with ecru French edging five eighths inch wide which have been butted together and zigzagged. Crisscrossing to form squares are rows of blue featherstitches made very tiny. In the center of each piece of ecru insertion in the weaving is a little machine embroidered heart in pale pink. The same featherstitching goes down the front of the gown and tiny pink machine embroidered hearts are stitched in between these two rows of blue machine featherstitch. Ecru French lace edging finishes the neckline and the armholes; wide ecru French edging finishes the front and back hemline. This gown is pretty enough for a bride and practical enough for a mom with four kids! Please make one like this for yourself.

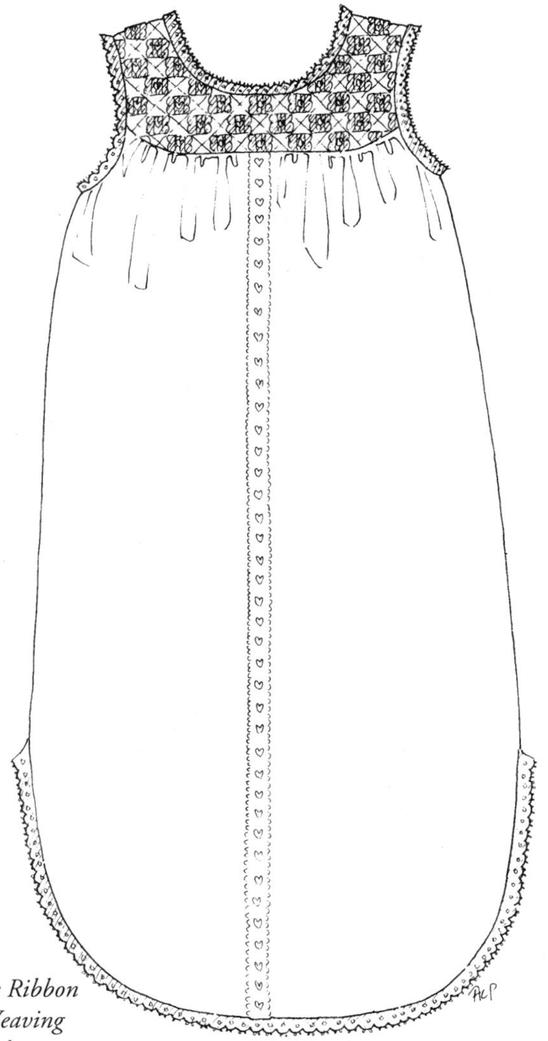

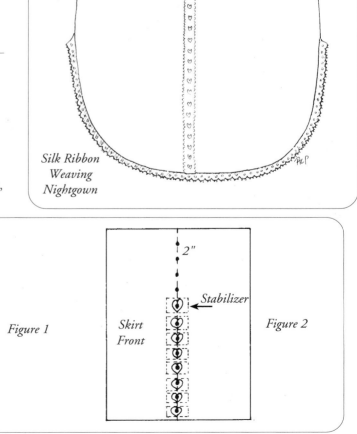

Silk Ribbon Weaving Nightgown

Supplies

In addition to the fabric yardages listed under general directions, you will also need the following supplies:

❧ 3 yds. of ¹/₂" edging (for neck and armholes)

❧ 9 yds. of ⁵/₈" edging (for yoke and skirt bottom)

❧ 2¹/₂ yds. of 32 mm silk ribbon

❧ decorative machine embroidery thread

A. Skirt Directions

1. Cut two skirt rectangles to the measurements given on the skirt chart found on page 122. Lay one piece aside, this piece will be the skirt back.

2. The remaining rectangle is the skirt front; starch and press. Mark the center front by folding the fabric in half, with the fold running from top to bottom; lightly press a crease (**fig. 1**).

3. Beginning 1¹/₂" from the top edge of the skirt, mark dots 2" apart, down the center front crease. Using the built-in stitches on the sewing machine, stitch a heart or other small design at each mark. Stablizer may be needed under the fabric for each design (**fig. 2**).

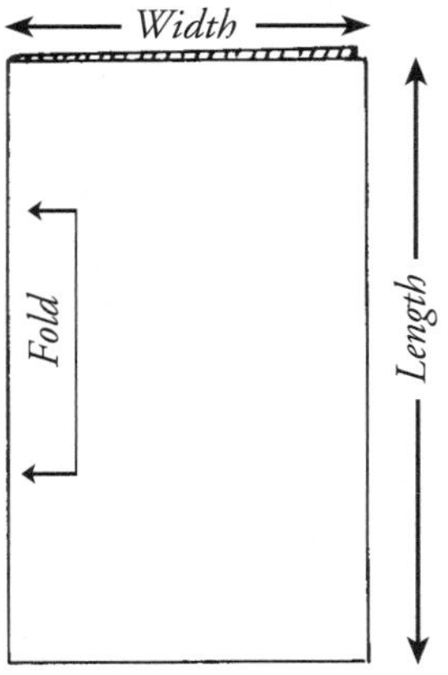

Width

Fold

Length

Figure 1

2"

Stabilizer

Skirt Front

Figure 2

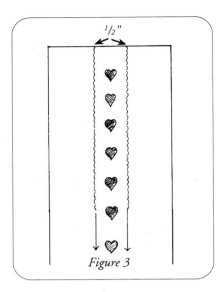

Figure 3

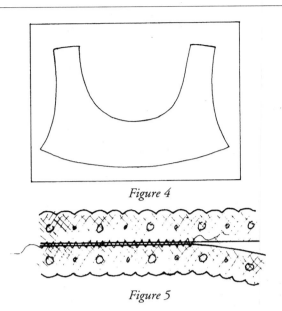

Figure 4

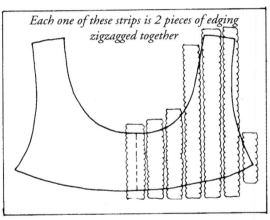

Figure 5

4. Stitch two rows of tiny feather stitch (or other decorative stitch) down the front of the gown, with one row $^1/_2$" to the left of the center crease, and the other row $^1/_2$" to the right of the center crease. You may mark the stitching lines with a washable pencil, or you may use the edge of your machine foot as a guide. You will need to starch the fabric until it is stiff, or use a stabilizer under the fabric (**fig. 3**).

5. Shape the skirt pieces (refer to General Directions, section II-A) and finish the skirt bottoms (refer to General Directions, section II-B.1).

B. Yoke Directions

1. Cut two yoke pieces; draw a third yoke onto a rectangle of fabric, but do not cut out (**fig. 4**).

2. Cut the remaining piece of $^5/_8$" edging in half. Join the two straight edges of the pieces together, using the technique "Lace to Lace." This makes one wide piece of lace to use in weaving the yoke (**fig. 5**).

3. Mark the center front on the drawn yoke. Pin the rectangle with the drawn yoke on a lace board.

4. Refer to the directions for lace and ribbon weaving found on page 226 for general weaving instructions.

5. Place the lace vertically on the drawn yoke, cutting strips to fit the drawn yoke with about $^1/_2$" extending past the drawn lines. One lace strip should be on top of the center line (**fig. 6**).

6. The horizontal strips will be the silk ribbon. Cut them the same as the lace. Weave the ribbon through the lace according to the general weaving instructions from Step 4 (**fig. 7**).

Each one of these strips is 2 pieces of edging zigzagged together

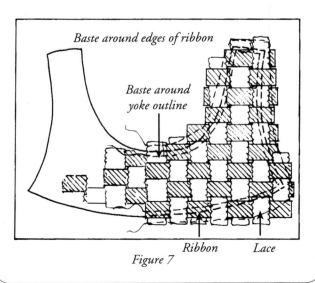

Figure 6

Baste around edges of ribbon

Baste around yoke outline

Ribbon   Lace

Figure 7

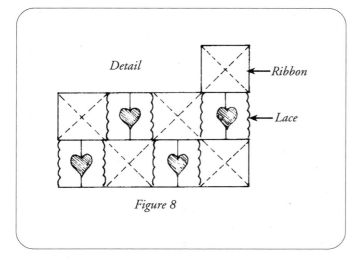

Detail

Ribbon

Lace

Figure 8

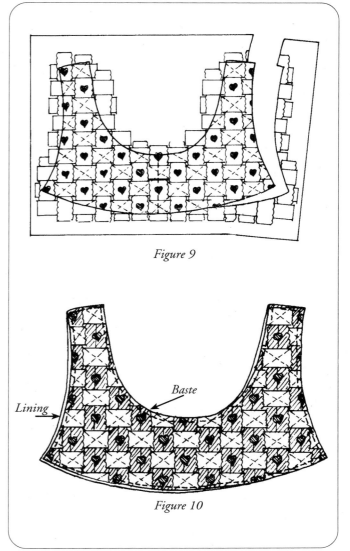

Figure 9

Baste

Lining

Figure 10

7. When all of the weaving is complete, baste the ribbon and lace to the fabric along the edges (**fig. 7**). Topstitch diagonally across the ribbon sections, using the same stitch used to decorate the skirt front. Work hearts or other small design in the centers of the lace squares (**fig. 8**).

8. Place the yoke pattern piece over the woven section, centering the center lace strip. Draw the yoke outline onto the woven piece; baste around the yoke outline and cut out the yoke (**fig. 9**).

9. Pin the woven yoke, right side up, over a plain yoke piece, which will be the lining. Baste the two pieces together and treat as one layer (**fig. 10**).

10. Attach the yokes to the skirts (refer to General Directions, section III-A)

C. Finishing the Gown

Refer to General Directions, section IV to finish construction of the gown. ✖

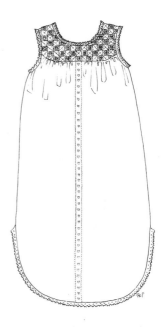

Sash Embellishments

To be sure that you have pulled out all of the stops on your next dress, how about decorating the sash ends in a very creative manner? I first saw gorgeous sash ends on Susan York dresses; I couldn't wait to see each of her dresses. Quickly after I looked at her dress masterpiece, I looked to see in what creative way that she had finished off her sash ends. I was never disappointed! In this section we have illustrated many different ways you might embellish the ends of your little girl's

sashes. Shaping lace, using organdy peek-a-boos, embroidering with silk ribbon, embroidering with floss, zigzagging lace pieces together or hemstitching—all will be beautiful and such a surprise for the ending of your dress. Let your imagination go wild and have your last little bit of fun sewing on that special dress by finishing the sash ends just the way your fancy tickles. ✳

Show 11

General Directions

The instructions and templates given are designed for sash tails with a finished width of 3¹/₂" to 4". You may make yours any width you want by changing the width of the design you use. Some of the sashes are hemmed before the design is attached, some are hemmed after the decorative work is done; the specific directions for each sash tail will refer you to the hemming directions at the correct time.

Hemming the Sash Edges

1. Stay-stitch a straight line ¹/₄" from each side edge of the sash tail (**fig. 1**).

2. Turn the edge to the inside along the stay-stitched line; press (**fig. 1**).

3. Turn the folded edge to the inside again; press (**fig. 2**).

4. Topstitch close to the first fold, approximately ¹/₄" from the sash edge (**fig. 3**). ✳

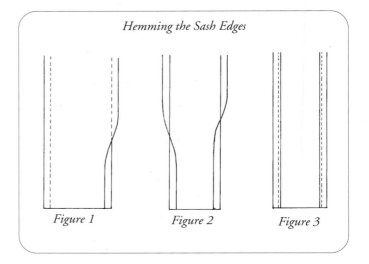

Hemming the Sash Edges

Figure 1   *Figure 2*   *Figure 3*

Specific Directions for Sash Tails

Specific Directions for Sash Tails are on the following pages.

Blue Nelona Flip-Flop Ribbon Bow Sash

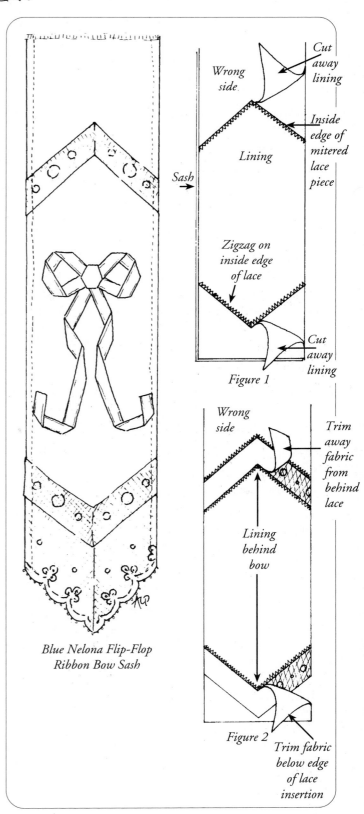

Supplies

In addition to the fabric needed for the sash pieces, you will also need the following supplies:

- ✿ two pieces of Nelona, 4¹/₂" x 12" each
- ✿ 1 yd. of ⁵/₈" lace insertion
- ✿ 1 yd. of lace edging at least 1" wide
- ✿ 1¹/₄ yds. of ³/₈" double-faced satin ribbon
- ✿ Sash template on page 273.

Sewing Directions

1. Cut two pieces of Nelona, 4" wide and as long as your sash needs to be. Lightly starch and press the sash pieces until they are dry.

2. Trace the design onto the Nelona sash pieces. Shape the ribbon bow onto the fabric (refer to the "Flip-flop Lace" instructions found on page 194); pin and stitch the bow in place with a tiny zigzag.

3. Pin the lace pieces over the design on the sash pieces, mitering the points (refer to the directions for "Fold-Back Mitered Lace" found on page 204). Place one of the 4¹/₂" x 12" pieces of Nelona behind the sash tail and pin the two pieces of fabric together, making sure that the lining piece completely covers the area behind the lace shapes.

4. Stitch with a tiny zigzag along the inside edges of the mitered lace pieces (you will be stitching inside the V-shapes). Cut away the extra fabric above and below the mitered lace pieces on the wrong side, leaving a lining behind the bow (**fig. 1**).

5. Zigzag the top edge of the top lace piece to the fabric. On the wrong side, trim away the extra Nelona from behind both pieces of the lace; be very careful not to cut the lace (**fig. 2**).

6. Stitch the gathered edging to the bottom edge of the bottom piece of mitered insertion lace using the technique "Lace to Lace" and mitering the edging at the point.

7. Lightly starch the sash tail and hem the edges according to the general directions at the beginning of this section. ✖

Blue Nelona Flip-Flop
Ribbon Bow Sash

Figure 1 — Wrong side, Cut away lining, Lining, Inside edge of mitered lace piece, Sash, Zigzag on inside edge of lace, Cut away lining

Figure 2 — Wrong side, Trim away fabric from behind lace, Lining behind bow, Trim fabric below edge of lace insertion

Robin's Egg Blue Nelona Pintucks and Curved Lace Sash

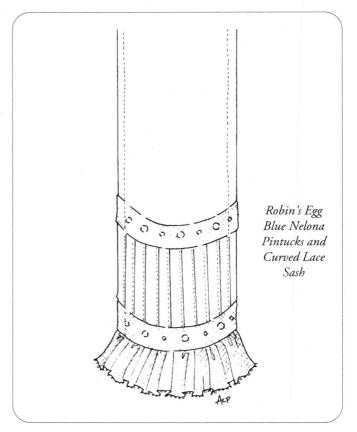

Robin's Egg Blue Nelona Pintucks and Curved Lace Sash

Supplies

In addition to the fabric needed for the sash pieces, you will also need the following supplies:

✿ ⁵/₈ yd. of ⁵/₈" lace insertion

✿ ⁵/₈ yd. of lace edging, at least 1" wide

✿ two pieces of Nelona 6" x 6"

✿ Template on page 272.

Sewing Directions

1. Pintuck the 6" x 6" pieces of Nelona (refer to "Pintucks" found on page 181.

2. Transfer the scallop designs onto the pintucked fabric. Shape the lace insertion along the scallops, pulling the heading threads to shape the lace to fit the curve (refer to "Lace Shaping" found on page 185.) Let the lace ends extend a little past the edges of the design.

3. With a tiny zigzag, stitch the inside edges only of the lace curves; this will be the bottom edge of the top piece, and the top edge of the bottom piece. Trim away the extra pintucked fabric on the wrong side, being careful not to cut the lace (**fig. 1**).

4. Pull the heading thread of the lace edging to gather it, making it fit the bottom edge of the bottom lace scallop; stitch the gathered edging to the bottom edge of the bottom scallop using the technique "Lace to Flat Lace."

5. Place the pintucked piece over the end of the sash piece, letting the top piece of lace overlap the sash and the bottom piece of lace drop below the edge of the sash; pin the pieces together.

6. Stitch the top lace edge in place with a tiny zigzag; trim away the extra sash fabric from behind the lace edge, being careful not to cut the lace (**fig. 2**).

7. Lightly starch the sash tails and hem the edges according to the general directions at the beginning of this section. �

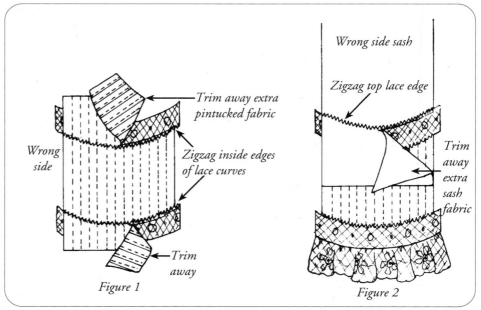

Trim away extra pintucked fabric

Wrong side

Zigzag inside edges of lace curves

Trim away

Figure 1

Wrong side sash

Zigzag top lace edge

Trim away extra sash fabric

Figure 2

Peach and Ecru Loop Insert Sash

Supplies

In addition to the fabric needed for the sash pieces, you will also need the following supplies:

- 2 pieces of ecru Nelona, 6" x 8" each
- 1 yd. of 5/8" lace insertion
- 1/2 yd. of 5/8" lace edging
- (Optional) silk ribbon, 4mm wide, in peach and green
- Template on page 272.

Sewing Directions

1. Trace the design onto the ecru Nelona pieces.
2. Shape the lace onto the ecru Nelona, using the lace edging to shape the bottom curve first, and then using the lace insertion to shape the loop; the ends of the loop will overlap the ends of the curve and extend to the edge of the fabric.
3. Stitch the inside edges of the lace pieces with a pinstitch; trim away the excess fabric, leaving only the ecru centers (**fig 1**).
4. Cut peach Nelona sash pieces 4" wide; place the lace shape over the sash end and stitch around the outer edge of the loop with a pinstitch. Trim the excess peach fabric away from behind the loop shape (**fig. 2**).
5. (Optional) Add the embroidery at this point.
6. Hem the sides of the sash.

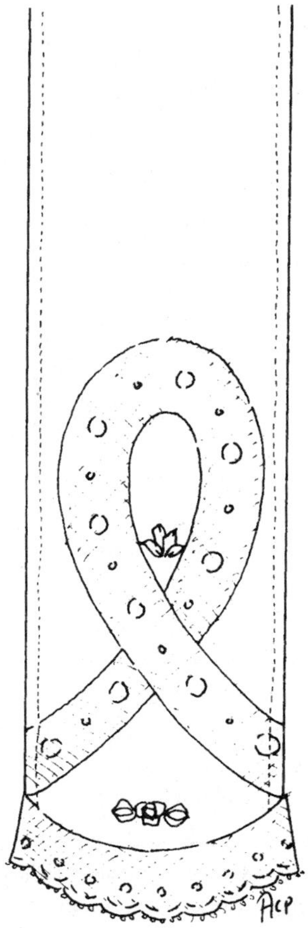

Peach and Ecru Loop Insert Sash

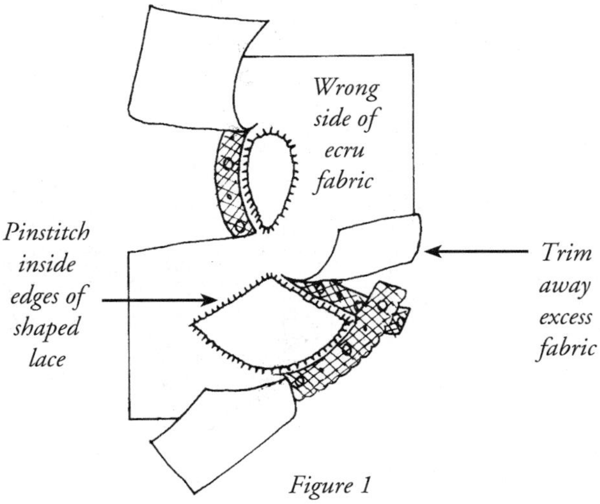

Figure 1

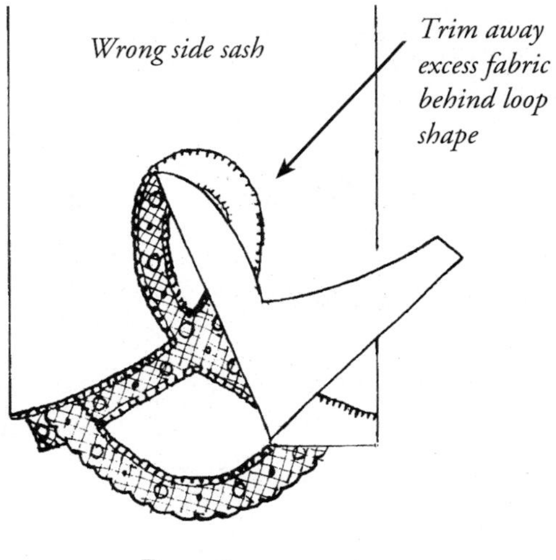

Figure 2

Lilac Nelona Sash with Elongated Lace Diamond

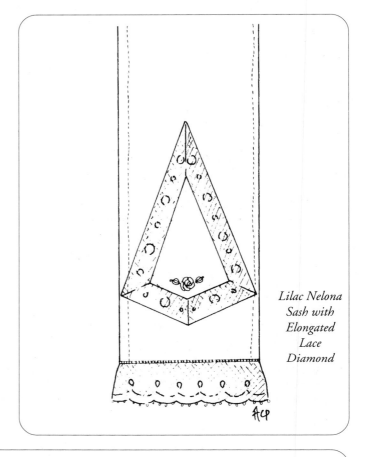

Lilac Nelona Sash with Elongated Lace Diamond

Supplies

In addition to the fabric needed for the sash pieces, you will also need the following supplies:

- ❀ 1 yd. of $^5/_8$" lace insertion
- ❀ $^1/_4$ yd. of entredeux
- ❀ $^1/_2$ yd. of 1" wide lace edging
- ❀ Water-soluble stabilizer (WSS)
- ❀ Template on page 275.

Sewing Directions

1. Place a piece of WSS over the design. Shape the lace insertion on top of the WSS to form the diamond; flat-pin the diamond to the WSS and stitch the miters, through the WSS (refer to "Fold-back Lace Miters" found on page 204).

2. Carefully remove the lace diamond from the WSS and trim the miters.

3. Cut lilac Nelona sash ends, 4" wide. Place the lace diamond over the sash end and stitch the inside edges of the diamond with a small zigzag, and also the outer edges of the diamond (**fig. 1**). Trim away the excess fabric from behind the lace (**fig. 2**).

4. Add entredeux and flat edging across the bottom edge of the sash, attaching the entredeux to the lace using the technique "Entredeux to Lace."

5. (Optional) Embroidery may be added at this point.

6. Hem the sides of the sash.

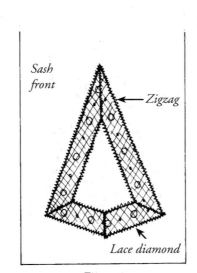

Sash front

Zigzag

Lace diamond

Figure 1

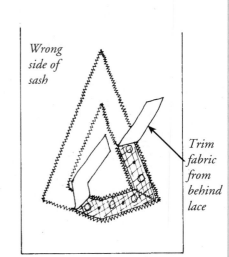

Wrong side of sash

Trim fabric from behind lace

Figure 2

White and Ecru Fancy Band Sashes

Supplies

In addition to the fabric needed for the sash pieces, you will also need the following supplies:

✿ Leftover pieces of fancy bands, 4" wide for each sash tail <u>OR</u>

✿ Lace scraps to make a fancy band section 4" wide for each sash tail

✿ ¼ yd. of entredeux for the top edge of the fancy band section

✿ ½ yd. of 1" or wider lace edging to make a bottom ruffle, if your fancy band doesn't have one

Sewing Directions

1. Make (or cut from leftover pieces) two fancy band sections 4" wide and 3" to 4" long .

2. Cut two Nelona sash tails, each 4" wide; attach entredeux to the bottom edge of the sash using the technique "Entredeux to Fabric."

3. Attach the fancy band section to the entredeux; add the lace edging ruffle to the bottom of the fancy band using the technique "Lace to Flat Lace".

4. Hem the sides of the sash tails. ▨

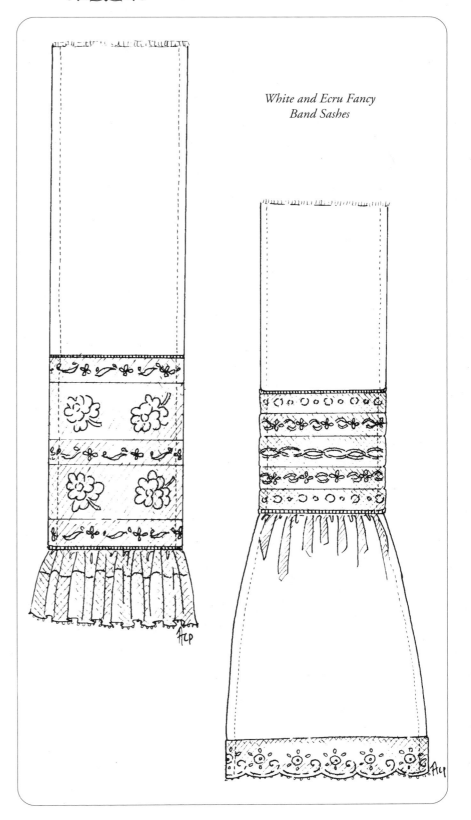

White and Ecru Fancy Band Sashes

Pink Nelona Heart with Netting Center

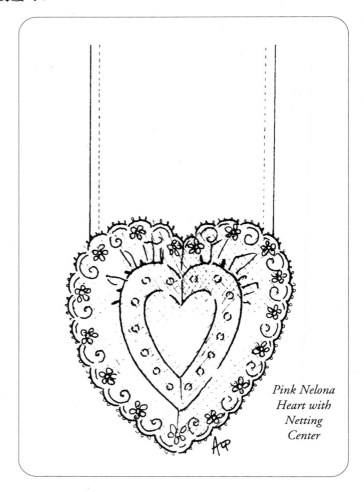

Supplies

In addition to the fabric needed for the sash pieces, you will also need the following supplies:

- ❀ 1 yd. of ⁵/₈" lace insertion
- ❀ 1 yd. of ⁵/₈" lace edging
- ❀ 2 pieces of netting, each 4" square
- ❀ Water-soluble stabilizer (WSS)
- ❀ Template on page 272.

Sewing Directions

1. Place a piece of netting over the heart design; shape the heart with lace insertion (refer to "Shaping a Lace Heart" found on page 204).

2. Flat-pin the insertion to the netting; lightly starch and press the heart dry. Stitch along the inside edge of the heart and trim away the excess netting. Stitch and trim the miters (**fig. 1**).

3. Place the heart over a piece of WSS. Shape the lace edging around the heart and flat-pin it to the WSS.

4. Stitch the edging to the outside edge of the heart, through the WSS; carefully remove the WSS. Stitch and trim the miters.

5. Cut two sashes from Nelona, 4" wide. Hem the sides of the sashes.

6. Place the heart over the end of the sash and pin in place. Stitch across the top edge of the heart with a small zigzag; trim away the excess sash fabric (**fig. 2**). ✠

Pink Nelona Heart with Netting Center

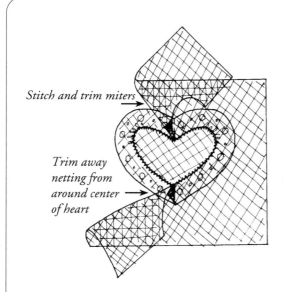

Stitch and trim miters

Trim away netting from around center of heart

Figure 1

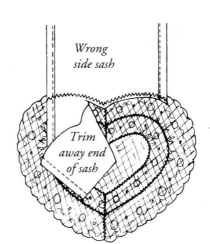

Wrong side sash

Trim away end of sash

Figure 2

Ecru Silk Sash Bow with Organdy Inserts

Supplies

In addition to the fabric needed for the sash pieces, you will also need the following supplies:

❀ 1¹/₂ yds. of ³/₈" to ¹/₂" lace edging

❀ 2 pieces of organdy, each 6" square

❀ Template on page 272.

Sewing Directions

1. Trace the design onto the organdy. Shape the edging over the design using the directions for lace shaping found on page 185.

2. Stitch along the inside edges of the lace design with a tiny zigzag; fold a small piece of the lace to make a bow knot and stitch it in place. Trim away the excess organdy (**fig. 1**).

3. Cut two sash pieces from silk. Hem the sides of the sashes.

4. Place the bow over the end of the sash. Stitch across the top edge of the bow, using a tiny zigzag. Trim away the excess fabric (**fig. 2**).

5. Stitch any loose edges where the lace overlaps. ❈

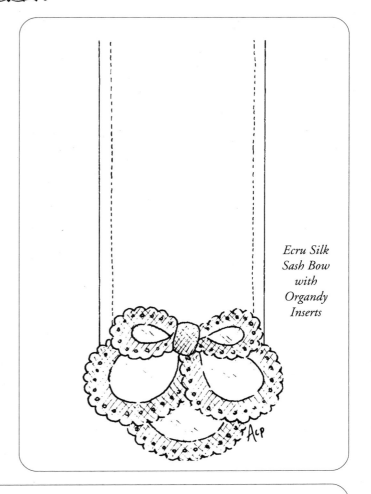

Ecru Silk Sash Bow with Organdy Inserts

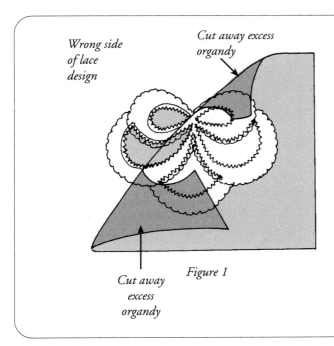

Wrong side of lace design

Cut away excess organdy

Cut away excess organdy

Figure 1

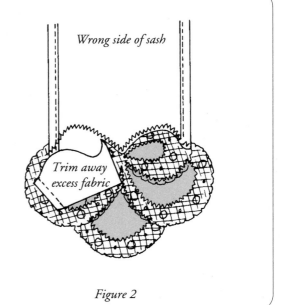

Wrong side of sash

Trim away excess fabric

Figure 2

Bib Knickers

When we were deciding on the patterns to include in this 400 series, *Martha's Attic*, we thought about a pattern which would be cute for a little boy or a little girl. Loving knickers has been a passion of mine for many years. They are cute on both boys and girls and they are appropriate for many occasions. Dress them up or dress them down, they still look precious. Coupled with a bib front, one can use them for smocking designs, woven ribbons, appliqué or lace work. I have seen velveteen knickers with lace shaping or the big, corduroy knickers with appliqué on the bib and cotton knickers with smocking on the bib. We feel that this pattern is so cute and that it will cover a world of clothing ideas for your little boys and girls.

One version has woven ribbons on the bib front. Two have smocking. The woven ribbon version has a white background fabric with tiny little flowers and lady bugs on it. The buttons are bright yellow, making for a festive outfit just right for summer occasions. Since everybody loves pockets, our knickers have two pockets in the front. The buttons do not really open at the waistline; they are just for looks. The buttons on the shoulders do unbutton and that is the way your little ones will come in and out of these knickers. The legs button also. There is elastic at the waistline and a cute high bib panel in the back. The front and back bibs are lined.

The two smocked versions have piping at the top and the bottom of the bib smocked inset. I believe your little ones will love this outfit and don't forget that you can make it as plain or as fancy as you want. ❋

Ribbon Bib Knicker

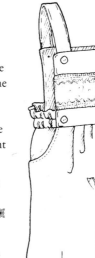

Smocked Heart Bib Knicker

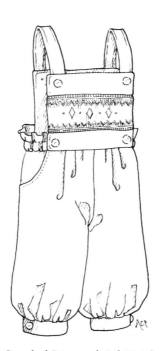

Smocked Diamond Bib Knicker

Bib Knickers

These knickers are shown in a smocked bib version and a woven ribbon bib version. Following the general directions, you will find directions for each specific bib.

General Directions

Fabric Requirements

Size	Fabric (woven ribbon or smocked)	Smocked Insert (smocked only)	Pleated Rows	Smocked Rows
2	1¹/₈ yds.	6"	8 - 10	6 - 8
3	1¹/₈ yds.	6"	8 - 10	6 - 8
4	1¹/₄ yds.	6"	9 - 11	7 - 9
5	1¹/₃ yds.	6"	10 - 12	8 - 10
6	1¹/₃ yds.	6"	12 - 14	10 - 12

Other Supplies

¹/₂ yd. of ¹/₂" elastic; six ¹/₂" to ⁵/₈" buttons; 8" x 10" piece of medium weight fusible interfacing; piping; DMC floss for the smocked bib; assorted ribbons for woven bib (see the specific directions for the woven bib yardage requirements); 6" x 9" piece of batiste for woven bib

Cutting Directions

The pattern is found on the pull-out section.

All seams are ⁵/₈" unless otherwise indicated.

1. Cut the following pieces: 2 pant fronts, 2 pant backs, 2 pocket facings, 2 pocket linings, 2 cuffs, 2 straps, 2 front bib pieces, 1 back bib facing.

2. The lining of the bib front will be cut after the bib insert is made.

I. Pants Front

1. With right sides together, stitch the pants center front seam. Clip the curves and finish the seam with a zigzag or serger (**fig. 1**).

2. Baste or pin the pleats in the upper pants front. The pleats will point to the sides (**fig. 2**).

3. Place the pocket facing to the pants front, with right sides together; stitch along the upper curve. Trim the seam to ¹/₄", clip curves and turn the facing to the inside of the pants and press (**fig. 3**). Top stitch along the pressed pocket edge (**fig. 4**).

4. Place the pocket lining to the pocket facing, with right sides together. The pocket lining will extend above the pocket facing. Stitch only the lining to the facing, starting at the sides and

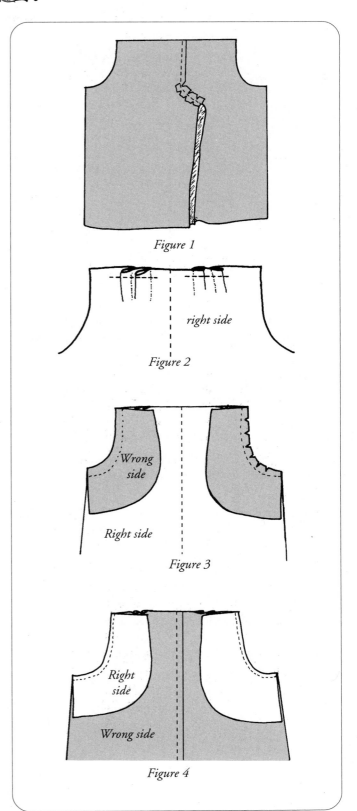

Figure 1

right side

Figure 2

Wrong side

Right side

Figure 3

Right side

Wrong side

Figure 4

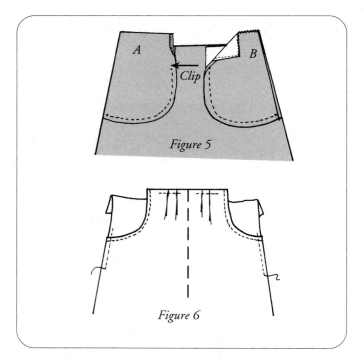

Figure 5

Figure 6

stitching to the dot; backstitch. Clip the seam allowance at the top of the stitching line. Turn the facing seam above the clip to the back side of the facing and stitch. Turn the lining seam above the clip to the inside of the lining and stitch (**fig. 5a**). Zigzag, serge or hem the top edge of the pocket lining (**fig. 5b**).

5. Pin or baste the pocket in place along the sides of the pants (**fig. 6**).

II. Pants Back

1. With right sides together, stitch the pants center back seam. Clip the curves and finish the seam edges with a zigzag or serger (**fig. 7**).

2. Straps: Fold the strap in half, right sides together, stitch along the long side and across the short straight side with a ³/₈" seam. Turn the strap to the right side through the pointed end. Press (**fig. 8**).

3. Pin the straps to the right side of the back bib with the points toward the center back. The edge of the strap should be ⁵/₈" from the side of the bib (**fig. 9**).

4. Finish the end of the bib facing (the long side) using a machine zigzag, serger or by turning up ¹/₄" to the wrong side, pressing and stitching with a straight stitch (**fig. 10**).

5. Place the back bib facing to the back bib, with right sides together. The straps will be between these two layers. Stitch as shown in (**fig. 11**). Clip the corners, turn and press (**fig. 12**).

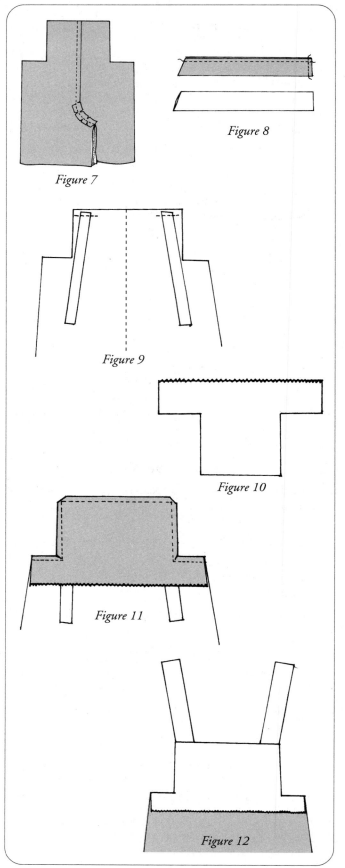

Figure 7

Figure 8

Figure 9

Figure 10

Figure 11

Figure 12

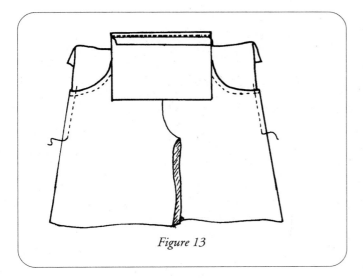

Figure 13

III. Bib Front

Follow the directions for each specific bib front.

IV. Attaching the Bib Front

1. Sew the right side of the bib to the right side of the pants front. Do not stitch through the lining. Trim the seam allowance to $^1/_4$" (**fig. 13**).

2. Turn the edge of the lining to the inside of the bib and whip to the seam (**fig. 14**).

V. Finishing the Knickers

1. Stitch the front pants to the back pants along the side seams, starting at the top of the pants and stitching to the placket extension; backstitch (**fig. 15**).

2. Fold each edge of the placket extension to the inside $^1/_8$", then $^1/_8$" again. Stitch (**fig. 16**).

3. The back extension will extend past the side seam by $^3/_8$". Fold to achieve this and pin in place. The front extension will be folded to the inside along the seam line (**fig. 17**).

4. Fold the cuff in half with right sides together; stitch the short sides together. Trim the seam and turn the cuff to the right side; press (**fig. 18**).

5. Run two gathering threads in the bottom of the pants at $^1/_8$" and $^1/_4$" (**fig. 19**).

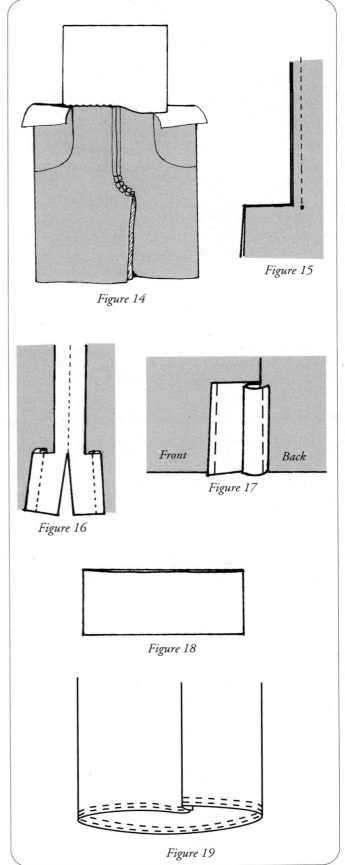

Figure 14

Figure 15

Figure 16

Front   Back

Figure 17

Figure 18

Figure 19

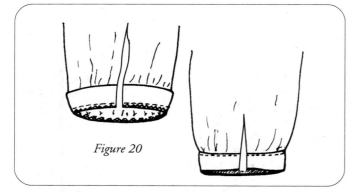

Figure 20

6. Pull the bobbin thread to gather the legs to fit the cuff. Pin the cuff to the pants, right sides together, and stitch, using a ¼" seam. Finish the seam with a zigzag or serge. Top stitch the seam allowance to the cuff (**fig. 20**).

7. Fold the top edge of the pocket lining to the inside even with the back bib facing. Top stitch along the fold and the edges of the back bib (**fig. 21a**).

   Elastic placement stitching lines:

   Measure ⅝" from the folded edge and straight stitch from the edge of the pocket facing/bib to 1" into the back bib. The second line is the same length as the first, and is ⅝" from the first stitching line (**fig. 21b**).

8. Cut two pieces of ½" elastic to the following measurements:

   Size 2 = 6½" ; size 3 = 7" ; size 4 = 7½" ; size 5 = 8" ; size 6 = 8½" .

9. Run the elastic through the casing. Stitch the ends of the elastic in place through the bib and bib lining; this will create a ruffle above the elastic (**fig. 22**).

VI. Buttonholes and Buttons

1. Work buttonholes in the front edge of the leg cuff. The buttonholes are made horizontally about ¼" to ½" from the edge. Buttonholes are also made in the upper bib strip. These buttonholes are made vertically about ¾" to 1" from the upper edge (**fig. 23**).

2. Attach buttons on the straps and back edges of the cuffs. Also attach the bottom bib strip to the pocket lining by sewing on the buttons through the pocket lining and the bib (you will stitch through the elastic) (**fig. 24a**); or you could make buttonholes in the bottom bib strip. The buttons, in this case, would be sewn on the pocket lining, through the elastic (**fig. 24b**). ▧

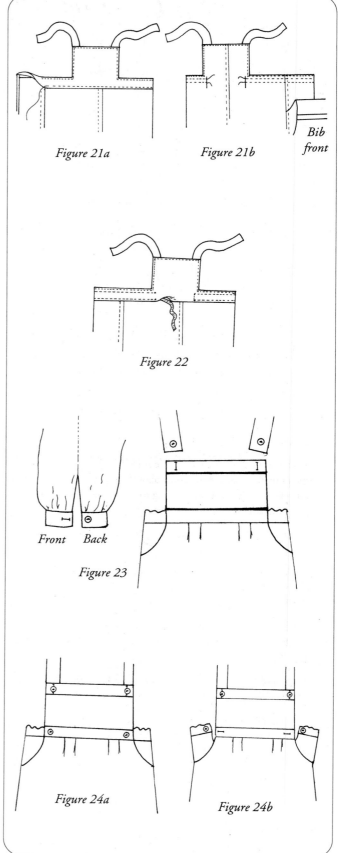

Figure 21a

Figure 21b

Bib front

Figure 22

Front   Back

Figure 23

Figure 24a

Figure 24b

Specific Directions for Knickers Bibs

A. Smocked Insert Bib

1. Tear a strip of fabric 6" for the insert. For geometric smocking designs, the strip should be 36" long; for picture smocking, make the strip 45" long.

2. Use the chart in the general instructions as a guide for the number of pleating rows; remember that you should pleat two rows more than you will smock.

3. Remove the pleating threads from a ⅝" seam allowance at each end of the panel. Pull up the pleating threads and tie off the pleated panel to the measurement for your size: size 2 = 6" ; size 3 = 6¼" ; size 4 = 6½" ; size 5 = 6¾" ; size 6 = 7" (these measurements are for the pleated area only, and do not include the seam allowances) (**fig. 1**).

4. Smock the design according to the instructions on the graph found on page 257.

5. Block the smocking to fit the bib strips. If the panel has been tied off too short, add strips to the sides of the panel to make it wide enough to fit the top and bottom strips (**fig. 2**).

6. Using a ⅝" seam allowance, attach corded piping to one long side of each top and bottom bib strip. Press the seam allowances toward the wrong side of the bib strips, exposing the piping along the folded edge (**fig. 3**).

7. Attach washout basting tape to the seam allowances on the wrong side of the bib strip, above the piping (**fig. 4**). Press the bib strips onto the inset, allowing the piping to fall between the first smocked row and the extra pleating row (**fig. 5**).

8. Stitch the bib strips to the top and bottom of the smocked panel; "stitch in the ditch" between the piping and the bib strip (**fig. 6**). Press the bib well.

9. See section "C. Lining the Bib."

B. Woven Ribbon Insert

Refer to "Lace and Ribbon Weaving" found on page 226.

1. Cut a rectangle of batiste 6" x 9" (the 6" side is the vertical, the 9" side is the horizontal). Pin the rectangle to a lace board or foam board, or ironing board.

2. Weave ribbon as directed in the "Lace and Ribbon Weaving" general directions, making sure that the batiste is completely covered with the ribbon.

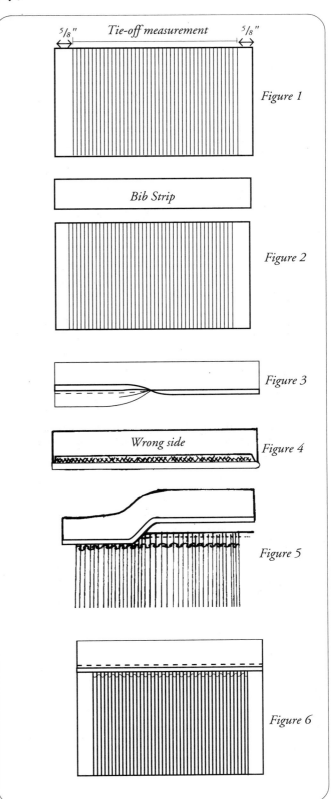

⅝" Tie-off measurement ⅝"

Figure 1

Bib Strip

Figure 2

Figure 3

Wrong side *Figure 4*

Figure 5

Figure 6

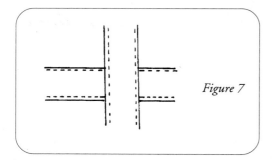

Figure 7

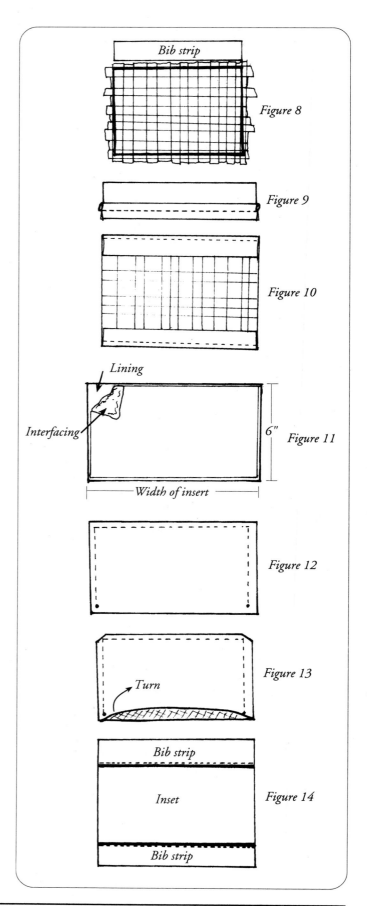

Bib strip — Figure 8

Figure 9

Figure 10

Lining — Interfacing — 6" — Figure 11

Width of insert

Figure 12

Turn — Figure 13

Bib strip — Inset — Bib strip — Figure 14

3. After all of the weaving is done, remove the pins from the board and flat-pin the ribbons to the batiste. Topstitch the ribbons down, stopping and tying off each time you come to an under lap. A straight stitch or zigzag may be used. You may match the thread color to the ribbons, or use an invisible thread (**fig. 7**).

4. Turn the panel to the wrong side and press well. Measure and mark the batiste to the correct size (6" x the length of the bib strips). Trim the batiste and ribbons to the correct size (**fig. 8**).

5. (Optional) To attach piping between the bib strips and the insert, stitch piping to one long edge of each bib strip, using a ⅝" seam (**fig. 9**). Refer to A. steps 6-8.

6. With right sides together, pin the bib strips to the top and bottom edges of the insert. Stitch with a ⅝" seam allowance. Press the seams toward the bib strips (**fig. 10**).

7. See section "C.-Lining the Bib."

C. Lining the Bib

1. Cut the bib lining the same size as the finished insert panel (**fig. 11**). Press a piece of fusible interfacing to the wrong side of the lining to add stability to the bib.

2. With right sides together, pin the bib and the bib lining together. Using a ⅝" seam allowance, begin stitching ⅝" from the bottom edge on one side, stitch up the side, across the top and down the other side, stopping the stitching ⅝" from the bottom edge (**fig. 12**).

3. Clip the corners and turn the bib to the right side; press the bib well (**fig. 13**).

4. Topstitch "in the ditch" between the piping and the bib strips; if there is no piping, stitch "in the ditch" between the bib strips and the insert. You will be stitching through all layers, to add stability (**fig. 14**).

5. Refer to sections IV, V and VI of the general directions to finish the knickers. ✻

Introduction To Silk Ribbon Embroidery

Contributed by YLI-Esther and Dan Randall

When Esther and Dan Randall purchased YLI Corporation in 1984 and transported the entire company in a U-Haul truck to Provo, Utah they had little thought where this decision would take them. But the two things they did know were that Dan was an experienced business executive and Esther loved fabrics and was an experienced, creative stitcher.

Because YLI's products included silk ribbon and silk thread, it didn't take Esther long to begin embroidering with silk. At first she used familiar iron-on patterns, but soon her creativeness took her artistic ability from her own flower garden to her embroidered needlework. She wrote in her book, Esther's Silk Ribbon Embroidery, "Before I begin a project I take an imaginary walk in a classic English flower garden, surrounded by an array of beautiful colors and hues. I pick an armful of flowers and mentally arrange them into a beautiful bouquet to adorn a favorite corner of my living room. This floral imagery is enhanced as I look at my basket of silk ribbons. Like the flowers in my imagined bouquet, my ribbons have all the delicate shades of color and are ready to portray in silk the exquisite shapes and colors of nature. No other stitching, I believe, can capture nature's floral beauty like silk ribbon embroidery."

Esther knew that silk ribbon embroidery was an ancient art and that through the ages it was found particularly in the Chinese, Japanese, European, and even early American cultures. Esther also knew she wanted to help bring this unique and exquisite needle art to those who love to do and those who love to view its beauty.

For many years Esther has made silk ribbon embroidery a focus of her creative needlework. She is well known for her artistic sewing, and particularly for her creative designs in silk ribbon embroidery. Her work has been featured in *McCall's Needlework, Sew Beautiful,* and *Creative Needle.* In addition, her needle work has been displayed at many trade shows. Esther has taught silk ribbon embroidery classes and seminars throughout the United States. Her book, *Esther's Silk Ribbon Embroidery,* has become well known internationally, and her designs and projects can be purchased as individual kits. Her great love of silk ribbon embroidery, her creative expertise, and her association with other needlework professionals have helped to associate her name with this international creative artwork. ▧

Silk Ribbon Embroidery And Ribbon Work

As you begin to embellish your special projects with silk ribbon you will find that it is actually much easier than it looks and it takes far less time than floss embroidery to complete a design. The craft of silk embroidery is little more than mastering a few basic stitches and using those stitches in combinations with each other. With a change in color and ribbon width, a basic leaf becomes a rose or a tulip. A French knot is babies' breath in one design and a rose or a hyacinth in another design simply by a change in the ribbon or number of twists on the needle. As you fill in your design you will find that silk ribbon is very forgiving and mistakes are easily corrected. You will become familiar with what works best for you as you play with different needles, ribbons, and fabrics. We use YLI Silk Ribbons. They're Gorgeous!

Fabrics

Many fabrics are suitable for silk ribbon embroidery; of course, some are easier to work with than others. All of the natural fiber fabrics are beautiful and very suitable. Some are cotton, linen, cotton velveteen, silk taffeta, raw silk, silk dupioni, natural silk, and batiste. The following synthetic fabrics are also useful; moiré taffeta, tapestry, lightweight polyester taffeta, organdy, and satin. Experiment with several.

Needles

There are a variety of needles used for silk ribbon work, as you experiment you will find what works best with which fabric and stitches. Remember, the higher the size number the smaller the needle.

Chenille Needle - A large, sharp point needle with a long eye. Sizes range 18 to 24. Good for wide ribbon and tightly woven fabrics because it punctures a hole that will accommodate a wide ribbon.

Crewel Needle - This needle has a long eye and a sharp point. Sizes range 1 to 10, however, sizes 3 to 9 is all you will ever need.

Tapestry Needle - A large eyed needle with a blunt end. It prevents snagging, and is great for passing through other ribbon; good for loosely woven fabrics. Size ranges 13 to 26, 18 to 26 being the most useful.

Straw Needle - This needle is a long, narrow needle which stays the same thickness from top to bottom, which means the needle does not get fatter at the eye. This aspect makes it a great needle for French and colonial knots.

Darner - A very large eyed, long needle used for wide ribbons and heavy thick threads. Sizes 14 to 18.

Beading needle - Used for assembling roses and gathering stitches and tacking beads. It is a thin, long needle with a small eye. ✠

Threading

For best results, work with ribbon no longer than 10 inches at a time. The ribbon becomes frayed and hard to work with quickly, so if the ribbon is longer the 10 inches it will probably be wasted before it can be used.

To keep the needle threaded insert the needle into the tail of the ribbon after it has been threaded through the eye of the needle (**fig. 1**). **Then,** pull the tail back over the main ribbon so that it forms a loop (**fig. 2**). Next, pull the main ribbon until the loop is closed (**fig. 3**). (This passes easily through the fabric and keeps the ribbon from coming unthreaded). ✠

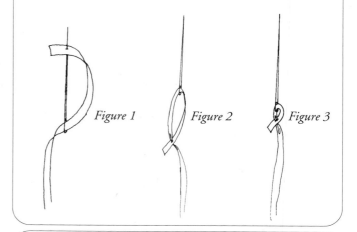

Figure 1 *Figure 2* *Figure 3*

Tying Off

There are two ways to tie on and to tie off the ribbon. One way is to simply tie knots. Knots are best for small projects. The second way is to leave about 1/2 inch of extra ribbon underneath the fabric and when the needle is inserted back through to complete a stitch, insert the needle through the extra ribbon to secure it. When cutting the ribbon, leave an extra 1/2 inch and insert the needle through it when making another stitch. This method helps keep the back side free of so many knots, which can eventually get in the way when working a complicated design. ✠

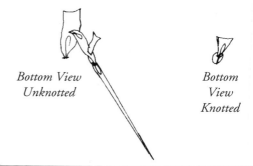

Bottom View Unknotted *Bottom View Knotted*

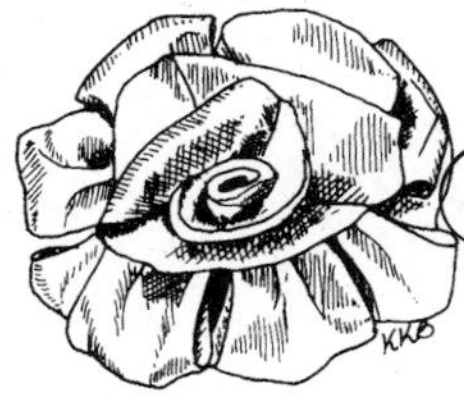

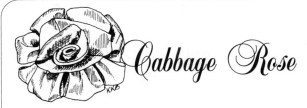

Cabbage Rose

Any project graced by this luxurious rose is instantly touched with a Victorian appeal. It is a wonderful ornament for hats, boxes, pillows, and especially on wedding dresses and veils. Technically, it is a variation of the hand wrapped rose taught on the Series 100 shows. It is made exactly the same way only there is a twist at the end. It takes a little practice so don't be discouraged the first time.

1. Beginning with a flat piece of ribbon about 15 inches long, fold down about three inches at a right angle (**fig. 1**). Fold again, this time fold the ribbon back on itself. This will create a triangle in the corner (**fig. 2**)

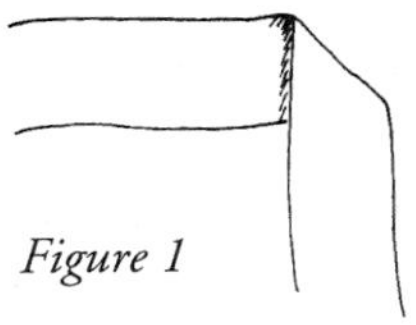

Figure 1

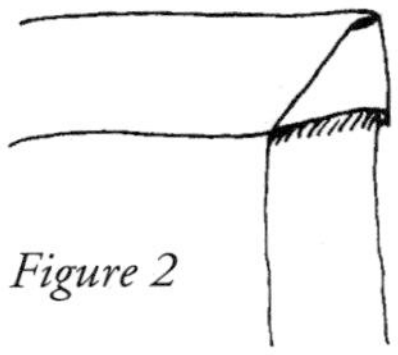

Figure 2

2. Place a pointed object such as the sharp tip of a chalk pencil or light colored pencil up through the "triangle" (**fig. 3**) and begin twisting with about two twists (**fig. 4**).

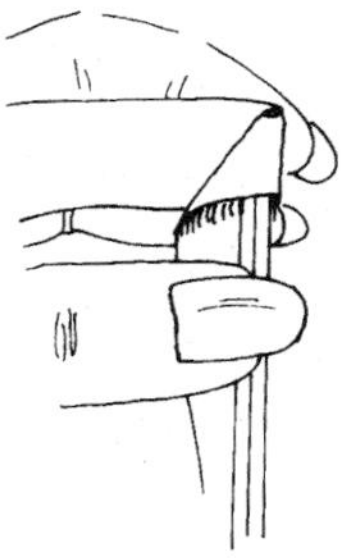

Figure 3

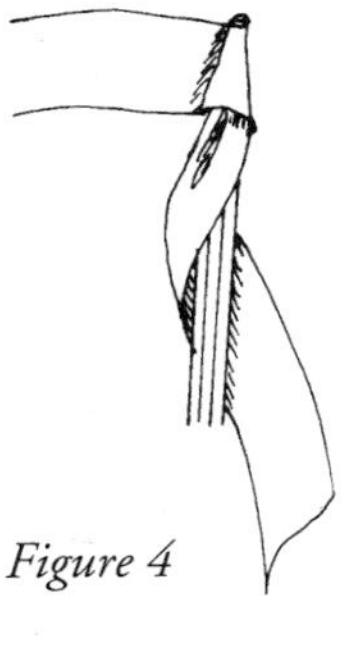

Figure 4

3. Begin folding the ribbon back while twisting the pencil (**fig. 5**). Continue folding and twisting until you have about 5 to 7 full twists for a full rose and about 4 twists for a small rosette.

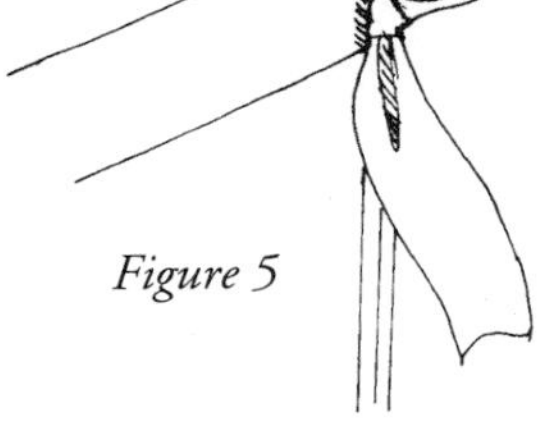

Figure 5

4. Remove the rose from the pencil and hold it between your thumb and finger. Tack the bottom securely with a needle and thread, leaving the tails dangling (**fig. 6**).

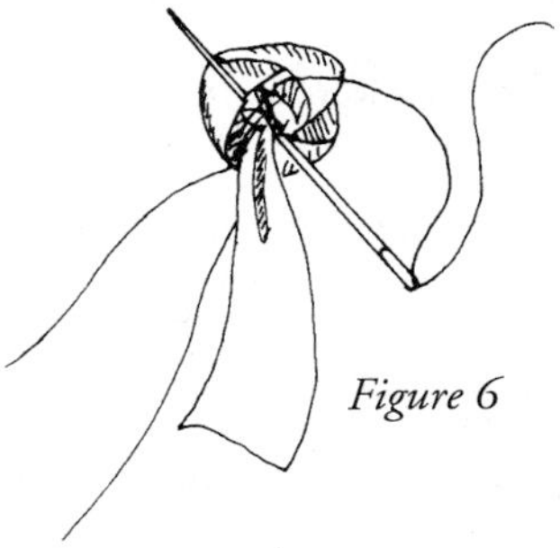

Figure 6

5. Now, here's the tricky part. After you have tacked the rose, to keep it from falling apart as you finish, take the tail of the ribbon and create loops as you would when making a Christmas bow (**fig. 7**). The point of the loop will be on bottom . Tack stitch each loop as it is formed to the bottom of the rose to secure it. Make four loops; one on each side of the rose. After the last loop, fold the raw edge under and stitch securely (**fig. 8**).

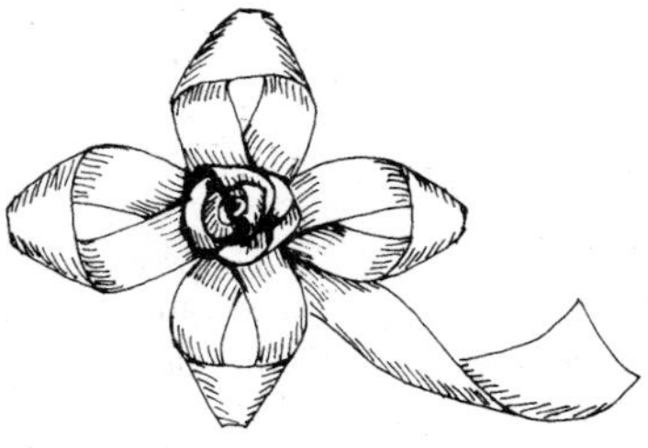

Figure 7

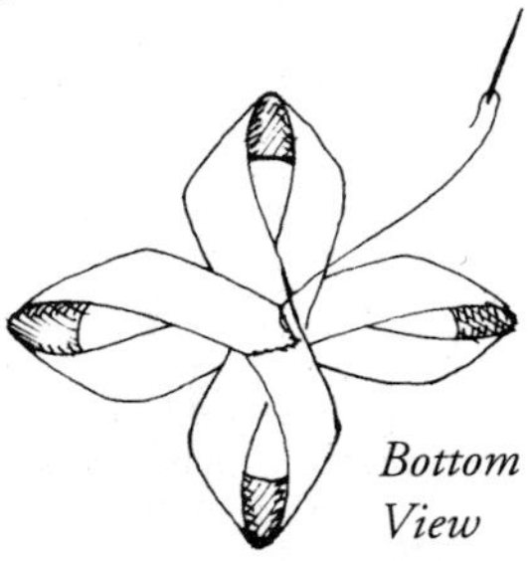

Figure 8

6. Pinch together the ends of the loop and take a couple of tiny stitches to secure (**fig. 9**). Gently pull the tacked ends to the bottom center and take loose stitches to hold it in place. Tie a knot and go to the next petal and repeat until all of the loops are tacked to the bottom . As you will notice, the tacked loops create puffy petals on the bottom of the rose and give the wrapped rose more volume (**fig. 10**). ⁂

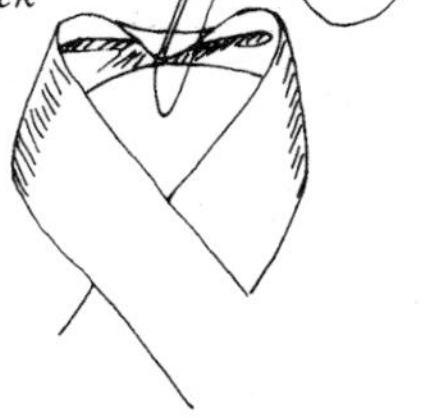

Figure 9

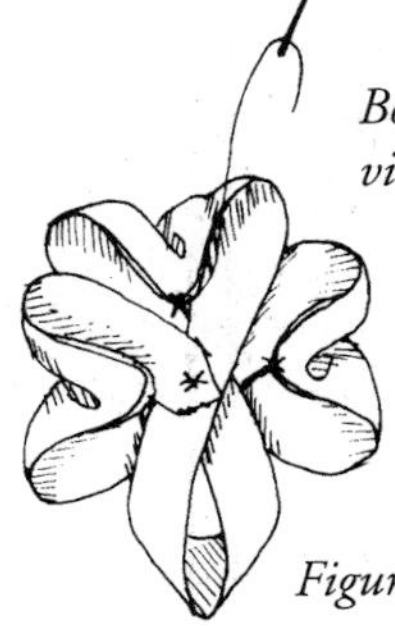

Figure 10

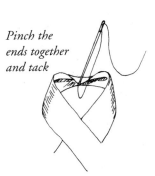

Concertina Rose

In my experience teaching silk ribbon, I have learned that not everyone can make a hand wrapped rose. The concertina rose doesn't take quite so many fingers and toes to make, and it can stand in the place of a wrapped rose just as nicely on any project.

Once you try one of these roses, you will probably be reminded of decorating for the prom in high school – remember folding all that tissue. Well, this rose is done the exact same way. And if you've never folded tissue, try this technique the next time you have to decorate for a party!

1. Cut a piece of 7 mm or wider ribbon 12 to 14 inches long and it fold in half.

2. Start by folding the ribbon at a 90° angle (**fig. 1**). Fold the bottom ribbon over the top ribbon (**fig. 2**). Continue folding the bottom ribbon over the top until it has at least a 1-inch tail at the end (**fig. 3**).

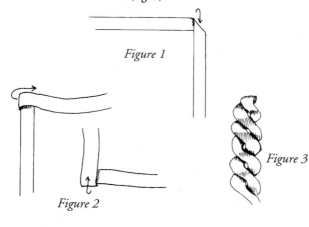

Figure 1

Figure 2

Figure 3

3. Hold the last folded edge of ribbon between your thumb and finger while your other thumb and finger pull the other ribbon tail gently until the folds have all collapsed on each other (**fig. 4**). You will see a rose forming from the top.

5. Stick a straight pin through the bottom to hold while you tack it secure with a needle and sewing thread. ✳

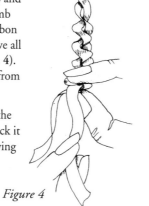

Figure 4

Feather Stitch

This is a great embellishing stitch for crazy patch and is also used for stems and vines.

Use a 2mm ribbon or floss.

1. Bring the needle up through the fabric in point "A" (**fig. 1**). Insert the needle down about $1/4$ to $3/8$ inch across from "A" into point "B". In the same stitch bring the needle back through about $1/4$ to $3/8$ inch down and center at point "C" (**fig. 2**). With the ribbon behind the needle, pull the ribbon through (**fig. 3**). This stitch is much like the lazy daisy only the needle does not insert into the same hole in which it came up. Notice that the stitch is simply a triangle.

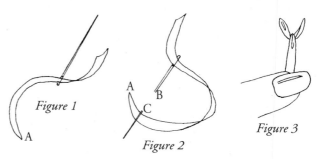

Figure 1

A   B
C

Figure 2

Figure 3

2. Now you will begin working your triangle from right to left, or left to right. Point "C" will now become point "A" for your next stitch. Repeat the stitch as in step 1 (**fig. 4**).

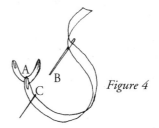

A   B
C

Figure 4

3. This time repeat the stitch on the other side (**fig. 5**). The trick is that "A" and "B" will always be straight across from each other and that all of the "A" points, "B" points, and "C" points will line up vertically (**fig. 6**). ✳

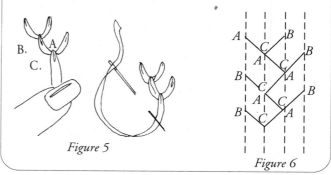

B.
C.   A

Figure 5

A   B
  C
    A   C   B
B   A
  C   C
    A   B
B   C   A

Figure 6

Fly Stitch

Appropriately named, this stitch looks like a fly. I prefer to see it as a bird myself, however the stitched is universally known as a fly stitch. A wonderful way to use this stitch is to tack the tails of bows. This creates a sweet fairy tale illusion of birds carrying ribbon in their beaks. This stitch is also great for creating fern leaves.

1. This is very similar to the lazy daisy stitch. This stitch is open where the lazy daisy stitch is closed. Bring the needle up through point A. Insert it down in point B and up through point C in the same stitch (**fig. 1**).

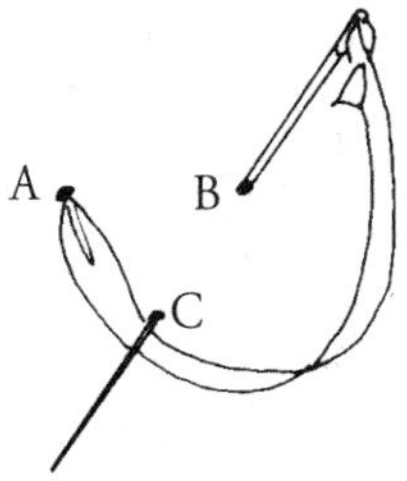

Figure 1

2. With the ribbon behind the needle, pull through (**fig. 2**). Secure the loop by inserting the needle straight down into the fabric at point C (**fig. 3**), or you may insert it a short distance beyond point C to create a longer anchor stitch (**fig. 4**). ✱

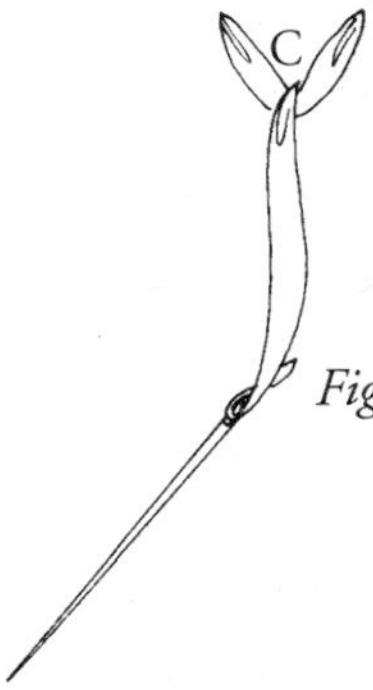

Figure 2

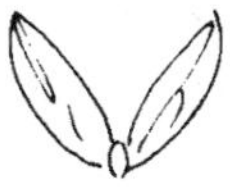

Figure 3

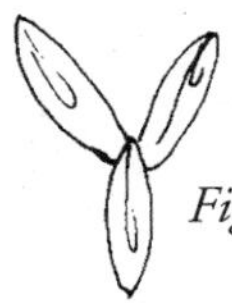

Figure 4

French Knot

Use a 2mm or 4mm ribbon for this stitch.

1. Bring the needle up through the fabric (**fig. 1**)

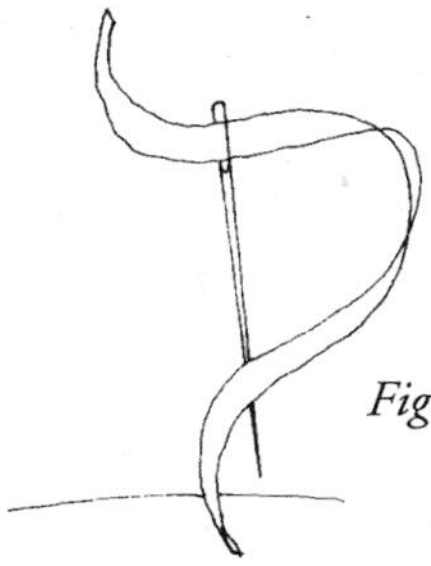

Figure 1

2. Hold the needle horizontally with one hand and wrap the ribbon around the needle with the other hand (**fig. 2**). One or two wraps create small knots; three to four wraps create medium knots; and five to six wraps create large knots, depending on the width of your ribbon.

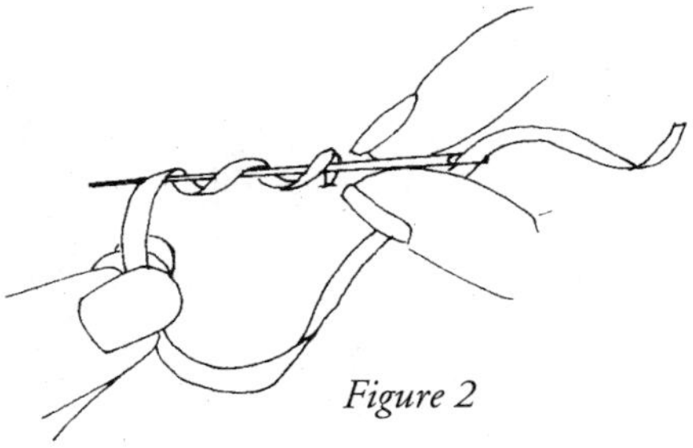

Figure 2

3. While holding the tail of the ribbon so that it does not unwind off the needle, bring the needle up into a vertical position and insert into the fabric just slightly beside where the needle came up (**fig. 3**). Pull the ribbon through while still holding the tail with the other hand. ✱

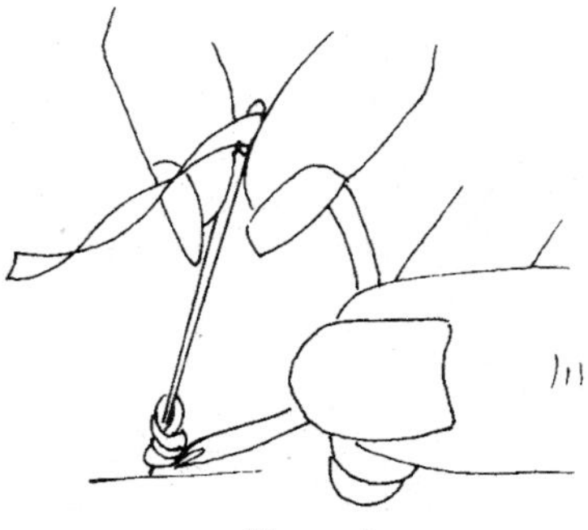

Figure 3

Herringbone Stitch

This beautiful line of stitching is a great decorative stitch for crazy patch. When doubled, this stitch becomes what Esther Randall calls a "Victorian stacking stitch." Use a 2mm ribbon for best results.

1. Make a long straight stitch from point A to point B (**fig. 1**). To practice you may want to mark dots on your fabric and label each point until you get the hang of it.

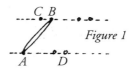

Figure 1

2. Bring the needle back up through the fabric at point C and make another long straight stitch to point D (**fig. 2**).

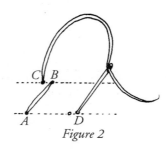

Figure 2

3. Repeat step 1 and 2 and continue the A, B, C, D pattern (**fig. 3**). Notice the sequence of overlaps; the current straight stitch overlaps the previous stitch. Also, notice that the crosses are high and low, not in the center. This is controlled by the distance set between point C and B and point A and D when bringing your needle up through the fabric for the next stitch. ▨

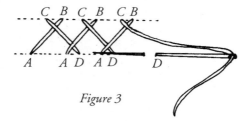

Figure 3

Ruching

Ruching is an age old technique seen on many antique garments. Most often strips of fabric were pleated, fluted, or gathered to embellish women's and children's clothing. What we know as "puffing" was actually called ruching in the old days. In France, as ribbon became popular, it was used to adorn clothing as well. The ribbon was gathered or pleated and stitched directly on top of the garments since the edges were finished and raveling was not a concern. This particular "applied" type of ruching is the technique we use with silk ribbon.

1. On a flat strip of 7mm or wider silk ribbon, run straight stitching, by hand or by machine, down the length of the ribbon to be gathered in a back and forth, zigzag direction (**fig. 1**). If hand stitching it helps if you have a long beading needle, because you can get more tiny stitches on the needle before you have to pull the thread through.

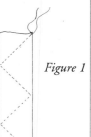

Figure 1

2. Once stitching is complete, pull the thread to gather the silk ribbon (**fig. 2**). Gather loosely or tightly as desired and tack with needle and thread or glue to project.

Figure 2

3. For a ruched carnation, simply coil the ruching. Gather the center tighter and loosen the gathering as you complete the outer petals (**fig. 3**) tacking with needle and thread as you coil.

Figure 3

4. For a ruched iris, roll the ruching up until you have rolled about five scallops. Pull two scallops up and three scallops down and wrap with thread. Tack to project and flare the petals (**fig 4**). ▨

Figure 4

Silk Ribbon Weaving

Nothing is more elegant than a ribbon weave. Weaving ribbon adds surface interest to a floral wreath, and it's the perfect stitch to make baskets for silk arrangements. This technique is very easy and can be stitched in any shape. It is always done first before the flowers are stitched.

Any size ribbon will make a weave, of course, it all depends on the size of your weaving shape. Once you get the hang of it, try different colors and different sizes together.

1. Trace the shape of the weave on the fabric. Begin at the top or the bottom of the shape and work to the other end. Bring the needle up through the fabric on one side of the traced line and insert it down through the fabric on the other side into the traced line (**fig 1**). Keep the ribbon completely flat and smooth. If fraying occurs switch to a bigger needle.

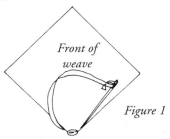

Front of weave

Figure 1

2. Make the next stitch come up through the fabric next to the last inserted stitch (**fig. 2**) so that the back side becomes simply an outline of the shape and not covered with ribbon (**fig. 3**). In other words, you will not carry the ribbon across the back side of the fabric. When bringing the needle up for another stitch allow room for the ribbon width. You want the ribbon edges to touch but not to overlap.

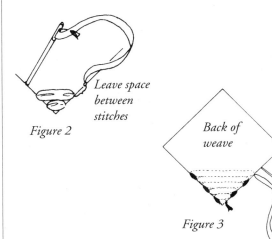

Leave space between stitches

Figure 2

Back of weave

Figure 3

Continued from Silk Ribbon Weaving

3. Continue filling the shape with horizontal stitches following the shape of the traced lines.

4. Once the shape is filled with horizontal stitches, it is time to repeat the process vertically, only this time you will weave the ribbon through the horizontal ribbons before you insert the needle on the other side (**fig. 4**).

5. Tie off when complete and embellish the edges with flowers and leaves. ✳

Figure 4

Satin Stitch

The satin stitch is used to fill in an area with color by using heavy thread coverage. All of the stitches line up in the same direction creating a smooth, sometimes shiny appeal when it catches the light, thus, looking like satin. To fill a given area takes patience because it is a slow moving stitch; the end result, however, is very pleasing.

1. It generally helps if you have the area to be filled traced on the project so that you have two definite lines to guide and maintain the varying width of the stitch as it fills different shapes. Secure in an embroidery hoop.

2. Begin at one end and work the needle from one side to the other stacking the thread up just below and next to the previous stitch (**fig 1**). Continue this wrapping process keeping the fabric secured and taut while the stitches are pulled with light tension so that the fabric will not tunnel. ✳

Figure 1

Margaret's Quilt

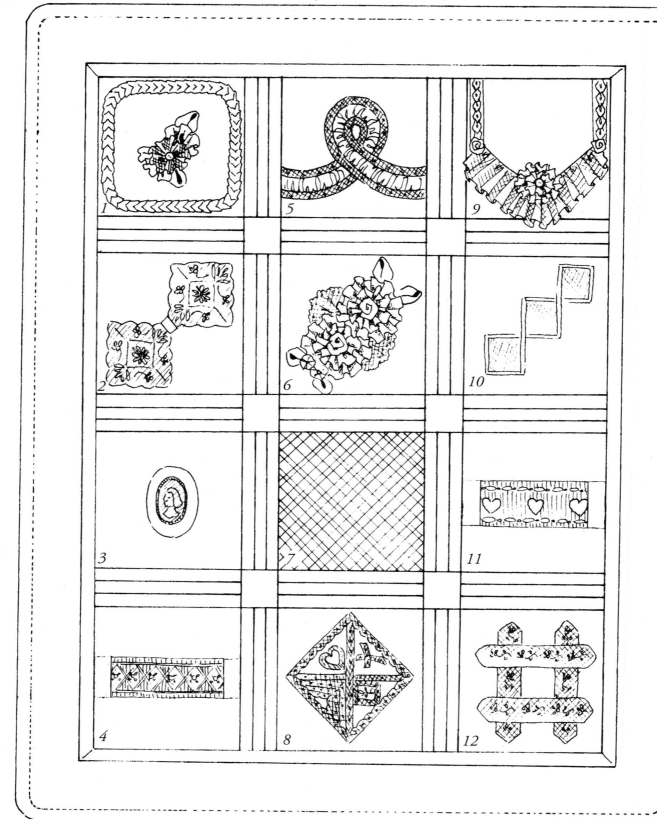

Introduction to Margaret's Quilt

Making this quilt is quick, fun and easy to do! Heirloom sewing takes a more traditional turn with this quilt, combining laces, ribbon manipulation, lace shaping, and quilting treasures. Imagination will be the only guideline when you formulate a similar quilt! Sampler quilts take me back to the first days when I was trying to learn heirloom sewing. I would try one technique and think, "There has to be an easier way to do this." Then, I would assemble my forces and try another method. After several years of this process, I began to write books believing that I truly had discovered simpler sewing traditions. When you practice the techniques used on the show, "Martha's Sewing Room," it seems likely that you would enjoy making a little square before you start on your christening dress or doll dress.

Using traditional quilting fabrics for the backgrounds and borders, this beauty is suitable for any room in your house. Your choices of fabrics make the central theme of the quilt either very dressy or very homespun. Don't be apprehensive about combining quilting fabrics and laces; this has been done for centuries.

When I look at this quilt, color is what I notice first. Teals, golds, hot pinks, and black blend together beautifully. The combination of color and textures set the mood for this Victorian feeling quilt. I love the antique brownish laces blended with the subtle colors of grosgrain ribbons. Speaking of mood; this quilt seems almost coquettish with its flirty flowers, intricate lace designs and shocks of the unexpected. Featuring nearly every shape–circles, ovals, squares, diamonds, and triangles–the interest level is fascinating. Expect the unexpected in feelings from this quilt.

The three dimensional effect of the ribbon shapes and the smocking inset are very unusual and different. Using grosgrain ribbon makes the quilt seem like a traditional breed of quilt since grosgrain has a dull finish rather than shiny. Many novel techniques combine to present this lovely piece of sewing joy on which you can exercise your favorite heirloom techniques. Fashioning a sampler quilt is a marvelous way for you to practice your heirloom sewing and have something spectacular when you put all of your squares together. Many sewing machine dealerships have a square of the month club and at the end of the year they sew all of the pieces together into a quilt. Some of you may already belong to one of these clubs.

From loops of puffing, three dimensional flowers, shadow shapes, smocking, ribbon weaving, to embroidery this quilt is one to value for your own domicile or for the home of someone you love very much. Beginning on a quilt like this is the way to start; the sooner the better as far as I am concerned. Following the easy directions given below, please start an heirloom quilt tradition. Remember, quilts last longer than people; they furnish wonderful memories of the one who made the quilt. It is for many reasons that I want you to make some heirloom quilts of your own. One of those reasons is that this type of quilt is so very easy. Need I say more? ✳

Quilt Sqaure Directions

Refer to Quilt Construction on page 163 for fabric requirements.

Square One-Ribbon Border with Ribbon and Lace Flowers

The hot pink background fabric has folded teal blue grosgrain ribbon encircling the border. Three dimensional flowers in pink, green and ecru are found in the middle. The center ecru flower is ecru English netting with a pearl button for the center of the flower. The ribbon folding technique could be used on many types of heirloom clothing. The flowers could be used on any number of different projects also.

Supplies

- 4 yds. of $^{7}/_{8}$" teal grosgrain ribbon for border (l" pleats only). If pleats are wider or smaller, see border instructions to determine amount of ribbon needed.
- 24" of wire edge green grosgrain ribbon
- 1 yd. of l" pink striped grosgrain ribbon
- $^{1}/_{3}$ yd. of l" wide lace edging
- shank pearl button, $^{1}/_{2}$", for center of lace flower
- Thread to match ribbon colors
- Quilting thread to match striped grosgrain ribbon
- 6" square of buckram
- 12$^{1}/_{2}$" by 12$^{1}/_{2}$" fabric square (pink)

Flowers

1. The striped grosgrain ribbon will make 3 flowers. Each flower uses l2" of ribbon. Cut striped ribbon into three 12 inch lengths.

2. Using quilting thread, run a basting stitch in a zigzag pattern from the top of the striped grosgrain ribbon to the bottom. (Refer to the ruching technique found on page 154).

3. Pull the quilting thread until the ribbon gathers into a circle.

4. Shape the flower by pulling petals into the center and petals to the outside. Shape as desired, take several backstitches to anchor the gathering thread.

5. Slipstitch the cut ends of the ribbons together.

6. Lace flower is made in the same manner.

Leaves

1. Cut the ribbon into l2" pieces. This will make two small leaves.

2. Fold the ribbon in half (wired edge to wired edge) (**fig. 1**). Fold the ends (cut edges) to the top wired edges.

3. Run a gathering thread along the folded side, across the bottom fold and up the other folded side (**fig. 2**).

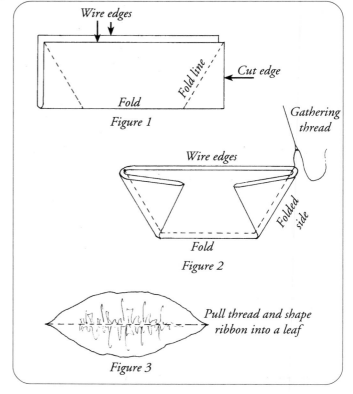

Wire edges

Fold line

Cut edge

Fold

Figure 1

Gathering thread

Wire edges

Folded side

Fold

Figure 2

Pull thread and shape ribbon into a leaf

Figure 3

4. Carefully pull the gathering thread, shaping the ribbon into a leaf.

5. Open the ribbon and arrange the gathers until the majority of them are in the center of the leaf and take several back stitches securing the thread (**fig. 3**).

Attaching to the Block

1. Place the leaves and flowers as desired. Stitch the leaves and flowers to the block in several places.

2. If one of the flowers is made of lace, stitch the pearl button in the center of the lace flower by stitching through all layers of fabric.

Border

1. The amount of ribbon needed for this single knife pleat border is calculated by multiplying the width of the pleat by 3, this figure by the number of inches needed for the completed length. Using a scrap of buckram, make a template the desired width of the pleat. This will make it easier to keep the pleats the same size. This template is 1".

2. Fold the ribbon into the width of the pleat desired. To anchor the pleats, pin the pleats in place. Using a knotted thread, bring the needle up through the back fold and through the top layer of ribbon at the center (point #1). Take one stitch along the upper fold, catching the fold only (point #2). Move across the upper

fold and take one stitch along the upper fold, catching the fold only (point #3). Take the needle to the back at point #1 (**fig. 4**). Pull the thread, creating a point. Tack the point and the upper fold in place (**fig. 5**). Move to the next pleat. Continue until the entire ribbon is stitched in place. Once you get accustomed to this stitching method, it will not be necessary to use pins.

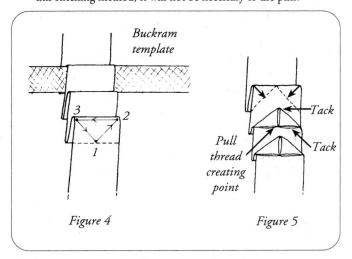

Figure 4   Figure 5

3. The ribbon is then placed on the quilt block and shaped to fit. Stitch to the block by hand. By working carefully with the ribbon, you should be able to join the cut edges of the ribbon underneath the first pleat to prevent a break in the pattern. ✖

— *Square Two-Lace Handkerchief Bow* —

Ecru linen forms the bow tie in the center. This handkerchief bow technique can be used on blouse fronts, linens for the home, skirts, pillows, doll dresses and many other garments. Using antique handkerchiefs in a creative way, this bow gives new ideas for what to do with that drawer full of Aunt Sadie's handkerchiefs which you inherited. Actually, I have seen this technique used with Swiss embroidered handkerchiefs, 1930's flowered hankies, as well as old lace ones. We might even call this square, "the recycling one."

Supplies

◄ 1 handkerchief large enough to make the size bow desired.
◄ 12 1/2" by 12 1/2" fabric square

1. Create handkerchief bow using the directions on page 225.

2. Place bow diagonally on the fabric square and stitch in place. ✖

— *Square Three-Oval With Motif* —

Swiss embroideries have been produced since the mid 1800's. It is almost impossible to imagine the wide variety of motifs which have been manufactured for over one hundred years. Sometimes, antique motifs are available; sometimes not. For this beautiful oval, a hot pink square is the background; the oval is of dark teal. Piping surrounds the oval cut out in the center and the motif is zigzagged down to the oval piece of fabric. The motif is ecru and has a picture of a lady's head with an entredeux stitching background.

Supplies

◄ 12 1/2" by 12 1/2" fabric square (pink)
◄ Oval motif (3 3/4" by 3 1/2")
◄ Cord for piping
◄ 1/3" yd. fabric for piping (teal)
◄ Oval template found on pattern pull-out.

1. Trace the oval template in the center of the fabric square. Note: A different size motif will require a different size template.

2. Make piping using bias strips of fabric and small cord. Clip the seam allowance of the piping every 1/8" to allow it to curve. Stitch the piping along the drawn line of the template with the seam allowance of the piping to the inside of the oval. At the beginning and end of the piping, crisscross and pull to the inside of the oval.

3. Trim the inside of the oval away along the cut edge of the piping. Clip the curve of the fabric under the piping. Turn the seam allowance of the piping to the inside of the oval. Press.

4. Cut a square of teal fabric 7" by 7". Center the motif on the square and stitch in place.

5. Place the motif/fabric in the center of the window. Stitch in place along the ditch of the piping. Trim the 7" square to the seam allowance of the piping. Press. ✖

— *Square Four-Geometric Smocking* —

Teal blue is the fabric choice for the background; the smocking inset is piped in hot pink and the background color of the smocked fabric is white. Teal blue geometric smocking forms the diamonds which are four step waves. The embellishment in the center of the waves is bullion roses in peach with teal lazy daisies on either side. In the center of each bullion rosebud is a pearl. What sweet geometric smocking!

Supplies

◄ 14" by 14" fabric square (teal)
◄ 3" by 6" fabric (teal)
◄ 3" by 45" fabric strip for smocking (white or ecru)
◄ cord for piping
◄ 1/4 yd. fabric for piping (pink)
◄ floss for smocking (DMC 964 light teal, DMC 3812 medium teal and DMC 754 pink)
◄ seed pearls
◄ Smocking plate and instructions found on page 259.

1. Pleat with 9 rows. Smock 7 rows. The top and bottom rows are stabilizing rows and will not be numbered on the graph. Remove pleating threads 1/2" from both sides for seam allowances.

2. Block smocking, pleat to pleat 9¹/₂". Make two pieces of piping 10¹/₂" long. Attach the piping just above the cable stitches of the top and bottom.

3. Cut the 3" by 6" fabric into two squares each 3" by 3". Stitch the fabric squares to each end of the smocked panel.

4. Cut the quilting square in half. Stitch one piece to the top of the panel and one piece to the bottom of the panel, just beyond the piping.

5. Trim the block to 12¹/₂" by 12¹/₂". ✷

Square Five-Loop of Puffing

Dark teal is the shade of the background square. Circling up in a loop is hot pink quilting fabric with ecru French cotton lace insertion on either side of the puffing. The teal fabric is cut away from behind the ecru lace making it peek a boo. Using this heavy quilting type cotton for puffing is very unusual since one usually thinks of puffing in a more delicate fabric. This heavier fabric is beautiful used in this way and one might expand one's creativity concerning puffing to include silk dupioni or handkerchief linen in addition to the more traditional Swiss batiste fabric.

Supplies

- 12¹/₂" by 12¹/₂" fabric square (teal)
- 1³/₄ yds. of ¹/₂" lace insertion
- 2 strips 2" by 45" for puffing (pink)
- Loop plate found on pattern pull-out

1. Stitch fabric strips together to form one long strip. Create puffing, stitching ¹/₂" on each side of the strip. Trim the seam allowance of the puffing to ¹/₈".

2. Trace lace puffing template on the fabric square. Shape the lace and puffing loop using the directions found on page 234. Do not cut teal fabric from behind the loop. ✷

Square Six-Ribbon Roses With Netting Buds and Ribbon Pods

Loving ribbon roses the way I do, it is easy to smile when I look at these. One large rose is pink; the other is medium blue. Both of them are made of grosgrain ribbon; the pink one is ombre in shades of deepest rose to palest pink. The centers of each flower are of black. English netting lace has been rolled in with the roses making some of the petals of lace. What a beautiful combination; ribbon and English netting lace. The pods are of ombre green taffeta ribbon and they are trimmed on each end with pink ribbon with picot edges. The leaves are dark green wired ribbon. There are two rolled roses made entirely of the bridal white English netting. The lace roses are in-between the blue and pink roses, one at the top and one at the bottom. The background fabric is hot pink.

Supplies

- 1¹/₂ yds. of 1¹/₄" teal grosgrain ribbon for flower
- 1¹/₂ yds. of 1¹/₄" pink variegated grosgrain ribbon for flower
- 2 yds. of 1¹/₄" organza ribbon or lace edging for each flower
- 1 yd. of 1¹/₄" netting lace or lace edging for each lace bud
- 8" of 1" picot edge ribbon for buds
- 1 yd. of wired ribbon for leaves
- 1 piece of florist wire
- Floral tape
- 2 cotton balls for stuffing
- 1 piece of buckram 8" long and 4" wide
- Optional: purchased pistils (flower centers)

Flowers

1. Each flower will use 1¹/₂ yds. of ribbon. To create the center of the grosgrain flowers, follow the directions given on page 151 for the Cabbage Rose. The center should use about 18" of the long ribbon piece. Do not cut the ribbon.

2. Run a gathering stitch ¹/₈" from the bottom edge of the remaining ribbon. When you are 1¹/₂" from the end of the ribbon, angle the gathering stitching up to the top of the ribbon. Pull the gathering thread to gather the ribbon (**fig. 6**).

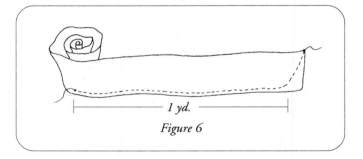

Figure 6

3. Place the center bud on the piece of buckram and stitch in place.

4. Wind the gathered ribbon around the bud and stitch from underneath the buckram. The rows of gathered ribbon should be ¹/₄" apart.

5. Use 1 yard of lace or ribbon per flower. Run a gathering thread along one edge of the lace or organza ribbon. If using lace, fold the cut edge of the lace at an angle before running the gathering stitch.

6. Pull the gathering thread in the lace or organza ribbon and gather the strip until it is 20" long.

7. Place the folded edge of the ribbon or lace close to the bud and begin stitching it in place between the rows of ribbon.

8. If desired, you may add pistils to the center of the cone with glue.

Netting Lace Buds

1. Use 18" of lace per bud.

2. Follow the directions for the center of the Cabbage Roses found on page 151.

Leaf

1. Use 9" per leaf.

2. Follow instructions given in Number One block above for leaves.

Pod

1. Fold the ribbon in half, right sides together, stitch the cut edges together to form a circle. Turn to the right side.

2. Run a gathering stitch around the top and bottom of the ribbon (**fig.** 7).

3. Pull one of the gathering threads until the ribbon is completely closed. Anchor the gathering threads with several back stitches (**fig.** 8).

4. Loop one end of the florist wire around the cotton ball and twist together (**fig.** 9).

5. Place the cotton ball in the circle of ribbon. Pull the last row of gathering threads on the ribbon as tightly as possible, causing it to enclose the ribbon and the florist wire. Anchor the gathering threads with several backstitches (**fig.** 10).

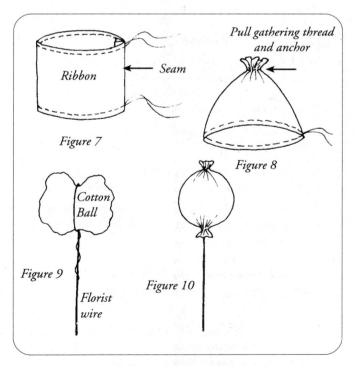

Ribbon

Seam

Figure 7

Pull gathering thread
and anchor

Figure 8

Figure 9

Cotton
Ball

Figure 10

Florist
wire

6. Wrap the florist wire with florist tape. Cut off the excess wire to use for the other bud.

7. Place the roses, leaves, and pods on the quilt block in any position desired. Stitch to the block by stitching through all layers. ⚕

— Square Seven-Ribbon and Lace Weaving —

Glorious grosgrain ribbon colors magnify the simple intricacy of this woven ribbon and lace square. Grosgrain ribbons in several shades of dusty pink, teal, gold, black and gold peek in and out of each other for a most interesting effect. One of the pinks has a picot edge; one is an ombre shade with pinks running from palest to burgundy. In three locations, English netting lace edging has been placed over the edge of a wide teal grosgrain ribbon and woven as if it were one piece. After the ribbons are woven, they are pressed onto a stabilizer to hold them in place for years of wonderful use on this quilt.

Supplies

- 14" x 14" piece of So Sheer™ interfacing or any lightweight fusible interfacing
- 10 yds. of ribbon in varying widths
- 2¹/₂ yds. of 1¹/₂" wide netting lace or lace edging

1. Pin the interfacing to a lace shaping board with the glue side up.

2. Refer to the technique "Lace and Ribbon Weaving" found on page 226 to complete the block. ⚕

Square Eight-Sash Block

Perhaps you are wondering why this square is called the sash block. Since we had a sash show, we wanted to make a quilt square using techniques from this show. The embellishments on this square are stitched onto a piece of netting which covers the whole hot pink background square piece of fabric. Ecru edging is stitched flat around the four sections which are made by crossing lace beading in the center. The lace edging around the edges has been mitered at the corners for a pretty, neat finish. On one square there is a tied bow; on another there is a tiny heart made from the narrow beading. On another there are two pieces of ecru lace insertion mitered with a piece of ecru lace edging at the top. On the fourth there is ecru lace edging stitched flat and mitered at the corners around an ecru Swiss motif. This netting square is attached to the pink background fabric with a zigzag around the largest side of the square through the heading of the edging lace.

Supplies

- 14" by 14" square of netting
- 12¹/₂" by 12¹/₂" fabric square (pink)
- 1 yd. of ¹/₂" lace edging (for the 8" square)
- 24" of ¹/₄" beading (for the X design)
- 1 motif - 2" square
- 12" of ¹/₂" lace edging to border the motif
- 9" of ⁵/₈" lace insertion for tied bow
- 9" of ¹/₄" beading for heart
- 12" of ⁵/₈" lace insertion for diamond point
- 12" of ¹/₂" lace insertion for diamond point
- 8" of ¹/₂" lace edging for diamond point
- Heart template found on pattern pull-out

1. Using a washout marker, draw an 8" square on the netting. Draw lines from corner to corner of the square.
2. Place the netting block on a lace shaping board. Center the 1/4" beading on the drawn lines of the X. Pin in place.
3. Using the 9" piece of lace insertion, tie a bow. Shape the bow and place in one of the four corners of the block. Pin in place and press.
4. Using the 9" piece of 1/4" beading, shape the heart (template found on the center pull-out) in one of the corners of the block. Pin in place. Press.
5. Place edging around the outer edges of the motif, mitering the corners. Stitch with a zigzag. Place the motif in one of the corners. Pin in place.
6. Using the remaining 12" pieces of 5/8" and 1/2" lace insertion, miter them to fit the remaining corner. Shape the 8" piece of 1/2" lace edging on top of the lace strip of insertion. Pin in place.
7. Remove from the lace shaping board. Stitch in place with a zigzag.
8. Shape the edging lace on the drawn lines of the square. Stitch in place with a zigzag.
9. Trim netting to 12 1/2" x 12 1/2".
10. Place the netting over the fabric square. Pin in place and treat as one layer fabric. ✠

Square Nine-Lingerie Bag

What a precious little lingerie bag which has been made into a quilt square. Using that wonderful hot pink quilt fabric as the background, the bag is trimmed with wide antique lace edging in a dark gold color. The ribbon flower at the bottom of the bag is made of ombre pink and teal grosgrain ribbons. There is a tiny little pearl button to trim the top of the flower. Along the edges of the flap to the bag, which really is a little bag which opens and closes with a clear snap, there is trim of teal and dusty pink grosgrain ribbon. The pink ribbon is folded in points to make a braid–like effect. There is a tiny cabbage rose at the bottom of each of the side pieces of ribbon trim; this ribbon is pink on one side and black on the other.

Supplies

- 2 fabric squares (pink) 12 1/2" x 12 1/2"
- 1 fabric piece 8 1/2" x 12 1/2" (pink)
- 1 yd. of 2 1/4" edging lace
- 5/8 yd. of 7/8" teal grosgrain ribbon for center flower and straight strips at top
- 9" of 1 1/4" pink grosgrain ribbon for outer flower petals on closure
- 1 shank pearl button, 1/2", for center flower closure
- 1 yd. of 3/8" satin ribbon for small flowers
- 2 1/2 yds. of 5/8" grosgrain ribbon for chevron border
- 2" by 2" square of buckram
- 1 snap

Flap

1. On one of the fabric squares, place a dot in the center 3" from the lower edge. Place dots along each side 5" from the top. Draw a line joining the side dots with the center dot. Cut along the lines. This will be the flap of the bag. Turn under 1/4" and 1/4" again on the 5" sides of the flap.
2. Fold the strip of lace edging in half and pin the center of the lace to the point of the flap.
3. Shape the lace edging into 1" box pleats along the pointed edge of the flap. Add extra lace at the point. Pin in place and press.
4. Turn the right side of the lace to the right side of the flap. Stitch in place, and overcast the edge with a zigzag.

Center Flower

1. Follow the instructions given in block Number One - Flowers, steps 2 to 5, to create the bottom layer of the center flower. Use the 1 1/4" wide pink ribbon.
2. Using 7/8" wide teal ribbon for the center flower, fold the ribbon in half, stitch closed to form a circle.
3. Turn the circle of ribbon to the right side and run a gathering thread along one of the edges. Pull the gathering threads to form the flower into a circle.
4. Place the circular flower on top of the bottom layer then place on the square of buckram. Stitch the flowers to the buckram. Add the pearl button for the center.

Ribbon Borders

1. Following the instructions given in block Number One - Border, step 2, create two pieces of folded ribbon to fit the hemmed sides of the flap. The template used for folding the small width ribbon is 5/8". Use the 5/8" wide ribbon.
2. Cut two pieces of 7/8" ribbon to fit the sides of the flap. Place the pleated ribbon on top of the 7/8" ribbon. Pin together.
3. Make two small roses, using the instructions for making roses from the Number Six block. Use the 3/8" satin ribbon.
4. Place the folded ribbon trim on the hemmed edges of the block. Stitch in place by hand. Attach the small ribbon flowers at the ends of each piece.

Block Construction

1. Hem one 12 1/2" side of the 8 1/2" by 12 1/2" fabric rectangle by turning under 1/4" and 1/4" again.
2. Place the hemmed rectangle on the 12 1/2" by 12 1/2" fabric square with the cut sides of the rectangle to the sides of the larger square. Pin along the cut edges. This creates a pocket.
3. Place the flap along the top edge of the square. Pin in place. Treat all layers as one layer of fabric. Note: When the sashing pieces are stitched to the sides of the block be careful not to catch the side of the flap in the stitching. ✠

Square Ten-Ribbon and Netting

Peekaboo pink fabric hides behind three cotton netting squares. One fourth inch wide ecru ribbon is stitched around each square and teal cotton is the top fabric. The teal fabric is cut away from behind the square sections; the pink and blue fabrics are joined with a tiny zigzag around both sides of the ecru satin ribbon.

Supplies

- 1 piece of netting 3" x 10"
- 1¼ yds. of ¼" double faced satin ribbon
- 12½" x 12½" fabric square (pink)
- 12½" x 12½" fabric square (teal)
- Diamond tempalte found on pattern pull-out

1. Using the quilt template in the center pull-out, trace the template on the teal fabric square.

2. Finish the ribbon and netting diamonds using the directions on page 229.

3. Place the top block on the pink block and treat as one layer of fabric. ✳

Square Eleven-Picture Smocking

Pretty picture smocked hearts are bordered with teal geometric borders on either side. Tiny pink rosettes fill in the sections of the picture smocking. This square uses the hot pink fabric as the base fabric and teal blue fabric is used for piping. Since the picture smocked piece was not long enough to place comfortably without stretching it too much, two end pieces of the hot pink fabric were added at either side.

Supplies

- 14" by 14" fabric square (pink)
- 5" by 8" fabric (pink)
- 5" by 45" fabric strip for smocking (white or ecru)
- cord for piping
- ¼ yd. fabric for piping (teal)
- floss for smocking (DMC 3808 teal and DMC 602 pink)
- Smocking Plate and smocking instructions on page 258.

1. Pleat with 12 rows. Smock 10 rows. The top and bottom rows are stabilizing rows and will not be numbered on the graph. Remove pleating threads ½" from both sides for seam allowances.

2. Block smocking, pleat to pleat, to 9". Make two pieces of piping 10½" long. Attach the piping just above the cable stitches of row 1 and just below row 10.

3. Cut the 5" by 8" fabric into two squares each 5" by 4". Stitch the fabric squares to each end of the smocked panel.

4. Cut the quilting square in half. Stitch one piece to the top of the panel and one piece to the bottom of the panel just above and below the piping.

5. Trim the block to 12½" by 12½". ✳

Square Twelve-Airplane Lace

Looking like an airplane, this old fashioned technique has been reinterpreted into a quilt square which is very unusual. Using English netting lace insertion, four pieces are placed parallel to each other and the ends are turned under into nice points. All are zigzagged to a pretty, dark teal piece of cotton fabric. The English netting looks so pretty on this dark fabric and this technique is one that isn't found everyday. That makes it unusual and special.

Supplies

- 12½" x 12½" fabric square (teal)
- 1⅓ yds. of 1¾" lace insertion
- Airplane lace template found on pattern pull-out

1. Trace the template onto the teal fabric.

2. Refer to the Airplane Lace technique found on page 210 to shape and stitch the lace. ✳

Quilt Construction

Basic Quilt Supplies

- ¼ yd. teal print (sashing)
- ¼ yd. pink print (sashing)
- ¼ yd. gold print (sashing)
- ¼ yd. black (inner border)
- 4½ yds. multi-print (outer border, backing, binding)
- ¾ yd. pink (squares)
- ¾ yd. teal (squares)
- Batting - finished quilt size 72" by 55"

Additional supplies for each block are listed under the specific square.

Each block created will be stitched using a square 12½" by 12½". Some of the squares will be created larger than 12½" by 12½" and then cut to this measurement. Refer to the specific square for dimensions.

I. Sashing

1. The sashing for this quilt is comprised of 3 strips of fabric in contrasting colors - light (gold print), medium (pink print), dark (teal print). Each strip for the sashing should be torn, if possible, 1½" wide by the width of the fabric. It is easier to work with the small strips of fabric if they are pressed before stitching. Tear 6 strips of each color.

2. Once the order is decided, stitch the strips together creating 6, three color strips.

3. Cut long strips of sashing into 12½" strips. Stitch the 12½" strips to the lower edge of all blocks except #4, #8 and #12, then stitch blocks 1 through 4 together, 5 through 8, and 9 through 12 together, creating 3 rows of 4 blocks. Press all seams to the dark side (**fig. 11**).

5. Cut 6 blocks of solid fabric 3½" square.

6. The long vertical sashing strips consist of four strips and three squares. Stitch a square to the lower end of three sashing strips. Stitch the strips together to make one long strip. The squares will fall in between the strips. Complete the long strip by stitching another small strip below the last square. Repeat for the second strip.

7. Stitch a vertical strip to the right side of blocks #1 - #4, matching the square to the horizontal sashing. Stitch the right side of blocks #5 - #8 in the same manner. Now stitch #1 - #4 to #5 - #8 and #5 - #8 to #9 - #12, matching the sashing strips. This completes the inner part of the quilt (**fig. 12**).

II. Inner Border

1. Cut 5 strips of (black) fabric 1½" wide for the inner border. Stitch the strips together to form one long strip.

2. Stitch the strip of fabric to the quilt top, right sides together, mitering the corners. Press the seam toward the border.

III. Cutting the Outer Border, Binding and Backing

The outer border, binding and backing are made from multi-colored printed fabric (shades of gold, teal and black).

1. Cut three strips of fabric 4½" by 45". This will be used for the binding.

2. Cut two pieces of fabric 72" by 45". Stitch the two pieces together along the 72" sides, creating one large rectangle. Press. Cut four 5" strips (outer border) and two 4½" strips (binding) from the outer sides of this large block. Refer to diagram (**fig. 13**).

3. The large piece will be used for the quilt back.

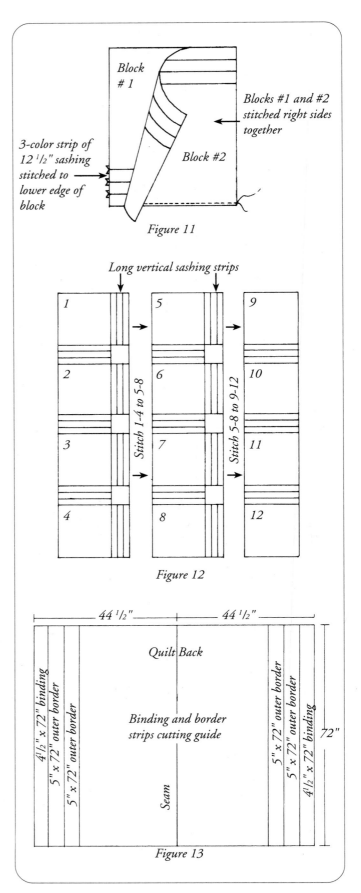

Figure 11

Figure 12

Figure 13

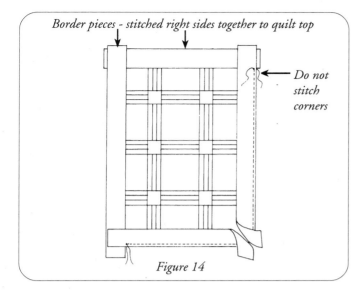

Border pieces - stitched right sides together to quilt top

Do not stitch corners

Figure 14

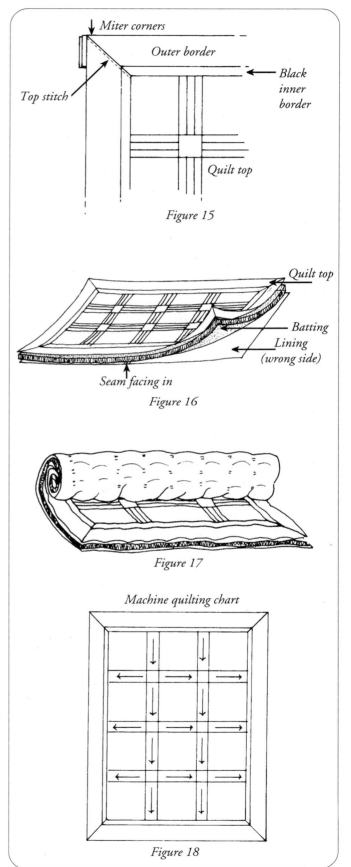

Miter corners

Outer border

Top stitch

Black inner border

Quilt top

Figure 15

Quilt top

Batting

Lining (wrong side)

Seam facing in

Figure 16

Figure 17

Machine quilting chart

Figure 18

IV. Outer Border

1. Place the border pieces along the outside edges of the quilt top, right sides together, allowing the pieces to extend above and below the quilt by 6". Stitch in place. Do not stitch the border pieces together at the corners (**fig. 14**).

2. Finish all four corners of the quilt using the fold back miter technique, allowing a slight overlap (**fig. 15**). Starch and press well. Stitch together with a topstitch along the folded edge. This completes the quilt top.

V. Assembling the Quilt

1. Layer the following on a large table: backing (right side to the table),batting, quilt top (right side up) (**fig. 16**). Note: The seam in the quilt back should fall in the center of the quilt top. Trim away the excess quilt backing from all sides. Secure all layers together, with safety pins or quilt tacks. As you pin the pieces together, make sure all wrinkles and folds are removed in the quilt and batting sandwich. The more pins or tacks used, the easier it will be to keep the pieces from slipping during quilting.

2. Roll the pinned quilt top and batting sandwich into a tube (**fig. 17**). When you start quilting, a great deal of bulk will be sent through the machine. Stitch distortion will occur if the quilt is pushed or pulled while being stitched. Using a walking foot or even feed foot for stitching is recommended.

3. The quilt featured in this program guide was simply quilted using a straight stitch (approximately 3 in length) and stitching in the ditch along the stitched lines of the sashing and blocks. In order to determine what stitch length works best on your machine, use scraps of the fabric, batting and fabric, make a batting sandwich and test stitch your machine length.

4. Follow the machine quilting chart for the direction and sequence of the stitching. Unroll the quilt as needed for stitching (**fig. 18**).

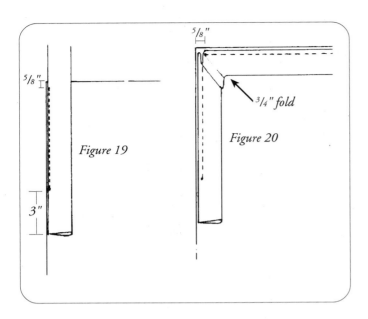

Figure 19

Figure 20

⁵/₈"

³/₄" fold

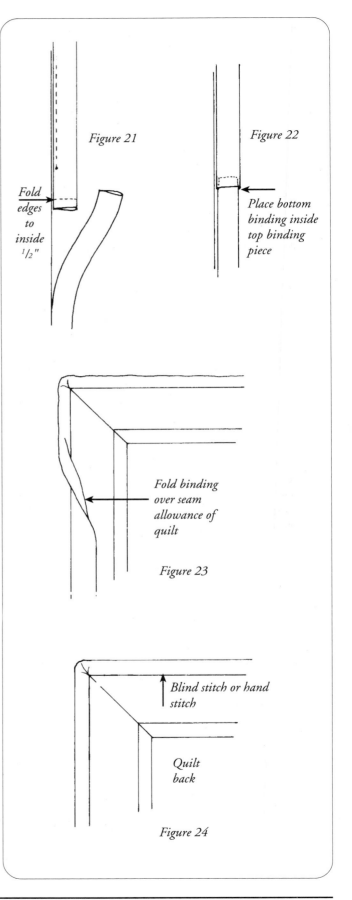

Figure 21

Figure 22

Fold edges to inside ¹/₂"

Place bottom binding inside top binding piece

Fold binding over seam allowance of quilt

Figure 23

Blind stitch or hand stitch

Quilt back

Figure 24

IV. Binding

1. Stitch the binding pieces together to form one long strip. Fold the binding in half so that the long piece measures 2¹/₄" in width. Press.

2. Place the cut edges of the binding to the edges of the quilt starting in the middle of any side. Pin in place. Start stitching 3" from the end of the binding with a ⁵/₈" seam. Stop stitching ⁵/₈" from the corner (**fig. 19**).

3. Use the following method to miter the corners of the binding. Place a ³/₄" fold in the binding and finger press toward the seam. Pin. Pull the cut edges of the binding to the second side of the quilt. Begin stitching again next to the previous stitching. The stitching will form a corner and the ³/₄" fold will fall at the center point of the corner (**fig. 20**). Continue for all sides and corners.

4. Allow the binding to overlap 1" at the ends. Turn the cut edges of the under piece to the inside ¹/₂" (**fig. 21**). Place the top binding piece inside the bottom binding (**fig. 22**). Stitch in place.

5. Fold the binding over the seam allowance of the quilt. Place the folded edge of the binding just beyond the stitching line along the back side of the quilt folding the miters in place at the corners. Stitch in place with a machine blind stitch or stitch by hand (**fig. 23 and 24**). ✄

Beginning French Sewing Techniques

Lace Straight Edge To Lace Straight Edge

Use this technique when applying: lace insertion to lace insertion; lace insertion to lace beading; lace insertion or lace beading to non-gathered straight edge of lace edging.

1. Spray starch and press each piece.

2. Place the two pieces, side by side, butting them together, but not overlapping. It is not important to match patterns in the lace (**fig. 1**).

3. Begin $^1/_4$ inch or $^3/_8$ inch from the ends of the pieces to be joined. This keeps the ends from digging into the sewing machine (**fig. 2**).

4. Zigzag the two edges together. Zigzag again if spaces are missed.

5. Stitch just widely enough to catch the two headings of the pieces of lace (or embroidery). Laces vary greatly in the widths of the headings. The stitch widths will vary according to the lace heading placement and your preference.

6. Stitch the length as tightly or as loosely as you wish. You don't want a satin-stitch; however, you don't want the dress to fall apart either. Work with your trims and your sewing machine to determine the length and width you want. Suggested stitch width and length:

    Width=2 to 3 — I prefer 2$^1/_2$
    Length=1 to 1$^1/_2$ — I prefer 1

Lace Flat Edge To Fabric

Use this technique when applying lace edging to a ruffle or skirt; embroidered insertion to straight edge of lace; lace edging to sleeve edge, as on smocked sleeve or bottom of sleeve with elastic casing; and Swiss edging (with scallops trimmed) to a flat surface or fabric edge, as on ruffles, sleeves, or collars.

Martha's Magic

1. Spray starch and press both the lace and the fabric.

2. Place right sides to right sides.

3. **NOTE:** Leave $^1/_8$ inch to $^1/_4$ inch of fabric edge before placing the lace to be joined (**fig. l**).

4. Zigzag with a satin stitch, going into the heading of the lace and all the way off the fabric edge (**fig. 2**).

5. Suggested stitch length:

    Width=3$^1/_2$ to 4
    Length=$^1/_2$ or as short as possible

NOTE: $^1/_8$ inch to $^1/_4$ inch of the fabric is exposed before the lace flat edge is put into place. The fabric edge will completely fold into the stitch when you are finished.

6. Why shouldn't you just place the edge of the lace and the edges of the fabric together and zigzag? They will come apart. There is not enough strength in the edge of the fabric without the extra $^1/_8$ inch or $^1/_4$ inch folded into the zigzag.

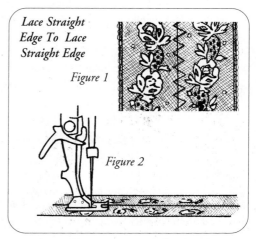

Lace Straight Edge To Lace Straight Edge

Figure 1

Figure 2

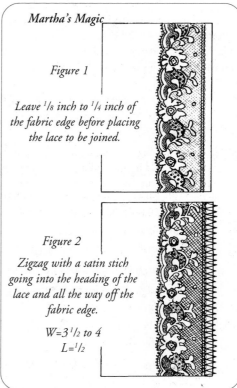

Martha's Magic

Figure 1

Leave $^1/_8$ inch to $^1/_4$ inch of the fabric edge before placing the lace to be joined.

Figure 2

Zigzag with a satin stich going into the heading of the lace and all the way off the fabric edge.

W=3$^1/_2$ to 4
L=$^1/_2$

7. Press the lace and fabric open. A common question is, "Which way do I press this roll?" Press the seam however it wants to lie. Naturally, it will fold toward the lace.

Top Stitching Lace

1. Work from the right side, after the lace has been pressed open.

2. Zigzag on top of the little roll which is on the back of the garment. Your width should be very narrow — just wide enough to go from one side of the roll to the other side. It should not be too short. You want it to be as invisible as possible (**fig. 3**).

3. This zigzag holds the lace down and gives added strength to the seam. Its main purpose, however, is to hold the lace down.

4. Stitch width and length: Width=$\frac{1}{2}$ to $1\frac{1}{2}$, Length=1 to 2

Cutting Fabric From Behind Lace
That Has Been Shaped and Zigzagged

I absolutely love two pairs of Fiskars Scissors for the tricky job of cutting fabric from behind lace that has been shaped and stitched on. The first is Fiskars 9491, blunt tip 5" scissors. They look much like kindergarten scissors because of the blunt tips; however, they are very sharp. They cut fabric away from behind laces with ease. By the way, both of the scissors mentioned in this section are made for either right handed or left handed people.

The second pair that I really love for this task are the Fiskars 9808 curved blade craft scissors. The curved blades are very easy to use when working in tricky, small areas of lace shaping. Fiskars are crafted of permanent stainless steel and are precision ground and hardened for a sharp, long lasting edge.

Repairing Lace Holes Which
You Didn't Mean To Cut!

Trimming fabric away from behind stitched-down lace can be difficult. It is not uncommon to slip, thus cutting a hole in your lace work. How do you repair this lace with the least visible repair? It is really quite simple.

1. Look at the pattern in the lace where you have cut the hole. Is it in a flower, in a dot series, or in the netting part of the lace (**fig. 1**)?

2. After you identify the pattern where the hole was cut, cut another piece of lace $\frac{1}{4}$ inch longer than each side of the hole in the lace.

3. On the bottom side of the lace in the garment, place the lace patch (**fig. 2**).

4. Match the design of the patch with the design of the lace around the hole where it was cut.

5. Zigzag around the cut edges of the lace hole, trying to catch the edges of the hole in your zigzag (**fig 3**).

6. Now, you have a patched and zigzagged pattern.

7. Trim away the leftover ends underneath the lace you have just patched (**fig. 3**).

8. And don't worry about a piece of patched lace. My grandmother used to say, "Don't worry about that. You'll never notice it on a galloping horse."

Piecing Lace Not Long Enough
For Your Needs

From my sewing experience, sometimes you will need a longer piece of lace than you have. Perhaps you cut the lace incorrectly or bought less than you needed and had to go back for more. Whatever the reason, if you need to make a lace strip longer, it is easy to do.

Top Stitching Lace

Figure 3

This top stiching is used to keep the lace from flipping toward the fabric when the fabric is gathered into a ruffle.

Cutting Fabric

Fiskars 9491 blunt tip

Fiskars 9808 curved blade

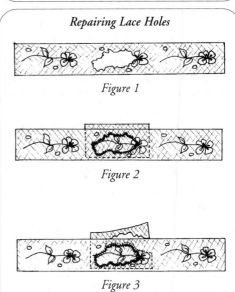

Repairing Lace Holes

Figure 1

Figure 2

Figure 3

1. Match your pattern with two strips that will be joined later (**figs. 1 and 3**).

2. Is your pattern a definite flower? Is it a definite diamond or some other pattern that is relatively large?

3. If you have a definite design in the pattern, you can join pieces by zigzagging around that design and then down through the heading of the lace (**fig. 2**).

4. If your pattern is tiny, you can zigzag at an angle joining the two pieces (**fig. 2**). Trim away excess laces close to the zigzagged seam (**fig. 4**).

5. Forget that you have patched laces and complete the dress. If you discover that the lace is too short before you begin stitching, you can plan to place the pieced section in an inconspicuous place.

6. If you were already into making the garment when you discovered the short lace, simply join the laces and continue stitching as if nothing had happened.

If Your Fancy Band Is Too Short

Not to worry; cut down the width of your skirt. Always make your skirt adapt to your lace shapes, not the lace shapes to your skirt.

Making Diamonds, Hearts, Tear-Drops, Or Circles Fit Skirt Bottom

How do you make sure that you engineer your diamonds, hearts, teardrops, or circles to exactly fit the width skirt that you are planning? The good news is that you don't. Make your shapes any size that you want. Stitch them onto your skirt, front and back, and cut away the excess skirt width. Or, you can stitch up one side seam, and zigzag your shapes onto the skirt, and cut away the excess on the other side before you make your other side seam.

Ribbon To Lace Insertion

This is tricky! Lace has give and ribbon doesn't. After much practice, I have decided that for long bands of lace to ribbon, as in a skirt, it is better to place the lace on top of the ribbon and straight-stitch (Length 2 to $2^{1}/_{2}$). For short strips of lace to ribbon, it is perfectly OK to butt together and zigzag.

Directions for Straight-Stitch Attachment (**fig. 1**):

1. Press and starch your ribbon and lace.

2. Place the heading of the insertion just over the heading of the ribbon and straight-stitch (Length=2 to $2^{1}/_{2}$).

Directions for Zigzag-Stitch Attachment (**fig. 2**):

1. Press and starch your ribbon and lace.

2. Place the two side by side and zigzag (Width=$1^{1}/_{2}$ to $2^{1}/_{2}$, Length 1-2).

Flat Lace To Entredeux

1. Trim one batiste side of the entredeux.

2. Spray starch and press entredeux and lace.

3. Lay trimmed edge of entredeux beside the flat side of the lace. These should be right sides up. Butt them together; they should not overlap. In other words, zigzag, side by side, right sides up.

4. Zigzag them together, trying to make one stitch of the machine go into one hole of the entredeux and over, just catching the heading of the lace (**figs. l and 2**).

5. Suggested Width=$2^{1}/_{2}$ to $3^{1}/_{2}$, Length=$2^{1}/_{2}$

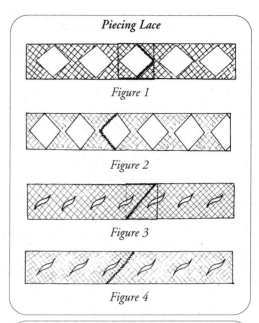

Piecing Lace

Figure 1

Figure 2

Figure 3

Figure 4

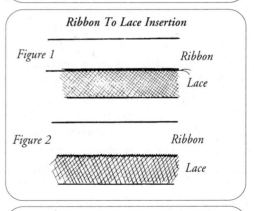

Center of Skirt

Leave Seam Allowance

Cut Off Excess Fabric

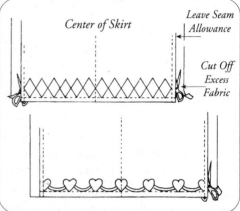

Ribbon To Lace Insertion

Figure 1   *Ribbon*

Lace

Figure 2   *Ribbon*

Lace

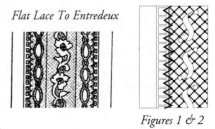

Flat Lace To Entredeux

Figures 1 & 2

Entredeux To Flat Fabric

Stitch-In-The-Ditch

1. Do not trim entredeux.

2. Spray starch and press fabric and entredeux.

3. Place together batiste edge of untrimmed entredeux and edge of the fabric. (This is similar to the sewing of any two seams of a dress. Place the edges and sew the seam.)

4. Sew in straight, short stitches along the right hand side of the entredeux (the side of the entredeux that is next to the body of the sewing machine.) This is called "stitch-in-the-ditch" because it is just that — you stitch in the ditch of the entredeux (Length= $2^1/_2$) (**fig. 1**).

5. Trim the seam, leaving about a $^1/_8$ inch seam allowance (**fig. 2**).

6. Zigzag a tight stitch (not a satin) to go over the stitch-in-the-ditch and all the way off the edge of the fabric edge. This zigzag will completely encase the fabric left on the entredeux and the straight stitch you just made (Width=$2^1/_2$ to 3, Length=1) (**fig. 3**).

7. Press the zigzagged seam toward the fabric. All of the holes of the entredeux should be showing perfectly.

8. This top stitching is not necessary if you are using entredeux to flat fabric; however, you may choose to make this stitching. When you make the top stitch, zigzag on top of the fabric. As close as possible, zigzag into one hole of the entredeux and into the fabric. Barely catch the fabric in this top zigzag stitch. Adjust your machine length and width to fit each situation (**fig. 4**).

9. My machine width and length: Width=$1^1/_2$ to 2, Length=2

10. You can choose to do top stitching from the back of the fabric. If you work from the back, you can hold the seam down and see a little better. On entredeux to flat fabric, the choice of top stitching from the top or from the bottom is yours.

Entredeux To Gathered Fabric

Method I

1. Press, don't spray starch the fabric.

2. Do not cut off the edges of the entredeux.

3. Run two rows of long gathering stitches on the fabric (Length=4). There are two methods for running these gathering stitches.

    a. Sew the first gathering row $^1/_4$ inch from the edge of the fabric. Sew the second gathering row $^3/_4$ inch from the edge of the fabric (**fig. 1**).

    b. Sew the first gathering row $^1/_4$ inch from the edge of the fabric. Sew the second gathering row $^1/_4$ inch below the first row. This is the more traditional method of running two gathering rows (**fig. 2**).

4. Gather by hand to adjust the gathers to fit the entredeux.

5. Lay right side of the entredeux to right side of the gathered fabric. This reminds me of the days when we put waistbands on very full gathered skirts. This is basic dressmaking.

    a. If you gathered with the first method ($^1/_4$ inch and $^3/_4$ inch gathering rows), place the ditch of the entredeux below the first gathering line. The ditch of the entredeux would be about $^3/_8$ inch from unfinished edge.

    b. If you used the second method ($^1/_4$ inch and $^1/_2$ inch gathering rows), place the entredeux on or a little below the second gathering row.

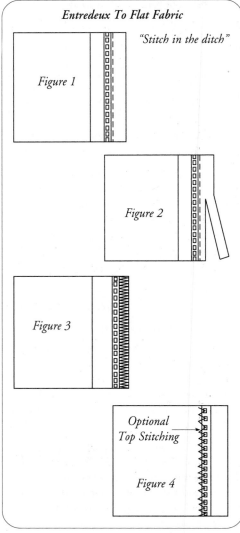

Entredeux To Flat Fabric

"Stitch in the ditch"

Figure 1

Figure 2

Figure 3

Optional Top Stitching

Figure 4

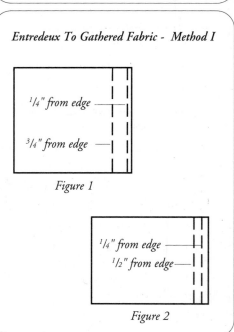

Entredeux To Gathered Fabric - Method I

$^1/_4$" from edge

$^3/_4$" from edge

Figure 1

$^1/_4$" from edge

$^1/_2$" from edge

Figure 2

6. Stitch in the ditch of the entredeux, using a short straight stitch. This stitch is on the right side of the entredeux. This side is closest to the body of the sewing machine (Length=2) (**fig. 3**).

7. Move over just a little and straight stitch the second time. This holds down the gathers under the entredeux (**fig. 4**).

8. Trim away both layers as close to the straight stitch as you can trim (**fig. 5**).

9. Zigzag to finish the process. This zigzag is not a satin stitch but close to a satin stitch. This zigzag stitch encloses the stitch-in-the-ditch seam, the second seam and goes off the side to catch the raw edges (Width=3 Length=$^3/_4$ to 1) (**fig. 6**).

10. Press the satin stitched roll toward the fabric.

11. Top stitch on the wrong side of the fabric. Zigzag into one hole of the entredeux and off into the zigzagged seam. This should be as narrow a seam a possible (Width=$1^1/_2$ to $2^1/_2$, Length=2) (**fig. 7**).

12. This last can be zigzagged from the top also. It is easier to zigzag it from the bottom if it is "entredeux to gathered fabric" because of the bulk of the zigzagged seam. When zigzagging entredeux to flat edge (as given in the section just preceding this one) it seems easier to zigzag the final time from the top.

Method II

1. Follow 1 through 6 of Method 1 (**fig. 1**).

2. Trim to within $^1/_8$ inch of the stitch-in-the-ditch (**fig. 2**).

3. Zigzag, going into one hole of the entredeux and all the way off of the edge of the fabric. This will roll the fabric/entredeux border right into the entredeux (Width=3 to 4, Length=$1^1/_2$) (**fig. 3**).

Serger Fever

Oh what a wonderful tool the serger is for French sewing by machine! I cannot say enough about how this machine has simplified the "Entredeux To Flat Fabric" technique and the "Entredeux To Gathered Fabric" technique. First of all, the serger does three things at once. It stitches in the ditch, zigzags, and trims. Secondly, the serger goes twice as fast as your conventional sewing machine. Probably you can eliminate two sewings and do that one twice as fast. Kathy McMakin has written a how-to book, "French Sewing By Serger." It gives complete instructions and settings on how to do these wonderful French sewing techniques by serger. It is available from Martha Pullen Company.

Another way to use the serger is for French seams. I always did hate those little things. Now, I serge my French seams. I serge in my sleeves! I serge the sleeves in my smocked bishops; you will not believe the improvement in getting bishops through the pleater!

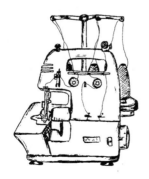

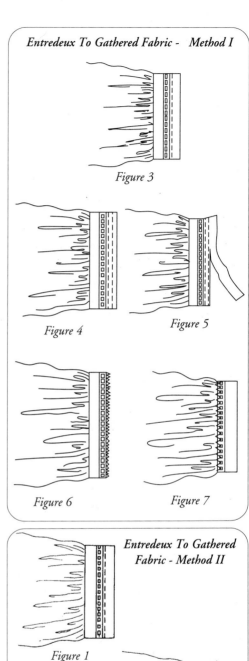

Entredeux To Gathered Fabric - Method I

Figure 3

Figure 4

Figure 5

Figure 6

Figure 7

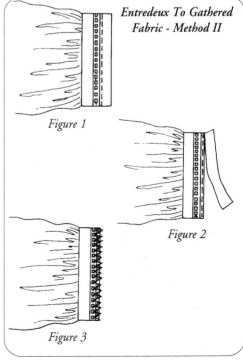

Entredeux To Gathered Fabric - Method II

Figure 1

Figure 2

Figure 3

Holidays And Vacations

It's not uncommon to find a hole in the seam of laces, or between the laces and fabrics that have been joined. This occurs when both pieces of lace do not get sewn together in the zigzag or the laces do not get caught in the lace-to-fabric, zigzagged seam. This is not a mistake. I refer to this as a holiday or vacation. Sometimes we take long vacations (long holes) and sometimes we are only gone for a few hours (very tiny holes). These vacations and holidays are easily fixed by simply starting above the hole and zigzagging over the hole, being careful to catch both sides of lace or fabric to repair the opening. No back-stitching is necessary. Clip the excess threads and no one will ever know about your vacation. ❈

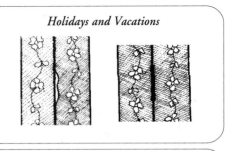

Holidays and Vacations

Plackets

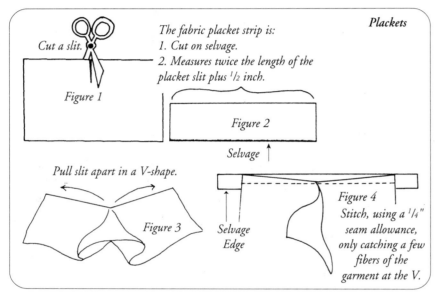

Plackets

Cut a slit.

Figure 1

The fabric placket strip is:
1. Cut on selvage.
2. Measures twice the length of the placket slit plus ¹/₂ inch.

Figure 2

Selvage ↑

Pull slit apart in a V-shape.

Figure 3

Selvage Edge

Figure 4
Stitch, using a ¹/₄" seam allowance, only catching a few fibers of the garment at the V.

Continuous Lap Placket

1. Cut a slit in the garment piece the length needed for the placket (**fig. 1**). Cut a placket strip from the fabric along the selvage ³/₄ inch wide and ¹/₂ inch longer than twice the length of the slit (**fig. 2**). Make the placket, using the following directions

2. Pull the slit apart in a V-shape (**fig. 3**).

3. Place the placket to the slit, right sides together. The slit is on the top and the placket is on the bottom. Note that the raw edge of the placket meets the V in the slit.

4. Stitch, using a ¹/₄ inch seam allowance, only catching a few fibers at the point. The placket strip will be straight. The skirt will form a V (**fig. 4**).

5. Press the seam toward the selvage edge of the placket strip. Fold the selvage edge to the inside (**fig. 5**). Whip by hand (**fig. 6**) or finish by machine, using the following directions.

6. Pin placket in place. From the right side of the fabric, top stitch ON THE PLACKET ¹/₁₆ inch away from the original seam (**fig. 7**).

7. Pulling the placket to the inside of the garment, fold the placket in half, allowing the top edges of the garment to meet (**fig. 8**). Sew a dart, starting ¹/₂ inch up from the outside bottom edge of the placket to the seam (**fig. 9**).

8. Turn back the side of the placket that will be on top when overlapped (**fig. 10**). ❈

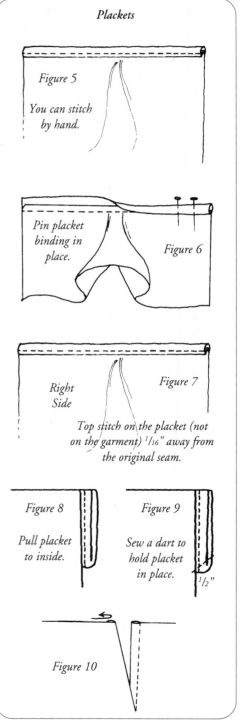

Plackets

Figure 5

You can stitch by hand.

Pin placket binding in place.

Figure 6

Right Side

Figure 7

Top stitch on the placket (not on the garment) ¹/₁₆" away from the original seam.

Figure 8

Pull placket to inside.

Figure 9

Sew a dart to hold placket in place.

¹/₂"

Figure 10

Gathering French Lace

Gathering French Lace

While Applying To Trimmed Entredeux Edge

NOTE: You must have a little extra lace when using this method. It may use more than the pattern requires. This method is easy and time saving. It can be used when attaching gathered lace around a collar that has entredeux at the bottom before the gathered lace. It is especially good when attaching gathered lace around a portrait collar. It is a great way to attach the gathered lace to an entredeux-trimmed neck edge. Actually, you can use this technique anytime you attach gathered lace to trimmed entredeux. It results in fairly even gathers, and saves you from having to pin, distribute, and straighten-out twisted lace.

1. Trim off the outside edge of the entredeux, after the other edge has been attached to the garment.

2. Press both the entredeux and the lace.

3. Side by side, right sides up, begin to zigzag with lace still straight (**fig. 1**).

4. About 6 inches out on the lace, pull one of the gathering threads. I find that using a little pick of some kind is effective. The same little pick that is used to pull a lace gathering thread, can also be used to push the gathers into the sewing machine. A pin will suffice if necessary (**fig. 2**).

5. In order to get the gathers to move in the right direction (toward the foot of the sewing machine), you will need to pull on the side of the thread loop closest to the sewing machine. If you pull on the other side, the gathers will not go toward the sewing machine. Pull the thread, and push the gathers toward the sewing machine (**fig. 2**).

6. Lift your pressure foot, and push a few gathers under it. Zigzag a few stitches (Width=3^1/$_2$, Length=2). You may notice that the width is a little wider than usual for zigzagging lace to entredeux. I have found that with gathered lace, it is necessary to make the width wider in order to catch all of the heading of the gathered lace. As always, you should adjust the width and length, according to the width of your entredeux and your lace heading. They vary so much it is hard to give one exact width and length. Lift your pressure foot again, and push a few more gathers under it. Continue, until all of your gathers on that one section have been stitched in (**fig. 3**).

7. Go out another 6 inches on your lace, and repeat the process. Continue, until all of the lace is gathered and stitched to the trimmed entredeux.

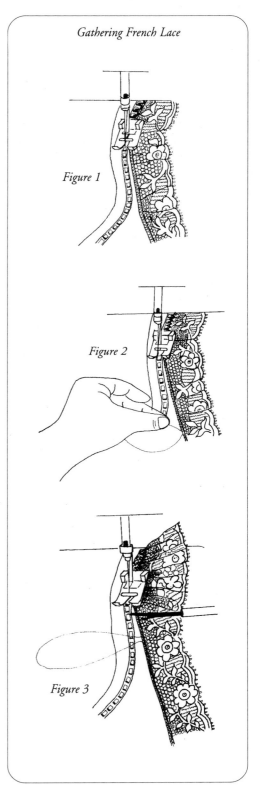

Gathering French Lace

Figure 1

Figure 2

Figure 3

Making An Entredeux And Lace String

The method "Gathering French Lace A Little At A Time, While Applying It To Trimmed Entredeux Edge" is the perfect way to make an entredeux/gathered lace trim for the yoke of a French dress. This is the easy way to trim your yoke with entredeux and gathered lace. The hard way would be to apply your entredeux in the seams of the yokes and the sleeves.

1. Follow the techniques found in the technique "Gathering French Lace By Machine, While Applying It To Trimmed Entredeux Edge."

2. Make the entredeux and lace string as long as you need it to be to travel around the entire yoke (front and back) and over the shoulders of the dress. After making this long strip of entredeux and gathered lace, simply trim the other side of the entredeux (**fig. 1**). Pin into place, around the yoke edges, and zigzag the entredeux and lace string right onto the finished dress (**fig. 2**).

Finishing The Neckline

With Entredeux/Gathered Lace

So many times, French dresses have an entredeux/gathered-lace neckline finish. Here is the technique I use.

1. Check the seam allowance on the neckline of your pattern. This is important.

2. Check the seam allowance on your entredeux. It is usually ¹/₂ inch; however, this is not always the case. Measure the seam allowance of your entredeux.

3. If the seam allowance at the neck of the pattern and the seam allowance of your entredeux do not match, trim the seam allowance of the entredeux to match the seam allowance of the neckline of your garment.

4. Using the techniques "Entredeux to Flat Fabric," attach the entredeux to the neckline of the garment.

5. Stitch in the ditch (**fig. 1**). Trim, leaving a ¹/₈ inch to ¹/₄ inch seam allowance (**fig. 2**).

6. Zigzag the seam allowance to finish (**fig. 3**).

7. Trim the remaining clipped seam allowance. Press the seam toward the body of the dress.

8. Gather the lace edging. Butt it to the trimmed entredeux and zigzag (**fig. 4**). ✳

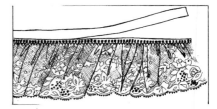

Making An Entredeux And Lace String

Figure 1

Figure 2

Finishing The Neckline

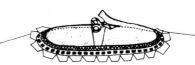

Figure 1

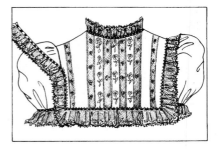

Figure 2

Figure 3

Figure 4

Machine Entredeux

Making Entredeux (Or Hemstitching) On Today's Computer Sewing Machines

About eight years ago I was conned into purchasing a 1905 hemstitching machine for $1500. I was told that it had a perfect stitch and that stitch (about 2 inches) was demonstrated to me by the traveling salesman. I was very happy to finally have one of those wonderful machines. Guess how long that wonderful machine lasted before it broke down? I stitched about 10 inches more which looked great; at that point, the stitching was awful. I called several repairmen. It never made a decent hemstitch again.

The good news to follow this sad story is that today's new computer machines do an excellent job of making hemstitching and they work! I am going to give our favorite settings for our favorite sewing machines. Before you buy a new sewing machine, if you love heirloom sewing, please go try out each of these machines and see if you love these stitches as much as we do.

Using A Stabilizer With Wing Needle Hemstitching Or Pinstitching

Before you do any hemstitching or any decorative work with a wing needle which involves lots of stitching on these wonderful machines, first let me tell you that **you must use a stabilizer**! You can use stitch-n-tear, computer paper, tissue paper (not quite strong enough but o.k. in certain situations), wax paper, physician's examining table paper, typing paper, adding machine paper or almost any other type of paper. When you are doing heavy stitching such as a feather stitch, I recommend that type of paper which physicians spread out over their examining tables. You can get a roll of it at any medical supply place. If you use stitch-n-tear or adding machine paper in feather stitch type stitches, it is difficult to pull away all of the little pieces which remain when you take the paper from the back of the garment. This physician's paper seems to tear away pretty easily.

I do not like the thin, plastic looking, wash away stabilizers for heavy stitching with a wing needle because it doesn't have enough body. There is another type of wash away stabilizer which is absolutely wonderful. It is the paint on, liquid kind. In this country it is called Perfect Sew. You simply paint it on with a paint brush; let it dry, and stitch. You don't have to use any other stabilizer underneath it. It washes out after you have finished your stitching. It is available in this country from Pati Palmer, Palmer/Pletsch Publishing, Perfect Sew, P.O. Box 12046, Portland, OR 97212. 1-800-728-3784.

Make your own wash away stabilizer by using some water in a container and by dropping this wash away plastic looking sheet of stabilizer into the container. Some of the brand names are Solvy™ and Aqua Solve™. Stir with a wooden spoon; keep adding the plastic looking wash away stabilizer sheets until it becomes the consistency of egg whites. Then, paint it on or brush it on with a sponge. Let it dry and then stitch. Both of the liquid, wash out stabilizers make batiste-type fabrics about as stiff as organdy which is wonderful for stitching. After stitching, simply wash the stabilizer away.

Preparing Fabric Before Beginning Hemstitching or Pinstitching

Stiffen fabric with spray starch before lace shaping or decorative stitching with the hemstitches and wing needles. Use a hair dryer to dry the lace before you iron it if you have spray starched it too much. Also, if you wet your fabrics and laces too much with spray starch, place a piece of tissue paper on top of your work, and dry iron it dry. Hemstitching works best on natural fibers such as linen, cotton, cotton batiste, silk or cotton organdy. I don't advise hemstitching a fabric with a high polyester content. Polyester has a memory. If you punch a hole in polyester, it remembers the original positioning of the fibers, and the hole wants to close up.

Threads To Use For Pinstitching Or Hemstitiching

Use all cotton thread, 50, 60, 70, 80 weight. If you have a thread breaking problem, you can also use a high quality polyester thread or a cotton covered polyester thread, like the Coats and Clark for machine lingerie and embroidery. Personally, I like to press needle down on all of the entredeux and pin stitch settings.

Pinstitching Or Point de Paris Stitch With A Sewing Machine

The pin stitch is another lovely "entredeux look" on my favorite machines. It is a little more delicate. Pin stitch looks similar to a ladder with **one of the long sides of the ladder missing**. Imagine the steps being fingers which reach over into the actual lace piece to grab the lace. The side of the ladder, the long side, will be stitched on the fabric right along side of the outside of the heading of the lace. The fingers reach into the lace to grab it. You need to look on all of the pinstitch settings given below and realize that you have to use reverse image on one of the sides of lace so that the fingers will grab into the lace while the straight side goes on the outside of the lace heading.

Settings For Entredeux (Hemstitch) And Pinstitch

Pfaff 7550

Pin Stitch

    -100 wing needle, A - 2 Foot, Needle Down
    -Stitch 112, tension 3, twin needle button, 4.0 width, 3.0 length

Entredeux

    -100 wing needle, A - 2 Foot, Needle Down

	width	length
Stitch #132	3.5	5.0
Stitch #113	4.0	2.0
Stitch #114	3.5	2.5
Stitch #115	3.5	3.0

Bernina

Pinstitch

    - 100 wing needle
    - 1230 stitch #26, SW - 2.5, SL - 2
    - 1530 menu H, pattern #10, SW - 2.5, SL - 2
    - 1630 menu G, Pattern #10, SW - 2.5, SL - 2

Entredeux

    - 100 wing needle
    - 1230 stitch #18, long stitch, SW - 3, SL - 1.5
    - 1530 menu H, pattern #2, long stitch, SW - 3, SL - 1.5
    - 1630 menu G, pattern #5, SW - 3.5, SL - 3

Viking#1+, 1100, 1090

Pinstitch

    - 100 wing needle
    -Stitch D6, width 2.5-3; length 2.5-3

Entredeux

    - 100 wing needle
    -Stitch D7 (width and length are already set in)

Elna 9000 and DIVA

Pinstitch

    - 100 wing needle
    -Stitch #120 (length and width are already set in)

Entredeux

    - 100 wing needle
    -Stitch #121 (length and width are already set)

Singer XL - 100

Pinstitch

    – 100 Wing Needle
    – Screen #3
    – Stitch #7
    – Width 4 (length changes with width)

Entredeux

    – 100 Wing needle
    – Screen #3
    – Stitch #8
    Width 5 (Medium) or 4 (small)

Attaching Shaped Lace

To The Garment With Machine Entredeux Or Pinstitching And A Wing Needle

Probably my favorite place to use the machine entredeux/wing needle hemstitching is to attach shaped laces to a garment. Simply shape your laces in the desired shapes such as hearts, diamonds, ovals, loops, circles, or bows, and stitch the stitch. In addition to stitching this gorgeous decorative stitch, it also attaches the shaped lace to the garment (**fig. 1**). Always use stabilizer when using this type of heavy hemstitching.

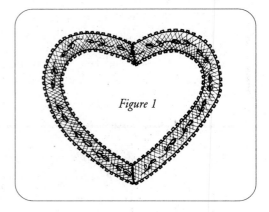

Figure 1

Attaching Two Pieces Of Lace With Machine Entredeux

There is nothing prettier than a garment which has entredeux in between each layer of fabric and lace. That would take a million years to stitch with purchased entredeux, not to mention the cost. Here is how you can use your hemstitch/machine entredeux stitch and wing needle and make your laces look as if they had been joined with entredeux.

1. Butt two pieces of lace insertion together. Since entredeux/hemstitching with a wing needle on your machine needs fabric underneath the stitching to hold the stitches perfectly, you need to put a narrow strip of batiste or other fabric underneath the place where these two laces will be joined.

2. Put a strip of stabilizer underneath the butted laces and the fabric strip.

3. Stitch using a wing needle and your hemstitching stitch. If your machine has an edge joining or edge stitching foot this is a great time to use it. It's little blade guides in between the two pieces of butted lace and makes it easy to stitch straight (**fig. 1**). You can see that the entredeux stitching not only stitches in one of the most beautiful stitches, it also attaches the laces.

4. When you have finished stitching, tear away the stabilizer and turn each side of the lace back to carefully trim away the excess fabric (**fig. 2**).

5. Now it looks as if you have two pieces of lace with purchased entredeux stitched in between them (**fig. 3**).

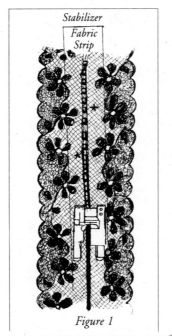

Attaching Two Pieces of Lace With Machine Entredeux

Stabilizer
Fabric Strip

Figure 1

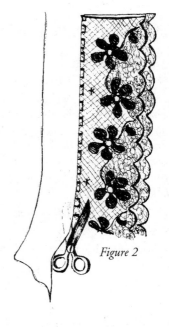

Attaching Two Pieces of Lace With Machine Entredeux

Figure 2

Making Machine Entredeux Embroidery Designs Or Initials

You can take almost any larger, plain embroidery design and stitch the entredeux stitch around it. You may find it necessary to put the design into an embroidery hoop for maximum effectiveness. I have some old handkerchiefs and some old tablecloths which actually look as if hemstitching has made the design. You can place several rows of entredeux stitching together to form a honeycomb effect which might be used to fill in embroidery designs.

Some of the prettiest monograms are those with hemstitching stitched around the letter. Once again, I think the liquid stabilizer and the embroidery hoop will be wonderful assets in doing this kind of wing needle work. Let your imagination be your guide when thinking of new and elegant things to do with these wonderful wing needle/entredeux stitches (**fig. 4**).

One of my favorite things to do with this entredeux stitch or pin stitch is simply to stitch it around cuffs, across yokes, around collars, down the center back or center front of a blouse. It is lovely stitched down both sides of the front placket of a very tailored woman's blouse. Some people love to machine entredeux in black thread on a black garment. The places you put this wing needling are endless. It is just as pretty stitched as a plain stitch as it is when it is used to stitch on laces. ✳

Figure 3

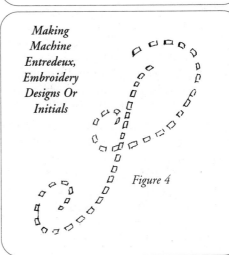

Making Machine Entredeux, Embroidery Designs Or Initials

Figure 4

Puffing Techniques

Gathering The Puffing Over A Quilting Thread Or Dental Floss

This method for making puffing simply rolls and whips the edges of the puffing strip by zigzagging over a quilting thread or dental floss. It has a finished edge which can be butted up to lace and zigzagged together. Although this is a good method for making puffing to curve around in a round portrait collar, I really do not believe that it is the easiest. Please read this method which is Puffing Method One. Then, if your machine has a gathering foot, read Puffing Method Two. Honestly, that is the easiest method. The choice is yours, of course.

1. Cut your puffing strip at least two times the length of the finished round portion of the collar to which it is to be attached.

2. A suggested puffing length is to cut two strips of 45-inch fabric about 2 inches wide.

3. Cut one of them in two pieces. Stitch these pieces to either end of the long strip. You can put in a French seam or serge these seams together (**fig. 1**). You may press the puffing strip but **do not starch.** Starching will affect the gathers of the puffing.

4. This puffing strip will probably be a little long for the collar. I like to have too much puffing and lace when I am working at portrait collars rather than too little. Since I like full puffing, I usually use the whole fullness. If it is fuller than you want, then simply put in the fullness you want and cut off the back at both sides after you have shaped your puffing.

5. Mark the center of this puffing strip before you roll and whip the edge. The two quarter points are already marked with the two side strips (**fig. 2**).

6. Roll and whip the edges using quilting thread or dental floss. To do this, simply place the quilting thread or the dental floss on the very edge of both sides and zigzag it into place. Be careful not to catch the quilting thread or dental floss in the stitching (**fig. 3**). Zigzag the edge of the fabric using approximately a $2^1/_2$ to $3^1/_2$ width and a 1-$1^1/_2$ length. You should zig going into the fabric and zag going all the way off of the fabric. The fabric will roll into a seam as you zigzag. The quilting thread will be rolled into that seam. Later you will use the very strong quilting thread to pull the gathers in your puffing (**fig. 4**).

7. **Note:** After you zigzag the quilting thread or dental floss into both sides of this puffing strip, you will probably see a few fuzzies and it may not look exactly perfect. This is normal because you used a relatively loose length (1-$1^1/_2$) for your zigzag. Using any tighter stitch tends to make the rolling and whipping too tight and makes the gathering of the puffing very difficult. Don't worry, when you zigzag your puffing to your lace, these fuzzies will go away.

8. Some sewing machines have a foot with a little hole in the center of the foot. If yours has this feature, put your quilting thread or dental floss in that little hole and your zigzagging will be perfectly in place and you won't have a chance of zigzagging through the quilting thread in the process of stitching.

9. After you finish your rolling and whipping on both sides, pull the gathering threads on both sides from both ends until it is gathered up to look like puffing (**fig. 4**).

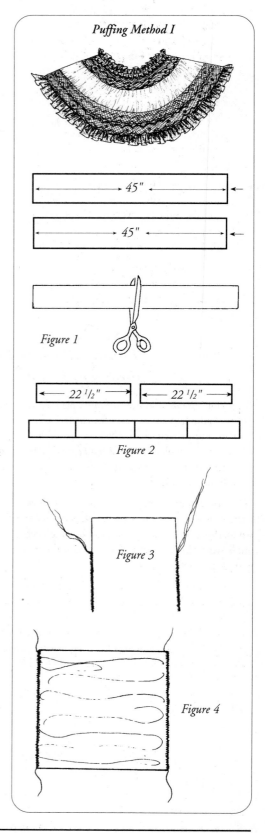

Puffing Method I

45"

45"

Figure 1

22 $^1/_2$"   22 $^1/_2$"

Figure 2

Figure 3

Figure 4

10. Pin the puffing to the fabric board right through the tissue paper that you have already pinned your lace strips to, matching the center front of the collar with the center front of the puffing. Pin by "poking" the pins into your fabric board, on the bottom side of the puffing (**fig. 5**).

11. Keep on playing with the gathers until you have them evenly distributed. Then, pin the top side (the smaller side) of the puffing. You treat the puffing exactly like you treated the laces. Pin the larger side first and then pin the smaller side (**fig. 6**).

12. Press the puffing flat after spray starching it. **Note:** On any garment which will be washed, it is necessary to press the puffing flat because you will have to do this after it is washed anyway. A puffing iron is perfect for this job, depending on how wide the puffing is. I love flat pressed puffing and there really isn't much choice in leaving it unpressed unless it will go into a pillow to put on the bed and not wash for a very long time.

13. Playing with and distributing your gathers carefully usually takes a long time. Don't become impatient. Just keep fiddling with the puffing to be sure you have distributed it carefully. This is a good project to save for evening t.v. watching so you can really make it perfect. After you have pinned your puffing where it looks beautiful, carefully remove the "poked" pins and pin it flat to the tissue paper where the edge of the puffing on the top exactly meets the bottom edge of the lace row above it (**fig. 7**). Width=1½ to 2½: Length=1 to 2

14. You are now ready to take the tissue paper with its rows of lace insertion and rows of puffing over to the sewing machine to zigzag your row of puffing to the top row of lace. Stitch right through the tissue paper. Leave the pins in the puffing after you stitch around the top row because you are now ready to shape the next piece of lace to the collar just exactly like you did the others.

15. Continue adding lace rows to the portrait collar to make it as wide as you wish it to be.

16. If you choose, you can add more puffing rows in between the lace rows to put several puffing rows onto the collar.

Puffing Method II

Gathering The Puffing Using The Gathering Foot On Your Machine

Two years ago, I wouldn't have told you that this was the easiest method of applying puffing into a round portrait collar. The reason being I didn't know how to make perfect puffing using the gathering foot for the sewing machine. I thought you used the edge of the gathering foot to guide the fabric underneath the gathering foot. This left about a ¼ inch seam allowance. It also made the gathers not perfect in some places with little "humps" and unevenness on some portions. Therefore, I wasn't happy with puffing made on the gathering foot. When I asked my friend, Sue Hausman, what might be wrong, she explained to me that to make perfect gathering, you had to move the fabric over so that you would have at least a ½ inch seam allowance. She further explained that there are two sides to the feed dogs; when you use the side of the gathering foot, then the fabric only catches on one side of the feed dogs. It works like magic to move your fabric over and guide it along one of the guide lines on the sewing machine. If your machine doesn't have these lines, simply put a piece of tape down to make a proper guide line.

Making Gathering Foot Puffing

1. The speed of the sewing needs to be consistent. Sew either fast or slow but do not sew fast then slow then fast again. For the beginner, touch the "sew slow" button (if available on your machine). This will help to keep a constant speed.

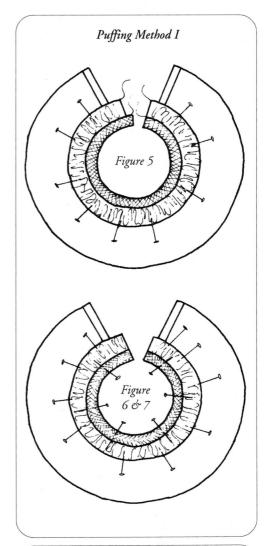

Puffing Method I

Figure 5

Figure 6 & 7

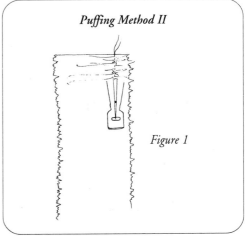

Puffing Method II

Figure 1

2. The puffing strip should be gathered with a ½ seam allowance, with an approximate straight stitch length of 4, right side up (**fig. 1**). Remember that you can adjust your stitch length to make your puffing looser or

fuller. Do not let the strings of the fabric wrap around the foot of the machine. This will cause to fabric to back up behind the foot causing an uneven seam allowance, as well as uneven gathers. Leave the thread tails long in case adjustments are needed. One side of the gathering is now complete (**fig. 2**).

3. Begin gathering the second side of the strip, right side up. This row of gathering will be made from the bottom of the strip to the top of the strip. In other words, bi-directional sewing (first side sewn from the top to the bottom, second side sewn from the bottom to the top) is allowed. Gently unfold the ruffle with the left hand allowing flat fabric to feed under the foot. **Do not** apply any pressure to the fabric (**fig. 3**). The feeding must remain constant. Leave the thread tails long in case adjustments are needed. The puffing strip in now complete.

Placing Machine Gathered Puffing Into A Collar

1. Cut your strips of fabric.

2. Gather both sides of the puffing, running the fabric under the gathering foot. Be sure you have at least a $^1/_2$ inch seam allowance. When you use a gathering foot, the moveability of the puffing isn't as great as when you gather it the other way.

3. You, of course, have two raw edges when you gather puffing with the gathering foot (**fig. 1**).

4. Shape the puffing around the fabric board below the row of lace (or rows of lace) that you have already shaped into the rounded shape. Place the pins into the board through the outside edge of the puffing. Place the pins right into the place where the gathering row runs in the fabric (**fig. 2**).

5. Pull the raw edge of the machine puffed strip up **underneath the finished edge of the curved lace**, so that your zigzagging to attach the puffing will be on the machine gathering line. Put the rounded lace edge on top of the puffing. Pin the bottom edge of the puffing first so you can "arrange" the top fullness underneath the curved lace edge which is already in place (the top piece of lace) (**fig. 2**).

6. It will be necessary to "sort of" arrange the machine gathered puffing, especially on the top edge which will be gathered the fullest on your collar, and pin it where you want it since the machine gathering thread doesn't give too much. After you have pinned and poked the gathering into place where it looks pretty on the top and the bottom, flat pin it to the tissue paper and zigzag the puffing strip to the lace, stitching right on top of the lace.

NOTE: **You will have an unfinished fabric edge underneath the place where you stitched the lace to the puffing.** That is o.k. After you have zigzagged the puffing to the lace, then trim away the excess fabric underneath the lace edge. Be careful, of course, when you trim this excess fabric, not to accidentally cut the lace.

7. If you have a machine entredeux/wing needle option on your sewing machine, you can stitch this beautiful stitch in place of the zigzagging. Since the fabric is gathered underneath the lace, you will have to be very careful stitching to get a pretty stitch.

8. Shape another piece of lace around the bottom of this puffing, bringing the inside piece of curved lace exactly to fit on top of the gathering line in the puffing. Once again, you will have unfinished fabric underneath the place where you will zigzag

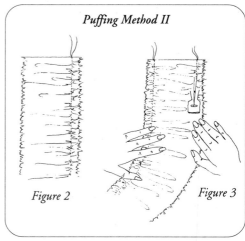

Puffing Method II

Figure 2   Figure 3

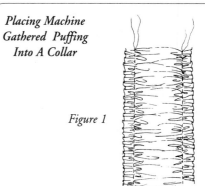

Placing Machine Gathered Puffing Into A Collar

Figure 1

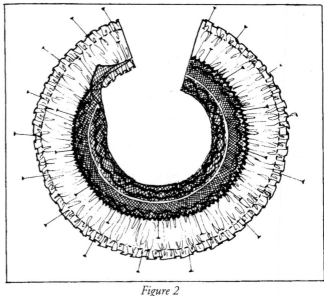

Figure 2

the lace to the puffing collar. After zigzagging the lace to the puffing collar, trim the excess fabric away.

9. Continue curving the rest of the laces to make the collar as wide as you want it to be. ▧

Basic Pintucking

Double Needles

Double needles come in different sizes. The first number on the double needle is the distance between the needles. The second number on the needle is the actual size of the needle. The chart below shows some of the double needle sizes. The size needle that you choose will depend on the weight of the fabric that you are pintucking (**fig. 1**).

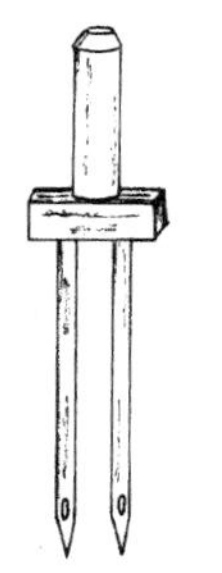

Let me relate a little more information for any of you who haven't used the double needles yet. Some people have said to me, "Martha, I only have a place for one needle in my sewing machine." That is correct and on most sewing machines, you probably still can use a double needle. The double needle has only one stem which goes into the needle slot; the double needles join on a little bar below the needle slot. You use two spools of thread when you thread the double needles. If you don't have two spools of thread of the fine thread which you use for pintucking, then run an extra bobbin and use it as another spool of thread. For most shaped pintucking on heirloom garments, I prefer either the 1.6/70, the 1.6/80 or the 2.0/80 size needle.

Figure 1

Fabric

a. 1.6/70 - Light Weight

b. 1.6/80 - Light Weight

c. 2.0/80 - Light Weight

d. 2.5/80 - Light Weight

e. 3.0/90 - Medium Weight

f. 4.0/100 - Heavy Weight

Pintuck Feet

Pintuck feet are easy to use and they shave hours off pintucking time when you are making straight pintucks. They enable you to space straight pintucks perfectly. I might add here that some people also prefer a pintuck foot when making curved and angled pintucks. I prefer a regular zigzag sewing foot for curved pintucks. Pintuck feet correspond to the needle used with that pintuck foot; the needle used corresponds to the weight of fabric. The bottom of these feet have a certain number of grooves 3, 5, 7, or 9. The width of the groove matches the width between the two needles. When making straight pintucks, use a pintuck foot of your choice. The grooves enable one to make those pintucks as close or as far away as the distance on the foot allows (**fig. 2**).

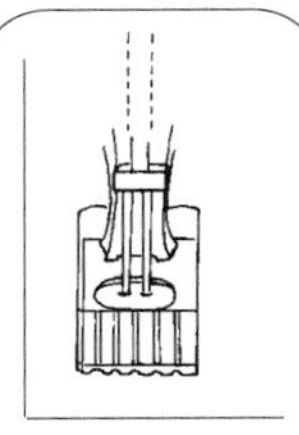

Figure 2

Preparing Fabric For Pintucking

Do I spray starch the fabric before I pintuck it? I usually do not spray starch fabric before pintucking it. Always press all-cotton fabric. A polyester/cotton blend won't need to be pressed unless it is very wrinkled. Tucks tend to lay flatter if you stiffen fabric with spray starch first; that is why I don't advise spray starching the fabric first in most cases. Pintuck a small piece of your chosen fabric with starch and one without starch, then make your own decision.

Straight Pintucking With A Pintuck Foot

Some of my favorite places places for straight pintucks are on high yoke bodices of a dress and along the sleeves. On ladies blouses, straight pintucks are lovely running vertically on the front and back of the blouse, and so slenderizing! One of the prettiest treatments of straight pintucks on ladies blouses is stitching about three to five pintucks right down the center back of the blouse. Tuck a little shaped bow or heart on the center back of the blouse; stitch several tiny pintucks and top them off with a lace shape in the center back. Horizontally placed straight pintucks are lovely running across the back yoke of a tailored blouse. Tucks are always pretty running around the cuff of a blouse. I love pintucks just about anywhere.

1. Put in your double needle. Thread machine with two spools of thread. Thread one spool at a time (including the needle). This will help keep the threads from becoming twisted while stitching the tucks. This would be a good time to look in the guide book, which came with your sewing machine, for directions on using pintuck feet and double needles. Some sewing machines have a special way of threading for use with double needles.

2. The first tuck must be straight. To make this first tuck straight, do one of three things: (**a.**) Pull a thread all the way across the fabric and follow along that pulled line. (**b.**) Using a measuring stick, mark a straight line along the fabric. Stitch on that line. (**c.**) Fold the fabric in half and press that fold. Stitch along that folded line.

3. Place the fabric under the foot for the first tuck and straight stitch the desired length of pintuck. (Length=1 to 2½; Needle position is center) (**fig. 1**).

4. Place your first tuck into one of the grooves in your pintuck foot. The space between each pintuck depends on the placement of the first pintuck (**fig. 2**).

5. Continue pintucking by placing the last pintuck made into a groove in the foot.

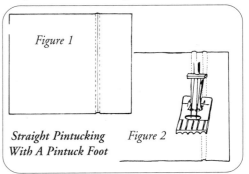

Figure 1

Straight Pintucking With A Pintuck Foot   *Figure 2*

Straight Pintucking Without A Pintuck Foot

1. Use a double needle. Use your regular zigzag foot.

2. Thread your double needles.

3. Draw the first line of pintucking. Pintuck along that line. At this point you can use the edge of your presser foot as a guide (**fig. 3**).

NOTE: You might find a "generic" pintuck foot for your particular brand of machine.

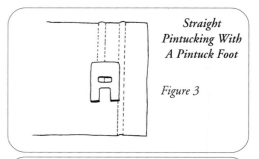

Straight Pintucking With A Pintuck Foot

Figure 3

Properly Tying Off Released Pintucks

A released pintuck is usually used to give fullness to a skirt. It is a perfectly elegant way to add detail to a garment which is easy to do using today's double needles. If you have a pintuck foot, please do use it for this treatment.

Straight pintucks that are made on a piece of fabric, cut out and stitched into the seams garment, do not have to be tied off. Why? When you sew the seam of the garment, the pintucks will be secured within that seam. Released pintucks stop at a designated point in the fabric. They are not caught in a seam and, therefore, have to be tied off. To make the most beautiful released pintuck possible, you must properly tie it off. If you want to take a short cut, then either back stitch on your machine or use the tie off feature that some of the modern machines offer. Please do not use a clear glue sold for tying off seams in sewing. One of my friends had a disastrous experience when making a lovely Susan York pattern featured in *Sew Beautiful* several years ago with over a hundred gorgeous released pintucks. She dabbed a little of this glue product at the end of each pintuck; when she washed and pressed the dress, each place on the Swiss batiste garment where that product had been touched on, turned absolutely brown. The dress with all of the money in Swiss batiste and French laces, had to be thrown away.

Properly tying off released pintucks is a lot of trouble. Remember, you can back stitch and cut the threads close to the fabric. The result isn't as pretty but it surely saves time. The choice, as always, is yours. If you are going to properly tie off those released pintucks, here are the directions.

1. End your stitching at the designated stopping point (**fig. 1**).

2. Pull out a reasonable length of thread before you cut the threads for this pintuck to go to the next pintuck. Five inches should be ample. You can use more or less.

3. Pull the threads to the back of the fabric (**fig. 2**). Tie off each individual pintuck (**fig. 3**).

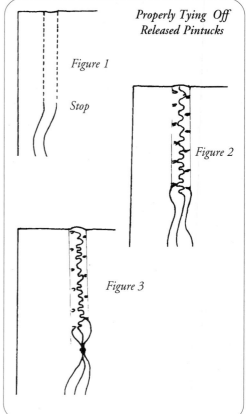

Properly Tying Off Released Pintucks

Figure 1

Stop

Figure 2

Figure 3

Bi-Directional Stitching Of Pintucks

The general consensus, when stitching pintucks, is to stitch down one side and back up the other side instead of stitching pintucks all in the same direction.

To prevent pintucks from being lopsided, stitch down the length of one pintuck, pull your sewing machine threads several inches, and stitch back up in the opposite direction (**fig. 4**).

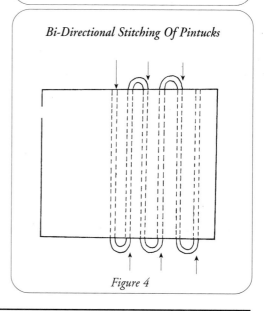

Bi-Directional Stitching Of Pintucks

Figure 4

Making Waffle Pintucks

1. Stitch pintucks all in the same direction to the width you desire.

2. Stitch pintucks in the opposite direction (**fig. 1**).

Cording Pintucks And Raised Pintucks

Cords make pintucks more prominent. Use Mettler gimp or #8 pearl cotton. Cording comes in handy when pintucks are being shaped. When pintucking across a bias with a double needle, you may get some distortion. The cord acts as a filler and will keep the fabric from distorting. Sometimes you might choose to use cording in order to add color to your pintucks. If you asked me, "Martha, do you usually cord pintucks? my answer would be no." However, just because I don't usually cord pintucks, doesn't mean that you won't prefer to cord them.

Some machines have a little device which sits in the base of the machine and sticks up just a little bit. That device tends to make the pintucks stand up a little more for a higher raised effect. Some people really like this feature.

1. If your machine has a hole in the throat plate, run the cord up through that hole and it will be properly placed without another thought (**fig. 2**).

2. If your machine does not have a hole in the throat plate, put the gimp or pearl cotton underneath the fabric, lining it up with the pintuck groove. Once you get the cording lined up under the proper groove, it will follow along for the whole pintuck.

3. You can stitch pintucks without a pintuck foot at all. Some sewing machines have a foot with a little hole right in the middle of the foot underneath the foot. That is a perfectly proper place to place the cord for shadow pintucks. Remember, if you use a regular foot for pintucking, you must use the side of the foot for guiding your next pintuck. ▨

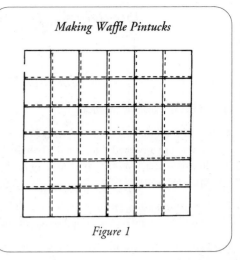

Making Waffle Pintucks

Figure 1

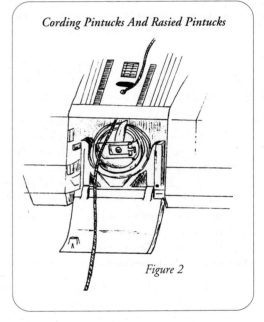

Cording Pintucks And Rasied Pintucks

Figure 2

Pintucking Questions And Answers

Shadow Pintucks

Q. What is a shadow pintuck?

A. Shadow pintucks are pintucks with a touch of color showing through. Some people simply put a colored thread in the bobbin. You might want to try this to see if you like the effect. To properly shadow pintuck, you must use sheer fabric — batiste, organdy, or pastel silk.

1. Using the cording techniques found in this section, choose #8 pearl cotton in a color you would like to peek through the batiste or silk.

2. Pintuck, using thread that matches your batiste in the regular sewing machine hook-up, and colored pearl cotton for the shadow. However, I have seen pintucks with colored thread for the regular sewing machine thread and color for the cording. The choice is certainly yours.

Pintucking On The Sewing Machine

Q. What do I do about puckering when I pintuck straight strips of fabric?

A. There are several things that you can try. Sewing machine pintucks tend to pucker slightly. You can shorten your stitch length. You can pull the fabric from the front and back as you sew. You can lightly starch your fabric before you pintuck. You can loosen your bobbin tension. If you do any or all of these things, you may prevent your fabric from puckering, but you will also change the look of the pintuck. Try various techniques on your particular sewing machine. Actually, I don't mind the tiny puckers. They add texture to the garment and make the pintucks stand out.

Q. Would I ever want to use a cord enclosed in my pintucks?

A. Cords will keep the fabric from puckering so much. They also keep the pintuck from smashing flat when you press it. Some people absolutely love cords in their pintucks. In fact, all of the students I met while teaching in Australia use cords within their pintucks.

Cords are also used decoratively with a darker color of cord under white or ecru batiste. One of the dresses in the first *Sew Beautiful* Sweepstakes, had dark peach cording under ecru batiste pintucks; it was fabulous.

Q. Can pintucks be run any way on your fabric, or do they have to run vertically or parallel with the straight of grain?

A. Pintucks can be run in any direction. Consider scalloped pintucks. The ease or difficulty of making pintucks depends on the fabric you use. When making straight pintucks, I prefer to make them on the straight of the grain, parallel to the selvage.

Q. Are there any fabrics to completely avoid for pintucking?

A. Yes. Dotted Swiss is terrible. Printed fabrics, on which the design has been stamped, does not pintuck well. Resulting pintucks are uneven. Stiff fabrics do not machine pintuck well. You will end up with parallel stitching lines with no fabric pulled up between the stitching lines.

Q. What happens when I put a pintuck in the wrong place or my pintuck is crooked? Can I take it out?

A. Yes. Pintucks are easy to take out. Turn your fabric to the wrong side, and slide your seam ripper underneath the bobbin thread, which looks like a zigzag on the underside. The parallel top-stitching lines will just come right out after you slice the underside stitching.

Q. How do I press pintucks?

A. I prefer to spray starch a series of tucks before pressing it. Don't be afraid to starch and press pintucks. You might want to pin the edges of the pintucked fabric to the ironing board, stretching it out as far as you can. (This is nothing more than blocking your pintucked fabric.) Slide the iron in one direction to make all the pintucks lay in that one direction. Starch and press again. This will take out most of the puckers. Then, remove the pins from the ironing board. Flip over the pintucked piece you have just blocked and pressed, and press again. Not everyone prefers pintucks that lay in the same direction. For a less stringent appearance, lay your pintucked fabric piece face down on a terry cloth towel for the first and last pressing. ✳

Lace Shaping Techniques

Glass Head Pins Are Critical To Lace Shaping!

Purchasing GLASS HEAD PINS is one of the first and most critical steps to lace shaping. **All of this type of work has to be spray starched and pressed right on top of the pins.** Since plastic head pins melt, obviously they won't do. About nine years ago, a dear student came to my school and I hadn't made my self clear enough about the use of glass pins. I thought I had told everybody in no uncertain terms, but apparently I hadn't. After she had shaped a perfectly beautiful round portrait collar, she went to the ironing board to press her curved lace. In a few minutes she called to me with anxiety in her voice and said, "Martha, something is wrong." When I arrived to view the collar, little pink, red, blue, orange, purple, and black circles were embellishing this lovely French lace round collar. I apologized profusely for my not being clear in my instructions; my assistant quickly helped her begin another collar which would be minus those little creative melted points of color.

Metal pins such as the iris pins with the skinny little metal heads won't melt; however, when you pin hundreds of these little pins into cardboard, your finger will have one heck of a hole poked into it. Please purchase glass head pins and throw away your plastic head pins. How many times have I heard the question, "Martha, can you tell which are plastic and which are glass?" Well, I have to answer, "No, I can't until I put an iron to them. Then it is too late!" Get the proper pins, please. I also find that it is easier to get the pins one at a time if you have a wrist pin holder. Years ago when I lived in Charlotte, N.C. I used to sew for hours nearly every day. I went to the local grocery store so many times with my "fine wrist jewelry" in place, that they called me the "pin lady."

Please don't stick your hands into a pin box. More than one time I have brought my hand out with a pin stuck in my finger when I have attempted to do this. If you don't have a wrist holder, then scatter some pins out on your fabric board so you can see where you are picking them up. This might seem a little trite for me to be telling you this; however, you really don't know how many pins you will work with when you begin shaping laces.

Please Read This Before Learning Anything New!

I would like to share with you a life changing philosophy of education that was taught to me by Dr. Bill Purkey, one of my most important mentors, while I was in graduate school at the University of Florida. Since learning to sew is education, perhaps you will enjoy reading this section. He told us that he was going to blow an old American adage (or Australian, New Zealand, English, Canadian, or whatever). Everybody in your life taught you "When something is worth doing, it is worth doing right! or well." I'm telling you that there is no truth at all in that statement. Does that blow your mind? Well, I would like for each person reading this book to think of one thing that you do extremely well! I mean you are really good at this something. Then I would like for you to raise your hand if you did this thing well the very first time you ever did it. Isn't that funny? I bet 99% of you didn't raise your hand, did you? If you will let me rephrase the old American adage to read another way, I think it will make more sense for my life, and possibly for yours. "When something is worth doing, it is worth doing very poorly at first or very awkwardly. Only then, do you ever have a chance of doing it over and over again to make it better and perhaps eventually as

perfect as it can be." Please think of something you really do well and think to yourself how long it took you to learn how to do that thing well. Then, please have patience with yourself and your family when you or they begin something new. I wish every teacher in the world working with children, would tell the class this adage. I think self concepts would be raised and little people would think that their first and awkward work was just the beginning of something wonderful after they practiced.

Drawing Shapes With Dots Rather Than A Solid Line

Margaret Boyles taught me years ago that it is simpler to draw your shapes on fabric by making dots about one half inch apart than it is to draw a solid line. This also means less pencil or marker to get out of the fabric when your lace shaping is finished (**fig. 1**).

Please mark the turn around areas such as the center top and center bottom of the heart in a solid line. Also, make a solid line when marking the insides (bottom and top) of the heart where you will fold back your laces to make your fold back miter. When I am marking diamonds, I also make a solid line at the four angles of the diamonds. I make little dots as I travel around the straight sides. I also make a solid line into the center of the diamonds where I will pin at the top and at the bottom for my fold back miter.

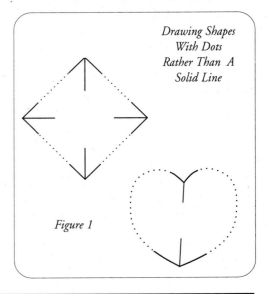

Drawing Shapes With Dots Rather Than A Solid Line

Figure 1

Shish Kabob Sticks For Pushing And Holding Everything

When we teach in Australia we learn so much from the women there who are expert seamstresses. Actually we learn so much from students we teach all over the world. I have always said that learning from my students is the most exciting part of our education no matter where we go. I first learned about using wooden shish kabob sticks from some of the technical school sewing teachers in Australia. By the way, where does one get these wooden shish kabob sticks? At the grocery store! If you can only find the long ones, just break them in half and use the end with the point.

Nearly every woman in Australia uses a wooden shish kabob stick (about 5 or 6 inches long, not the super long ones) to push and to hold with her right hand as the sewing goes into the sewing machine. These sticks are used instead of the usual long pin or worse still, seam ripper that I have used so often. The sticks are wonderful for holding all fabrics, are inexpensive, have no sharp point to damage fabric or sewing machine needles and really are easy to hang on to. I shudder to think what would happen if a sewing machine needle landed on a metal seam ripper as one was sewing one hundred miles per hour.

At several of our sewing seminars, we have handed out the wooden shish kabob sticks and the ladies have loved using them. The idea is that you can have something to hold your fabric or shaped lace on fabric as it feeds through the sewing machine which won't damage anything. Also, it keeps fingers away from the actual needle. Although I have never run a needle through my hand, I have certainly known of others who have done this. Using this stick is a safety technique as well as an efficient technique.

Making A Fabric Board

Fabric boards have become a must for lace shaping or any kind of working-in-the-round in heirloom sewing. They double as portable ironing boards also. At my School of Art Fashion in Huntsville, we make these boards in the double-wide version for collar classes and in the single-wide version for single lace shaping of hearts, diamonds, ovals, loops, and other shapes. Instructions for the double board follow, since it is the most convenient to have. You can also purchase a June Taylor Quilting Board for lace shaping also. We recommend that you make a little "sheet" just like a fitted sheet on your bed if you purchase this type of quilting board for your lace shaping. Since we use so much starch, the little sheet can be removed and washed and not ruin the surface of your quilting board. If you don't want to make this little sheet, then simply use a pillowcase over your June Taylor Board. Cardboard cake boards, covered with one layer of fabric or paper, also work well. You can also use just a sheet of cardboard. Another alternative is to go to any store which has old shipping boxes to throw away and cut the side out of a cardboard box. Cover the cardboard with paper or fabric and use this as your fabric board. One of my favorite lace shaping boards is a child's bulletin board. Another good one is a ceiling tile. Just staple or pin white typing paper or butcher paper over the board before you begin lace shaping.

One thing I don't particularly like in lace shaping is a padded board with a lot of bounce. I think it is easier to get the laces shaped properly without a lot of padding such as quilt batting. The simpler the better is my philosophy. �

Shaping A Lace Scalloped Skirt

I have always loved scalloped skirts. The first one that I ever saw intimidated me so much that I didn't even try to make one for several years after that. The methods which I am presenting to you in this section are so easy that I think you won't be afraid to try making one of my favorite garments. Scalloping lace can be a very simple way to finish the bottom of a smocked dress or can be a very elaborate way to put row after row of lace scallops with curved pintucks in-between those scallops. Plain or very elaborate—this is one of my favorite things in French sewing by machine. Enjoy!

Preparing The Skirt For Lace Scallops

Before I give you the steps below, which is one great way to prepare scallops on a skirt, let me share with you that you can also follow the instructions found under the beginning lace techniques for scallops as well as diamonds, hearts, teardrops or circles. These instructions are that you can use any size scallop that you want to for any width skirt. How do you do that? Stitch or serge up one side seam of your whole skirt.

1. Pull a thread and cut or tear your skirt. I usually put 88 inches in my skirt, two 44-inch widths - one for the front and one for the back. Make the skirt length the proper one for your garment (**fig. 1**).

2. Put in a French seam (or serge) one side seam only. You now have a flat skirt, which is approximately 88 inches wide (**fig. 1**). Probably by now you know that I really don't

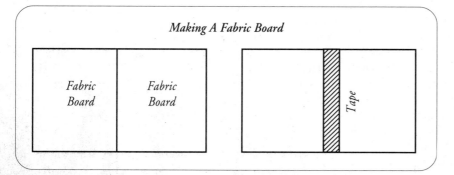

Making A Fabric Board

Fabric Board | Fabric Board

Tape

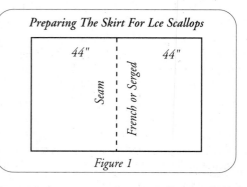

Preparing The Skirt For Lce Scallops

44" | 44"

Seam

French or Serged

Figure 1

make French seams anymore; I use the rolled hem finish on the serger. It is beautiful, strong, and prettier than most French seams.

3. Fold the skirt in half at the seam line (**fig. 2**). Press. Fold it again (**fig. 3**). Press. Fold it again (**fig. 4**). Press. Fold it again (**fig. 5**). Press. When you open up your skirt, you have 16 equal sections (**fig. 6**). This is your guideline for your scallops. Each section is 5¹/₂ inches wide.

4. You can make a template which fits between your folds by using a saucer, a dinner plate, an artist's flexible curve or whatever has a curved edge. Make one template which has only one full sized scallop and the points of two more. Draw a straight line bisecting each top point of the scallop; make this line extend at least 2 inches above and below the point of the scallop (**fig. 7**). Make this template on a piece of paper so you can slip the bottom of the piece of paper along the bottom of the fabric and draw only one scallop at a time. You will slip this template between the folds that you made earlier by folding and pressing. This is the simplest way to get those scallops drawn on the whole skirt.

5. Draw your scallops between these folds or pressed in creases (**fig. 8**). You can place the scallops anywhere on the skirt bottom that you want to place them. For maximum use of the fabric, use the following guidelines for placing the scallops near the bottom of the skirt fabric. The bottom of the scallop (**Line A to B**) is at least 1¹/₂ inches from the bottom of the skirt fabric (**fig. 9**).

6. Draw a line at the top of each scallop, bisecting the top of the scallop, approximately 2 inches tall. On **figure 9** the top of each scallop is **point C**; this 2-inch line extending above the scallop is **point D** (**fig. 9**). These bisecting lines going out of the top of each scallop are very important in the new fold back method of miters which follow.

Placing Your Skirt On The Fabric Board

1. Get a fabric board. This board is approximately 23 inches, which will allow you to work effectively with four scallops at one time. It does not matter how many scallops you work with at one time. The size of your board determines that.

2. Working from the left side of your skirt, place the left side of the skirt on the fabric board, right side up (**fig. 8**). If you are right handed, it is easier to work from left to right. You can also work from the right of the skirt or from the center of the skirt which has been French seamed or serged together.

Pinning The Lace Insertion
To The Skirt Portion On The Fabric Board

1. Cut enough lace insertion to go around all of the scallops on the skirt. Allow at least 16 inches more than you measured. You can later use the excess lace insertion in another area of the dress. If you do not have a piece of insertion this long, remember to piece your laces so that the pieced section will go into the miter at the top of the scallop.

2. Pin the lace insertion to the skirt (one scallop at a time only) by poking pins all the way into the fabric board, through the bottom lace heading and the fabric of the skirt. Notice on (**figure 10**) that the bottom of the lace is straight with the pins poked into the board. The top of the lace is rather "curvy" because it hasn't been shaped to lie flat yet.

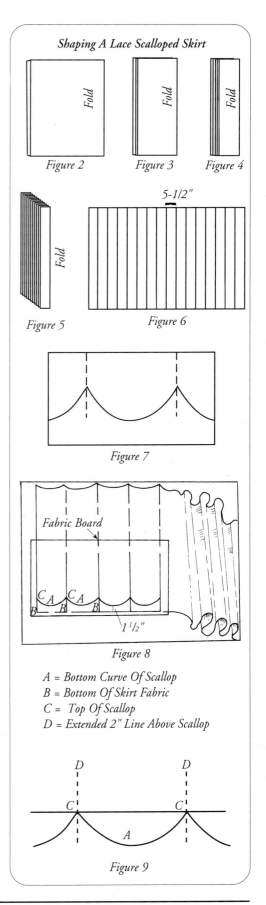

Shaping A Lace Scalloped Skirt

Figure 2   Figure 3   Figure 4

Figure 5   Figure 6

Figure 7

Figure 8

A = Bottom Curve Of Scallop
B = Bottom Of Skirt Fabric
C = Top Of Scallop
D = Extended 2" Line Above Scallop

Figure 9

3. As you take the lace into the top of the first scallop, carefully place a pin into the lace and the board at **points C and D.** Pinning the D point is very important. That is why you drew the line bisecting the top of each scallop (**fig. 10**). Pin the B point at exactly the place where the flat lace crosses the line you drew to bisect the scallop.

4. Fold back the whole piece of lace onto the other side (**fig. 11**). Remove the pin at **C** and repin it to go through both layers of lace. Leave the pin at point **D** just as it is.

5. Then fold over the lace to place the next section of the lace to travel into the next part of the scallop (**fig.12**).

NOTE: If a little bit of that folded point is exposed after you place the lace into the next scallop, just push it underneath the miter until the miter looks perfect (**Fig. 13**). I lovingly call this "mushing" the miter into place.

6. To shape the excess fullness of the top of the scallop, simply pull a gathering thread at the center point of each scallop until the lace becomes flat and pretty (**fig. 14**).

7. Place a pin in the lace loop you just pulled until you spray starch and press the scallop flat. Remember, it is easier to pull the very top thread of the lace, the one which makes a prominent scallop on the top of the lace. If you break that thread, go in and pull another one. Many laces have as many as 4 or 5 total threads which you can pull. Don't worry about that little pulled thread; when you zigzag the lace to the skirt or entredeux stitch it to the skirt, simply trim away that little pulled thread. The heaviness of the zigzag or the entredeux stitch will secure the lace to the skirt.

8. Spray starch and press each scallop and miter after you finish shaping them.

9. After finishing with the section of scallops you have room for on that one board, pin the laces flat to the skirt and begin another section of your skirt (**fig 15**). You have the choice here of either zigzagging each section of the skirt as you complete it, or waiting until you finish the whole skirt.

10. If you choose to use a decorative stitch on your sewing machine (entredeux stitch with a wing needle) you will need to stitch with some sort of stabilizer underneath the skirt. Stitch 'n Tear is an excellent one. Some use tissue paper, others prefer wax paper or adding machine paper. Actually, the paper you buy at a medical supply store that doctors use for covering their examining tables is great also. As long as you are stitching using a wing needle and heavy decorative stitching, you really need a stabilizer.

11. If you have an entredeux stitch on your sewing machine, you can stitch entredeux at both the top and bottom of this scalloped skirt (**fig. 16**). There are two methods of doing this:

Method Number One

12. After you finish your entredeux/wing needle stitching on both the top and the bottom of the scalloped skirt, trim away the fabric from behind the lace scallop.

13. Carefully trim the fabric from the bottom of the skirt also, leaving just a "hair" of seam allowance (**fig. 17**).

14. You are now ready to zigzag over the folded in miters (**fig. 18**). Use a regular needle for this zigzag.

15. Now zigzag the gathered laces to the bottom of this machine created entredeux.

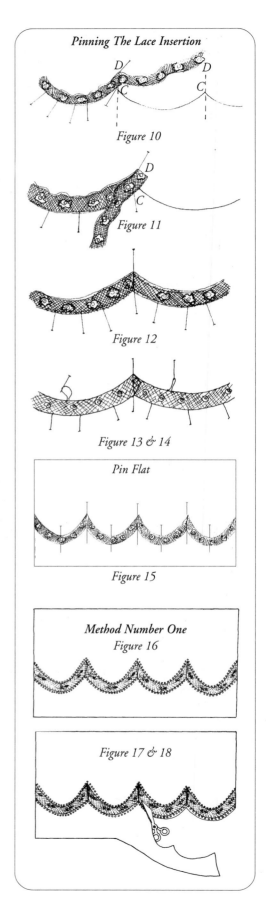

Pinning The Lace Insertion

Figure 10

Figure 11

Figure 12

Figure 13 & 14

Pin Flat

Figure 15

Method Number One
Figure 16

Figure 17 & 18

Method Number Two

12. Machine entredeux the top only of the scallop (**fig. 19a**). Don't cut anything away.

13. Butt your gathered lace edging, a few inches at a time, to the shaped bottom of the lace scallop. Machine entredeux stitch in between the flat scalloped lace and the gathered edging lace, thus attaching both laces at the same time you are stitching in the machine entredeux (**fig. 19b**). Be sure you put more fullness at the points of the scallop.

14. After the gathered lace edging is completely stitched to the bottom of the skirt with your machine entredeux, cut away the bottom of the skirt fabric as closely to the stitching as possible (**fig. 20**).

15. Zigzag over your folded in miters (**fig. 20a**).

16. If you are going to attach the lace to the fabric with just a plain zigzag stitch, you might try (Width=1¹⁄₂ to 2, Length=1 to 1¹⁄₂). You want the zigzag to be wide enough to completely go over the heading of the laces and short enough to be strong. If you are zigzagging the laces to the skirt, zigzag the **top only** of the lace scallops (**fig. 21**).

17. After you zigzag the top only of this skirt, carefully trim away the bottom portion of the fabric skirt, trimming all the way up to the stitches (**fig. 21**).

18. Now you have a scalloped skirt. Later you might want to add entredeux to the bottom of the scalloped skirt. It is perfectly alright just to add gathered laces to this lace scallop without either entredeux or machine stitched entredeux. Just treat the bottom of this lace scallop as a finished edge; gather your lace edging and zigzag to the bottom of the lace (**fig. 22**).

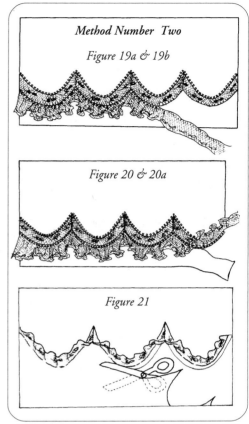

Method Number Two

Figure 19a & 19b

Figure 20 & 20a

Figure 21

Finishing The Center Of The Miter

After Attaching It To The Skirt and Trimming Away
The Fabric From Behind the Scallops

I always zigzag down the center of this folded miter. You can leave the folded lace portion in the miter to make the miter stronger or you can trim away the folded portion after you have zigzagged over the miter center (**fig. 22**).

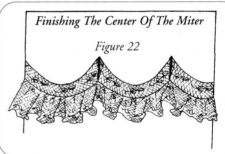

Finishing The Center Of The Miter

Figure 22

Shaping And Stitching Purchased
Entredeux To Scallops

1. Trim off one side of the entredeux completely (**fig. 23**).

2. Slash the other side of the entredeux (**fig. 23**).

3. **You must pin, starch, and press the entredeux before sewing it to the scallops. It won't hang right, otherwise.**

4. Here is a great trick. In order to pin the entredeux into the points of the scallops most effectively, trim entredeux about 1¹⁄₂ inches on either side of the point. This allows you to see exactly where you are placing the entredeux (**fig. 24**).

5. After pinning the entredeux into the points, starch, and press the entredeux into its shape.

6. Remove the pins from the skirt.

7. Zigzag the lace to the entredeux trying to go into one hole and off onto the lace (W=3, L=1¹⁄₂).

8. As you go into the points with the entredeux, simply "smush" the entredeux into the point, stitch over it, and turn the corner (**fig. 25**).

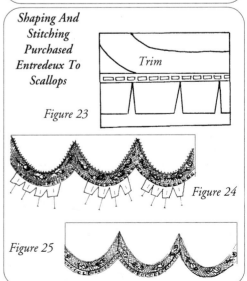

Shaping And Stitching Purchased Entredeux To Scallops

Trim

Figure 23

Figure 24

Figure 25

9. There is an optional method for sewing entredeux on to scallops. Some people prefer to put entredeux on the bottom of a lace shaped skirt by using short pieces of entredeux which go only from top of the curve to top of the next curve (**fig. 26**). Treat it exactly as you did in steps 1-6 in this section. Overlap the trimmed edges in each point. When you attach the gathered laces by zigzagging, these cut points will be zigzagged together.

Adding Gathered Lace To The Entredeux At the Bottom of Scallops

1. Measure around the scalloped skirt to get your measurement for the gathered lace edging you are going to attach to finish the skirt bottom.

2. Double that measurement for a 2-1 fullness. Remember that you can piece your laces if your piece of edging isn't long enough.

3. Cut your lace edging.

4. Using the technique "Sewing Hand-Gathered French Lace To Entredeux Edge," zigzag the gathered lace to the bottom of the entredeux (**fig. 27**).

5. You can also choose to use the method "Gathering French Lace By Machine, While Applying It To Trimmed Entredeux Edge" to attach this lace edging.

Gathering French Laces By Hand

Pull Thread In the Heading of Laces

On the straight sides of French or English cotton laces are several threads called the "heading." These threads serve as pull threads for lace shaping. Some laces have better pull threads than others. Before you begin dramatically-curved lace shaping, check to be sure your chosen lace has a good pull thread. The scallop on the top of most laces is the first pull thread that I pull. Most French and English laces have several good pull threads, so if you break the first one, pull another. If all the threads break, you could probably run a gathering thread in the top of the lace with your sewing machine.

1. Cut a length of lace 2-3 times the finished length to have enough fullness to make a pretty lace ruffle.

2. To gather the lace, pull one of the heavy threads that runs along the straight edge or heading of the lace (**fig. 28**).

3. Adjust gathers evenly before zigzagging.

Sewing Hand-Gathered French Lace To Entredeux Edge

1. Gather lace by hand by pulling the thread in the heading of the lace. I use the scalloped outside thread of the heading first since I think it gathers better than the inside threads. Distribute gathers evenly.

2. Trim the side of the entredeux to which the gathered lace is to be attached. Side by side, right sides up, zigzag the gathered lace to the trimmed entredeux (Width=1½; Length=2) (**fig. 29**).

3. Using a wooden shish kabob stick, push the gathers evenly into the sewing machine as you zigzag. You can also use a pick or long pin of some sort to push the gathers evenly into the sewing machine.

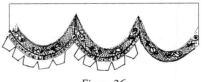

Shaping And Stitching Purchased Entredeux To Scallops

Figure 26

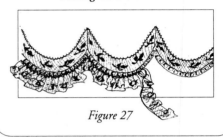

Adding Gathered Lace

Figure 27

Gathering French Laces By Hand

Heading of the lace

Pull thread

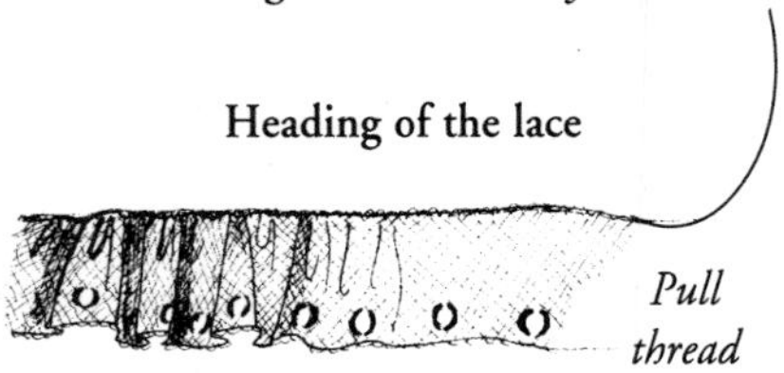

Figure 28

Sewing Hand-Gathered French Lace To Entredeux Edge

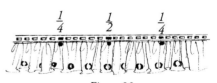

Figure 29

Figure 30

Hint: To help distribute the gathers evenly fold the entredeux in half and half again. Mark these points with a fabric marker. Before the lace is gathered, fold it in half and half again. Mark the folds with a fabric marker. Now gather the lace and match the marks on the entredeux and the marks on the lace (**fig. 30**). ✂

Shaping Lace Diamonds

Making Lace Diamonds

Lace diamonds can be used almost anywhere on heirloom garments. They are especially pretty at the point of a collar, on the skirt of a dress, at angles on the bodice of a garment, or all the way around a collar. The easiest way to make lace diamonds is to work on a fabric board with a diamond guide. You can make your diamonds as large or as small as you desire. I think you are really going to love this easy method of making diamonds with the fold back miter. Now, you don't have to remove those diamonds from the board to have perfect diamonds every time.

Making Lace Diamonds

Materials Needed

♦ Spray starch, iron, pins, fabric board

♦ Lace insertion

♦ Diamond guide

1. Draw the diamond guide or template (**fig. 1**).

2. Tear both skirt pieces. French seam or serge one side only of the skirt.

3. Working from the center seam you just made, draw diamonds all the way around the skirt. This way you can make any sized diamonds you want without worrying if they will fit the skirt perfectly. When you get all the way around both sides of the skirt you will have the same amount of skirt left over on both sides.

4. Simply trim the excess skirt away. Later you will French seam or serge the skirt on the other side to complete your skirt. This is the easy way to make any type of lace shaping on any skirt and it will always fit perfectly (**fig. 2**).

5. The guide or template, which you have just drawn, will be the outside of the diamond. Draw lines going into the diamond, bisecting each angle where the lace will be mitered. This is very important, since one of your critical pins will be placed exactly on this line. These bisecting lines need to be drawn about 2 inches long coming in from the angles of the diamonds (**fig. 3**). If you are making a diamond skirt, it is easier to draw your diamond larger and make your diamond shaping on the inside of the diamond. That way, the outside points of your diamond can touch when you are drawing all of your diamonds on the skirt.

6. As I said earlier, you can shape the laces for diamonds on either the outside or the inside of the template. I actually think it is easier to shape your laces on the inside of the template.

7. Place your skirt with the drawn diamonds on a fabric board.

8. Place the lace flat and guiding it along the inside of the drawn template, put a pin at **point A** and one at **Point B** where the bisecting line goes to the inside (**fig. 4a**). The pin goes through both the lace and the fabric into the fabric board.

9. Guiding the edge of the lace along the drawn template line, place another pin into the fabric board through the lace (and the fabric skirt) at **point C** and another one at **point D** on the bisecting line (**fig. 4b**).

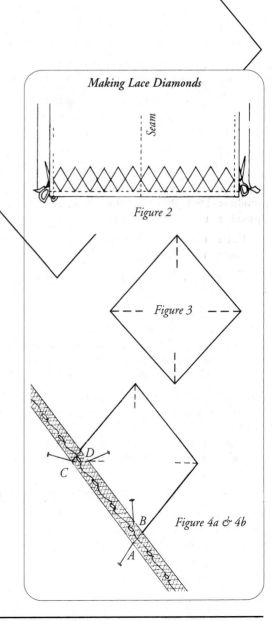

Figure 1

Making Lace Diamonds

Seam

Figure 2

Figure 3

D
C
B
A

Figure 4a & 4b

10. Fold back the lace right on top of itself. Remove the pin from the fabric board at **point D**, replacing it this time to go through both layers of lace rather than just one. Of course, the pin will not only go through both layers of lace but also through the skirt and into fabric board (**fig. 5**).

11. Take the lace piece and bring it around to once again follow the outside line. You magically have a folded miter already in place (**fig. 6**).

12. Guiding further, with the edge of the lace along the inside of the drawn template line, place another pin into the fabric board through the lace at **point E** and another at **point F** on the bisecting line (**fig. 6**).

13. Fold the lace right back on top of itself. Remove the pin at **point F**, replacing it this time to go through both layers of lace rather than just one (**fig. 7**).

14. Take the lace piece and bring it around to once again follow the outside line. You magically have a folded miter already in place (**fig. 8**).

15. Guiding further, with the edge of the lace along the inside of the drawn template line, place another pin into the lace at **point G** and another pin at **point H** on the bisecting line.

16. Fold the lace right back on top of itself. Remove the pin at **point H**, replace it this time to go through both layers of lace rather than just one.

17. Take the lace piece and bring it around to once again follow the outside line. You magically have a folded miter already in place (**fig. 9**).

18. At the bottom of the lace diamond, let the laces cross at the bottom. Remove the pin at **point B** and replace it into the fabric board through both pieces of lace. Remove the pin completely at **point A** (**fig. 10**).

19. Taking the top piece of lace, and leaving in the pin at **point B** only, fold the lace under and back so that it lies on top of the other piece of lace. You now have a folded in miter for the bottom of the lace.

20. Put a pin in, now, at **point B** (**fig. 11**). Of course you are going to have to cut away this long tail of lace. I think the best time to do that is before you begin your final stitching to attach the diamonds to the garment. It is perfectly alright to leave those tails of lace until your final stitching is done and then trim them.

21. You are now ready to spray starch and press the whole diamond shape. After spray starching and pressing the diamonds to the skirt, remove the pins from the fabric board and flat pin the lace shape to the skirt bottom. You are now ready to zigzag the diamond or machine entredeux stitch the diamond to the garments. Suggested zigzag settings are Width=2 to 3, Length=1 to 1¹/₂.

Finishing The Bottom Of The Skirt

These techniques are for finishing the bottom of a Diamond Skirt, a Heart Skirt, a Bow Skirt, or any other lace shaped skirt where the figures travel all the way around the bottom touching each other.

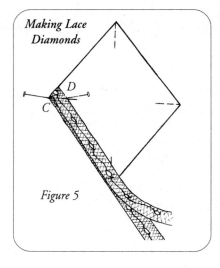

Making Lace Diamonds

Figure 5

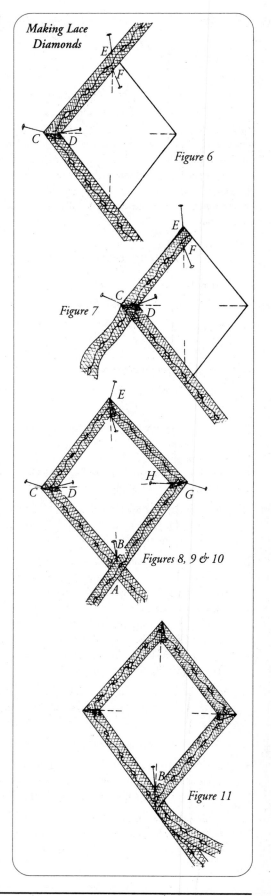

Making Lace Diamonds

Figure 6

Figure 7

Figures 8, 9 & 10

Figure 11

Method One

Using Plain Zigzag To Attach Diamonds (Or Other Shapes) To The Skirt

1. First, zigzag across the top of the diamond pattern, stitching from **point A** to **point B**, again to **point A** and finish the entire skirt (**fig. 12**). Your lace is now attached to the skirt all the way across the skirt on the top. If your fabric and diamonds have been spray starched well, you don't have to use a stabilizer when zigzagging these lace shapes to the fabric. The stitch width will be wide enough to cover the heading of the lace and go off onto the fabric on the other side. The length will be from ¹/₂ to 1, depending on the look that you prefer.

2. Zigzag all of the diamonds on the skirt, on the inside of the diamonds only (**fig. 13**).

3. You are now ready to trim away the fabric of the skirt from behind the diamonds. Trim the fabric carefully from behind the lace shapes. The rest of the skirt fabric will now fall away leaving a diamond shaped bottom of the skirt (**fig. 14**). The lace will also be see through at the top of the diamonds.

4. If you are going to just gather lace and attach it at this point, then gather the lace and zigzag it to the bottom of the lace shapes, being careful to put extra fullness in the points of the diamonds (**fig. 15**). If your lace isn't wide enough to be pretty, then zigzag a couple of pieces of insertion or edging to your edging to make it wider (**fig. 16**).

5. If you are going to put entredeux on the bottom of the shapes before attaching gathered lace to finish it, follow the instructions for attaching entredeux to the bottom of a scalloped skirt given earlier in this lace shaping section. Work with short pieces of entredeux stitching from the inside points of the diamonds to the lower points of the diamonds on the skirt.

Finishing The Bottom Of The Skirt

Method Two

Using A Wing Needle Machine Entredeux Stitch To Attach Diamonds (Or Other Lace Shapes) To The Skirt

1. If you are going to use the wing needle/entredeux stitch on your sewing machine to attach your diamonds or other lace shapes to the skirt, use the entredeux stitch for all attaching of the lace shapes to the skirt. Remember **you must use a stabilizer** when using the entredeux stitch/wing needle on any machine.

2. Place your stabilizer underneath the skirt, behind the shapes to be stitched. You can use small pieces of stabilizer which are placed underneath only a few shapes rather than having to have a long piece of stabilizer. Just be sure that you have stabilizer underneath these lace shapes before you begin your entredeux/wing needle stitching.

3. First, stitch the top side of the diamonds entredeux stitching from point A to point B all the way around the skirt. (**fig. 17**).

4. Secondly, stitch the inside of the diamonds using the entredeux stitch (**fig. 18**). Do not cut any fabric away at this point. Remember to continue using stabilizer for all entredeux/wing needle stitching.

5. You are now ready to gather your lace edging and machine entredeux it to the bottom of the skirt, joining the bottom portions of the diamonds at the same time you attach the gathered lace edging. If your machine has an edge joining or edge stitching foot with a center blade for guiding, this is a great place for using it.

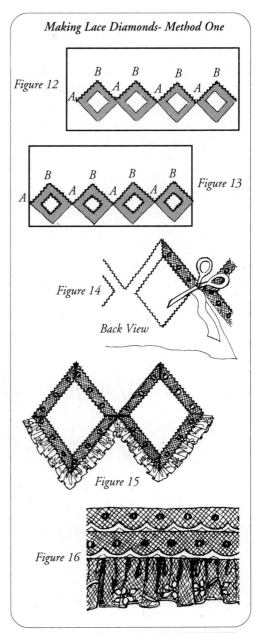

Making Lace Diamonds- Method One

Figure 12

Figure 13

Figure 14

Back View

Figure 15

Figure 16

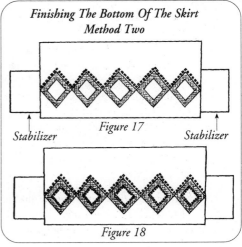

Finishing The Bottom Of The Skirt
Method Two

Stabilizer *Figure 17* *Stabilizer*

Figure 18

6. Gather only a few inches of lace edging at a time. Butt the gathered lace edging to the flat bottom sides of the diamonds.
7. Machine entredeux right between the gathered lace edging and the flat side of the diamond. Remember, you are stitching through your laces (which are butted together, not overlapped), the fabric of the skirt and the stabilizer (**fig. 19**). Put a little extra lace gathered fullness at the upper and lower points of the diamonds.
8. After you have stitched your machine entredeux all the way around the bottom of the skirt, you have attached the gathered lace edging to the bottom of the skirt with your entredeux stitch.
9. Trim the fabric from behind the lace diamonds. Trim the fabric from underneath the gathered lace edging on the bottom of the skirt (**fig. 20**).
10. Either zigzag your folded miters in the angles of the diamonds or simply leave them folded in. I prefer to zigzag them (**fig. 21**). You also have the choice of cutting away the little folded back portions of the miters or leaving them for strength. ✻

Finishing The Bottom Of The Skirt - Method Two

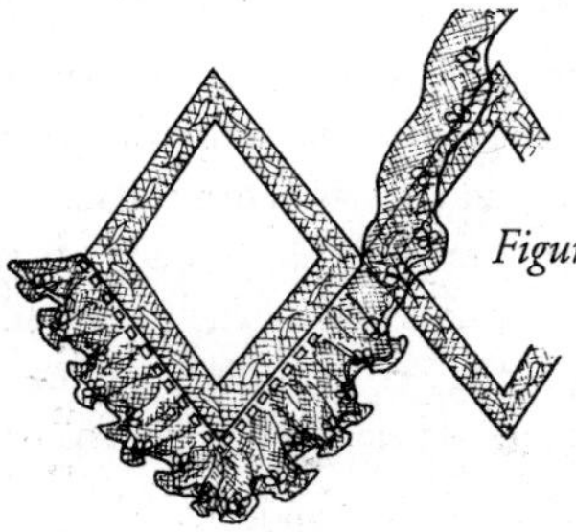

Figure 19

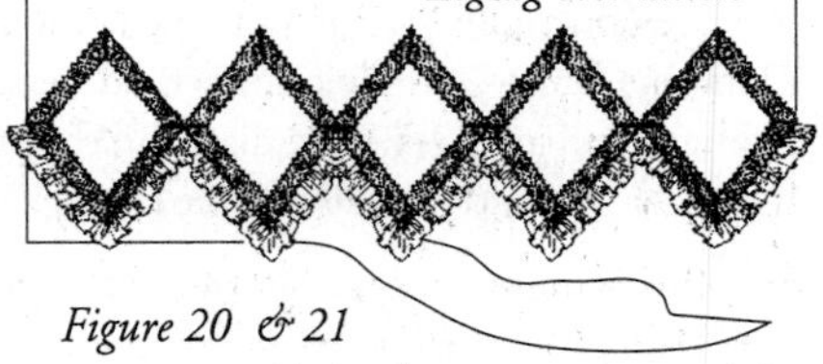

Figure 20 & 21

Shaping Flip-Flopped Lace Bows

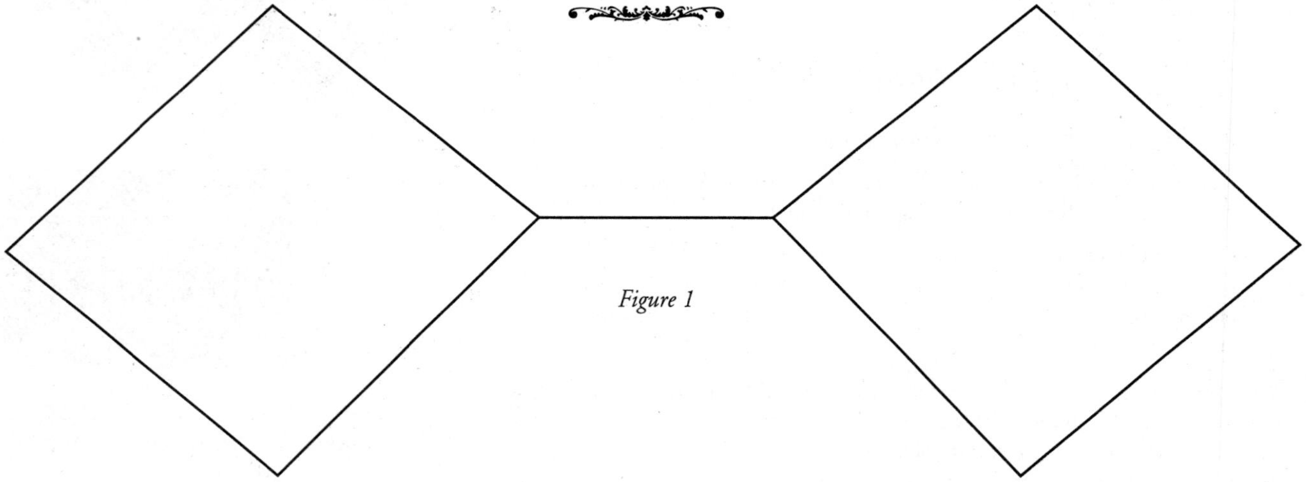

Figure 1

I make lace bows using a technique called "flip-flopping" lace — a relatively unsophisticated name for such a lovely trim. I first saw this technique on an antique teddy I bought at a local antique store. It had the most elegant flip-flopped lace bow. Upon careful examination, I noticed the lace was simply folded over at the corners, then continued down forming the outline of the bow. The corners were somewhat square. Certainly it was easier than mitering or pulling a thread and curving. I found it not only looked easier, it was easier.

Follow the instructions for making a flip-flopped bow, using a bow template. This technique works just as well for lace angles up and down on a skirt. You can flip-flop any angle that traditionally would be mitered. It can be used to go around a square collar, around diamonds, and around any shape with an angle rather than a curve.

Flip-Flopping Lace

1. Trace the template onto the fabric exactly where you want to place bows (**fig. 1**). Remember, the easy way to put bows around a skirt is to fold the fabric to make equal divisions of the skirt. If you want a bow skirt which has bows all the way around, follow the directions for starting at the side to make the bows in the directions given for a diamond skirt.

2. Draw your bows on your garment or on a skirt, where you want this lace shape.

3. Place your garment on your fabric board before you begin making your bow shapes. Beginning above the inside of one bow (**above E**), place the lace along the angle. The template is the inside guide line of the bow (**fig. 2**).

4. At the first angle (**B**), simply fold the lace so that it will follow along the next line (**B-C**) (**fig. 3**). This is called flip flopping the lace.

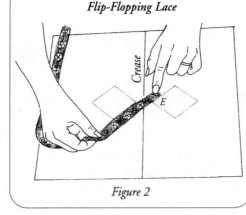

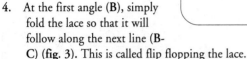

Flip-Flopping Lace

Figure 2

5. Place pins sticking through the lace, the fabric, and into the shaping board. I like to place pins on both the inside edges and the outside edges. Remember to place your pins so that they lie as flat as possible.

6. The lines go as follows: A-B, B-C, C-D, D-A, A-E, E-F, F-G, G-H, H-E. Tuck your lace end under E, which is also where the first raw edge will end (**fig. 4**).

7. Cut a short bow tab of lace that is long enough to go around the whole tie area of the bow (**fig. 4**). This will be the bow tie!

8. Tuck in this lace tab to make the center of the bow (**fig. 5**). Another way to attach this bow tie is to simply fold down a tab at the top and the bottom and place it right on top of the center of the bow. That is actually easier than tucking it under. Since you are going to zigzag all the way around the bow "tie" it really won't matter whether it is tucked in or not.

9. Spray starch and press the bow, that is shaped with the pins still in the board, with its bow tie in place (**fig. 6**). Remove pins from the board and pin the bow flat to the skirt or other garment. You are now ready to attach the shaped bow to the garment.

10. This illustration gives you ideas for making a bow two ways. First, the "A" side of the bow has just the garment fabric peeking through the center of the bow. Second, the "B" side of the bow illustrates what the bow will look like if you put a pintucked strip in the center. Both are beautiful (**fig. 7**).

11. If you prefer the bow to look like side (A), which has the fabric of the garment showing through the middle of the bow, follow these steps for completing the bow. Zigzag around the total outside of the bow. Then, zigzag around the inside portions of both sides of the bow. Finally, zigzag around the finished bow "tie" portion (**fig. 8**). The bows will be attached to the dress.

12. If you prefer the bow to look like side (B), which will have pintucks (or anything else you choose) inside, follow the directions in this section. (These directions are when you have bows on areas other than the bottom of a skirt or sleeve or collar. If you have bows at the bottom of anything, then you have to follow the skirt directions given in the diamond skirt section.)

13. Zigzag the outside only of the bows all the way around. Notice that your bow "tie" will be partially stitched since part of it is on the outside edges.

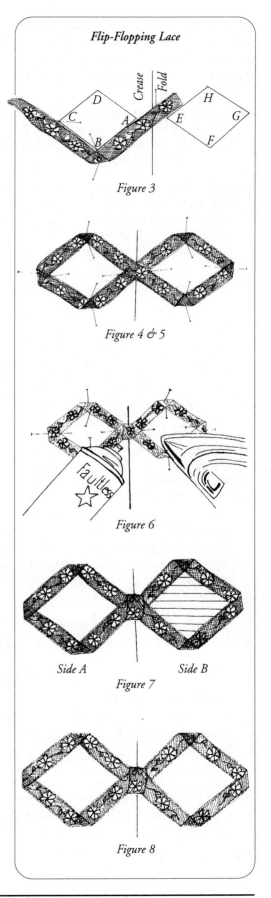

Flip-Flopping Lace

Figure 3

Figure 4 & 5

Figure 6

Side A   *Side B*

Figure 7

Figure 8

14. I suggest pintucking a larger piece of fabric and cutting small sections which are somewhat larger than the insides of the bows (**fig. 9**).

15. Cut away fabric from behind both center sections of the bow. I lovingly tell my students that now they can place their whole fists inside the holes in the centers of this bow.

16. Place the pintucked section behind the center of the lace bows. Zigzag around the inside of the bows, which will now attach the pintucked section. From the back, trim away the excess pintucked section. You now have pintucks in the center of each side of the bow (**fig. 10**).

17. Go back and stitch the sides of the bow "tie" down. After you have zigzagged all the way around your bow "tie," you can trim away excess laces which crossed underneath the tie. This gives the bow tie a little neater look. ❈

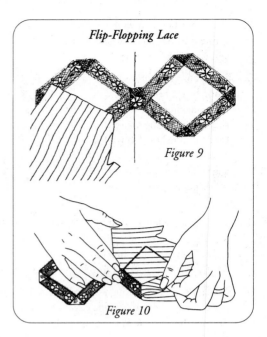

Flip-Flopping Lace

Figure 9

Figure 10

Tied Lace Bows

This method of bow shaping I saw for the first time years ago in Australia. It is beautiful and each bow will be a little different which makes it a very interesting variation of the flip flopped bow. Your options on shaping the bow part of this cute bow are as follows:

1. You can flip flop the bow, or
2. you can curve the bow and pull a string to make it round, or
3. you can flip flop one side and curve the other side. Bows can be made of lace insertion, lace edging, or lace beading. If you make your tied lace bow of lace edging, be sure to put the scalloped side of the lace edging for the outside of the bow and leave the string to pull on the inside.

Tied Lace Bow

Materials Needed

✧ 1 yd. to 1¹/₄ yds. lace insertion, edging or beading for one bow

Directions

1. Tie the lace into a bow, leaving equal streamers on either side of the bow.

2. Using a lace board, shape the bow onto the garment, using either the flip flopped method or the pulled thread curved method.

3. Shape the streamers of the bow using either the flip–flopped method or the pulled thread method.

4. Shape the ends of the streamer into an angle.

5. Zigzag or machine entredeux stitch the shaped bow and streamers to the garment. ❈

Round Portrait Collar

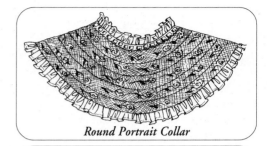

Round Portrait Collar

Round Portrait Collars

Materials Needed

* Sizes 4 and Under: 4 yards of $^1/_2$ " to $^3/_4$" insertion; 2 yards of edging; $1^3/_4$ yards entredeux

* Sizes 5-12: 5 yards of $^1/_2$" to $^3/_4$" insertion; 2 yards of edging; 2 yards entredeux

* Adult: 6 or 7 yards of $^1/_2$" to $^3/_4$" insertion (This will depend on how wide you want to make your collar, of course.); 3 yards of edging; $2^1/_2$ yards entredeux

NOTE: If you are using wider insertion, you need less yardage. If you are using narrow insertion, you need more yardage. You may want your collar wider than the shoulder/sleeve point. Get more lace. And vice versa. There is really no exact lace amount.

* Glass head pins or Iris Super Fine Nickel-Plated Steel Pins.

NOTE: Do not use plastic head pins. They will melt when you press your laces into curves!

* Iron

* Sizing or spray starch

* Make a double-wide fabric board using the directions given earlier in this chapter. You can ask your fabric store to save two empty bolts for you.

* Lightweight threads to match your laces

* A large piece of white tissue paper like you use to wrap gifts

* Scissors

Making A Fabric Board

Use the directions found earlier in this lace-shaping section.

Preparing The Paper Guide

1. Trace your collar guide onto a piece of tissue paper.

2. If your pattern doesn't have a collar guide, you can make one.

3. Cut out the front yoke and the back yoke of your paper pattern (**fig. 1**). Put the shoulder seams of your paper pattern together to form the neckline. Be sure to overlap the seam allowance to get a true seam line at the shoulder (**fig. 2**). Subtract the seam allowance around the neckline. This is the neck guide to use for your paper pattern. Trace the neckline off. Mark the center-back lines, which will be evident from your pattern pieces (**fig. 3**). As you look at **figure 3**, you will see that a large circle is on the outside of this pattern piece. You can draw this large circle on if you want to; however, you only need the neckline shape and the center back. You must draw the center back the length of your collar.

4. Mark the fold-back line. To get your fold-back line, measure the width of the gathered lace that will be used around the bottom of the collar and up the center back on both sides. Take that measurement off of the center-back point and mark the fold-back line (**fig 3**).

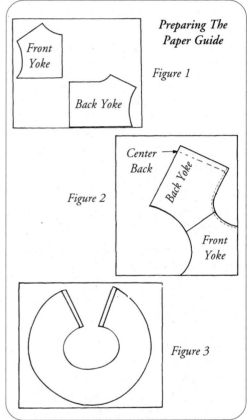

Preparing The Paper Guide

Figure 1

Front Yoke

Back Yoke

Center Back

Back Yoke

Figure 2

Front Yoke

Figure 3

5. You will probably notice that the neckline isn't really round, but oval shaped. That is the true neckline on any pattern, not an exact circle. Use that shaped neckline as your neckline guide.

6. This neckline guide and the center-back line on the pattern are the only lines that you need to shape the circular laces around the collar. You will use the fold-back line after the lace shaping is done to finish the back of the collar. You only use the neckline guide for the first piece of lace. After that, you use the previously-shaped piece of rounded lace as your guide.

— Making The First Two — Rows Of Insertion

1. Shape the neckline row first. Then work from the neckline down to complete the collar width you want.

2. Cut your lace for the neckline or first row of your collar. **NOTE:** Cut extra. You will want to cut your laces longer than the center-back line of the collar you have marked. I suggest at least $3/4$ inch to 1 inch longer than the exact center back.

3. Place the tissue paper guide on the fabric board.

4. Using your fabric board as your work base and your tissue paper collar guide, you are now ready to begin shaping your collar.

5. Pin the outside of the lace so that the inside will touch the neck guide when it is pressed down. The outside lace will have the pins jabbing through the lace and the tissue paper, right into the fabric board. This outside line is not gathered at all. The inside will be wavy. At this point, the inside has no pins in it (**fig. 4**).

6. After you have pinned the outside of the lace onto the fabric board, gently pull the gathering string in the heading of the INSIDE EDGE of the lace. The lace will pull flat (**fig. 5**). Gently distribute the gathers by holding the lace down. Be certain that it is flat on the fabric board. You can pull your gathering rows from both ends. It is now time to put pins on the inside of the first row (**fig. 5**). Jab them into the fabric board. Spray starch lightly and steam.

7. Now that the first row is pretty and flat, you are ready to do the same thing with the second row. Pin the OUTSIDE edge to the board by jabbing the pins, just like you did on the first row. Be sure the inside of the lace touches the first row when you press it down with your fingers (**fig. 6**). After you have gone all the way around with the second row of lace, pull from both ends to gather the inside row, just like you did the first row (**fig. 7**).

8. If you will remove the pins where the two rows butt (and where you will zigzag in a few minutes) and leave pins on the two outside rows, you will find it easier to press them (**fig. 8**).

9. Spray starch the two rows (**fig. 9**). Don't worry if spray starch gets on the tissue paper, because when you spray the two rows, it naturally gets on the tissue paper. It looks a little soggy; however, it will dry nicely with a hair dryer.

10. Using a hair dryer, dry the starch and the tissue paper where the starch made it wet. If you do not dry the paper before you steam the laces, the paper will tear easily. If your tissue paper tears anytime during the process of making this collar, simply put another piece of tissue paper behind the whole collar and stitch through two pieces.

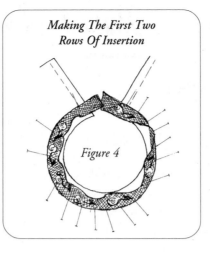

Making The First Two
Rows Of Insertion

Figure 4

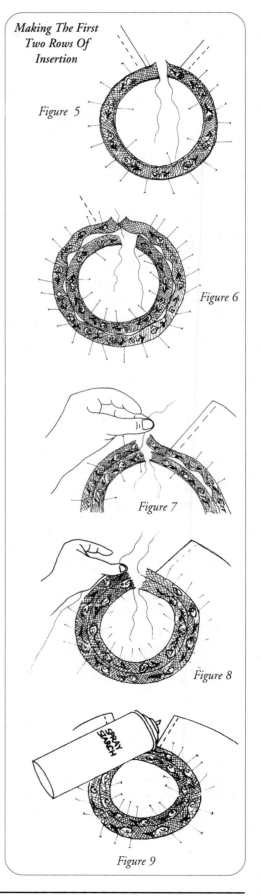

Making The First
Two Rows Of
Insertion

Figure 5

Figure 6

Figure 7

Figure 8

Figure 9

11. After you have dried the starch, press and steam the laces right on the paper (**fig. 10**).

12. Remove the jabbed pins, one at a time, and flat pin the lace to the paper on both rows. Pin with the points toward the neckline. This makes it a lot easier when you stitch your collar, because when the pins are in this position, you can pull them out as you zigzag. If they are pinned the other way, it is difficult to remove the pins as you stitch. Never sew over pins, please! It is easier to remove the pin than it is to replace the needle.

13. (Stitch right through the tissue paper and the lace. Later, you will tear away the tissue paper.) Move to your sewing machine, and zigzag (Width=1$^1/_2$ to 2, Length=1$^1/_2$ to 2) (**fig. 11**). This width and length are just suggestions. Actually, the width and length will depend on the width of the laces and the heading of your particular lace. The stitch length will depend upon your preference. If you like a heavier, closer together look, make your stitch length shorter. If you like a looser, more delicate look, make your stitch length longer.

14. The first two rows should now be zigzagged together.

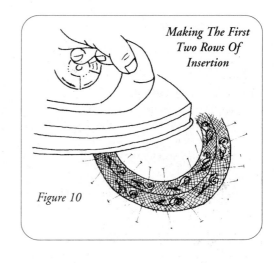

Making The First Two Rows Of Insertion

Figure 10

Making The Rest Of The Rows Of Insertion

— *Making The Rest Of The Rows Of Insertion* —

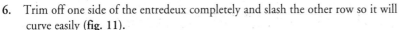

1. Following the directions given for applying the second row, pin, and stitch the rest of the rows that you want to have on your collar. Make the collar as wide as you want it (**fig. 11**).

2. Here is a little trick that I have learned through experience. After you have pinned, pressed, starched, pressed, and zigzagged your first two rows together, the remaining rows can be made on the paper pattern at the same time. You don't have to stitch each row of insertion right after shaping it (**fig. 11**). You might choose to stitch after each row of shaping. The choice is yours.

3. Shape the laces on the rest of the collar by pinning, pressing, starching, pressing, and letting dry (**fig. 11**).

4. After all the lace rows are shaped and the tissue paper is completely dry, pin them flat, remembering to place the pins with the points toward the neckline and the heads away from the neckline (**fig. 11**). Zigzag the laces together.

5. Cut a piece of entredeux with enough length to go completely around the outside row of lace insertion, allowing for plenty of excess. You don't want to run out.

6. Trim off one side of the entredeux completely and slash the other row so it will curve easily (**fig. 11**).

8. Pin the entredeux around the outside row of lace, jabbing pins into the holes of the entredeux about every 2 inches or so. After the entredeux is all the way around the curved lace collar, press, starch, press again, and allow to dry. You can always dry it with a hair dryer if you want to begin stitching immediately (**fig. 11**).

9. Pin the entredeux to the tissue paper at several places. You are now ready to begin stitching the first row of lace insertion that is not already stitched. Remember, if you have chosen to stitch each row of insertion after it was shaped, you might have already stitched all of your laces at this time.

10. Stitch each row, starting with the unstitched one closest to the neckline. Move outward with each row for your stitching. Remove the pins, one at a time, as you are stitching.

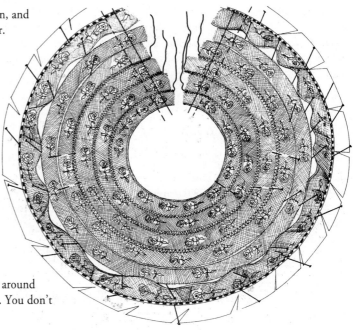

Figure 11

11. With each successive row, carefully remove the pins, and be sure to butt the lace edges exactly as you stitch around the collar.

12. The entredeux to the last row of insertion may or may not be the last row that you will stitch, while the tissue paper is still on the collar. You will have to make a decision concerning whether you want to use Method I or Method II a little later on in the instructions.

Using The Center Back Of The Collar

Check The Fold Back Line

1. The center back of a garment is just that - where the backs meet. This collar will not end at the center back point unless you are not putting laces up the center back of the collar.

2. You can choose to put no laces and no entredeux up the center back. In this case, you will work on the center back line. The best way to finish the back of the collar, if you make this choice, is to serge or overlock the collar just outside of the center-back line (**fig. 1a**). Then fold your serged seam to the back, and straight-stitch it to the collar (**fig. 1b**). That leaves just a finished lace edge as the center back.

3. If you are adding lace edging and entredeux up the back of the collar, you will have to use the fold-back line you made in the beginning on your pattern. Laces don't need to overlap at the center back, but meet instead. Check to be sure that your fold-back line is as wide as your lace edging is from the center-back line on your pattern.

Method I For Adding Entredeux

1. Make a straight row of stitching on the fold-back line. You are still stitching through the tissue paper.

2. Trim away the laces, leaving about $^1/_8$ inch of raw lace edge (**fig. 2a**).

3. Zigzag very tightly (Width=$1^1/_2$, Length=$^1/_2$) to finish the lace edge (**fig. 2b**). You can also serge the back of the collar to finish it.

4. Butt the entredeux to the finished edge (**fig. 3a**) and zigzag, going into the holes of the entredeux and off (**fig. 3b**).

Method II For Adding Entredeux

1. Using the technique "Entredeux To Flat Fabric," attach the entredeux to the back of the collar. Stitch in the ditch (**fig. 1**), trim (**fig. 2**), and zigzag (**fig. 3**).

2. You have two options when finishing this straight line of stitching. Either serge or zigzag along this line. You will make the decision in the next section. For right now, don't trim away any laces along the foldback line; just leave the collar like it is.

3. Trim away the other side of the entredeux. It is now ready for gathered lace to be attached to it. ✳

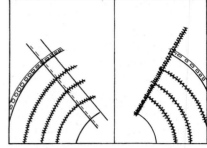

Using The Center Back Of The Collar

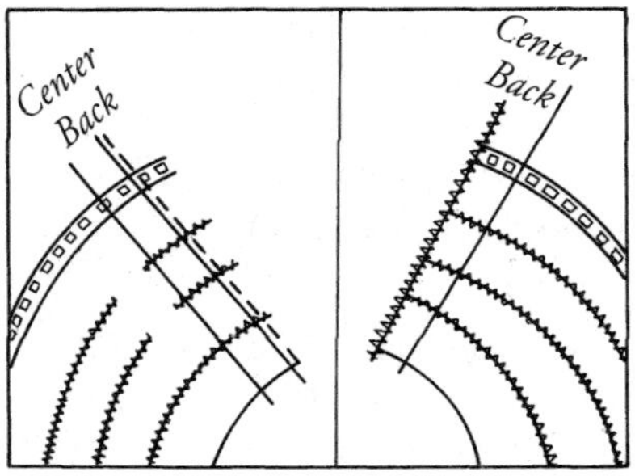

Figure 1b   *Figure 1a*

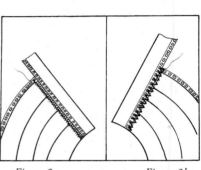

Method I For Adding Entredeux

Figure 2a   *Figure 2b*

Figure 3a   *Figure 3b*

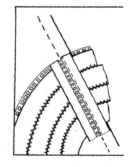

Method II For Adding Entredeux

Figure 1

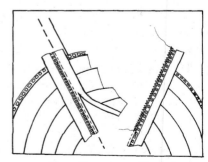

Figure 2   *Figure 3*

Round Lace Portrait Collar

Finishing The Collar
Method I

For Attaching Gathered Lace To Entredeux On The Outside Edge of the Collar With Tissue Paper

Question: When would you use Method I?

For some, this method is the easiest for distributing lace evenly because you can put the quarter points exactly where you want them and control the fullness. If you have a machine which isn't up to par, stitching laces on tissue paper is easier than working without it. So, for some people the method of stitching the gathered lace on while tissue paper is still attached is the easiest.

1. Cut lace edging to be gathered around the bottom and up the back of the collar. Use a $1\frac{1}{2}$ - 1 fullness or a 2 - 1 fullness, depending on the amount of lace desired.

2. After cutting your lace, (allow about 2 inches to turn each back corner and about 10 inches to gather and go up each back of the collar) fold the rest of the lace in half, and mark the center of the lace. Fold once again, and mark the quarter points. This will allow you to distribute the fullness accurately.

3. Pull the gathering thread in the top of the edging. Pin the center of the lace to the center of the entredeux edge of the collar. Pin the quarter points of the lace to the approximate quarter points of the collar. You should have about 12 inches of lace on each end to go around the corner of the collar and to gather it up the back of the collar. After figuring out these measurements, begin to distribute and pin the gathered lace to the bottom of the collar entredeux. Distribute the gathers carefully. Pin all the way around.

4. Stitch the gathered lace (Width=$1\frac{1}{2}$ to 2, Length=$\frac{1}{2}$) to the entredeux, still stitching through the tissue paper. You are only going to stitch around the bottom of the collar. Leave the laces unattached at this point, coming up the center back.

5. Carefully tear away the tissue paper from collar.

6. If you are not going to use a serger, trim away the lace ends $\frac{1}{4}$ inch away from the fold-back line of the collar where you have stay-stitched. This $\frac{1}{4}$ inch gives you a seam allowance to zigzag to finish. If you plan to serge the outside of this line, you do not have to trim away the lace since the serger does this for you.

7. Zigzag tightly over this stay-stitched line (Width=1 to 2, Length=$\frac{1}{2}$).

8. If you have a serger, serge this seam rather than zigzagging over it.

9. If you serged this seam, fold back the serged edge, and straight-stitch it down.

10. If you zigzagged over this seam, use this rolled and whipped edge as the finished edge of this seam.

Finishing The Application

Of Entredeux and Gathered Lace Edging

1. Now that your fold-back line is finished, you are ready to finish gathering the lace edging and zigzag it to the back of the collar.

2. Trim the other side of the entredeux up the back of the collar.

3. Put extra gathers in the lace edging when going around the corner. This will keep it from folding under.

4. After gathering the lace edging, butt the gathered laces to the trimmed entredeux and zigzag to the collar.

5. Fold down the top of the lace edging before completely zigzagging to the top of the collar. That way you have a finished lace edge on the top of the collar.

Method II

For Attaching Gathered Lace To The Entredeux of the Collar Without Tissue Paper

Question: When would you use Method II?

If the tension is good on your sewing machine, use Method II. If you don't mind the laces not being exactly the same gathering all the way around, use Method II. By the way, the laces won't be distributed evenly using Method I either. I haven't found a way to perfectly distribute and gather laces and attach them using any method, including hand sewing! However, Method II is the easiest.

1. Tear away the tissue paper from your collar.

2. Cut the lace edging, which will be gathered around the bottom of the collar and up the back of the collar. You can use a $1\frac{1}{2}$ - 1 fullness or a 2 - 1 fullness. It really depends on how much lace you wish to use.

3. Now that your fold-back line is finished, you are ready to finish gathering the lace edging and zigzag it to the back of the collar.

4. Trim the other side of the entredeux.

5. Using the techniques found in "Gathering French Lace By Machine, While Applying It To Trimmed Entredeux Edge," attach your lace to the bottom of the collar and up the back edges. ❇

Round Portrait Collar Variations

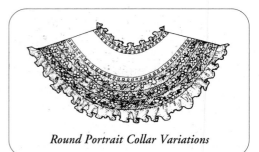

Round Portrait Collar Variations

Adding A Fabric Neckline Piece

Portrait collars are lovely when they start with a fabric circular piece finished with entredeux at the bottom. After your entredeux is attached, then complete the portrait collar exactly as you would if the fabric weren't there. If you are adding a fabric neckline piece, **you must use the actual dress or blouse pattern to make your round portrait collar guide.** If you are making a lace only portrait collar, you can use a general neckline guide since lace can be shaped to go into many shapes. For the fabric neckline, you must make an exact pattern to fit the neckline of the garment.

Materials Needed

Round Portrait Collar Variations

- ∞ Laces and entredeux for portrait collar given in the portrait collar section
- ∞ ¹/₃ yard batiste for adult collar
- ∞ ¹/₄ yard for infant or small child's collar
- ∞ 1 extra yard of entredeux for use at the bottom of the fabric portion of the collar (Optional if you have a machine which makes machine entredeux with a wing needle.)

1. Refer to the directions for Preparing The Paper Guide which tells you how to get your neckline curve for your actual garment. If you are putting in this fabric around the neckline, you must cut an actual pattern by the neckline of the garment to which it will be attached.

2. Be certain when you cut the collar fabric piece that you mark in a seam allowance exactly like the one on the garment neck edge.

3. Cut out a circular neckline piece extending beyond the center back neck edge. You're not going to use this excess, it is only for security in case you want to make the center backs a little wider after you try on the collar! Also, when you zigzag entredeux and laces together, sometimes the fabric shrinks up just a little because of all of that heavy stitching (**fig. 1**).

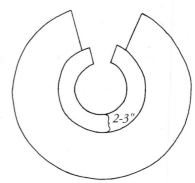

Figure 1

Method I

Purchased Entredeux Added To Bottom Of Fabric Collar

4. Cut enough entredeux to go around this curve with a little excess on either side. Trim one side only of the entredeux. Slash the other side so it will curve around the neckline edge.

5. With the slashed side of the entredeux meeting the cut curved edge of the collar, pin, using the fabric board, the entredeux around the outside edge of this fabric neck line piece (**fig. 2**).

6. Spray starch and press.

7. Using the method, entredeux to flat fabric (stitch in the ditch, trim and zigzag or serge the whole thing with a rolled hem), stitch the entredeux to the outside edge of the curve. You can also serge this curved entredeux onto the collar. I suggest that first, before you serge the entredeux on, you straight stitch in the ditch to be sure that it is perfectly placed. Then, using your rolled hemmer, serge it to the collar.

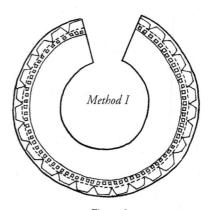

Figure 2

8. Press the entredeux down. You now have completed the fabric circle with the trimmed entredeux already attached. You have a trimmed entredeux edge to shape the laces onto, with the first row of shaped laces which will come next (**fig. 3**).

9. Place this fabric/entredeux piece on the piece of tissue paper which you also drew to match this neckline edge. You are now ready to shape the laces and finish the collar following all directions in the Round Portrait Collar section.

Method II

Stitching The First Row of Laces To The Collar Using Machine Entredeux Stitch And Wing Needle

10. Skip the entredeux altogether. Shape the first row of laces overlapping the raw edge of the fabric portion of the collar by about 1/4 inch; you can choose to overlap more if you want to (**fig. 4**).

11. After pinning and shaping the first row of rounded laces to overlap this fabric collar, stitch a row of machine entredeux stitching at the seam line. Now, it looks as if you have entredeux on your collar and it was so much easier than actually applying entredeux. If you have excess fabric underneath your stitching, simply trim away this excess fabric from your collar after the whole collar is finished (**fig. 5**).

12. To finish the collar, simply follow all directions in the Round Portrait Collar section. ✻

Round Portrait Collar Variations - Method I

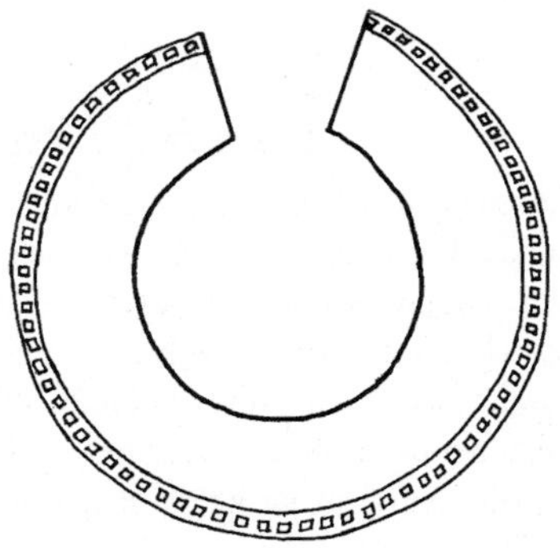

Figure 3

Round Portrait Collar Variations - Method II

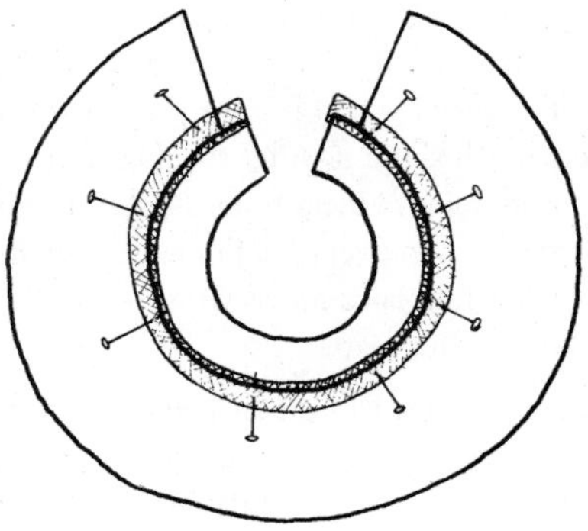

Figure 4

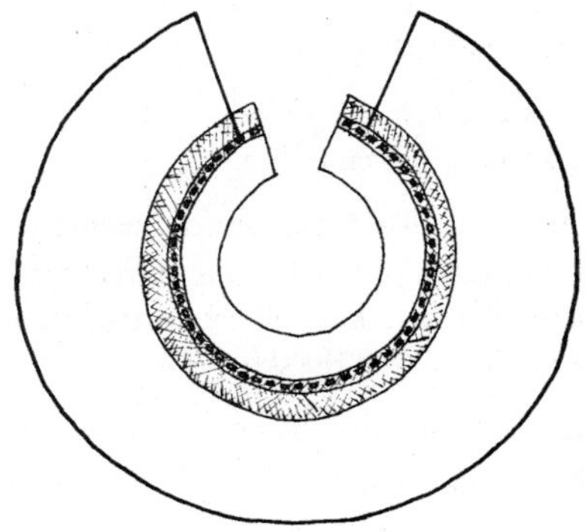

Figure 5

Hearts-Fold-Back Miter Method

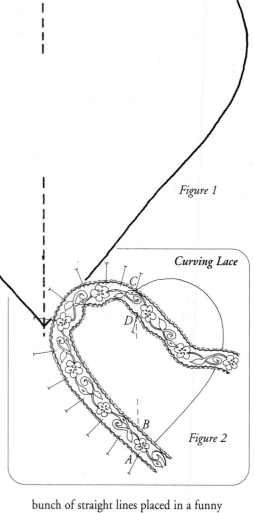

Curving Lace

Since many heirloom sewers are also incurable romantics, it's no wonder hearts are a popular lace shape. Hearts are the ultimate design for a wedding dress, wedding attendants' clothing, or on a ring bearer's pillow. As with the other lace shaping discussed in this chapter, begin with a template when making hearts. When using our heart template, we like to shape our laces inside the heart design. Of course, shaping along the outside of the heart design is permitted also, so do whatever is easiest for you.

With the writing of the *Antique Clothing* book, I thought I had really figured out the easy way to make lace hearts. After four years of teaching heart making, I have totally changed my method of making hearts. This new method is so very easy that I just couldn't wait to tell you about it. After shaping your hearts, you don't even have to remove them from the skirt to finish the heart. What a relief and an improvement! Enjoy the new method of making hearts with the new fold-back miters. It is so easy and you are going to have so much fun making hearts.

1. Draw a template in the shape of a heart. Make this as large or as small as you want. If you want equal hearts around the bottom of a skirt, fold the skirt into equal sections, and design the heart template to fit into one section of the skirt when using your chosen width of lace insertion.

2. Draw on your hearts all the way around the skirt if you are using several hearts. As always, when shaping lace, draw the hearts onto the fabric where you will be stitching the laces.

3. Draw a 2-inch bisecting line at the top into the center and at the bottom of the heart into the center (**fig. 1**).

NOTE: I would like to refresh your memory on lace shaping along the bottom of a skirt at this time. You make your hearts (or whatever else you wish to make) above the skirt while the skirt still has a straight bottom. Later after stitching your hearts (or whatever else) to the skirt, you cut away to make the shaped skirt bottom.

4. Lay the fabric with the hearts drawn on top, on top of the fabric board. As always, pin the lace shaping through the lace, the fabric and into the fabric board.

5. Cut one piece of lace which will be large enough to go all the way around one heart with about 4 inches extra. Before you begin shaping the lace, leave about 2 inches of lace on the outside of the bottom line.

6. Place a pin at **point A**. Beginning at the bottom of the heart, pin the lace on the inside of the heart template. The pins will actually be on the outside of the lace insertion; however, you are shaping your laces on the inside of your drawn heart template.

7. Work around the heart to **point C**, placing pins at ¹/₂-inch intervals. Notice that the outside will be pinned rather tightly and the inside will be curvy. **Note:** One of our math teacher students told me years ago, while I was teaching this lace shaping, a very important fact. She said, "Martha did you know that a curved line is just a

bunch of straight lines placed in a funny way?" She said this as I was trying to explain that it was pretty easy to get the straight lace pinned into a curve. Since I remembered as little about my math classes as possible, I am sure that I didn't know this fact. It makes it a lot easier to explain taking that straight lace and making a curve out of it to know that fact.

8. After finishing pinning around to the center of the heart, place another pin at **point D** (**fig. 2**).

9. Lay the lace back on itself, curving it into the curve that you just pinned (**fig. 3**). Remove the pin from **Point C** and repin it, this time pinning through both layers of lace.

10. Wrap the lace to the other side and begin pinning around the other side of the heart. Where you took the lace back on itself and repinned, there will be a miter which appears just like magic. This is the new fold-back miter which is just as wonderful on hearts as it is on diamonds and scalloped skirts.

11. Pin the second side of the lace just like you pinned the first one. At the bottom of the heart, lay the laces one over the other and put a pin at **point B** (**fig. 4**).

12. It is now time to pull the threads to make the curvy insides of the heart lay flat and become heart shaped. You can pull threads either from the bottom of the heart or threads from the center of each side of the heart. I prefer to pull the threads from the bottom of the heart. Pull the threads and watch the heart lay down flat and pretty. (**fig. 5**). After teaching literally hundreds of students to make hearts, I think it is better to pull the thread from the bottom of the heart. You don't need to help the fullness lay down; simply pull the thread. On other lace shaped curves such as a scalloped skirt, loops, or ovals, you have to pull from the inside curve.

13. Spray starch and press the curves into place.

14. To make your magic miter at the bottom of the heart, remove the pin from **Point A**, fold back the lace so it lays on the other piece of lace, and repin **Point A**. You now have a folded–back miter which completes the easy mitering on the heart (**fig. 6**). You are now ready to pin the hearts flat onto the garment and remove the shaping from the fabric board.

15. You can trim these bottom "tails" of lace away before you attach the heart to the garment or after you attach the heart to the garment. It probably looks better to trim them before you stitch (**fig. 7**).

16. You can attach the hearts just to the fabric or you can choose to put something else such as pintucks inside the hearts. If you have hearts which touch going all the way around a skirt, then follow the directions for zigzagging which were found in the diamond section.

17. If you have one heart on a collar or bodice of a dress, then zigzag the outside first. If you choose to put something on the inside of each heart, cut away the fabric from behind the shape after zigzagging it to the garment. Then, put whatever you want to insert in the heart behind the heart shape and zigzag around the center or inside of the heart. Refer to the directions on inserting pintucks or something else in the center of a lace shape in the flip-flopped bow section.

18. You can certainly use the entredeux/wing needle stitching for a beautiful look for attaching the hearts. Follow the directions for machine entredeux on the lace shaped skirt found in the diamond section of this lace shaping chapter.

19. After you cut away the fabric from behind the hearts, go back and zigzag over each mitered point (**fig. 8**). You then have the choice of either leaving the folded over section or of cutting it away. Personally, I usually leave the section because of the strength it adds to the miters. The choice is yours. ✽

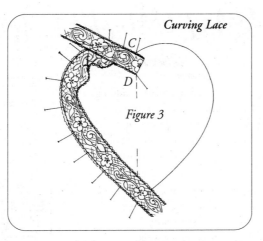

Curving Lace

Figure 3

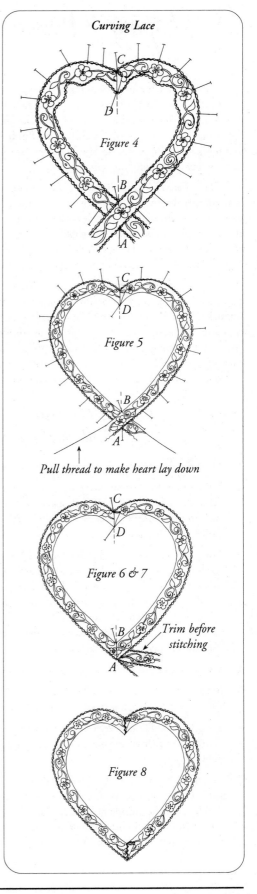

Curving Lace

Figure 4

Figure 5

Pull thread to make heart lay down

Figure 6 & 7

Trim before stitching

Figure 8

Shaping Curves And Angles With Pintucks

Pintucks are inexpensive to make. They add texture and dimension without adding cost to the dress. They're rarely found on store-bought clothing. One of my favorite things in the whole world to do is to follow lace shapes with pintucks or decorative stitches on your machine for an enchanting finish. Or you may simply use your template and pintuck the shape instead of using lace. For threads, use white-on-white, ecru-on-ecru, or any pastel color on white or ecru.

The effect of shaped pintucks is so fabulous and so interesting. Virtually everybody is afraid that she doesn't know how to make those fabulous pintucks thus making a garment into a pintuck fantasy. It is so easy that I just can't wait to share with you the tricks. I promise, nobody in my schools all over the world ever believes me when I tell them this easiest way. Then, everybody, virtually everybody, has done these curved and angled pintucks with absolute perfection. They usually say, "This is really magic!"

The big question here is, "What foot do I use for scalloped pintucks?" For straight pintucks, I use a pintuck foot with the grooves. That foot is fine for curved or scalloped pintucks also, but I prefer either the regular zigzag foot or the clear applique foot, which is plastic and allows easy "see through" of the turning points. Try your pintuck foot, your regular sewing foot, and your clear applique foot to see which one you like the best. Like all aspects of heirloom sewing, the "best" foot is really your personal preference. Listed below are my absolute recommendations for curved and angled pintucks.

Martha's General Rules Of Curving And Angling Pintucks

1. Use a regular zigzag foot, or a pintuck foot (**fig. 1**).

2. Either draw on your pintuck shape, or zigzag your lace insertion to the garment. You can either draw on pintuck shapes or follow your lace shaping. My favorite way to make lots of pintucks is to follow lace shaping which has already been stitched to the garment.

3. Using a ruler, draw straight lines with a fabric marker or washable pencil, bisecting each point where you will have to turn around with your pintuck. In other words, draw a line at all angles where you will have to turn your pintuck in order to keep stitching. This is the most important point to make with curved and angled pintucks. When you are going around curves, this bi-secting line is not necessary since you don't stop and pivot when you are turning curves. Everywhere you have to stop and pivot, these straight lines must be drawn (**fig. 2**).

4. Use a 1.6 or a 2.0 double needle. Any wider doesn't curve or turn well!

5. Set your machine for straight sewing, L=1.5. Notice this is a **very short stitch**. When you turn angles, this short stitch is necessary for pretty turns.

6. Press "Needle Down" on your sewing machine if your machine has this feature. This means that when you stop sewing at any time, your needle will remain in the fabric.

7. Stitch, using either the first line you drew or following around the lace shaping which you have already stitched to your garment. The edge of your presser foot will guide along the outside of the lace shape. When you go around curves, turn your fabric and keep stitching. Do not pick up your foot and pivot, this makes the curves jumpy, not smooth (**fig. 3**).

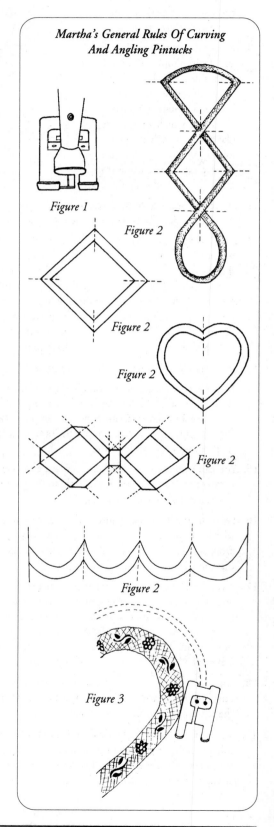

Martha's General Rules Of Curving And Angling Pintucks

Figure 1

Figure 2

Figure 2

Figure 2

Figure 2

Figure 2

Figure 3

8. When you come to a pivot point, let your foot continue to travel until you can look into the hole of the foot, and see that your double needles have **straddled the line you drew on the fabric**. Remember your needles are **in the fabric** (**fig. 4**).

9. Sometimes, the needles won't exactly straddle the line exactly the way they straddled the line on the last turn around. Lift the presser foot. (Remember, you needles are still in the fabric.) Turn your fabric where the edge of the presser foot properly begins in a new direction following your lace insertion lace shaping or your drawn line, lower the presser foot, and begin sewing again (**fig. 5**).

10. Wait A Minute! Most of you are now thinking, "Martha, You Are Crazy. There are two major problems with what you just said. You said to leave the double needles in the fabric, lift the presser foot , turn the fabric, lower the presser foot and begin sewing again. If I do that I will probably break my double needles, and there will be a big wad or hump of fabric where I twisted the fabric to turn around to go in a new direction. That will never work!" I know you are thinking these two things because everybody does. Neither one of these things will happen! It is really just like MAGIC. TRY THIS TECHNIQUE AND SEE WHAT I AM SAYING. Ladies all over the world absolutely adore this method and nobody believes how easy it is.

11. After you get your first row of double needle pintucks, then you can use the edge of your regular zigzag sewing machine foot, guiding along the just stitched pintuck row as the guide point for more rows. The only thing you have to remember, is to have made long enough lines to bisect each angle that you are going to turn. You must have these turn around lines drawn so you can know where to stop sewing, leave the needles in the fabric, turn around, and begin stitching again. These lines are the real key.

Making A Skirt For Curved Pintuck Scallops Or Other Fancy Design

I always like to give the easiest way to do anything. Probably most of you know that by now! To divide any garment piece (skirt, bodice, collar or whatever) into equal parts, fold it in half. This marks the half-way point. Continue to fold in halves until the piece is divided the way you want it. If you are to mark the bottom of a skirt, seam (French seam, flat lock or rolled serger hem) one side seam first so that you can work on the entire skirt (**fig. 1**).

If you want to use this skirt for curved pintucks only, that is great. If you want to use the drawn scallop to make a scalloped piece of lace insertion, then you will guide your regular zigzag sewing machine foot with the double needles along the scalloped lace insertion later for your curved pintucks. Remember, those bisecting straight lines are the most significant part of making pintucks turn around properly at angles.

1. Take your skirt, sleeve, bodice, or pattern part and fold it in half. Press (**fig. 2**).

2. Fold that in half again. Press. If you have a skirt with the front and back already stitched together on one side, you now have it folded in quarters. The seam will be on one side. Press on that seam line.

3. Fold in half again. Press. Your piece is now divided into eighths (**fig. 3**).

4. Repeat this process as many times as necessary for you to have the divisions that you want.

5. Open up your garment part. Use these fold lines as your measuring points and guide points (**fig. 4**).

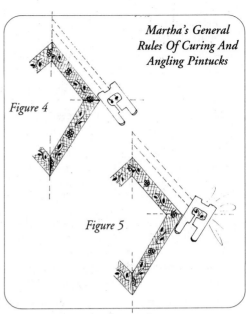

Martha's General Rules Of Curing And Angling Pintucks

Figure 4

Figure 5

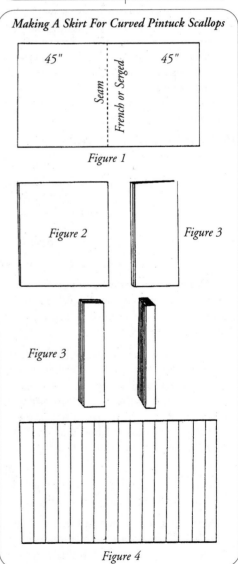

Making A Skirt For Curved Pintuck Scallops

45"   *Seam French or Serged*   45"

Figure 1

Figure 2   Figure 3

Figure 3

Figure 4

6. It is now time to make one template which will fit between the scallops. Using this illustration make one template, only, with partial scallops on either side of this template. Use a piece of typing paper or notebook paper (**fig. 5**). You can go to the cupboard and get a dinner plate, a saucer, or a coffee can or whatever to draw your one scallop which goes between the folds. Measure up evenly on each side of the scallop before you make this one pattern. Where the curve of the scallop meets the folded line of the skirt must be evenly placed on either side. After you have made your one pattern, you are ready to trace the first row of scallops on the skirt.

7. Make the template pattern where the bottom of the piece of paper lines up with the bottom of the skirt. Each time you move the paper over to mark a new scallop you can always line up the bottom of this template with the bottom of the skirt. Draw the scallops and the dotted A-B lines also.

8. Draw dotted lines bisecting the tops and bottoms of the scallops (**fig. 5**). Make these lines as tall as you want your pintuck sets to go. These lines serve as the turn around points for all of your pintucks. **They are absolutely necessary for correct turning around at the angles. These lines are the real keys to perfect sets of pintucks traveling in any angle and turning around at the proper point.**

9. Trace with a fabric marker the scallops between the fold lines (**fig. 6**). Since you made your pattern where the bottom of the piece of paper follows along the bottom of the skirt, your scallops will be equally spaced and be properly aligned with the bottom of the fabric. You will move your template from fold to fold, marking the whole scallop and a part of the next one. Mark the straight up and down lines bisecting each scallop. These lines will be along the fold lines. When you move your template over to the next fold to mark the next scallop, you will line up three things: the last piece of the scallop which overlaps, the straight lines, and the bottom of your template along the bottom of the skirt.

10. Use the curved lines for making only the first row of machine pintucks. After that you can use the edge of your sewing machine foot for guiding the next row of scallops.

11. Follow directions from "Martha's General Rules Of Curving And Angling Pintucks".

Making Strips Of Pintucking To Insert In Center Of Lace Shapes

One of the prettiest things to do in lace shaping is to make a strip of double needle pintucks and insert these pintucks behind the center of a heart, a diamond, a bow, or an oval. There are several methods of inserting this pintucked strip behind a lace shape. I think the one below is the easiest.

1. Make your heart, diamond, or bow and zigzag or machine entredeux stitch (**outside edge only**) to the garment skirt, collar, bodice, or whatever. In other words, make all of the shapes that you are going to make and zigzag the outside only to the garment (**fig. 1**). **Note:** If you are making a heart, diamond, oval or bow skirt, go ahead and stitch all the hearts around the skirt (**outside stitching only**) (**fig. 2**). Trim away the inside fabric of the diamonds, several at a time. Stitch the pinstitching in each of those trimmed hearts before trimming the inside fabric of the next hearts.

2. Make a straight strip of machine pintucks longer that the actual insides of the shapes, and a little bit taller also (**fig. 3**).

3. After zigzagging or machine entredeux stitching the **outside only of the lace shape** (diamond, heart, bow, loop or whatever) to the garment, cut away the whole fabric inside of the lace shape. It is alright to cut almost to the stitching since the heavy

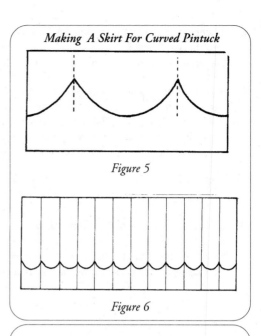

Making A Skirt For Curved Pintuck

Figure 5

Figure 6

Making Strips Of Pintucking To Insert In Center Of Lace Shaapes

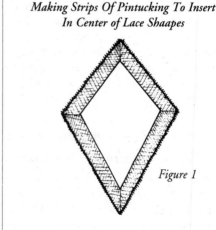

Figure 1

Figure 2

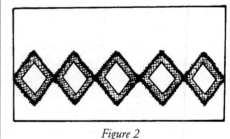

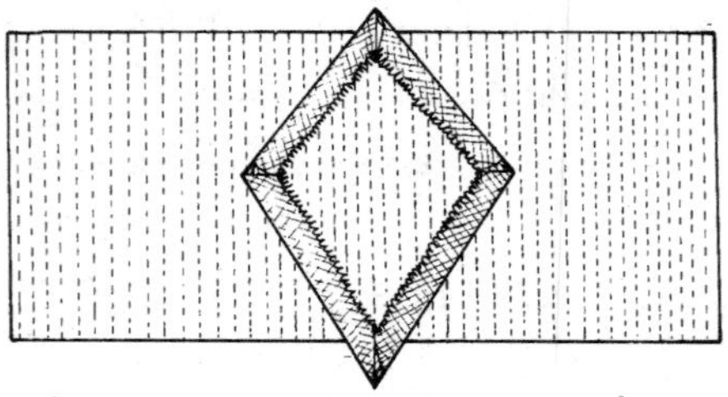

Figures 3 & 4

stitching of a heavy zigzag or the machine entredeux stitching has hundreds of stitches holding the shape to the garment (**fig. 3**). **Note:** If you are making a heart, diamond, oval or bow skirt, go ahead and stitch all the hearts around the skirt (**outside stitching only**). Trim away the inside of the hearts several at a time. Stitch the pinstitching in each of those trimmed hearts before trimming the inside fabric of the next hearts.

4. Place the pintucked strip behind one shape at a time. Stitch around the inside of the shape, attaching a portion of the pintucked strip (**fig. 4**). You can either zigzag , machine entredeux stitch or machine pin stitch.

5. Trim away the pintucked strip very close to the zigzagging from behind the lace heart, diamond, bow or oval.

Stitching One Or Two Rows Of Pintucks Inside A Fancy Lace Shape

Unlike inserting a strip of pintucks into a lace shape, when you want to stitch only one or two rows of pintucks following the shape within a heart, bow, diamond, oval or whatever, you do not have to cut away the fabric. You will use your double needles, a regular zigzag foot , and the drawn lines bisecting each turn around point.

1. Make your desired lace shape such as a heart, bow, diamond, oval or whatever. Attach to garment.

2. After shaping your desired lace shape, simply draw the bisecting lines to intersect the turn around points. Draw the lines only to the inside of the shape if you are only going to put pintucks on the inside of the shape (**fig. 1**).

3. Using your regular zigzag foot and your 1.6 or 2.0 pintuck double needles, travel around the inside of the lace shape using the edge of the zigzag foot to guide along your lace shapes. Use a needle down position and a straight stitch with a length=1.5.

4. Using the directions for making curved and angled pintucks, stitch within the figure.

Making Double Needle Shadow Embroidery Designs

When I was in Australia, one of my students who is a sewing teacher in New Zealand asked me if I had ever made shadow embroidered double needle designs. I replied that I hadn't but that I was certainly interested. She then painted on liquid stabilizer, let it dry and placed this piece of fabric in an embroidery hoop. She then drew a shadow work design from my shadow work embroidery book, put in 2.0 double needles, white thread, and proceeded to stitch all the away around that shadow work bow simply straight stitching with a short stitch (1.5 length) and made a perfectly acceptable looking shadow embroidered bow. She used a regular zigzag sewing foot, not a pintuck foot, with her double needles. Now, shadow work embroidery, it isn't; however, it is very lovely and very quick. You might want to try it (**fig. 1**). ❈

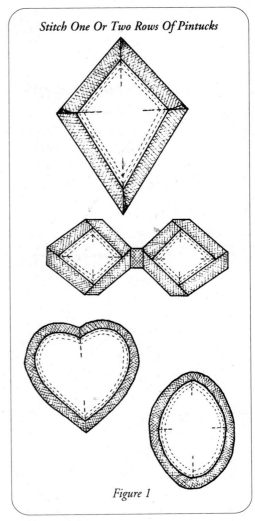

Stitch One Or Two Rows Of Pintucks

Figure 1

Making Double Needle Shadow Embroidery Designs

Figure 1

Airplane Lace Technique

Directions For Airplane Lace Shaping

1. Choose the spot for your lace airplanes.

2. Place your lace pieces from the background to the foreground on the fabric. In the case of this antique airplane shaping, the little motif was put down for the center and the four strips were placed on top of that.

3. Turn under the cut ends of the lace strips for the airplane wings.

4. Zigzag around the shapes.

5. Trim away the fabric from behind the shapes. ✳

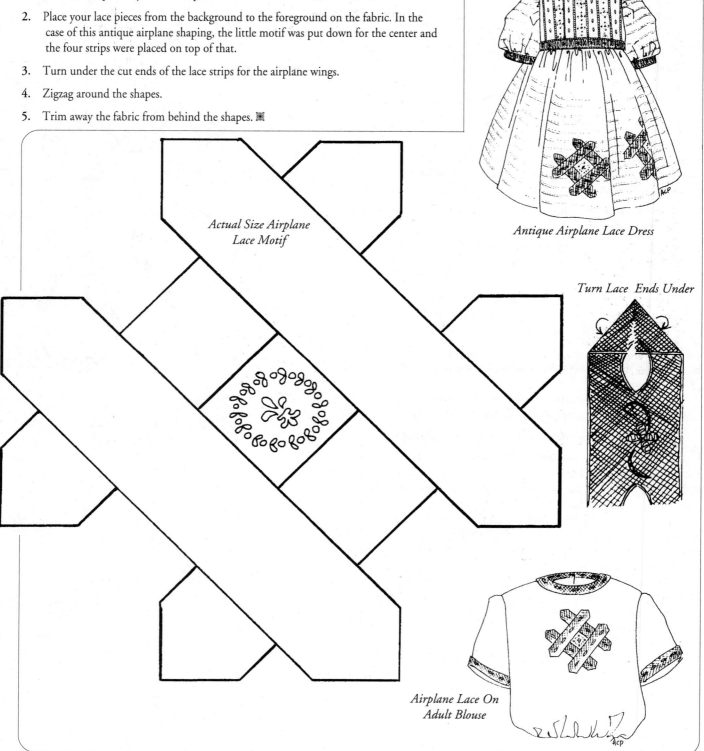

Actual Size Airplane Lace Motif

Antique Airplane Lace Dress

Turn Lace Ends Under

Airplane Lace On Adult Blouse

Appliqué

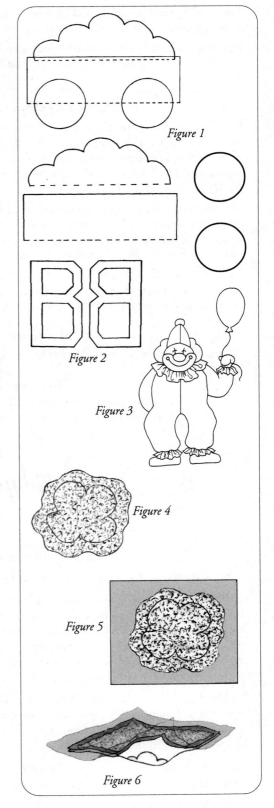

Figure 1

Figure 2

Figure 3

Figure 4

Figure 5

Figure 6

Each appliqué design can be dissected into smaller pieces. Some of the appliqué pieces may extend under other appliqué pieces. Some appliqué designs are drawn with a dotted line extending from the appliquéd piece. This shows that the fabric extension is under another piece. When dissecting these designs, watch for these dotted lines. When you are tracing your pattern which will later be used for cutting out your appliqué fabric, include the dotted extension as a part of your pattern.

For example, on the coal car of the train, the coal pattern piece extends under the body of the car and the body of the car extends under the wheels (**fig. 1**). This is the appliqué design. Here are the dissected pieces.

Some appliqué patterns have a definite right and left side (**fig. 2**). For example, letters of the alphabet (B, E, R), or a clown holding balloons with his left hand (**fig. 3**). Other patterns do not, such as the letter A (uppercase) or O. Keep this in mind when following the directions below.

1. Tracing Pattern On Bonding Agent

If Wonder Under™ or another paper-backed bonding agent is used, **trace each individual pattern piece on paper backing**, with a permanent fine-tip marker. Since the pattern is placed on the wrong side of the fabric, and if it has a definite right and wrong side, the pattern should be traced in reverse. Any design traced exactly as it is featured in this book will appear in reverse on the project.

Take the clown appliqué as an example. If the clown were holding balloons in his left hand and that is how you want it to look on the garment, the design would need to be traced in reverse. If the balloons on the completed project need to be in the clown's right hand, trace as is. All samples in this book were traced in reverse first.

Tracing A Pattern In Reverse Image

1. Photocopy or trace the design from this book.

2. Hold the design to a window with the design facing outside.

3. Trace the design on the back of the paper.

4. This newly traced design is your reverse image.

2. Roughly Cut Pattern

Roughly cut out pattern pieces to separate, leaving about ¼ inch to ½ inch around pattern lines. **Do not cut** pattern on cutting lines at this time (**fig. 4**).

3. Fusing

Follow the bonding agent instructions and fuse to the wrong side of a square of appliqué fabric. Be sure the bonding agent does not extend past the edges of the fabric to be appliquéd (**fig. 5**).

4. Cutting Out Appliqué

Cut out appliqué pieces along cutting lines. Remember to use the dotted extensions where indicated as the cutting lines.

* Fine Fuse™ or Stitch Witchery™ (**fig. 6**)

a. An appliqué pressing sheet is required. Plastic coated freezer paper or lightweight iron-on stabilizer is also needed.

b. Trace pattern pieces onto paper side of freezer paper or stabilizer with a fine-tip permanent marker. Since the pattern is placed on the right side of the fabric the pattern should be traced as is, no reversal is necessary.

c. Press to right side of appliqué fabric.

d. Fuse bonding agent to wrong side of fabric using the pressing sheet between bonding agent and iron. Iron according to manufacturer's instructions.

e. Peel off pressing sheet. Cut out pattern pieces along lines traced on the stabilizer. There will be paper on the right side and the bonding agent on the wrong side of each piece.

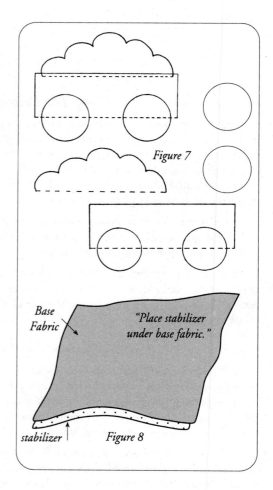

Figure 7

5. Placing Appliqué Pieces

a. Place pattern pieces on base fabric in desired position, fitting pieces together as you would a puzzle. Remember when putting the pieces together, the background pieces may extend under foreground pieces (designated by dotted lines). This will help you to see how the final design will look, as well as decipher where each piece will be fused (**fig. 7**).

b. Slide appliqué to the side, away from placement of design. While looking at the total design, remove paper backing from first piece to be fused. If paper is difficult to remove try scratching an X or a line in the paper backing with a straight pin or needle. This will help release the paper from the appliqué piece.

c. Fuse in position. Repeat in order for other pieces. Fusing order instructions are given for each design. **Note:** The background pieces are fused first, layering perspectively to the foreground to complete the fusing of the design.

Base Fabric

"Place stabilizer under base fabric."

stabilizer

Figure 8

6. Stabilizer

Place stabilizer under base fabric in the area of the appliqué (**fig. 8**).

7. Stitching

Satin stitch each piece, background to foreground. Satin stitch maneuvers, including straight lines, curves, corners, and points will be discussed in the section, *Stitch Maneuvers.* ▨

Appliqué Stitch Maneuvers

General Directions

1. Never start stitching at a corner or point; start at a straight side or curve.

2. Preferably, the appliqué piece should be positioned so that the left swing of the needle (zig) stitches on the appliqué piece and the right swing of the needle (zag) stitches off the appliqué piece (**fig. 1**). **All stitch maneuver directions are given with appliqué piece positioned on the left needle swing unless otherwise indicated.** Sometimes the appliqué piece should be placed on the right needle swing (**fig. 2**). Appliqué piece position is provided in such maneuvers.

3 **Tie-On** (**fig. 3**). Using a short straight stitch, take one complete stitch on the fabric right next to the appliqué. Pull gently on the top thread, bringing the bobbin thread to the top side of the fabric. Place threads under and behind foot. Take several straight stitches on base fabric just off appliqué.

4. Set the machine for a zigzag, medium width and satin or buttonhole length. Slightly loosen the top tension to allow the thread to "wrap" to the wrong side. If "needle

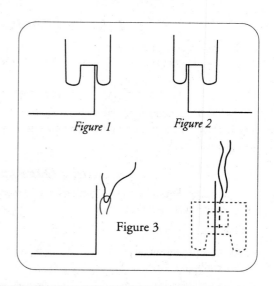

Figure 1   Figure 2

Figure 3

down" is available on your machine, it will be helpful in satin stitching and pivoting. Reposition appliqué so that zigzag stitches are placed mostly on the appliqué but extend completely off the edge of the appliqué. This will stitch the appliqué piece on in a neat fashion encasing the raw edges of the appliqué. If the entire stitch is taken on the appliqué, fuzzy may occur on the edge of the appliqué piece. If you don't stitch enough on the appliqué fabric, the appliqué may pull from the stitching.

5. Take all stitches perpendicular to the edge of the appliqué.

6. Stitch individual pieces and detail lines (that identify arms, legs, flower petals, etc.), working background to foreground.

7. Do not push or pull but simply guide the fabric through the machine. Let the machine do the work. A gentle nudge may be required when crossing over previous stitching.

8. **Tie-Off (fig. 4).** Change to a short straight stitch, reposition appliqué, and take several straight stitches just beside the satin stitch.

9. Cut threads very close to the stitching.

10. Complete design using steps 1-8 on this page.

11. With a water-soluble marker, transfer any straight stitch detail not previously satin stitched (eyes, mouth, hair, nose, glasses). These will be stitched using free-motion embroidery or hand embroidery.

Straight Lines

Follow steps in General Directions (**fig. 5**).

Curves
Outside and Inside

1. Zigzag along the appliqué as described in steps 1 - 7 of the *General Directions*. While stitching along a curve, the stitching will fail to be perpendicular to the appliqué, therefore pivoting is required. There is more area to cover along the outside edge of the curve, so the pivot must be taken with the needle down at this outside edge (**fig. 6**).

2. To pivot on a curve, leave the needle in the **outside edge of the curve** (not specifically on the zig or the zag). Raise the foot and pivot very slightly, keeping the stitches perpendicular to the edge of the appliqué. It is better to pivot too often than not often enough. If the needle is left in the inside edge of the curve while pivoting, a V will occur in the stitching.

Note: When stitching around a curve, the tendency is to force the stitching without pivoting. This will cause the appliqué edge to be wavy, therefore pivoting is very important!

Pivoting Rule For Curves: To pivot on an outside curve, the needle is left in the fabric right next to the appliqué piece. To pivot on an inside curve the needle is left in the appliqué piece itself.

Corners
Block Corners

Any zigzag sewing machine will accomplish this very simple method of turning corners.

Outside Block Corner
Method 1

1. Zigzag along the appliqué as described in steps 1 - 7 of the *General Directions*.

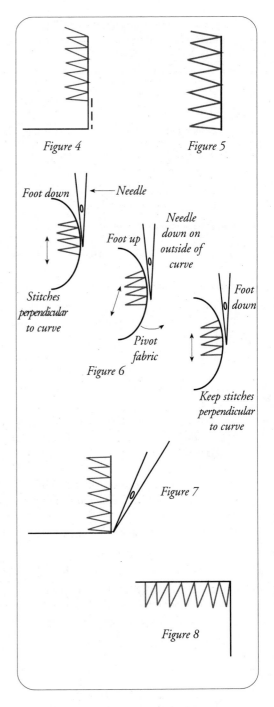

Figure 4

Figure 5

Foot down ← Needle

Foot up

Needle down on outside of curve

Foot down

Stitches perpendicular to curve

Pivot fabric

Figure 6

Keep stitches perpendicular to curve

Figure 7

Figure 8

2. Stitch down first side to corner, stopping with the needle down at the point of the corner (**fig. 7**).

3. Pivot 90° (**fig. 8**). Walk the machine by using the fly wheel to take the first stitch that should be placed in the edge of the previous stitching.

4. Continue stitching along the second side (**fig. 9**). Some machines may need a little push to begin satin stitching the second side at the corner. To keep the machine from bogging down at this point, push gently by placing fingers along the sides of the foot to help move the stitching over the previous satin stitch at the corner.

Outside Block Corner
Method 2

1. Zigzag along the appliqué as described in steps 1 - 7 of *General Directions*.

2. Stitch down first side to corner, stopping with the needle down on the left swing [not on the point of the corner (zag) but on the other side (zig)] (**fig. 10**).

3. Pivot 90°. Raise needle out of fabric, raise presser foot, and reposition so that the needle pierces the same hole of the last stitch before the pivot (**fig. 11**). Lower foot.

4. Continue stitching.

Inside Block Corner
Method 1

1. Bisect corner using a water-soluble marker (**fig. 12**).

2. With appliqué on left needle swing, zigzag along the appliqué as described in steps 1 - 7 of the General Directions. Continue stitching until the left needle swing hits the drawn line (**fig. 13**).

3. With needle in fabric, raise foot, pivot 90°, walk the machine by using the fly wheel to take the first stitch that should be placed in the edge of the previous stitching (**fig. 14**), lower foot and continue stitching along the second side.

4. Some machines may need a little push to begin satin stitching the second side at the corner. To keep the machine from bogging down at this point, push gently by placing fingers along the sides of the foot to help move the stitching over the previous satin stitch at the corner.

Inside Block Corner
Method 2

1. Bisect corner using a water-soluble marker (**See fig. 12**).

2. With appliqué on left needle swing, zigzag along the appliqué as described in steps 1 - 7 of the General Directions.

3. Continue stitching until the left needle swing hits the drawn line (**fig. 15**).

4. On the next stitch, leave the needle down on the right swing (**fig. 16**). Raise foot, pivot 90°, lower foot, raise needle out of fabric, raise presser foot, and reposition so that the needle pierces the same hole of the last stitch before the pivot (**fig. 17**).

5. Continue stitching along the second side.

Mitered Corners

Before beginning the maneuvers of miters and points it will be helpful to practice on stabilized scrap fabric, increasing and decreasing the stitch width with the right hand while guiding fabric with the left. Watch where the needle is stitching, not the stitch width knob or lever. Also practice this stitching method using right and left needle position, if available.

Mitering corners can be done if your machine has the capability of changing needle positions (right, left or both) and being able to change the stitch width while stitching in any of these needle positions. Note: Once the needle position is changed, it may stay in that position to continue stitching until the next maneuver (corner or point) is reached.

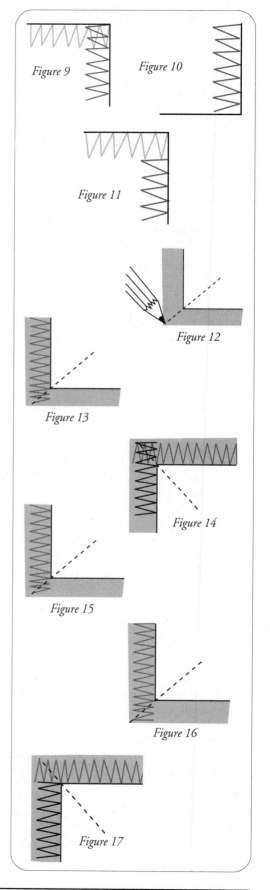

Figure 9   Figure 10

Figure 11

Figure 12

Figure 13

Figure 14

Figure 15

Figure 16

Figure 17

Sewing Machines with Right and Left Needle Position
Outside Corner

1. Place appliqué pieces on the left swing of the needle.

2. Zigzag along the appliqué as described in steps 1 - 7 of the General Directions.

3. Stitch down first side to corner, stopping with the needle down at the point of the corner (**fig 18**).

4. Pivot 90° (**fig. 19**). Lower the foot. Note the stitch width used.

5. Raise needle from fabric, change to right needle position and a 0 stitch width. Reposition so that the needle pierces the same hole of the last stitch before the pivot.

6. Guide the fabric with the left hand while gradually increasing stitch width with the right hand, stopping at the original width setting. Changing the width from 0 to the original width should be completed when the edge of the previous stitching of the first side is reached (**fig. 20**). It will be helpful to watch where your needle is stitching, not the stitch width knob or button.

Inside Corner

1. Place the appliqué pieces on the left swing of the needle.

2. Bisect inside corner with water-soluble marker (**fig. 21**).

3. Zigzag along the appliqué as described in steps 1 - 7 of the General Directions.

4. Stitch down first side until the left swing of the needle intersects drawn line (**fig. 22**).

5. Leaving the needle down, raise the foot, pivot 90° (**fig. 23**), lower foot. Note the stitch width being used.

6. Raise needle from fabric. Change to left needle position and a 0 stitch width. Reposition so that the needle pierces the same hole of the last stitch before the pivot.

7. Guide the fabric with the left hand while gradually increasing stitch width with the right hand, stopping at the original width setting. Changing the width from 0 to the original width should be completed when the edge of the previous stitching of the first side is reached. It will be helpful to watch where your needle is stitching, not the stitch width knob or button (**fig. 24**).

Sewing Machines with Right Needle Position Only–Outside Corner

Refer to Mitered Corners - Outside Corners.

Inside Corner

1. Refer to Mitered Corners - Inside Corner. However, appliqué piece must be positioned on the right needle swing.

2. Stitch until the right swing of the needle intersects the drawn line leaving the needle down (**fig. 25**).

3. Raise the foot, pivot 90°, lower foot (**fig. 26**).

4. Note the stitch width being used. Raise needle from fabric. Change to right needle position and a 0 stitch width.

5. Reposition so that the needle pierces the same hole of the last stitch before the pivot.

6. Guide the fabric with the left hand while gradually increasing stitch width with the right hand, stopping at the original width setting. Changing the width from 0 to the original width should be completed when the edge of the previous stitching of the first side is reached (**fig. 27**). It will be helpful to watch where your needle is stitching, not the stitch width knob or button.

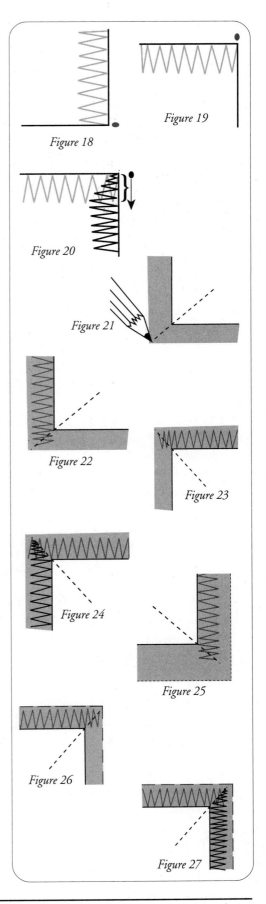

Figure 18

Figure 19

Figure 20

Figure 21

Figure 22

Figure 23

Figure 24

Figure 25

Figure 26

Figure 27

Sewing Machines with Left Needle Position Only Outside Corner

1. Appliqué piece must be positioned on the right needle swing.

2. Stitch down first side to corner, stopping with the needle down at the point of the corner (**fig. 28**).

3. Raise foot, pivot 90°, lower foot. Note the stitch width being used. Raise needle from fabric, change to left needle position and a 0 stitch width. Reposition so that the needle pierces the same hole of the last stitch before the pivot (**fig. 29**).

4. Guide the fabric with the left hand while gradually increasing stitch width with the right hand, stopping at the original width setting. Changing the width from 0 to the original width should be completed when the edge of the previous stitching of the first side is reached (**fig. 30**). It will be helpful to watch where your needle is stitching, not the stitch width knob or button.

Inside Corner

The inside corner directions are the same directions given under *Mitered Corners - Right and Left Needle Position - Inside Corners.*

*Optional Decorative Stitch Used for Mitered Corners

There are several machines that have a solid triangle as a decorative stitch. All or part of this stitch can be used to miter a corner. On a stabilized scrap fabric, work one complete pattern starting at the beginning of the pattern.

- If the pattern looks like (**fig. 31**), only half of the pattern will be used and it is in right needle position.

- If the pattern looks like (**fig. 32**), only half of the pattern will be used and it is in left needle position.

- If the pattern looks like (**fig. 33**), it is stitching in a right needle position and the entire pattern is used.

- If the pattern looks like (**fig. 34**), it is stitching in left needle position and the entire pattern is used.

- If your machine has mirror image this pattern can be stitched in either right or left needle position.

Follow directions above for appropriate needle position through the pivot.

—— *Directions For Built In Decorative Stitch Triangle* ——

1. Stitch down first side to corner stopping with the needle down at the point of the corner (**fig. 35**).

2. Raise foot, pivot 90°, lower foot. Note the stitch width and length being used.

3. Raise needle and engage decorative stitch matching the length and width of the original satin stitch. Stitch pattern through widest point (**fig. 36**).

4. Raise needle. Engage original satin stitch taking the first stitch by reentering the hole of last stitch. Continue (**fig. 37**).

———— *Points* ————

All points are stitched in center needle position.

Outside Point

1. Appliqué piece on left needle swing.

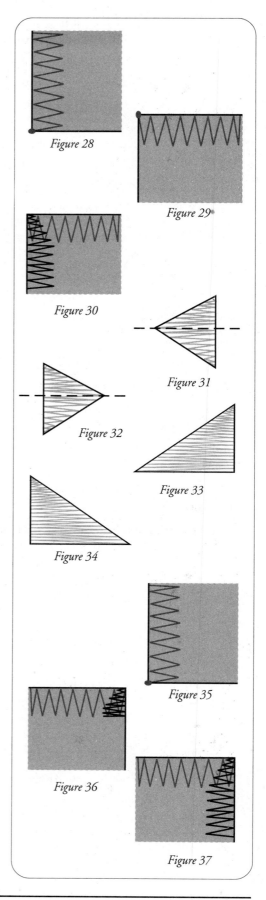

Figure 28

Figure 29

Figure 30

Figure 31

Figure 32

Figure 33

Figure 34

Figure 35

Figure 36

Figure 37

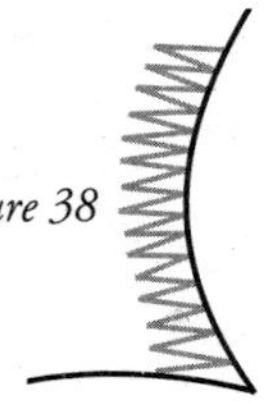
Figure 38

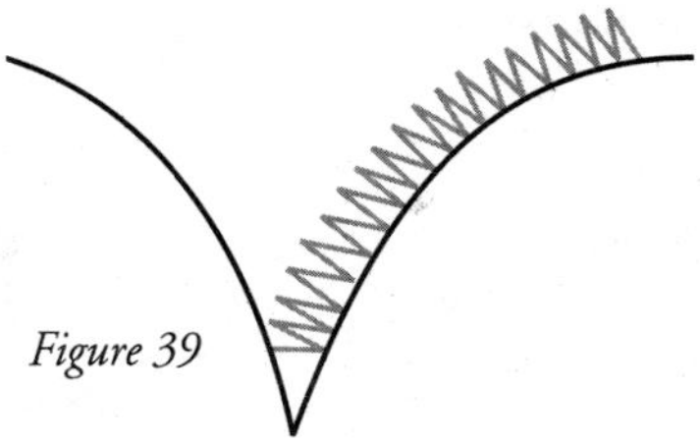
Figure 39

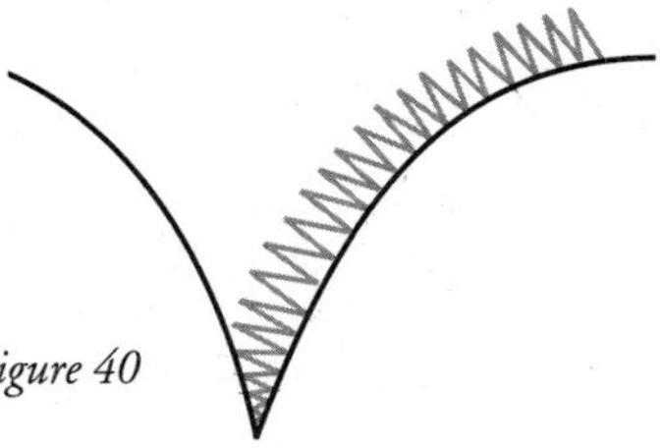
Figure 40

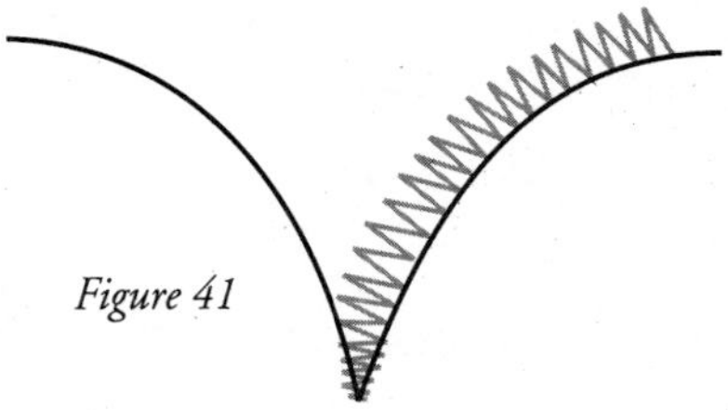
Figure 41

2. Zigzag along the appliqué as described in steps 1 - 7 of the General Directions. Zigzag toward point until needle is stitching off both sides of the appliqué piece. Leave needle down on left side (**fig. 38**).
3. Raise foot, pivot so that point is directly toward you (**fig. 39**).
4. Note stitch width. Continue stitching to the point guiding the fabric with your left hand, while decreasing stitch width with your right hand to cover appliqué piece.
   a. For a sharp point it will be necessary to take the stitch width down to 0 (**Fig. 40**).
   b. For a blunt point, taking the width to 0 is not necessary (**fig. 41**).
5. Lower needle, raise foot, pivot 180° (the point of the appliqué piece is pointed away from you) (**fig. 42**).
6. Lower foot, raise the needle and reposition so that the first stitch will reenter the hole of the last stitch.
7. Continue stitching away from the point, guiding the fabric with your left hand, while increasing the stitch width with your right hand to the original width. Continue stitching (**fig. 43**), pivoting as necessary to keep the satin stitches perpendicular to the appliqué edge.

Inside Point

1. Appliqué piece on left needle swing.
2. Bisect the point using a water-soluble pen (**fig. 44**).
3. Zigzag along the appliqué as described in steps 1 - 7 of the General Directions. Continue stitching until the right swing of the needle is off the appliqué at the point (**fig. 45**).
4. Note original stitch width. Guide the fabric with your left hand, so that the right needle swing hits the bisected line as you decrease stitch width gradually to 0 (**fig. 46**).
5. With the needle down, raise the foot, pivot approximately 180° positioning unstitched edge of appliqué under the foot. Lower the foot and continue stitching as you gradually increase the stitch width to the original width keeping the right needle swing butted up against the edge of the previous stitching. Continue stitching (**fig. 47**), pivoting as necessary to keep the satin stitches perpendicular to the appliqué edge.

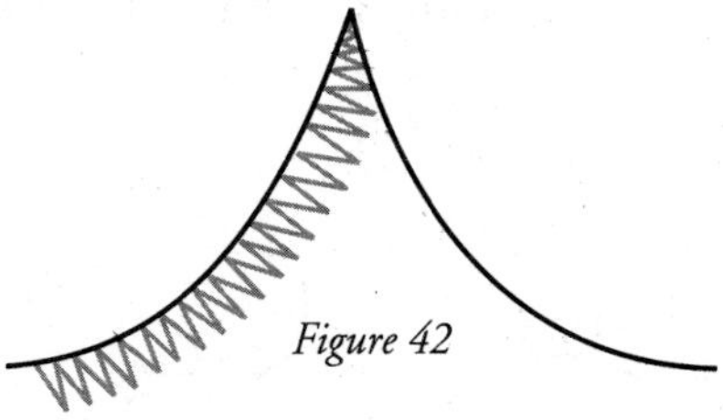
Figure 42

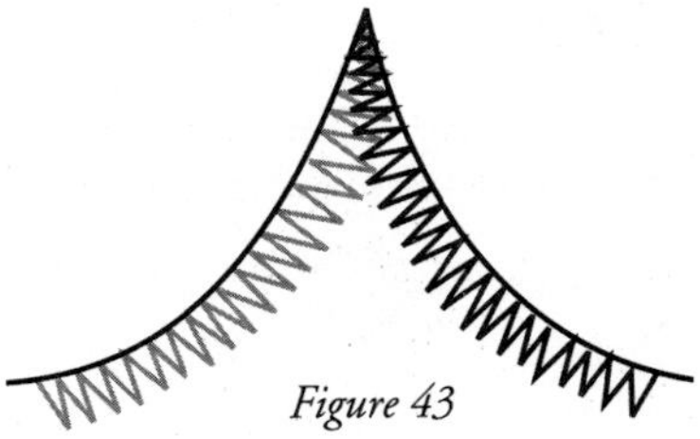
Figure 43

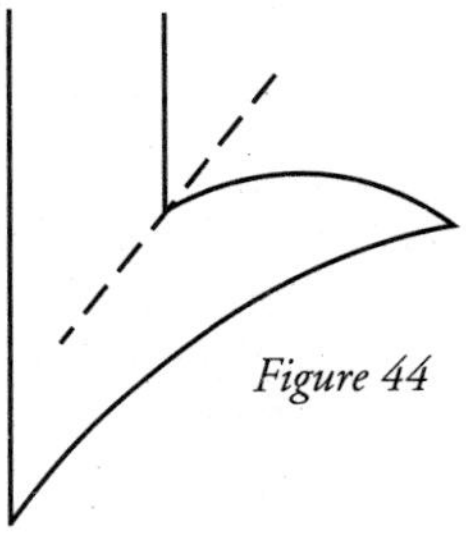
Figure 44

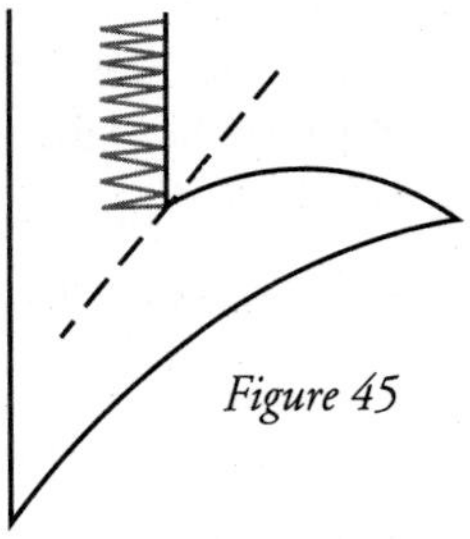
Figure 45

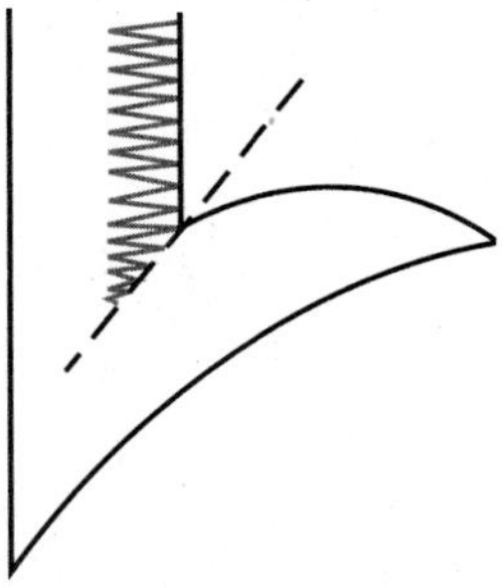
Figure 46

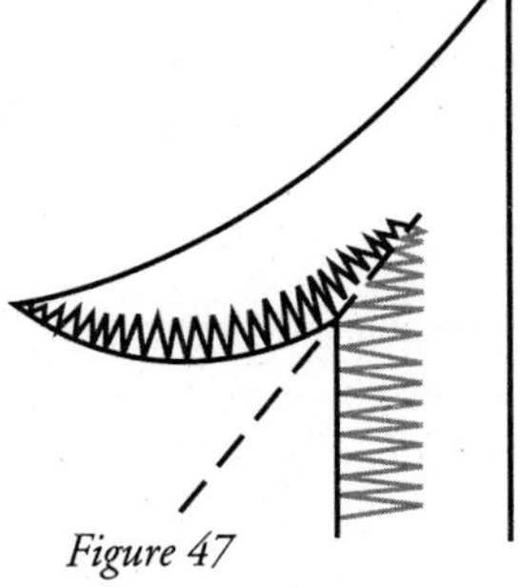
Figure 47

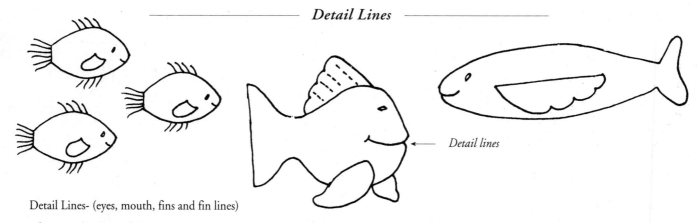

Detail lines

Detail Lines- (eyes, mouth, fins and fin lines)

After completing appliqué, stitch detail lines using straight stitches, zigzag stitches or decorative stitches. Detail lines can also be stitched by hand. ✖

Shadow Appliqué

Different colored fabrics can be applied to the wrong side of a sheer fabric to give a shadow effect. This simple technique can be applied to collars, blouse fronts, cuffs, and skirt hems. An open zigzag, blanket stitch or other decorative stitch can be used to apply the colored fabrics to the base fabrics.

Supplies

- ✖ Sheer Base Fabric (blouse, collar, etc.)
- ✖ Bright or Dark Appliqué Fabric
- ✖ Open Toe Appliqué Foot
- ✖ Machine Embroidery Thread
- ✖ Size 70 to 80 Needle
- ✖ 6" to 8" Hoop (Wooden machine embroidery or spring tension)
- ✖ Marking Pens or Pencils, Water or Air Soluble
- ✖ Small, Sharp Pointed Scissors
- ✖ Appliqué Scissors

Shadow Appliqué Fabrics

1. Base Fabric

The base fabric should be a sheer fabric so that the fabric appliqué will show through from the wrong side. If a fabric other than white is used, experiment to see how it will change the color of the appliqué fabric. The appliqué will show more distinctly after it is lined.

2. Appliqué Fabric

The appliqué color should be bright enough to show through base fabric. Some colors will look "muddy" under the base fabric. Always test appearance of color by placing a single layer of appliqué fabric between two layers of the base fabric.

General Shadow Appliqué
Directions

1. To determine the size of base fabric to be shadow appliquéd, consider the position of the appliqué. The fabric should extend beyond the appliqué design in all directions, so that it may be placed in the hoop. For example, when doing shadow appliqué on a pocket edge, even though the pocket pattern itself is small, you must start with a piece of fabric large enough to fit in the hoop (**fig.** 1). Another example would be when placing shadow appliqué near the edge of a collar, the base fabric must be large enough to contain the whole collar pattern plus enough fabric on the edges to hold in the hoop (**fig.** 2).

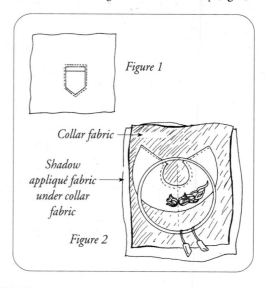

Figure 1

Collar fabric

Shadow appliqué fabric under collar fabric

Figure 2

2. Press and starch the pretreated fabric to remove all of the wrinkles and give the fabric some body. Several applications of starch can be used.

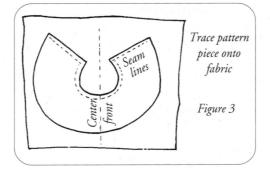

Trace pattern piece onto fabric

Figure 3

3. Trace the pattern piece (cutting lines, seam lines and center front line and all other necessary markings) (**fig. 3**). Trace the design, within the pattern stitching lines, to the base fabric in the desired position (**fig. 4**). When tracing, especially the design for the appliqué, maintain as fine a line as possible since you will be stitching ON this line. A washable marking pencil with a sharp point is helpful. To trace the design, place the base fabric in a hoop large enough to encompass the design. This will help to hold the fabric flat and keep it from shifting while tracing. Don't pull fabric too tight in hoop.

4. To determine the thread color to use, place a piece of each of the appliqué fabrics between two layers of base fabric. Match the thread to the color that shows through the base fabric. It will be lighter than the actual appliqué fabric. Use this color for the top thread. White or base fabric color thread can be used in the bobbin throughout the project.

   The upper thread tension should be loosened so that the bobbin thread will pull the top thread to the wrong side. It should not be so loose that the bobbin thread forms a straight line on the wrong side. Test to make correct adjustments.

5. Decide what stitch to use to attach the appliqué fabric to the base fabric. There are several choices.

   a. A narrow open zig zag can be used, a stitch width of about 1 mm and a length of 1 mm (**fig. 5**). This is not a satin stitch, but a short, narrow zig zag stitch.

   b. A pin stitch or blanket stitch can also be used if your machine has this capability (**fig. 6**). The pin stitch generally has a heavier look than the blanket stitch. The stitch width should be narrowed to about 1 mm and the length may also need to be adjusted. Test on a sample to make adjustments.

6. With machine shadow appliqué, the appliqué fabric is placed to the wrong side of the base fabric and you must work from foreground to background (opposite from regular machine appliqué). Place both fabrics in a hoop, layered with the right side of the appliqué fabric to the wrong side of the base fabric. When learning to do shadow appliqué by machine, have the appliqué fabric large enough to be placed in the hoop with the base fabric. As you become more accustomed to this technique it is not necessary to place the fabrics in a hoop (**fig. 7**). When the stitching is done, care should be taken to keep the appliqué fabric from shifting or wrinkles being stitched in. Pin in place if necessary or use a touch of water soluble glue stick to hold the fabric in place. Spray starching the appliqué fabric again will help it to remain flat.

   Decide on the starting point, generally not a corner or a point. Pull up bobbin thread and tie on by taking several tiny straight stitches on the drawn line of the appliqué pattern. Stitch on design line to completely enclose area in that color (**fig. 8**). When using the pin stitch or blanket stitch, the straight part of the stitch should be on the design line and the "fingers" part or "ladder steps" of the stitch should be INTO the appliqué (**fig. 9**). You may need to engage "mirror image" if your machine has this capability or stitch in the opposite direction to place the stitch correctly.

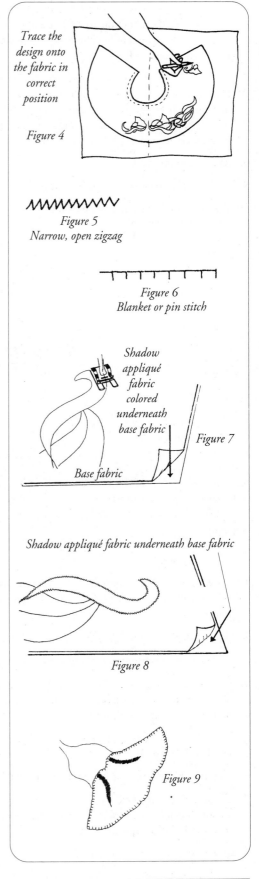

Trace the design onto the fabric in correct position

Figure 4

Figure 5
Narrow, open zigzag

Figure 6
Blanket or pin stitch

Shadow appliqué fabric colored underneath base fabric

Base fabric

Figure 7

Shadow appliqué fabric underneath base fabric

Figure 8

Figure 9

6. Trim the <u>appliqué</u> fabric close to the stitching lines, being careful not to cut the stitches (**fig. 10**). If both the base fabric and the appliqué fabric are in the hoop, remove the hoop, and re-hoop just the base fabric. Trimming will be easier if the base fabric remains in the hoop.

7. Working foreground to background, place the next color to be appliquéd under the base fabric as above and stitch. For areas that touch each other, the stitching must be done on BOTH sides of the appliqué (**fig. 11**) Allow the regular zigzag stitches to just touch each other (not overlap) or the straight part of the pin or blanket stitch to be beside each other (**fig. 12**).

8. Continue in this manner until all of the appliqué pieces are attached and trimmed.

9. Wash fabric to remove all of the markings.

10. Press with the right side down on a towel. ▓

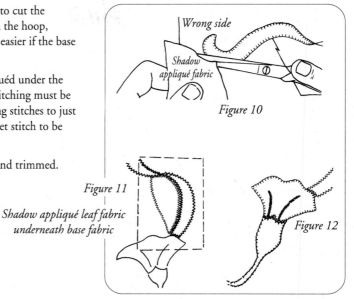

Figure 10

Figure 11

Shadow appliqué leaf fabric underneath base fabric

Figure 12

Puffy or Padded Appliqué

This appliqué design will give a three-dimensional affect. Balloons and clown bodies are the perfect designs for this technique. Reverse Appliqué Stitching techniques combined with batting for a puffy effect, make up Puffy Appliqué.

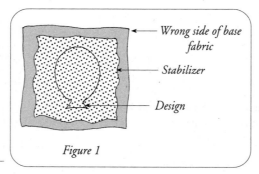

Figure 1

Directions

1. Trace the entire design onto the stabilizer. Place the stabilizer in position on the wrong side of the base (or garment) fabric (**fig. 1**). Remember to work background to foreground.

2. Place batting, next, on right side of base (or garment) fabric.

3. Place the wrong side of the appliqué fabric on top of the batting (**fig. 2**).

4. Stitch (width = 1, length = 1) along the pattern lines drawn on the stabilizer. Right side of the appliqué fabric will be next to the feed dogs. In other words, you are stitching on the wrong side of the garment.

5. Trim excess batting and appliqué fabric with appliqué scissors, close to the stitching on the right side (**fig. 3**).

6. Continue this process, one piece at a time until the design is finished.

7. If regular fabrics are used, re-stitch each pattern piece on right side as described in section, Stitch Maneuvers, on page 170 (**fig. 4**). If the fabric does not ravel, as in tricot-backed lamé, you are finished.

8. Remove stabilizer on the wrong side. ▓

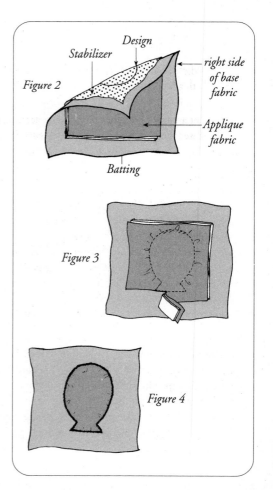

Figure 2

Figure 3

Figure 4

Basic Crazy Patch

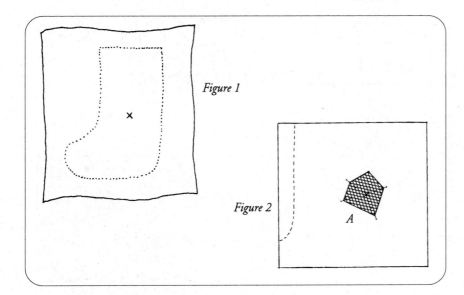

Figure 1

Figure 2

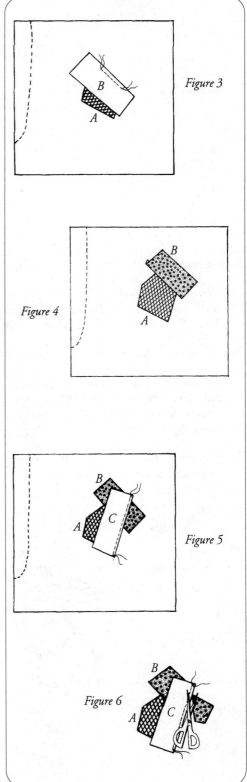

Figure 3

Figure 4

Figure 5

Figure 6

Directions

1. Cut a piece of base fabric larger than each pattern piece to be crazy patched. This base fabric can be any fabric since it will not show when the crazy patch is complete. We prefer to use unbleached muslin as the base fabric.

2. Outline the pattern piece on the base fabric. Find the center of the base fabric and mark with a fabric marker (**fig. 1**).

Optional: For a quilted look, batting may be placed under the base fabric. Pin the batting to the base fabric in several places to prevent the batting from slipping.

3. For the patchwork, start with a multi-sided fabric piece (patch "A") with at least five sides.

4. Pin patch "A" to the center of the base fabric (**fig 2**).

5. Place patch "B" to patch "A", right sides together. Line up one side of patch "B" with one side of patch "A". Patch "B" will overhang patch "A". Stitch using a ¹/₄" seam the length of the edge of patch "A" (**fig. 3**). This stitching will be made through the two patch pieces and the base fabric. The stitch length should be about a 3, which is a little longer than a normal stitch. Use a straight stitch.

6. Flip patch "B" to the right side and press (**fig. 4**).

7. Place one of the straight sides of patch "C" overlapping patches "A" and "B". The edge of patch "C" may extend beyond the length of the patches underneath. The patches underneath may extend above the straight edge of patch "C" (**fig. 5**).

8. Stitch along the straight edge of patch "C" the length of the under pieces. Trim away any excess of the "A" and "B" patches (**fig. 6**).

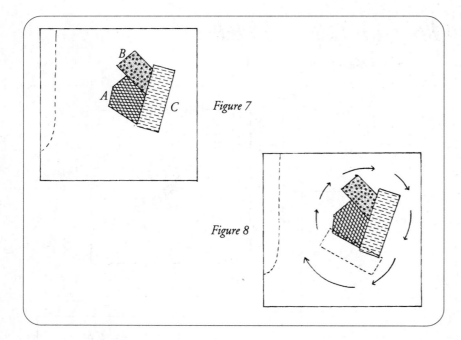

Figure 7

Figure 8

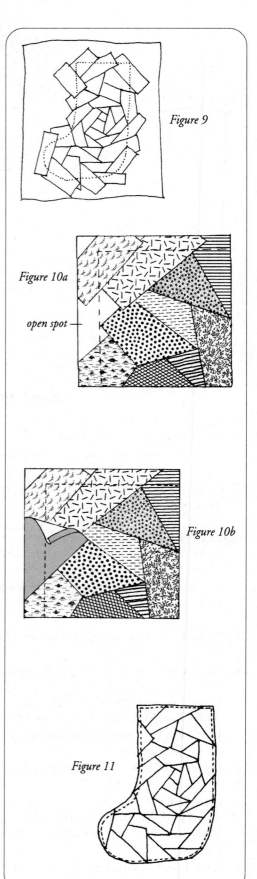

Figure 9

Figure 10a

open spot —

Figure 10b

Figure 11

9. Flip patch "C" to the right side and press (**fig. 7**).

10. Continue working in a clockwise direction adding patches until the needed base fabric is covered (**fig. 8**). The patches should extend beyond the traced pattern lines. This will insure that the crazy patch design will fit the pattern piece (**fig. 9**).

Note: Eventually, when stitching crazy patch, an unusual angle will develop or you will come to an unfinished space. A piece of ribbon, lace or any trim can be hand or machine stitched in that space or a piece of fabric can be used to cover the space by turning the edge or edges of the fabric under and top stitching in the desired area. In other words, use anything and any technique to cover these unusual or hard-to-stitch spaces (**fig. 10a and 10b**).

11. Place the pattern piece on top of the crazy patch fabric. Trace around the pattern and stitch just inside the traced line. Cut out the pattern piece (**fig. 11**). ❋

Extra-Stable Lace Finishing

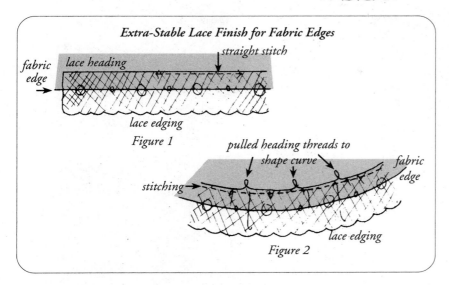

Extra-Stable Lace Finish for Fabric Edges

fabric edge — lace heading — straight stitch

lace edging

Figure 1

pulled heading threads to shape curve

stitching — fabric edge

lace edging

Figure 2

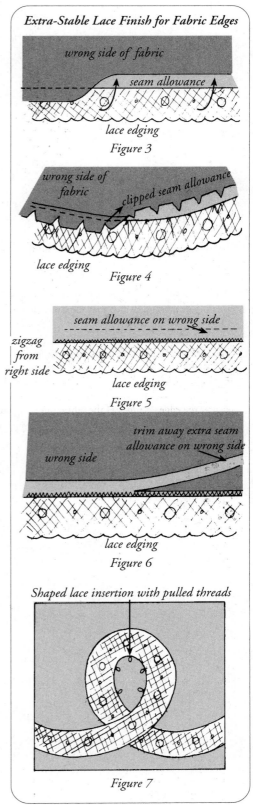

Extra-Stable Lace Finish for Fabric Edges

wrong side of fabric

seam allowance

lace edging

Figure 3

wrong side of fabric — clipped seam allowance

lace edging

Figure 4

seam allowance on wrong side

zigzag from right side

lace edging

Figure 5

wrong side — trim away extra seam allowance on wrong side

lace edging

Figure 6

Shaped lace insertion with pulled threads

Figure 7

A. Extra-Stable Lace Finish for Fabric Edges

1. If the lace is being attached to a straight edge of fabric, pin the heading of the lace to the right side, ¼" or more from the cut edge, with the right side of the lace facing up and the outside edge of the lace extending over the edge of the fabric. Using a short straight stitch, stitch the heading to the fabric (**fig. 1**).

2. If the lace is being attached to a curved edge, shape the lace around the curve as you would for lace shaping; refer to "Lace Shaping" found on page 185. Pull up the threads in the lace heading if necessary. Continue pinning and stitching the lace as directed in Step 1 above (**fig. 2**).

3. Press the seam allowance away from the lace, toward the wrong side of the fabric (**fig. 3**). If the edge is curved or pointed, you may need to clip the seam allowance in order to press flat (**fig. 4**).

4. On the right side, use a short, narrow zigzag to stitch over the lace heading, catching the fold of the pressed seam allowance (**fig. 5**).

5. On the wrong side, trim the seam allowance close to the zigzag (**fig. 6**).

B. Extra-Stable Lace Finish for Lace Shapes

1. Trace the lace design onto the fabric. Shape the lace according to the directions in "Lace Shaping" found on page 185 (**fig. 7**).

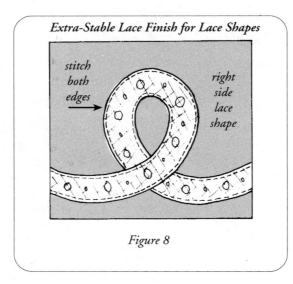

stitch both edges →

right side lace shape

Figure 8

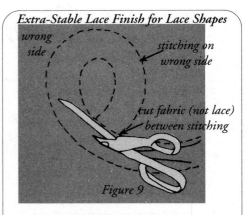

wrong side

stitching on wrong side

cut fabric (not lace) between stitching

Figure 9

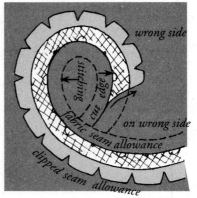

wrong side

stitching

cut edge

fabric seam allowance

on wrong side

clipped seam allowance

Figure 10

2. Using a short straight stitch, stitch the heading to the fabric on both edges of the lace (**fig. 8**).

3. After both sides of the lace have been stitched, carefully slit the fabric behind the lace, cutting in the middle between the two stitching lines. Be very careful not to cut through the lace (**fig. 9**).

4. Press the seam allowance away from the lace, toward the wrong side of the fabric. If the edge is curved or has a corner, you may need to clip the seam allowance in order to press flat (**fig. 10**).

5. On the right side, use a short, narrow zigzag to stitch over the lace heading, catching the fold of the pressed seam allowance (**fig. 11**).

6. On the wrong side, trim the seam allowance close to the zigzag (**fig. 12**). ✻

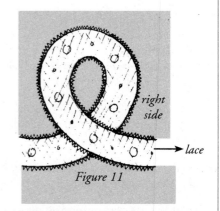

right side

→ lace

Figure 11

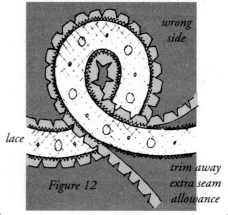

wrong side

lace

Figure 12

trim away extra seam allowance

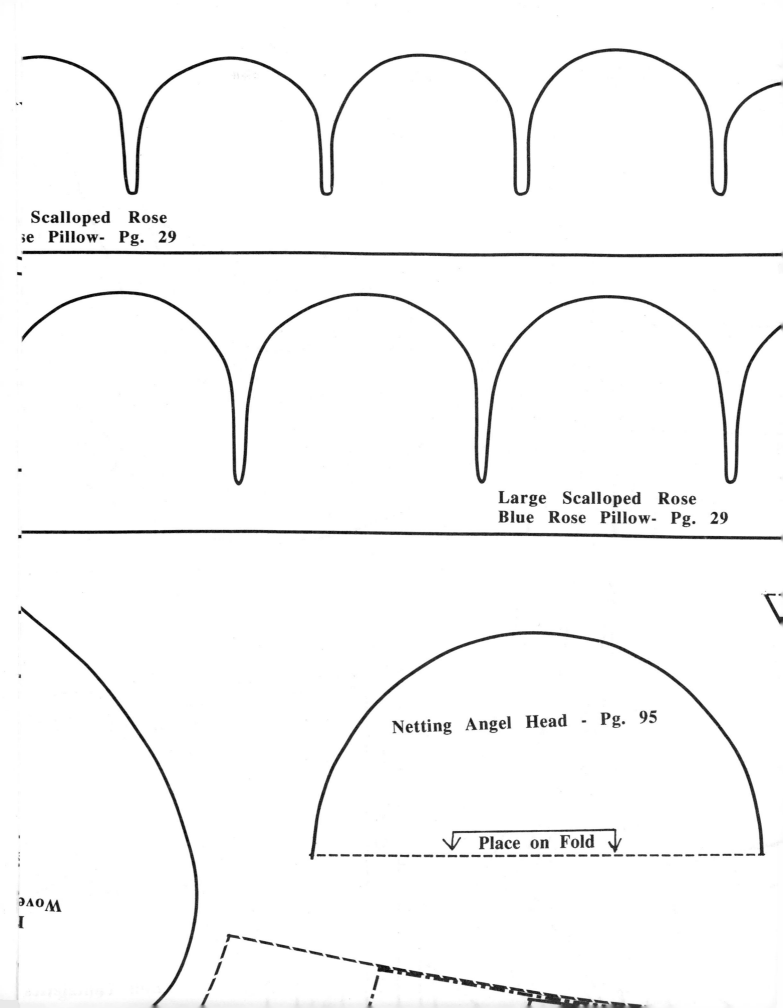

Scalloped Rose
se Pillow- Pg. 29

Large Scalloped Rose
Blue Rose Pillow- Pg. 29

Netting Angel Head - Pg. 95

↓ Place on Fold ↓

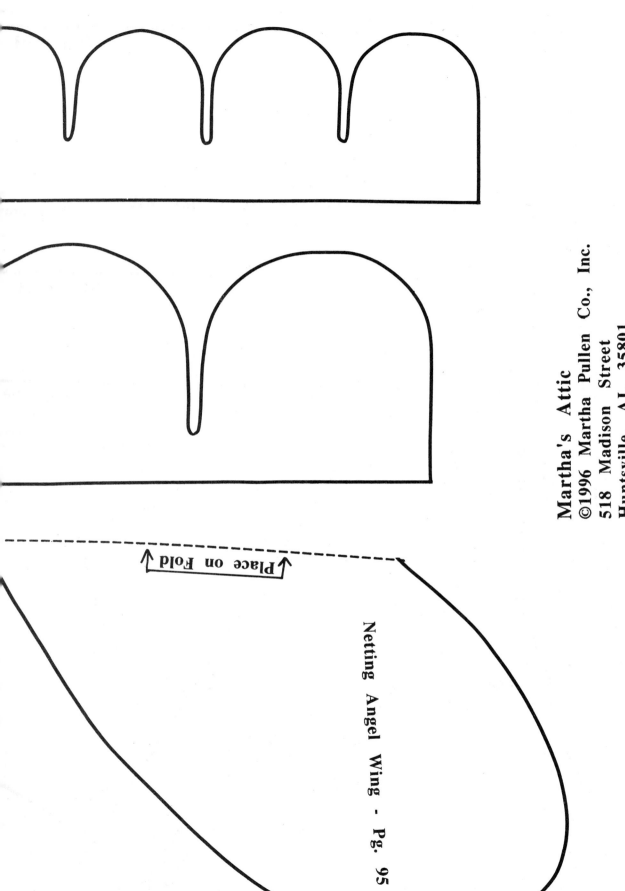

Martha's Attic
©1996 Martha Pullen Co., Inc.
518 Madison Street
Huntsville, AL 35801
1-800-547-4176

↑ Place on Fold ↑

Netting Angel Wing - Pg. 95

Handkerchief Bow

To make this easy bow, use one decorative handkerchief, 10" to 12" square. The four corners of the handkerchief will be used to make up the bow "loops." The bow knot will be made from the remaining decorative part of the handkerchief.

Instructions

1. Fold the handkerchief in half, with right sides together.

2. Mark the center on the long edge. Measure down $3\frac{1}{2}$" along the sides and mark. Draw two diagonal lines joining the dots.(**fig. 1**).

3. Cut along the traced lines. Pin each set of corners together along the cut edges (**fig. 2**).

4. Stitch the cut edges together with a $\frac{1}{4}$" seam and press the pieces open. This forms the bow "loops" (**fig. 3**).

5. Place the two bow loops with right sides together. Stitch the two triangles together 1" from the point (**fig. 4**). Open and press (**fig. 5**).

6. Cut a piece from the remaining handkerchief fabric 3" square. Fold the square in half with wrong sides together. This will make the bow knot.

7. Sew a $\frac{1}{4}$" seam along the long edge. Press the piece flat with the seam hidden underneath (**fig. 6**).

9. Wrap the knot around the middle of the bow letting the ends meet in the back. Pull the knot as tight as desired. Sew the two ends together. Trim the seam (**fig. 7**).

10. Place the finished bow on the garment or project you are making. Pin.

11. Use a small zigzag, not quite a satin stitch, to stitch the bow in place around the edges. You may trim the fabric from behind the bow if you wish.

Note: Additional bow designs, blouse pattern and skirt pattern can be found in Patty Smith's book <u>Simple Patterns with Elegant Bows</u>. This book can be purchased from Martha Pullen Company. ✳

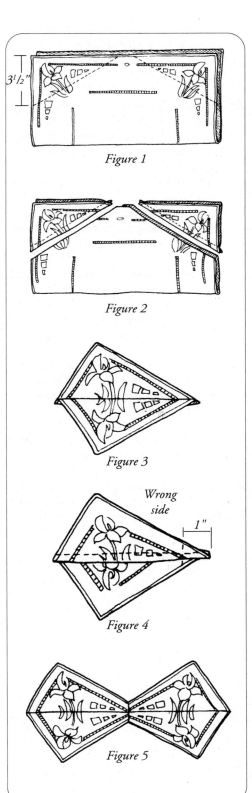

Figure 1

Figure 2

Figure 3

Wrong side

1"

Figure 4

Figure 5

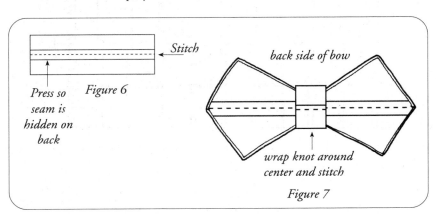

Stitch

Press so seam is hidden on back

Figure 6

back side of bow

wrap knot around center and stitch

Figure 7

Lace and Ribbon Weaving

1. Cut a piece of fusible interfacing larger than the desired woven area or pattern piece. Trace the pattern piece on the interfacing with a washout marker or pencil.

2. Place the fusible interfacing, fusible side up, on the ironing board or lace shaping board. Cut lace and/or ribbon strips to the length of the interfacing. Center the strips on top of the interfacing with the edges touching but not overlapping. Pin the top of the strips in place. Place a piece of wash away basting tape $1/8$" away from the outer strips. The paper backing of the wash away basting tape will be removed as the sticky surface is needed (**fig. 1**).

3. Cut strips of ribbon or lace to the width of the interfacing. Start weaving the strips. As the pieces are woven, use the sticky tape on each side to hold the strip in place. Continue working until the pattern outline is covered (**fig. 1**).

4. Lay a press cloth on the woven strips. Press lightly to secure strips. Turn up-side-down and press on the interfacing side to make sure all pieces are fused.

5. Re-trace the pattern on the woven piece. Stitch just inside the traced lines. Cut out (**fig. 2**).

6. Optional: For extra stability stitch along the strips with clear, nylon thread or add machine decorative stitches with colored thread as desired. ✳

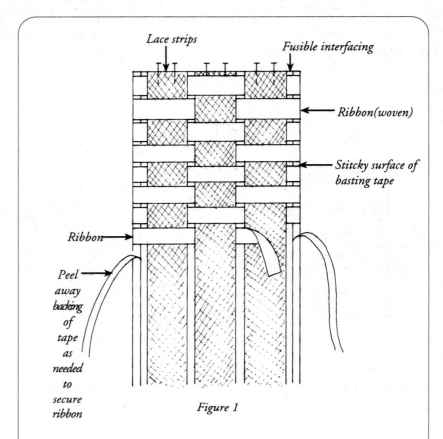

Lace strips

Fusible interfacing

Ribbon(woven)

Stitcky surface of basting tape

Ribbon

Peel away backing of tape as needed to secure ribbon

Figure 1

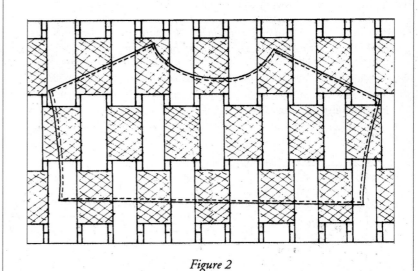

Figure 2

Log Cabin Lace Technique

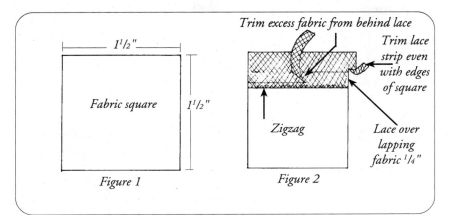

Trim excess fabric from behind lace

Trim lace strip even with edges of square

Fabric square

1¹/₂"

1¹/₂"

Figure 1

Zigzag

Lace over lapping fabric ¹/₄"

Figure 2

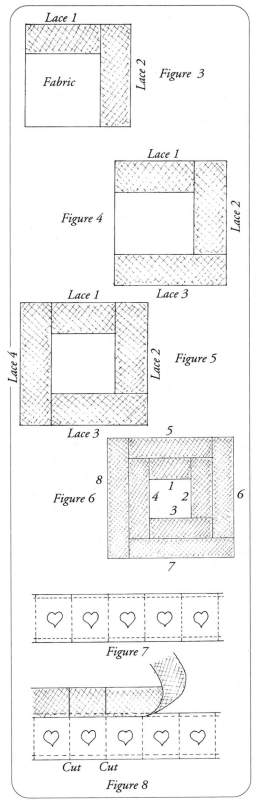

Lace 1

Fabric

Lace 2

Figure 3

Lace 1

Figure 4

Lace 2

Lace 3

Lace 1

Lace 4

Lace 2

Figure 5

Lace 3

5

8

1 2

4

3

6

Figure 6

7

Figure 7

Cut   Cut

Figure 8

The Log Cabin Lace (Making One Square)

1. Begin with a square of fabric 1¹/₂" by 1¹/₂" (**fig. 1**).

2. Place a piece of lace overlapping one side of the square ¹/₄". The lace and fabric are both right side up. Stitch the lace in place with a zigzag. Trim excess fabric from behind. Trim lace strip even with the edges of the square. (**fig. 2**).

3. Place a second strip of lace along the second side of the fabric/lace using the same technique found in step 2 (**fig. 3**).

4. Continue stitching lace to all sides (**fig. 4 and 5**).

5. Repeat lace attachment until the desired size square is achieved (**fig. 6**).

Assembly–Line Log Cabin Lace Squares (Making Many Squares)

A. Preparing the center squares:

1. Begin with a 1¹/₂" wide strip of fabric marked in squares of 1¹/₂". If embroidered insertion is used for the center square, measure the distance from the center of one design to the center of the next design, then measure the width of the insertion. Whichever of the two is smaller will determine the size of the square. Mark into squares. Note: When marking make sure all of the sides are square, not slanted. Do not cut the squares apart (**fig. 7**).

B. Assembling the first round of lace "logs":

1. Once you have marked the squares, lace "logs" will be stitched around the squares. Four different laces will be needed. Label, or sort, the laces into piles of "A," "B," "C," and "D;" alternate white and ecru (if "A" is white, "B" is ecru, etc.).

2. Beginning with lace A, place the lace heading on top of one long edge of the fabric strip or embroidered insertion, letting the heading meet the seam line, ¹/₄" inside the edge or drawn line. Both pieces are right side up (**fig. 8**).

3. With a small zigzag, stitch the lace to the insertion.

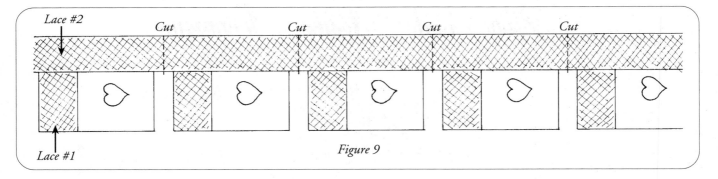

Figure 9

4. On the wrong side, carefully trim away the excess seam allowance, being careful not to cut the lace or get too close to the stitches.

5. Using a ruler to keep the lines straight, extend the drawn lines from the fabric strip or embroidered insertion across the lace piece just sewn; cut the pieces apart along the drawn lines. A rotary cutter and mat make this easier (**fig. 8**).

6. Stack the pieces right side up, with the last side you stitched on the right (the last side stitched is the one with no seams across it).

7. Keeping right sides up, rotate the squares 90 degrees so that the last lace piece stitched is now at the top. The next piece of lace will be added to the side of the squares that is now closest to the needle.

8. Using lace B, place the lace with right side up, under the machine foot.

9. Take the top block from the stack and slide it under the left edge of lace B until the lace heading lies on the $^1/_4$" seam line, inside the drawn line.

10. Stitch the lace to the embroidered insertion with a small zigzag over the lace heading. When you get to the end of the seam, leave the block under the machine foot.

11. Take the next block from the stack and repeat steps 9-10, leaving $^1/_4$" - $^3/_8$" between the edges of the blocks.

12. Repeat steps 7-9 until all of the blocks are sewn onto the lace "string." When you remove the last block from the machine, trim off the excess lace so that there is about $^1/_4$" left beyond the edge of the block.

13. Trim as in step 4.

14. Cut the blocks apart in the middle of the lace between the blocks, leaving a lace "tab" on each side of the block. Try to make the cuts straight across, not slanted (**fig. 9**).

15. Repeat steps 6-14 with lace C and lace D.

16. Stack and rotate the pieces as before.

— C. Assembling the second — round of lace "logs":

1. Place lace C under the machine foot.

2. Take the top square from the stack and slide it under the left edge of lace C until the headings on the two lace edges are overlapped; the lace "tab" you left on the square will extend under lace C.

3. Stitch with a small zigzag. When you come to the end of the seam, leave the block under the foot as before.

4. Slide the next block under lace C, leaving $^1/_4$" - $^3/_8$" between squares; stitch as before. Trim the lace "tabs" to $^1/_8$" if needed.

5. Cut the squares apart as before; stack and rotate the squares before adding each new lace.

6. Repeat steps 1-4 for laces D, A and B, in that order.

7. To add more rounds of lace, repeat steps 1-6, going back to laces A, B, C, D for the next, then to laces C, D, A, B for the following round until the square is as large as you want. ❀

Ribbon and Netting Diamonds

Shape the diamonds using double-faced ribbon (¹/₄" for small diamonds, and wider ribbon for larger diamonds). Cotton netting is used for the centers.

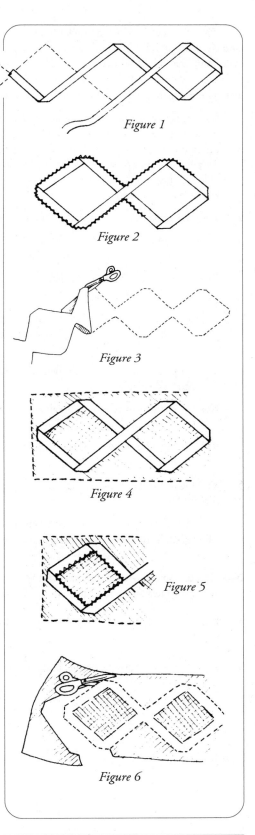

Figure 1

Figure 2

Figure 3

Figure 4

Figure 5

Figure 6

Requirements

✹ Cotton netting

✹ Double-faced satin ribbon

✹ Water soluble stablizer

✹ Washable marker

✹ Thread to match ribbon

✹ Template on pattern pull-out.

Instructions

1. Trace the diamond template onto the fabric. Place a piece of water-soluble stabilizer (WSS) on the right side of the fabric, over the template lines.

2. Place ribbon on top of the WSS along the template lines, using the "flip-flop" method (page194) for lace shaping. Pin in place. Start the ribbon at a point where two diamonds meet. Travel in a zigzag motion from one end of the template to the other, then zigzag back in the other direction, hiding the end of the ribbon under the beginning intersection (**fig. 1**).

3. Stitch along the <u>outer edge only</u> of the ribbon with a small zigzag, not quite a satin stitch (**fig. 2**).

4. On the wrong side, trim away the fabric from the inside of the diamond shapes, leaving the WSS in place to support the open space (**fig. 3**).

5. Place a strip of netting behind the cut-out diamonds, piecing the netting behind the intersections of the ribbon if necessary (**fig. 4**).

6. Using the same zigzag as before, stitch over the edges of the ribbon around the <u>inside</u> edges of the diamonds (**fig. 5**).

7. On the wrong side, trim away the excess netting (**fig. 6**).

8. Rinse the item in cold water to remove the WSS. ▨

Shadow Work Embroidery ── From The Back

With this method, you embroider from the wrong side of the fabric. When the fabric is loaded into the hoop, the wrong side of the fabric will be facing out. The design is traced onto that side. The stitches, a closed herringbone, are rather like "sewing" with a bite taken out of the top of the design and a bite taken out of the bottom. I prefer this method more than working from the front, because it is easiest.

1. Trace your design onto the wrong side of the fabric. If you are using an alphabet, be sure that the letters are properly reversed (**fig. 1**). An easy way to reverse letters or a design onto the wrong side of the fabric is to use a photocopy machine. Copy the design onto a clear plastic sheet like you would use for an overhead projector. This is called a transparency. Flip the transparency over. Run a copy on paper this time. It will be reversed properly.

2. Insert the fabric into the embroidery hoop.

3. Cut a piece of embroidery floss approximately 18 - 22 inches long (**fig. 2**). Remember to knot the cut end, although you will later cut that knot away.

4. There are two ways of placing the loose end (the knotted end of the floss) while you stitch your shadow embroidery.

   a. Lay the end of the floss (rather a long one) outside the embroidery hoop and close the hoop over it. This gives you plenty of floss to later weave into the completed design (**fig. 3**).

   b. Bring your knot up through the circle of fabric as far away from your first stitch as possible.

   Note: Sometimes there is not enough embroidery floss "tail" to easily weave into the completed design.

   Following the illustrations given, using the leaf shape (**fig. 4**), begin your stitching.

5. With the thread below the needle, bring the needle down at (A) (**fig 5**) and up at (B) (**fig. 6**). Pull through.

7. Move down. Thread above the needle, put your needle down at (C) (**fig. 7**) and up at (B) (**fig. 8**). Move into the exact same hole as your needle made on the first bite at (B).

Note: In order to easily remember whether the thread is above or below the needle, see the "Cat And The Courthouse Story" in the *Smocking Techniques*.

8. With the thread below the needle, bring the needle down at (D) (**fig. 9**) and up at (A) (**fig. 10**).

9. With the thread above the needle, bring the needle down at (E) (**fig. 11**) and up at (C) (**fig. 12**).

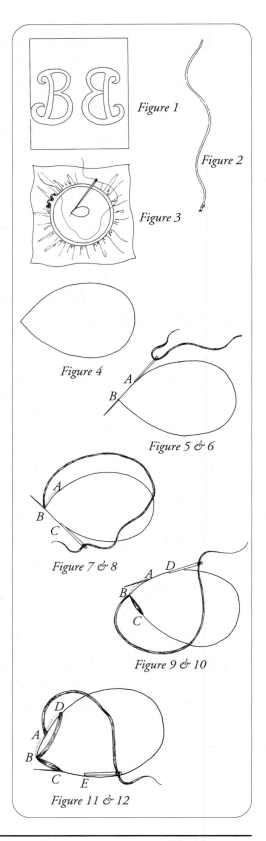

Figure 1

Figure 2

Figure 3

Figure 4

Figure 5 & 6

Figure 7 & 8

Figure 9 & 10

Figure 11 & 12

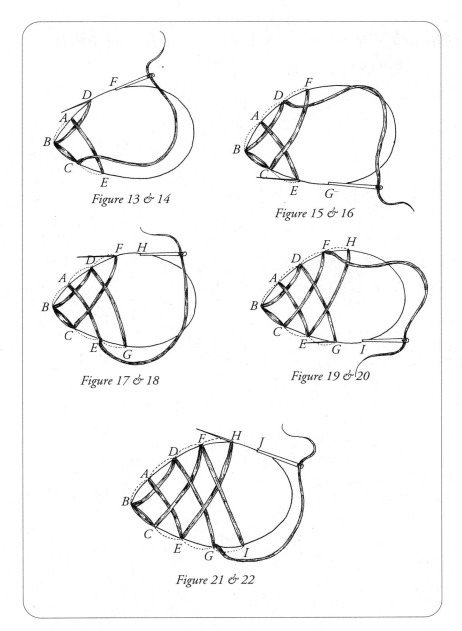

Figure 13 & 14

Figure 15 & 16

Figure 17 & 18

Figure 19 & 20

Figure 21 & 22

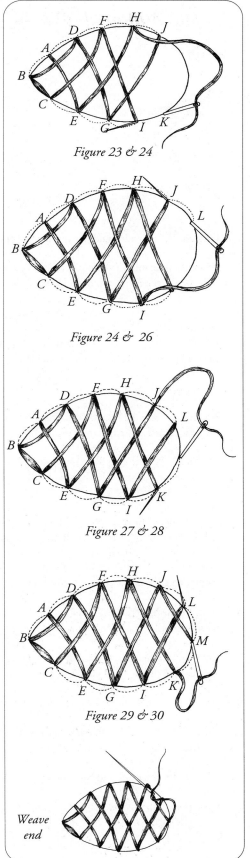

Figure 23 & 24

Figure 24 & 26

Figure 27 & 28

Figure 29 & 30

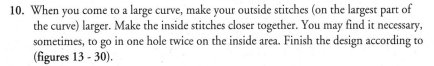

Weave end

10. When you come to a large curve, make your outside stitches (on the largest part of the curve) larger. Make the inside stitches closer together. You may find it necessary, sometimes, to go in one hole twice on the inside area. Finish the design according to (**figures 13 - 30**).

11. Keep turning your work so that the portion of the design you are currently working on is horizontally in front of you and so that you are working from left to right.

12. When you have finished your work, weave the tail of the thread through the stitching on the sides. As with most needlework, never knot your thread. Just weave it.

13. After you have finished with a design or with the amount of floss you have in your needle, weave that end into the design. Clip the knotted end which is either in the upper section of the fabric or held outside the embroidery hoop. Re-thread the needle with this end, and weave this end into the work as well. ❈

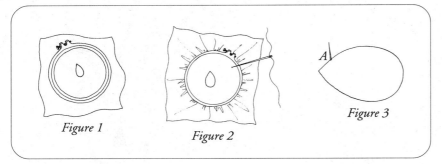

Figure 1

Figure 2

Figure 3

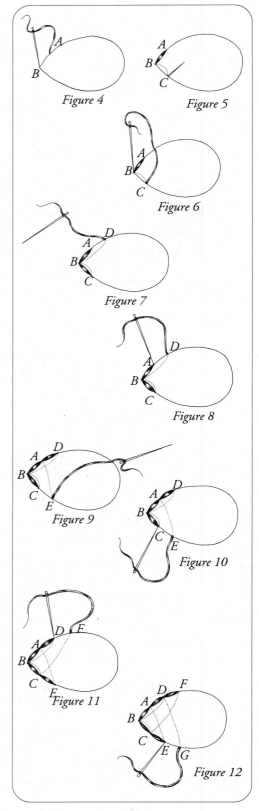

Figure 4

Figure 5

Figure 6

Figure 7

Figure 8

Figure 9

Figure 10

Figure 11

Figure 12

1. Trace the design you would like to shadowwork on the right side of the fabric (**fig. 1**).

2. Place the fabric into the embroidery hoop centering the design to be stitched. The right side of the fabric will be facing you.

3. Cut a piece of embroidery floss approximately 18 - 22 inches long. Separate the strands of floss. Thread one strand of floss through your favorite shadowwork needle. I suggest using a 10 sharp, 10 Crewels, or a 26 tapestry needle. Remember to knot the cut end of the floss, although you will later cut that knot away.

4. Securing the thread.

    Method 1. Place the knot on the wrong side of the fabric between the hoop and the fabric. Close the hoop (**fig. 2a**).

    Method 2. Place the needle in the right side of the fabric as far away from your first stitch as possible. The knot will end up on the right side of the fabric (**fig. 2b**).

    Either of these methods will put the needle/thread on the back side of the fabric. Note: This thread tail will need to be long enough to weave back through the stitching after the design is complete.

5. Bring the needle to the right side of the fabric at the beginning point (A) (**fig. 3**).

6. To make the first stitch, take the needle down at point (B) to the wrong side of the fabric (**fig. 4**).

7. Move to the other side of the design and bring the needle up at (C) (**fig. 5**) and back down at (B) (**fig. 6**). Pull gently.

8. Bring the needle up from the backside at (D) (**fig. 7**) and back down at (A) (**fig. 8**).

9. Move down to the other side and come up through (E) (**fig. 9**) and go back down at (C) (**fig. 10**).

10. Move to the other side and come up at (F) and back down at (D) (**fig. 11**).

12. Move to the other side and come up through (G) and down at (E) (**fig. 12**).

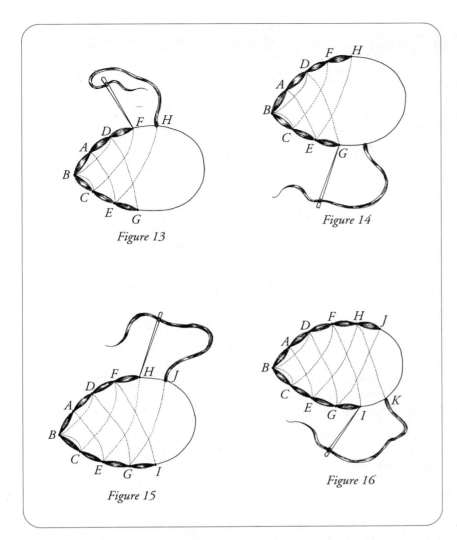

Figure 13

Figure 14

Figure 15

Figure 16

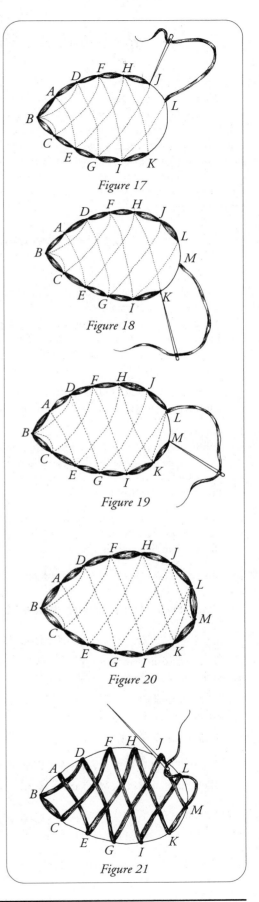

Figure 17

Figure 18

Figure 19

Figure 20

Figure 21

13. When you come to large curve, make your outside (on the largest part of the curve) larger. Make the inside stitches closer together. You may find it necessary to go in one hole twice on the inside area. Finish the design according to (**figures 13 - 20**).

14. After you have finished with a design or with the amount of floss you have in your needle, weave that end into the design. Clip the knotted end which is either in the upper section of the fabric or held outside the embroidery hoop. Rethread the needle with this end, and weave this end into the work as well (**fig. 21**). ▧

Shaped Puffing

Narrow puffing strips can be shaped in many of the same ways in which wide lace insertion can be shaped. This technique for puffing should be used only for decorative effects, and not on sleeve cuffs, for yoke-to-skirt attachments, or any place where there is stress on the fabric, because it is not as strong as puffing made with entredeux. It is a lovely treatment for skirts or collars. The loops and teardrops shown here have a little Swiss embroidered motif in the center; however, you could use lace insertion or a lace rosette in the center.

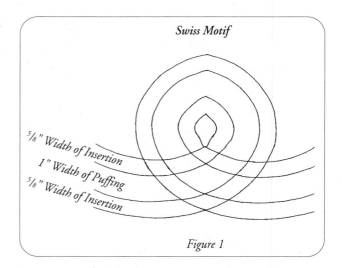

Swiss Motif

⁵⁄₈" *Width of Insertion*
1" *Width of Puffing*
⁵⁄₈" *Width of Insertion*

Figure 1

Puffing Directions

Method I

1. On paper, trace around the Swiss motif. Draw another line the width of the insertion away from the motif outline. Draw another line 1" (or desired width of puffing) beside second line. Draw another line the width of insertion outside the third line. Draw lines at the bottom to continue into smooth scallops (**fig. 1**).

2. Cut lots of puffing strips ³⁄₄" wider than your finished puffing. Run gathering threads ¹⁄₈" and ¹⁄₂" from each long edge. Use cotton covered polyester thread, loosened top tension, stitch length 2.5, stitch with bobbin thread on right side of strips (**fig. 2**).

3. Gather puffing strip to approximately 2:1 fullness and distribute gathers evenly. Place puffing strip over fabric (over fabric board), and pin in place as you would shaped insertion. Pull up gathering threads on inner curves to make puffing lay flat, just as you would pull the thread in the heading of lace insertion. Use your fingernail to distribute gathers (**fig. 3**).

4. Baste or pin puffing in place close to raw edges. Shape insertion along drawn lines. Remove pins from fabric board. Zigzag in place except for very center of loop (**fig 4**). Trim all layers from behind lace and puffing.

5. Place Swiss motif in center of loop and zigzag to lace.

Narrow Puffing With A Gathering Foot

Method II

You can use the gathering foot on your sewing machine to make this narrow puffing around the curves. Cut strip 1" wider than desired finished puffing. It really does work!

1. Use a gathering foot ¹⁄₂" from the edge, trim the seam allowance to ¹⁄₄". Run a row of gathers down both sides of the strip.

2. Pin as shown in (**fig. 3**).

3. With your fingers, "mush" the inside gathers into place.

4. Follow directions as in 4 and 5 above. ✶

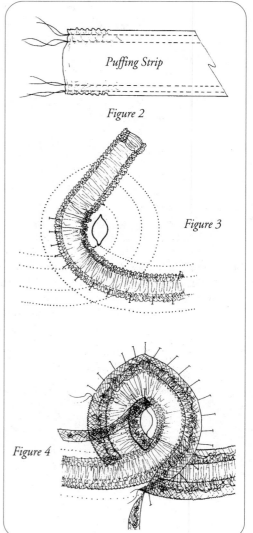

Puffing Strip

Figure 2

Figure 3

Figure 4

*Teardrop Or
Candlelight Puffing*

Loop Puffing

Preparing To Smock

Needles

Generally, a #8 crewel embroidery needle is used in smocking

For smockers with bad vision, it may not be comfortable to thread a #8 crewel needle with three or four strands of embroidery floss. If this is the case, use a #6 or #7 crewel needle.

Some needles work better for certain fabrics. For example:

a. for fine batiste or batiste blend, use a #8 or #9 crewel needle. Use a smaller size when using fewer strands of floss.

b. for fine to medium fabrics, such as broadcloth or quilting fabric, use a #7 or #8 crewel needle.

Personal preference for some smockers is to use milliner's needles. These needles are long and have a straight needle eye opening. Other smockers prefer to use #7 darners or #7 long darners.

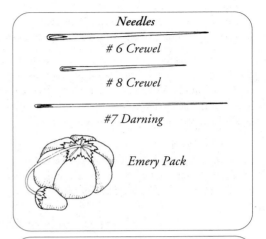

Needles

6 Crewel

8 Crewel

#7 Darning

Emery Pack

Embroidery Floss

The general rule of thumb is to use three strands of embroidery floss when working with fine to medium fabrics. However, there are exceptions:

a. For a different look with fine fabrics, try using two strands. It is pretty and delicate.

b. For picture smocking, most designers recommend four strands.

c. For some heavier fabrics, such as corduroy and velveteen, use up to five or six strands. Experiment with heavier fabrics to find the right weight of floss for the desired look.

d. It is perfectly acceptable to use Pearl Cotton #8 for smocking.

e. In order to prepare your embroidery floss for smocking, you must first make sure that it is put on grain properly. All thread has a grain. With DMC floss, it is easy to make sure the floss is on grain properly. Look at the two paper wraps on the embroidery floss. One has the round DMC symbol. The other has the color number and a picture of two hands pulling the floss out of the package. Follow these directions. Place your left hand on the floss, and with your right hand, pull the floss out of the package. Always knot the end that you cut. If I am smocking, I separate all six strands, then I put three strands back together and knot those three strands. I put the other three strands back together and knot those at that time also.

f. If for some reason you forget which end you cut and therefore, which end to knot, here is a simple solution. One end of the floss "blooms" more than the other. The cut end of the floss does not fuzz out as much. The knot will go on the less fuzzy end.

g. Needles also have a right and wrong side. Think about sewing machine needles that only go in one way. If you have difficulty threading a needle, flip it to the other side. One side will usually thread more easily than the other.

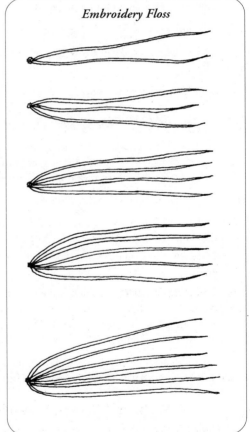

Embroidery Floss

Fabric

Some favorite fabrics to smock are the blends of 65 percent polyester and 35 percent cotton. Sometimes, a higher polyester count does not pleat well. However, using all of the half spaces of the Pullen Pleater, we have pleated lingerie - 100 percent nylon - without a pucker. Ginghams, Pima cottons, 100 percent cottons for quilting, challis, Swiss batiste, velveteen, soft corduroy, and silks are also good for smocking.

Fabrics, such as calico prints, which are 100 percent cotton, should be washed and dried before pleating. Fabrics with a polyester content generally do not shrink, and thus do not need to be washed prior to pleating. It is not necessary to preshrink Imperial batiste, Imperial broadcloth, 100 percent Swiss batiste (Nelona, Finella, Finissima), wool challis from Switzerland, and velveteen.

Note: When a 45 inch piece for the front and one for the back of a yoke dress is necessary, it is easier to tear those skirt lengths first and preshrink them separately. Then, preshrink the remaining fabric from which the bodice, sleeves, and collars will be cut. It is easier to preshrink and put fabric "on grain" in smaller pieces.

Putting Fabric On Grain

Follow these directions for putting fabric on grain.

Tear both ends. Most fabric stores tear wovens (**fig. 1**).

Or, pull a thread and clip across from selvage to selvage. I always do this on Swiss batiste (**fig. 2**).

Fabric may be preshrunk after having "torn" or "pulled a thread" and cut the fabric.

Tying Off Pleating Threads Before Smocking

Much of the fitting is done before any smocking is done. Measure the piece to which the smocking is to be attached. The general rule is that the smocking is to be tied off 1 to 1½ inches smaller than the finished piece will be.

Figure 3 Is an example of where the whole skirt will be used in the smocked garment.

Figure 4 Is a typical short yoke dress where a portion of the armhole curve must be cut away out of the skirt. Do not smock that portion. Do not count that portion when figuring the 1 to 1½ inches rule of tying off.

This rule is sometimes called "smocking to size." It is a must to size the smocking before beginning to smock. The smocking will have to be stretched too much to fit the dress if this rule is not followed. This causes ripples and waves at the yoke after the dress is constructed. I suppose that the opposite could be true (smocking too loosely); however, I have never found beginning smockers to smock too loosely.

The width of fabric, before being pleated, should be three times as wide as the finished smocked piece will be. A little more or a little less fullness is acceptable.

Right and Wrong Side of Pleated Fabric

Pleated fabric has a right and wrong side. The secret to figuring out which side of the fabric to smock, assuming that the fabric does not already have a designated right or wrong side, is easy to remember - **Long is Wrong**.

Stretch out the pleated fabric (**fig. 5**). Look at the length of stitches on both sides. The flat stitches are longer on one side than they are on the other . This is the wrong side. The right side of the fabric, the side to be smocked, has the shorter stitches (**fig. 6**). Hence, the rule - **Long is Wrong**.

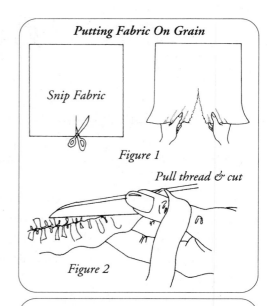

Snip Fabric

Figure 1

Pull thread & cut

Figure 2

Tying Off Peating Threads Before Smocking

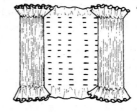

Figure 3

This is a "longish" yoke dress where the whole 45" gathered skirt will be used in the garment. Tie off the skirt gathering threads before smocking so that the total skirt is from 1" to 1½" smaller than the yoke to which it will be attached after the smocking is completed.

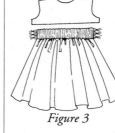

Figure 4

Right and Wrong Side of Pleated Fabric

"Long Is Wrong"

Figure 5

"Pulling Pleating Apart So Stitches Can Be Seen"

Roll Down Long Stitches

Figure 6

Short Stitches

Another way to determine the right and wrong side of the pleated fabric is by the height of the pleats. Flip the pleated fabric back and forth to see which side has the tallest pleats from the gathering row up to the top of the pleat. The right side of the pleated fabric has the tallest pleats.

When running fabric through the pleater, the right side of the fabric should face the floor or the bottom of the pleater. If you are using a fabric with a designated right or wrong side (corduroy or printed fabric), run it through the pleater with the right side facing down to the floor.

Tying Off Gathering Threads Before Smocking

After opening the pleated fabric to the desired width, it is time to tie off the excess gathering threads (**fig. 7**).

Tie off as many threads as is comfortable. I usually work with three threads (**fig. 8**).

It is not necessary to tie off gathering threads at all. Many smockers will work with them hanging long. As a beginner, you might find that the long hanging threads tangle. If so, tie them.

It is hard to keep the spongy quilting thread from coming untied. I find that a surgical knot does the trick.

Tying A Surgical Knot

1. Tie one knot. Do not take this first knot down to the fabric, but leave it about 1 inch away from the fabric edge (**fig. 9**).

2. Hold the knot with your right hand. Wrap the left hand strings around the knot one more time (**figs. 10 and 11**). Reverse if you are left handed.

3. Tie one more knot, just like the first one (**fig. 12**). This last knot is pulled tightly for a very tight knot (**fig. 13**).

4. Clip off the excess threads after tying each knot. Clip the threads to within 2 inches of the knot.

Centering Smocking Design

The easiest way to mark the center of the fabric is to fold it in half and mark. Counting the pleats to determine the center will also work. There are two methods of centering the smocking.

• Method One

1. Begin smocking in the exact center of the skirt or dress. Tie knots at this point, as if this were the left hand side of the smocking.

2. Knot the floss. Bring it in on the left hand side of the middle pleat of the skirt. Smock half the skirt to the right side.

3. Turn the work upside down. Smock the other side, working from the middle to the other side.

• Method Two

This method avoids the two knots on the center pleats (**fig. 14**).

1. Leave a long thread with the first stitch.

2. Take this first stitch from the front of the smocking. Do not bring the thread from the back. Leave your long, unknotted thread hanging on the front.

3. Smock all the way over to the right and tie off.

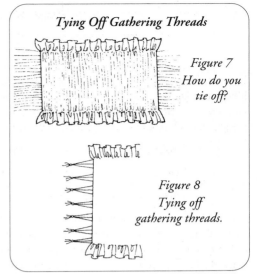

Tying Off Gathering Threads

Figure 7
How do you tie off?

Figure 8
Tying off gathering threads.

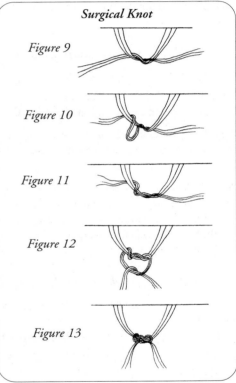

Surgical Knot

Figure 9

Figure 10

Figure 11

Figure 12

Figure 13

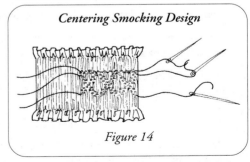

Centering Smocking Design

Figure 14

4. Turn the work upside down. Re-thread the long thread. Finish the first stitch you started. Smock the rest of the work to the other side.

Crazy Cat and The Courthouse Story

Many beginner smockers get frustrated with the rule: When you move up, the thread is down, when you move down, the thread is up. For a beginner, this is the most difficult concept to learn. I made up a simple, and very silly, story to help beginners remember this principle. I was a little embarrassed the first time I told the story, but several years and smockers later, I can honestly say the story works.

Setting - courthouse with lots of tall steps leading to the door.

Characters - A Tabby cat with a very long tail, Martha Pullen.

Time - During business hours.

Tabby Cat wants to drive a car and knows she must first have a driver's license. Martha Pullen drives Tabby Cat to the courthouse and parks at the side of the building to let Tabby Cat out. Tabby Cat climbs the long steps until she gets almost to the top. There, she remembers that you have to have money to pay for a license. Tabby Cat turns around, climbs down the long flight of steps and goes back to the car to get some money from her purse.

• Important Points To This Story:

Point A. Tabby Cat's tail is the thread.

Point B. When Tabby Cat climbs stairs, her tail points downward (**fig. 15**). In smocking, when the needle is moving up, the tail of the thread is down.

Point C. When Tabby Cat climbs down steep stairs, her tail points upward (**fig. 16**). In smocking, when you are moving to take a stitch downward, the tail of the thread is up.

Point D. When Tabby Cat turns around at the top of stairs, at the landing, her tail swings around before she can begin to climb back down the stairs. This symbolizes a top cable before the wave or trellis moves downward. When Tabby Cat turns around at the bottom of the stairs to begin upward, this symbolizes a bottom cable before the climb back up.

Bringing In The Needle To Begin Smocking

There are two schools of thought on where to make the first stitch.

Method One

1. Bring in the needle on the left hand side of the first pleat that begins your smocking (**fig. 17**).

2. Bring in the needle just above the gathering thread (**fig. 18**).

3. It is acceptable to bring in the needle in the same hole as the gathering thread, on this left side of the pleat.

4. This method leaves the knot of the floss hidden within the first pleat on the back of the smocking.

Method Two

1. Bring in the needle on the left hand side of the second pleat, rather than on the left hand side of the first pleat (**fig. 19**).

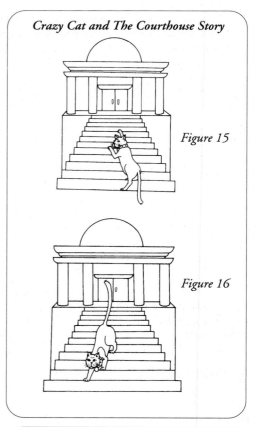

Crazy Cat and The Courthouse Story

Figure 15

Figure 16

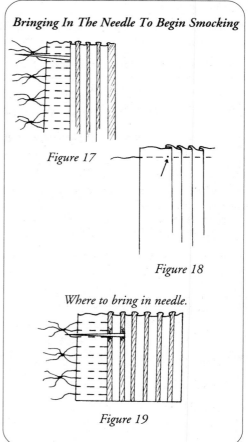

Bringing In The Needle To Begin Smocking

Figure 17

Figure 18

Where to bring in needle.

Figure 19

2. Go through the gathering holes of the first pleat to bring the needle out of the left hand side of the first pleat where smocking begins. This hides the knot in the second pleat and is stronger and more secure. The knot will less likely pull out with wear and washing since it is one pleat over from the edge of the smocking (**fig. 20**).

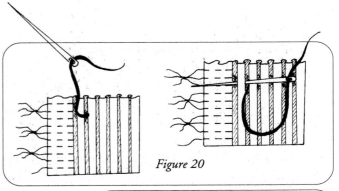

Figure 20

Stitch Bite

Nearly all smocking books advise picking up from ¹/₃ to ¹/₂ of the pleat above the gathering threads (**fig. 21**).

I have tried my best to figure out how there is enough space using a #8 crewel embroidery needle to pick up ¹/₃ of the space above the gathering threads, when there is only about ¹/₁₆ of an inch in that distance. A #8 crewel needle is almost that wide.

I suggest picking up ⁵/₈ to ⁷/₈ of the distance from the gathering thread to the top of the pleat. Some people may pick up as little as ¹/₂ of the pleat above the gathering row.

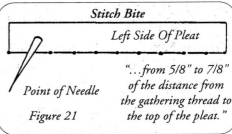

Stitch Bite

Left Side Of Pleat

Point of Needle

Figure 21

"…from 5/8" to 7/8" of the distance from the gathering thread to the top of the pleat."

Tangled Thread

Your thread may become tangled after making some stitches. There are several ways to fix this. Hold the smocking over, so that the threaded needle can hang loose. Let the thread untangle by twirling around until it stops (**fig. 22**).

With the needle still threaded, push the needle all the way down to the fabric. Separate the strands of floss, untangling them all the way down to the needle which is slipped all the way down to the fabric. After separating the strands, carefully rub them together again, slip the needle up and begin to smock again (**fig. 23**).

Some people use beeswax for smocking. It does keep threads from tangling, somewhat. Be aware that beeswax may compress the threads more than you like (**fig. 24**).

I think a better substitute for beeswax is to run the threads (already threaded and knotted) over a dry bar of Ivory Soap. This gives a little lubrication (**fig. 25**)

Always remember to have floss running with the grain with the cut end knotted (**fig. 26**). Always remember to separate the floss, strand by strand, before knotting.

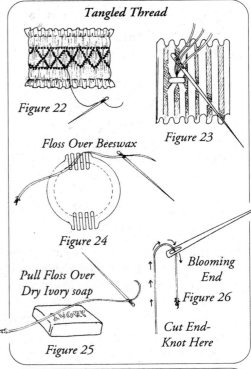

Tangled Thread

Figure 22

Figure 23

Floss Over Beeswax

Figure 24

Pull Floss Over Dry Ivory soap

Figure 25

Blooming End

Figure 26

Cut End- Knot Here

Slip-Snail Knot

Tying Off Your Thread

When you run out of thread in the middle of a row, when you change colors, or when you end a row of smocking, you must properly tie off your thread. I like to use a slip snail knot.

1. Take the thread to the back of the smocking.

2. Turn the work to the back and notice that the needle is in one pleat. This is the pleat on which you will want to put the knot.

3. Make a stitch in that one pleat (**fig. 27**).

4. Tighten that stitch but leave a little loop (**fig. 28**).

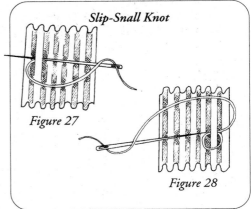

Slip-Snall Knot

Figure 27

Figure 28

5. Take the needle and slip it through the loop (**fig. 29**).

6. Pull the thread to form a little knot (**fig. 30**). This is where the slip snail knot comes in. Slip the needle through the loop and slip a little knot in the thread. This knot should look like a snail.

7. If you want to tie the second knot, follow the same instructions in the same pleat.

Tie-Off, Re-thread, and Begin Again In Middle

Since smocking is best worked with 15 to 20 inch lengths of thread, tie off and begin again in the middle of the row. It is easiest to tie off on a level stitch, using the following technique.

1. Take the smocking stitch, whatever that stitch may be.

2. Take the needle to the back by going between the last two pleats involved in that last stitch. Slip the needle down very close to the stitch before taking the thread straight back to the back (**fig. 31**).

3. Tie a slip snail knot. You may want to tie two.

4. Re-thread. Tie a knot in the end of the thread.

5. Bring the new thread in on the left hand side of the last pleat that already has smocking on it. It may be difficult to do, since the stitch will already be secured and tied off (**fig. 32**).

6. Try to bring the needle in at exactly the same place that the smocking thread has travelled in the left hand side of that last pleat. The thread will appear as if it were not tied off at all, coming through the same hole as described.

NOTE: Try to bring the needle point in at exactly the same place that the smocking thread has already made a hole in the left hand side of that last pleat. If you can come in at that same hole, the thread will be as if it were not tied off at all.

Specific Stitch Tie-Off Situations

Thread placement depends on whether the next stitch moves upward or downward.

- **Example A** You have just completed a two-step wave, coming down. You have made the down-cable, at the bottom. This is the turnaround stitch. Tie off the thread, and bring the new thread in the left hand side of the last pleat of the down-cable you just took. Bring the thread in on the top side of that down-cable because you are preparing to go back up in your two-step wave (**fig. 33**).

- **Example B** You have just completed a two-step wave, going up. You have made the up-cable at the top of the wave. Tie off your thread and bring the new thread in on the left hand side of the last pleat of that up-cable you just took. Bring your thread in on the bottom side of that up-cable because you are preparing to go back down in your two-step wave (**fig. 34**).

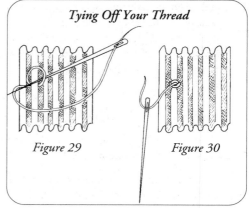

Tying Off Your Thread

Figure 29   *Figure 30*

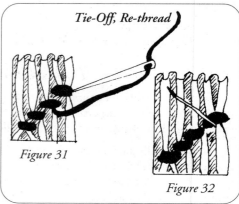

Tie-Off, Re-thread

Figure 31

Figure 32

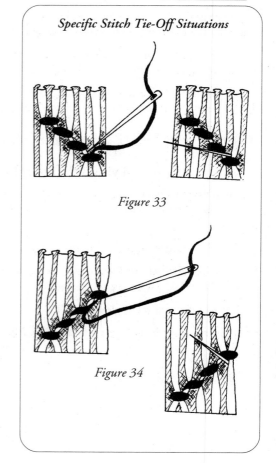

Specific Stitch Tie-Off Situations

Figure 33

Figure 34

Smocking Completed

1. Always block your smocking before constructing the garment. After smocking is completed, carefully remove all gathering row threads except the top gathering thread.
2. Set your steam iron on the lowest setting you can get and still have steam.
3. Pin the smocked piece to the board at the top, middle, and sides (**fig. 35**). Gently stretch it out to the exact measurement of the yoke to which it will be attached. I pin the smocking right side up to be sure the smocking design is straight.
4. Hold the steam iron at least one or two inches above the smocking. Do not touch the smocking with the iron. Steam the piece (**fig. 36**). Allow it to dry thoroughly before unpinning the piece from board. ⌘

Smocking Completed

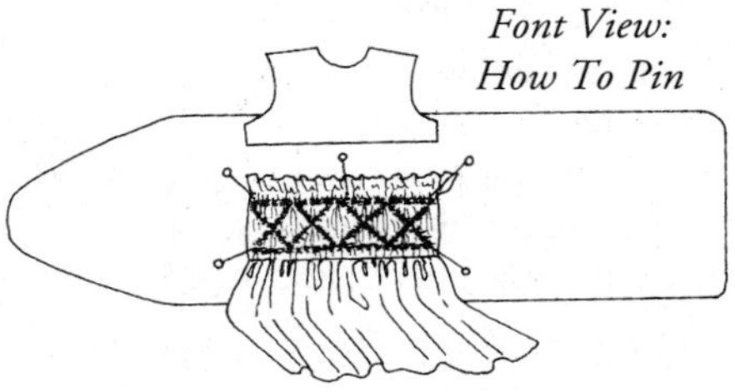
Font View:
How To Pin

Figure 35

Steam Pleating

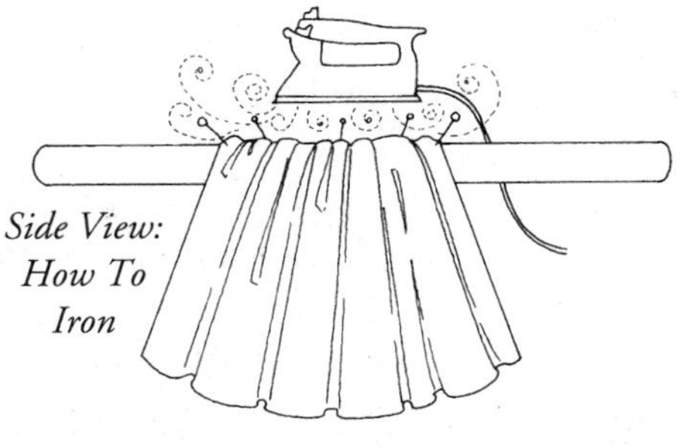
Side View:
How To
Iron

Figure 36

The Pleater

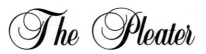

I have taught beginning smocking to more than 2,000 people. The single largest problem for the beginners was guessing the location of the half spaces, between the two rows of pleats. Many beginners ended up with half-space smocking which looks like a snake crawling through the rows. Needless to say, it was very frustrating.

Pleater

Important Parts

1. Left hand end plate
2. Right hand end plate
3. Base of the machine
4. Needles inserted into the grooves
5. Drop-in roller
6. Keeper and keeper screw
7. Knob
8. Left hand groove for fabric to pass through
9. Right hand groove for fabric to pass through in certain pleating instances

Important Pleater Parts

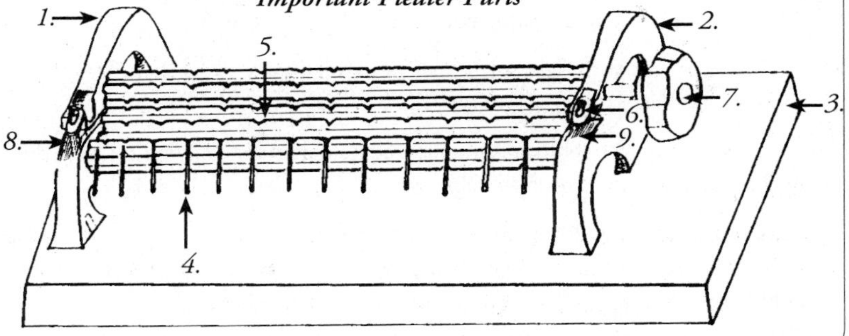
1.
2.
3.
4.
5.
6.
7.
8.
9.

Pleater Needles

Replacing

1. Loosen the keeper screw. Complete removal of the keeper and the screws is not necessary; just slide the keeper forward on the loosened screw (**fig.1**).
2. Tilt the machine back and prop it on a book. Tilting the pleater keeps the needles from falling out.
3. With the thumb, gently roll the small, drop-in roller up and off of the machine (**fig. 2**).

Replacing Pleater Needles

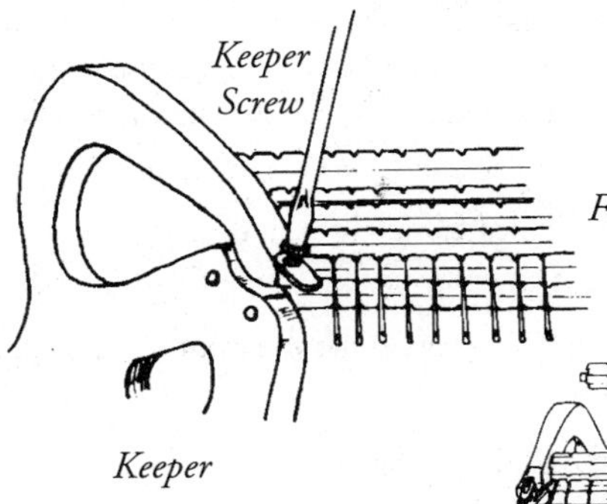
Keeper
Screw
Keeper

Figure 1

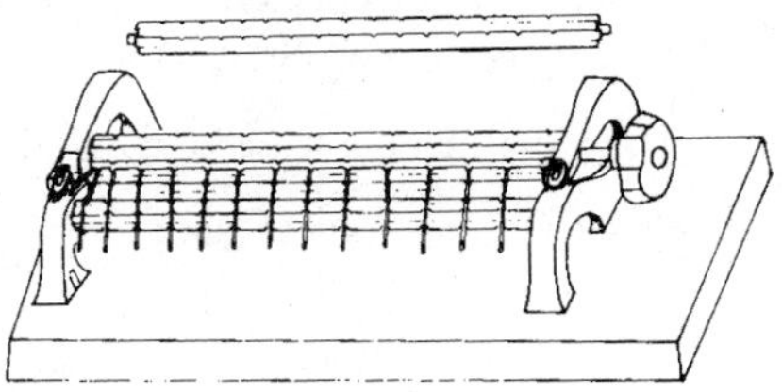
Roller

Figure 2

4. Reposition the needles according to the specific pleating needs (**fig. 3**).

5. Gently roll the drop-in roller back into place. Be sure to align the half spaces of the drop-in roller with the half space grooves on the pleater.

6. Tighten the screw just until resistance is felt. Then turn just a tiny bit more. Do not overtighten. Loosen the screws when pleating heavier fabrics; tighten them for sheer fabrics.

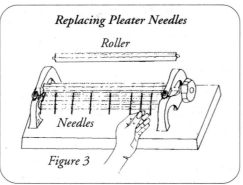

Replacing Pleater Needles

Roller

Needles

Figure 3

Note: To hold your pleater in place during pleating, try this. Purchase a spool of 2" duck tape.

Cut enough of this tape to put across the back of the pleater. Put the pleater on a flat surface with the duck tape across the back of the pleater and on the flat surface.

Preparing To Pleat

1. Thread the required number of needles. I use a 36" long piece of quilting thread for each needle. Thread from the top. Pull 6". Let the long end hang (**fig. 4**).

2. Do not cut off the armholes of a yoke dress until after the fabric has been pleated.

3. The right side of the pleating should be downwards when going though the machine. The tallest pleats come from the bottom of the pleater (**fig. 5**).

4. Lay the fabric flat with right sides down, and roll onto a dowel stick. Run the fabric through the pleater, right side down (**fig. 6**).

Note: If you are using a bobbin continuous feed holder or system, your quilting thread may become spongy. This may help.

Soak your spool of quilting thread in warm water. Place the spool in front of the refrigerator vent overnight to gently dry the thread. You may then wind it onto bobbins or put the spools into your smocking machine holder.

Dowel Sticks

Usually I use a ¼", wooden, craft-type dowel stick, about 36" long. However, some people like small, thin, steel rods which give some weight for holding the fabric and dowel in place while pleating. Others like a cafe curtain rod which opens or closes as much as needed for garments. The size of the dowel should be compatible with the type fabric used, no larger than 1" (**fig. 7**).

1. Put the dowel stick, covered with the rolled fabric, through the left hand side of the pleater.

2. Line up the exact rows to pleat. Eyeball the groove that you must use as a guideline in order to run the pleating through evenly (**fig. 8**).

3. Leave one whole pleater space for the guideline (**fig. 9**).

4. Hold the fabric and begin to guide it through.

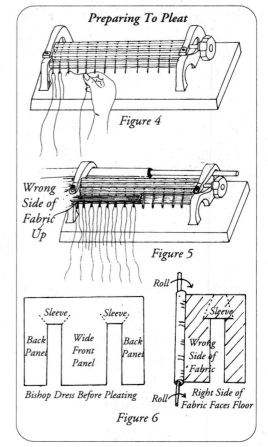

Preparing To Pleat

Figure 4

Wrong Side of Fabric Up

Figure 5

Roll

Sleeve   Sleeve

Back Panel | Wide Front Panel | Back Panel

Bishop Dress Before Pleating

Sleeve

Wrong Side of Fabric

Roll

Right Side of Fabric Faces Floor

Figure 6

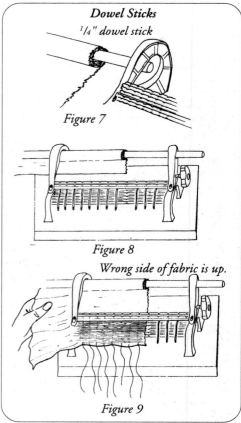

Dowel Sticks

¼" dowel stick

Figure 7

Figure 8

Wrong side of fabric is up.

Figure 9

5. As your fabric goes through the pleater it is important to gently pull the fabric edge hanging out the left side. Gently pull parallel with the rollers. This will keep bumps from forming in the pleats. Let the rollers and the handle pull the fabric through (**fig. 10**).

6. As the fabric comes onto the needles, stop and gently, gently, guide the fabric off of the needles. Do not force or jerk, since this could bend the needles.

Pleater

General Instructions

1. The fabric edge to be fed into the machine should be cut straight and started evenly to avoid a crooked pleat and for pleating with ease. Gently "rocking" the fabric into the pleater may get it going.

2. Do not force or pull the fabric into the roller gears to get it started. Align the fabric straight into the gears and let the gears grab the fabric as you start turning. Although unlikely, if the fabric should jam and some of the needles start moving wildly, the pleater may become very difficult to turn. Remove the drop-in roller gear and remove the needles and fabric. "Cutting out the pleating" will be avoided this way.

3. Always be sure to trim the selvage on heavier fabrics, such as corduroy and broadcloth. This is a good idea with any fabric, but especially with the heavier fabrics.

4. A strip of wax paper, run through the pleater prior to pleating, will lubricate the needles and allow the fabric to pass more freely. It is not recommended to pleat over French seams because of the bulk of fabric that the pleater needles must penetrate. It is recommended that you serge the seams together using a rolled hem. If, however, you find it necessary to pleat over French seams, rub a bar of soap on the seams before pleating them. Rubbing the bar of soap over the edge of heavier fabric edges works well also (**fig. 11**).

5. Fabric may tend to pile up on the needles as it comes out of the pleater and make it hard to turn. If this occurs, gently slide the fabric along the needles onto the thread as it accumulates on the needles (**fig. 12**).

6. Always use the exact number of needles. Leaving excess needles in the pleater may cause wear and tear and even breakage of the needles.

7. To minimize dulling of the needles and machine wear, avoid turning the pleater without fabric in it.

8. Replace bent and dull needles. If not replaced, they can jam the cloth and break in the machine. A bent needle is easy to identify: it moves excessively while the pleater is turning, it has an unusual angle compared with the other needles, and it makes pleating more difficult.

9. Needles do need to be changed after excess usage because they will dull.

10. If the machine becomes stiff to operate, chances are that you have wound some threads into the machine or around the shaft of the roller. Pick these out carefully with a small needle and cut them.

11. Because the pleater's needles will rust when exposed to moisture, keep the pleater in a dry place. ✳

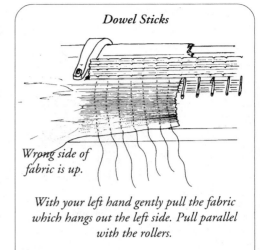

Dowel Sticks

Wrong side of fabric is up.

With your left hand gently pull the fabric which hangs out the left side. Pull parallel with the rollers.

Figure 10

Rub a bar of Ivory soap over French seams before pleating them.

A strip of wax paper, run through the pleater prior to pleating, will lubricate the needles and allow the fabric to pass more freely.

Figure 11

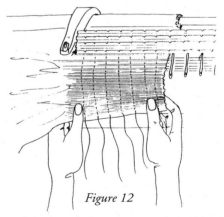

Figure 12

Fabric may tend to pile up on the needles as it comes out of the pleater and make it hard to turn. If this occurs, gently slide the fabric along the needles onto the thread as it accumulates on the needles.

Smocking Stitches

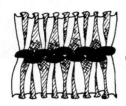

Cable Stitch

Cable Stitch

General Instructions

- This stitch is worked from left to right. It consists of alternating up and down cables. Start the thread on the left hand side of the pleat to smock.

- Take every stitch with the needle running parallel to the gathering line, taking care to keep the needle parallel as you take the stitches.

- The needle always "bites the fabric" exactly on top of the gathering row. It may appear that one stitch goes a tiny bit above the gathering thread and one stitch goes a tiny bit below. The up cable (top cable) and down-cable (bottom cable) portions of the stitch gives this appearance. Be sure you keep each stitch exactly on top of the gathering thread.

- A down cable is made by stitching into the pleat with the thread below the needle. An up cable is made by stitching into the pleat with the thread above the needle.

- Take one cable stitch in every pleat. Throw the thread to the bottom in one stitch, to the top in the next.

Directions

1. Bring in the thread on the left hand side of the first pleat.

2. Move to the second pleat and take a stitch there with the thread below the needle. This is a down cable (**fig. 1**).

3. Move to the third pleat and take a stitch with the thread above the needle. This is an up cable (**fig. 2**).

4. Move to the fourth pleat and take a stitch with the thread below the needle. This is another down cable.

5. Move to the fifth pleat and take another stitch with the thread above the needle. This is another up cable.

6. Every two to four stitches, with the needle or a fingernail, push the cable stitches together to be sure the fabric does not show through.

Note: To make beautiful cable stitches, try this. After taking the stitch, begin to tighten by pulling upward on a down-cable and downward on an up-cable. Before actually pulling the final stitch to the fabric, place your thumbnail next to the stitch and guide the stitch into its exact position. ❖

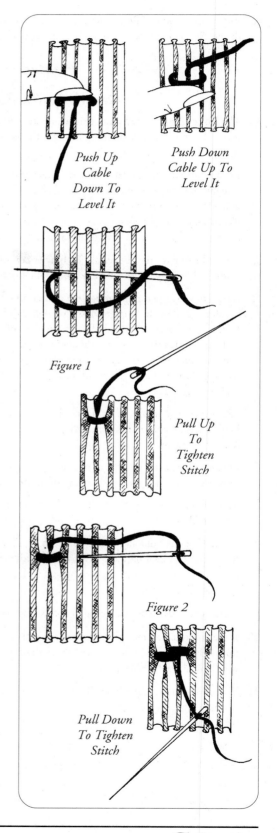

Push Up Cable Down To Level It

Push Down Cable Up To Level It

Figure 1

Pull Up To Tighten Stitch

Figure 2

Pull Down To Tighten Stitch

Outline Stitch

Directions

This stitch is worked from left to right.

1. Bring the thread in on the left hand side of the first pleat (**fig. 1**).

2. The outline stitch is a continuous row of up cables. The thread is thrown above the needle for every stitch (**fig. 2**).

3. Run the needle in parallel to the gathering row, on exactly the top of the gathering row. Tighten each up-cable by pulling down. Always tighten up cables in this manner (**fig. 3**).

4. After tightening each stitch, gently pull upward to align the whole row with the gathering row (**fig. 4**). ❈

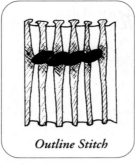

Outline Stitch

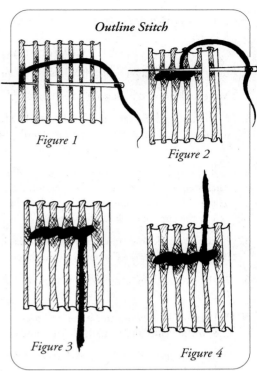

Outline Stitch

Figure 1

Figure 2

Figure 3

Figure 4

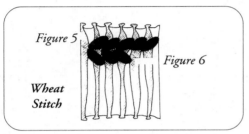

Figure 5

Figure 6

Wheat Stitch

Wheat Stitch

A wheat stitch derives its name because of the similarity in its looks to wheat. The wheat stitch is really two rows of stitching.

Directions

1. The first row is the outline stitch (**fig. 5**).

2. Work a row of stem stitches directly under the outline stitch row (**fig. 6**). ❈

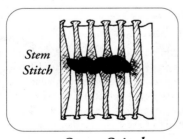

Stem Stitch

Stem Stitch

This stitch is worked from left to right.

1. Bring the thread in on the left hand side of the first pleat (**fig. 7**).

2. The outline stitch is a continuous row of down cables. The thread is thrown down below the needle for each stitch (**fig. 8**).

3. Take each stitch by running the needle in parallel to the gathering row on exactly the top of the gathering thread. Next, tighten each down cable by pulling up (**fig. 9**).

4. After you do the up tighten on each stitch, gently pull downward to pull the whole row back in line with the gathering row (**fig. 10**). ❈

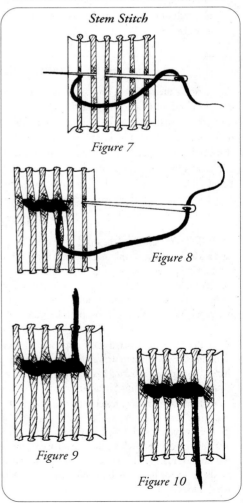

Stem Stitch

Figure 7

Figure 8

Figure 9

Figure 10

Wave/Chevron Stitch or Baby Wave

Directions

1. Bring the thread in on the left hand side of the first pleat.

2. Move to the second pleat and make a down cable (**fig. 1**).

3. Make another down cable at the half-space line (marked with a gathering thread on the pleat). Remember the Cat and the Courthouse story. When the cat goes up the courthouse steps, the tail drops down (**fig. 2**).

4. Make an up cable on the half-space line also (**fig. 3**). It may look as if the second stitch went in between the bottom row and the half-space row. Looks are deceiving. The second bottom cable and the top cable (the turnaround stitch) are placed on exactly the same line - the half-space line.

5. Now move back down to the whole line. Make an up-cable at the starting line (**fig. 4**). Remember the Cat and the Courthouse tale.

6. At the same bottom row, make another down-cable. This is the turnaround stitch (**fig. 5**).

NOTE: Half-space chevrons end at the half space on the smocking rows. Whole-space chevrons are taller and go all the way to another row.

Half-space chevrons are easy if you own a Pullen pleater because the gathering thread is in the half spaces in addition to the whole spaces. Half-space refers to the fact that the stitch only goes from the main row to the halfway point and back again to its main row. ✄

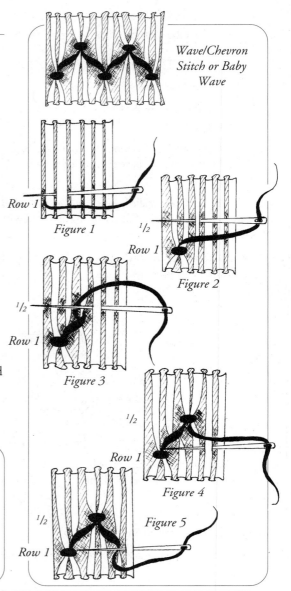

Wave/Chevron Stitch or Baby Wave

Row 1
Figure 1

½
Row 1
Figure 2

½
Row 1
Figure 3

½
Row 1
Figure 4

½
Row 1
Figure 5

Sitting In Martha's Smocking Class

"Bring the thread in on the left hand side of the first pleat, on Row 1. Move over one pleat and make a down cable. Move over to the next pleat at the same time moving up to the ¹/₂ space and make another down cable. **At the same ¹/₂ space point**, move over another pleat and make an up cable. This is your turn around stitch. Notice that two stitches were placed with your needle at the ¹/₂ space on your diagrams. Move over one pleat and make an up cable back at Row 1. Move over another pleat and make a down cable also at Row 1. That last stitch was your bottom turn around stitch." ✄

Reflections From Martha On Smocking

The very thought of the word, smocking, brings joy to my heart. The first smocking I ever stitched was begun in 1968 when I bought a soft coral fabric and a McCall's pattern with iron on dots. This lovely little bishop dress was lovingly constructed by me and then those dratted dots were ironed on. The commercial pattern instructed me to draw up each dot as I stitched a little wave design. My very nerves were shattered as I hunted among the stitches for the next dot to draw up. Actually, I gave up on completing the dress; however, I didn't throw it away. Years later, about 1978 to be exact, I found the little unfinished dress. Since I had begun my first smocking class at that time, I decided that it would be good to finish it for Joanna. The original plans for the dress were for a friend's little girl. Those plans fell through! I was so proud of my completing it, I even took Joanna for a picture in the dress which took 10 years to make!

I had a pleater ordered at that time and was very grateful for a teacher who would pleat for me until mine came. Back in the "olden days of smocking" (around 1978) you had to wait about a year for a smocking machine. Worse yet, the price was $165 for a small pleater. My pleater finally came and the rest is history, I suppose. Smocking has been one of the great joys of my life and smocking for grandchildren has brought the smocking bug back into my life in full swing. I'm even perfecting picture smocking.

I have a funny story to relate to you. About 1982, when I still had a smocking shop, the phone rang one day and a sweet sounding lady asked me to mail order her a smocking needle. Customarily, one orders several needles for the pleater, but I figured that she had broken only one pleater needle and that she only wanted to spend $1. I wrapped one pleater needle carefully and mailed it to her. A few weeks later she wrote me a letter thanking me for this wonderful needle. She related that it had taken hours off of her smocking to have that interesting little crooked needle! Mortified, I picked up the phone and reconfirmed my fear that she had used that pleater needle to smock a whole dress. I apologized profusely, telling her that I thought she had wanted a pleater needle. Since she had never heard of a pleater, I sold her a pleater over the phone and she promised that she would never again use her crooked needle for hand smocking. ✄

Two, Three, or Four-Step Wave (Trellis)

My Misunderstanding

This stitch can be known as a wave or a trellis. Either is correct; I choose to call it a wave.

When I was a beginner, just learning to smock, one thing always confused me about waves. So, let's try to clear it up first. When looking at a two-step wave, I counted four stitches going up on one side and three stitches coming down on the other. How could this stitch be called a two-step wave with all these stitches. Each wave must have a cable at the bottom and a cable at the top. These are "level" or "turnaround" stitches. And counting these as steps to the two-step wave is where I got confused.

Correct Way To Count A Two-Step Wave

Stitch 1 is a bottom-cable working as a turnaround stitch.

Stitch 2 is moving up as **Step 1** in the two-step wave.

Stitch 3 is moving up as **Step 2** in the two-step wave.

Stitch 4 is a top-cable working as a turnaround stitch. ✽

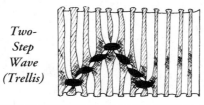

Two-Step Wave (Trellis)

Two-Step Wave (Trellis)

Directions

This is worked from left to right. Move over one pleat at a time as you move up and down between the rows.

A two-step wave can have various heights, depending on your design. **Example:** A two-step wave which goes from row 1 to row $^1/_2$ above it (technically called a half-space, two-step wave) is done like this:

1. Bring the needle in on the left side of the first pleat. Begin with a down-cable on Row 1 (**fig. 1**).

2. Move up halfway between row 1 and row $^1/_2$ (a $^1/_4$ space) for the next stitch, a down cable (**fig. 2**).

3. Move up to the half-space for the next stitch, another down cable (**fig. 3**).

4. At this same half-space point, move over one pleat and do a top cable (turn-around stitch) (**fig. 4**).

5. Move down $^1/_4$ space, do a top cable.

6. Move down to row 1 and do another top cable.

7. Complete the stitch sequence with another turn-around stitch (a bottom cable). ✽

"Now, there is a common misunderstanding concerning 2 step waves. I will try to clear this up. Look at the illustration showing a completed 2 step wave. It appears that the two middle steps are stitched on the $^1/_3$ and $^2/_3$ points between the bottom cable and the top cable. That is only its appearance! In reality the two stitches are taken at the $^1/_4$ point and at the $^1/_2$ space itself."

Correct Way To Count A Two-Step Wave

Top Cable
(Turn Around)

Two

One

Bottom
Cable

2   1   One

Two

Bottom Cable
(Turn
Around)

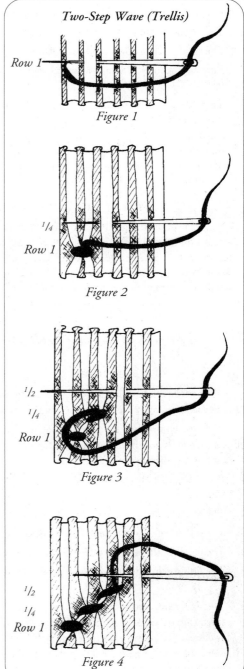

Two-Step Wave (Trellis)

Row 1

Figure 1

$^1/_4$

Row 1

Figure 2

$^1/_2$

$^1/_4$

Row 1

Figure 3

$^1/_2$

$^1/_4$

Row 1

Figure 4

Three-Step Wave (Trellis)

Directions

This is worked from left to right. Move over, one pleat at a time, as you move up and down between the rows.

A three-step wave can have various heights, depending on your design. **Example:** A three-step wave, which goes from one major gathering row to the next, for a distance of $^3/_8$ inch (the usual distance between gathering rows on a pleater) is done like this:

1. Row 1 begins with a down-cable on the gathering row (**fig. 1**).

2. The second stitch, a down cable, will be placed $^1/_3$ of the way up (**fig.2**).

3. The third stitch, a down cable, will be placed $^2/_3$ of the way up (**fig. 3**).

4. Row 2 is the fourth stitch, a down cable, placed on the next gathering row line (**fig. 4**).

5. The fifth stitch, an up cable, will be placed on the same gathering row (Row 2) as stitch number four (**fig. 5**). Look at the finished work. The fourth and fifth stitches will appear to be at different levels, with the fourth stitch slightly below the gathering row. However, the last down cable moving up the row is placed at the same level as the turnaround stitch, the up-cable at the top. ✽

Three-Step Wave (Trellis)

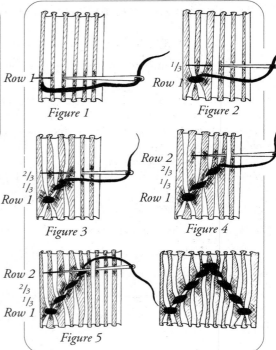

Figure 1   Figure 2

Figure 3   Figure 4

Figure 5

Sitting In Martha's Smocking Class

"One of the things I like to do when I count my three-step waves when going across a row is to say, 'Bottom cable, 1, 2, 3, top cable, 1, 2, 3, bottom cable, 1, 2, 3, top cable, 1, 2, 3.' Some people like to say, 'Turn around, 1, 2, 3, turn around, 1, 2, 3, turn around 1, 2, 3.' Always count by realizing that the three steps are in the middle with a cable at the top and a cable at the bottom." ✽

Four-Step Wave (Trellis)

Directions

This is worked from left to right. Move over, one pleat at a time, as you move up and down between the rows.

A four-step wave can have various heights, depending on your design. It goes from one major gathering row (Row 1) to the next gathering row (Row 2).

1. Row 1 begins with a down-cable on the gathering row (**fig. 1**).

2. The second stitch, a down cable, will be placed $^1/_4$ of the way up (**fig. 2**).

3. The third stitch, a down cable, will be placed on the half-space (**fig. 3**).

4. The fourth stitch, a down cable, will be placed on the $^3/_4$ space (**fig. 4**).

5. The fifth stitch, a down cable, will be placed on the top gathering row, Row 2 (**fig. 5**).

6. The sixth stitch, an up cable, is placed on the same gathering row (Row 2) as the fifth stitch (**fig. 6**). Look at the finished work. The fifth and sixth stitches will appear to be at different levels, with the fifth slightly below the gathering row. However, the last down cable moving up the row is placed at the same level as the turnaround stitch, the up cable at the top. ✽

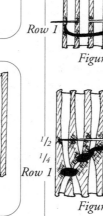

Four-Step Wave (Trellis)

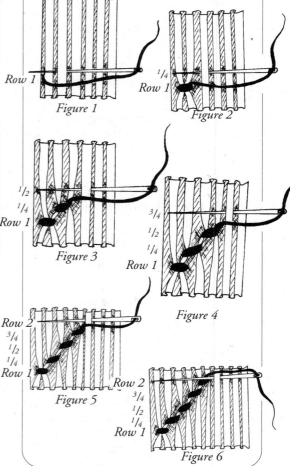

Four-Step Wave (Trellis)

Figure 1   Figure 2

Figure 3   Figure 4

Figure 5   Figure 6

Double Wave or Diamond Stitch

Directions

A double wave means the second wave is worked in the opposite directions of the first, making a diamond shape.

1. The top portion of the diamond wave (one-, two-, three-, four-wave) begins with a down-cable, and moves upward.

2. The bottom portion of the diamond wave begins with a top cable and moves downward.

3. Stack the cables the to meet in the middle. A trick to matching the cables perfectly is to slip your needle between the pleats and slide it up. This will enable you to stitch very close to the first pleat. ✄

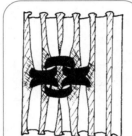

Six-Step Flowerette

Directions

Work from left to right.

1. Bring the needle up on the left side of pleat 1 or the left side of the first pleat to be involved in the flowerette.

2. With the thread below the needle, insert the needle on the right side of pleat 2 , picking up only pleat 2 (**fig. 1**).

3. With the thread above the needle, insert the needle on the right side of pleat 3, picking up only pleat 3 (**fig. 2**).

4. With the thread below the needle, insert the needle on the right side of pleat 4, picking up only peat 4 (**fig. 3**).

5. Carry the thread to the back of the fabric between the last two pleats (pleats 3 and 4). Turn the work, as well as the illustration, upside down.

6. Bring the needle out on the left side of pleat 4, below the last down cable made (**fig. 4**).

7. With the thread below the needle, insert the needle on the right side of pleat 3, picking up only pleat 3 (**fig. 5**).

8. With the thread above the needle, insert the needle on the right side of pleat 2, picking up only pleat 2 (**fig. 6**).

9. With the tread below the needle, insert the needle on the right side of pleat 1, picking up only pleat 1 (**fig. 7**).

10. Carry the thread to the wrong side of the fabric by inserting in between the last two pleats used, (pleats 1 and 2), and tie off. ✄

Sitting In Martha's Smocking Class

"Just because we have stopped our instructions with a four step wave doesn't mean that you can't make a five step wave or a six step wave or even more. Always remember that when you call a stitch a four step wave, that you have a bottom cable at the bottom before you make four stitches upward and that you have a top cable at the top before you make four stitches downward. Don't forget to count the four-step wave as follows. Bottom cable, 1, 2, 3, 4, top cable, 1, 2, 3, 4, bottom cable, 1,2, 3, 4, top cable."

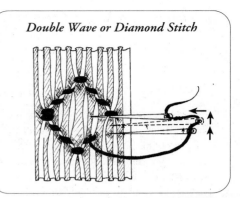

Double Wave or Diamond Stitch

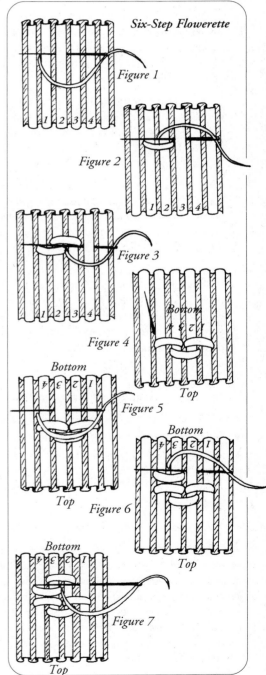

Six-Step Flowerette

Figure 1

Figure 2

Figure 3

Figure 4

Figure 5

Figure 6

Figure 7

Picture Smocking

1. Thread

1. In picture smocking, you should always use a good quality thread. You are not limited to just a good six strand cotton embroidery floss. There are many things on the market that are wonderful when used in smocking. It is acceptable to use yarns, silk ribbon threads, pearle cotton, floche, or other fibers as long as they can be stitched and pulled through the fabric. A word of caution, think about the care of the garments and try to match a like thread to it. For example, use silk on silk or cotton on cotton.

2. Always remove floss from the wrapper by pulling from the end with the hands on the wrapper. Cut your piece of floss no more than 18-24 inches long. A piece of floss longer than this has a tendency to fray, tangle, and wear, which in turn will cause problems with your coverage.

3. When you cut your floss, you will notice a difference in the two ends. One end will unravel more than the other and thereby appear fuller. The fuller end of the floss should always be threaded in the eye of the needle and the cut end should always be knotted. In order to keep from getting confused when separating the six strands of floss, always knot the cut end of the floss.

4. Once you have cut your floss to the correct length, separate each strand. Put the correct number of strands of floss back together. Then pull these strands of floss between the thumb and forefinger to strip them. This will give a more ribbon like appearance to the floss. Another method that is used frequently is to pull these strands through a fabric softener dryer sheet.

5. As you smock, the thread will twist and not lie flat. In order to obtain the best coverage, the thread must lie flat when making the stitches. You may untwist the thread by simply holding the end of the floss straight up and running the eye of the needle down the floss to the fabric and back up again, thereby straightening the floss as you go. Another method used frequently is simply turning the pleated fabric upside down and allowing the needle to dangle, using the weight of the needle to untwist the floss.

2. Number of Strands to Use for Smocking

The following chart lists the recommended strands of floss to use when doing the various types of smocking.

3 Strands for all Geometrics

4 Strands for Stacking (Picture Smocking)

2 Strands for Backsmocking

1-2 Strands for Detail Work

If you are using thread heavier than the normal six strand embroidery floss, it will be necessary to adjust the number of strands recommended above. As with any type of smocking, always refer to your smocking plate for the suggested number of strands to use. Sometimes, it will be necessary to use more than the recommended number of threads, especially if you are smocking with white. It is recommended that you always do a small test area for coverage. Caution: If you are using a dark color thread, think about where you are doing your practice piece because when it is removed, it is possible that "fuzz" from the thread will be left in the fabric.

3. Stitches

When picture smocking, there will be times that the stitch will not lie as it should. To correct this problem, simply take the needle and lay it lengthwise on top of the stitch and press down toward the previous row. If all stitches are made correctly, you should have no problems in getting the stitches perfectly level.

If, at any time, you find that you have made an error in stitch placement or the stitch doesn't lie correctly, it is always best to remove that stitch. Even though it seems that you can "work around" the mistake, it will come back to cause you problems later in your smocking. To remove the unwanted stitch, unthread your needle and use the eye of the needle to remove it. If there is a large number of stitches to remove, clip every 4th or 5th stitch with your embroidery scissors and pull them out with the eye of the needle. Remember, if you make a mistake, it is always best to remove it.

4. Tension

More often than not, the problem with picture smocking is tension. Tension is the most important thing in smocking. In order to achieve the desired finished look, stitches should not be tight nor should they be loose. Each stitch is critical and necessitates patience and accuracy. For the design to be correct, the tension should be equal on all stitches.

When completing a stitch, don't jerk the thread through the fabric. Gently pull the floss through the fabric by hand or with the needle. Carefully lay the stitch on the pleats making sure that the thread is not twisted. If you see "open areas" between the stitches where the fabric shows or if your pleat is distorted, your tension is too tight (**fig. 1**) or your pleats are too far apart. If the

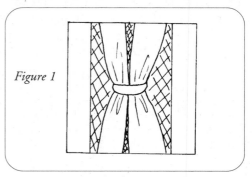

Figure 1

stitches have the appearance of "hanging off" the fabric, your tension is to loose (**fig. 2**). Correct tension will allow the thread to gently "hug" the pleats (**fig. 3**).

5.. Fabric

When smocking, do not be limited to just lightweight fabrics. You can smock any fiber that is not tightly woven. Linen, silk batiste, satin, 100% featherwale corduroy, some velvets and velveteens, cotton, poly-cotton blends, and lightweight challis are good choices. When trying to decide whether or not a piece of fabric will pleat, always try pleating a sample piece first and see if it will go through the pleater without having to force it through.

When pleating a tightly woven fabric such as Imperial broadcloth, it is always best to remove the selvage first. You may also find that with broadcloth, it is easier to pleat if you rinse the fabric to remove some of the sizing put in during manufacturing. If you choose not to wash the broadcloth before pleating, try rubbing a bar of Ivory soap over the back of the fabric to make it easier to pleat or run a sheet of waxed paper through the pleater before pleating.

6. Seams

It is recommended that you do not pleat fabric with French seams because of the bulk of fabric that the needles must penetrate. Often times, French seams will cause your pleater needles to break or skip stitches. When putting together a garment that calls for French seams, such as a bishop, simply serge the seam using a rolled hem or stitch the seam together by machine, press it open and then pleat the fabric.

7. Smocking Plates

Smocking directions are given on the back of each plate. The directions give the order in which to work the geometric rows as well as the figures. Most smocking designs need to be centered, especially picture smocking. Smocking plates are designed for straight as well as round yokes. When doing a round yoke, make sure you have a plate that will give you a variation for the round yoke.

The most common problem with smocking plates is the confusion caused when reading the rows of stitches. The confusion comes from reading the bottom stitches as one row and the top stitches as another. Remember, it takes both rows of stitches to make a single row of cables (**fig. 4**).

In the beginning, you may find it easier to read the graph by taking a colored pencil and coloring every other row. This will make the graph easier to read and less confusing.

8. Changing Colors

When doing picture smocking, you will find that more than one color is used in the design, therefore making it necessary to use more than one needle. To avoid continuous tying off of the threads, simply thread the different colors of floss in different needles before starting. When it becomes necessary to change colors, allow the needle you were using to hang at the back of the smocked fabric or place it on the back side of the fabric so it will not get in your way. Start your next cable with a new color and smock the required number of stitches. This step is repeated for every color used in your graph.

9. Scissors and Needles

One of the most important tools needed for smocking is a good pair of embroidery scissors. The small, sharp pointed scissors are a must when cutting the floss close to the fabric and for snipping unwanted threads close to the fabric for easy removal.

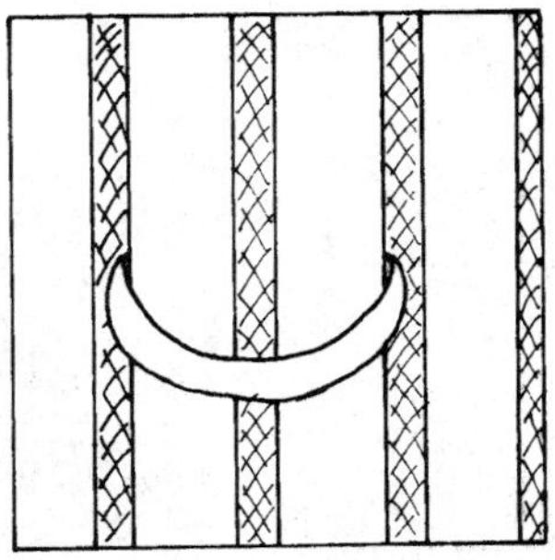

Figure 2

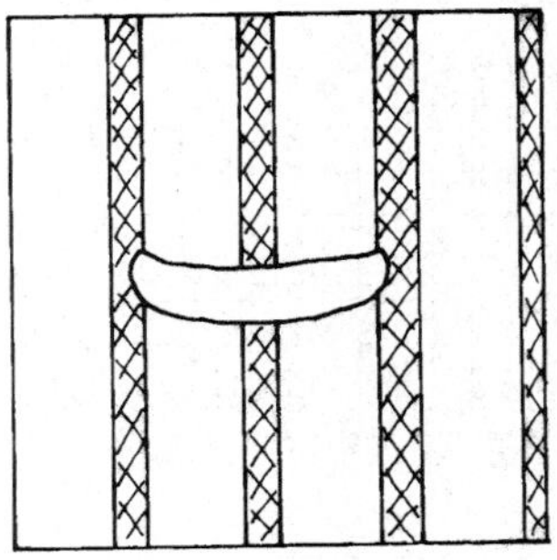

Figure 3

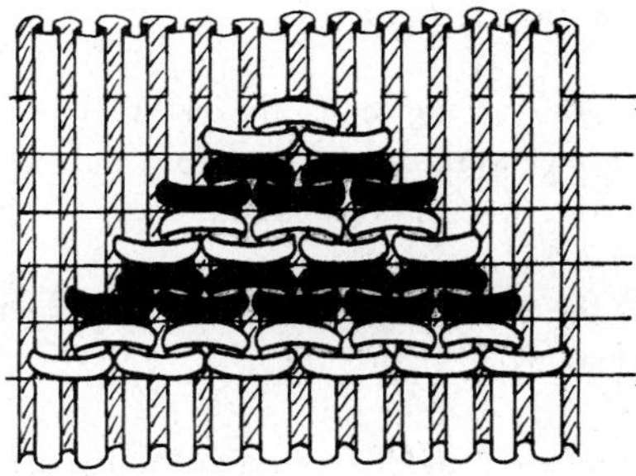

Figure 4

We recommend using a size 7 or 8 crewel needle for smocking. The crewel needle is used because it will make holes large enough for four strands of floss to pull through easily.

If you have difficulty grasping a size 7 or 8 crewel needle for any reason, you may use a size 7 or 8 long darner. This needle is wonderful for those smockers who have arthritic hands and find it difficult to work with the short needles. ✻

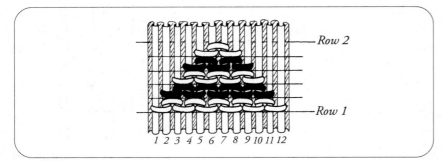

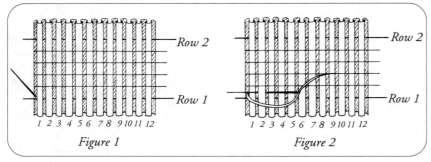

Figure 1   *Figure 2*

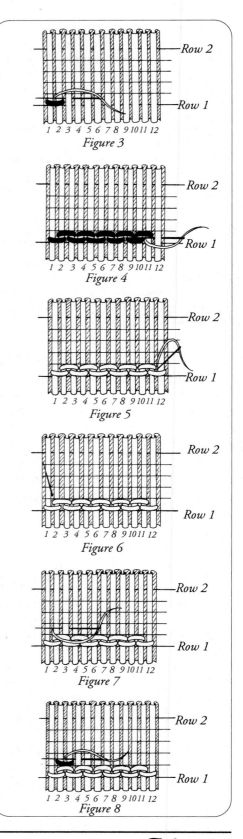

Figure 3

Figure 4

Figure 5

Figure 6

Figure 7

Figure 8

1. Bring the floss up on the left side of gathering row 1, pleat 1, (**fig. 1**).

2. With the tread below the needle, insert the needle on the right side of pleat 2, picking up only pleat 2 (**fig. 2**).

    You will notice that the first stitch of each row comes up on the side of the pleat to be worked, skips that pleat, and picks up the next one. In other words, your first stitch contains two pleats.

3. With the thread above the needle, insert the needle on the right side of pleat 3, picking up only pleat 3 (**fig. 3**).

4. Repeat steps 2 and 3 until you have made a total of 11 cable stitches (**fig. 4**). This completes row 1.

5. Take the thread to the back of the pleated fabric by sticking your needle between the two pleats (11 & 12) taken in by the last stitch. In other words, insert your needle back into the valley that your thread is coming out of (**fig. 5**).

6. For the purpose of this practice piece, allow your thread to travel across the wrong side of the fabric to begin row 2. Do not pull it tight or it will distort your triangle.

7. Begin row 2 by bringing the needle up on the left side of pleat 2 (**fig. 6**).

8. With the thread below the needle, insert the needle on the right side of pleat 3, picking up only pleat 3 (**fig. 7**).

9. With the thread above the needle, insert the needle on the right side of pleat 4, picking up only pleat 4 (**fig. 8**).

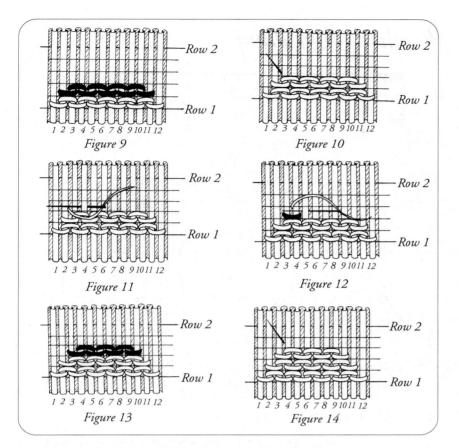

Figure 9

Figure 10

Figure 11

Figure 12

Figure 13

Figure 14

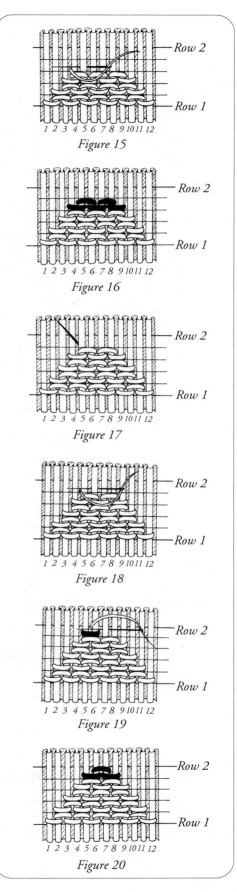

Figure 15

Figure 16

Figure 17

Figure 18

Figure 19

Figure 20

10. Continue across the row until you have a total of 9 cables. This completes row 2 (**fig. 9**).

11. Carry the thread to the wrong side of the fabric as referred to in Step 5. Bring the needle up on the left side of pleat 3 (**fig. 10**).

12. With the thread below the needle, insert the needle on the right side of pleat 4, picking up only pleat 4 (**fig. 11**).

13. With the thread above the needle, insert the needle on the right side of pleat 5, picking up only pleat 5 (**fig. 12**).

14. Continue across the row until you have a total of 7 cables (**fig. 13**).

15. Carry the thread to the wrong side of the fabric as referred to in Step 5. Insert the needle on the left side of pleat 4 (**fig. 14**).

16. With the thread below the needle insert the needle on the right side of pleat 5, picking up only pleat 5 (**fig. 15**).

17. Continue across the row until you have completed a total of 5 cables. This completes row 4 (**fig. 16**).

18. Carry the thread across the back of the fabric as instructed in step 5. Bring the needle up on the left side of pleat 4 (**fig. 17**).

19. With the thread below the needle, insert the needle on the right side of pleat 6, picking up only pleat 6 (**fig. 18**).

20. With the thread above the needle, insert the needle on the right side of pleat 7, picking up only pleat 7 (**fig. 19**).

21. Continue across the row until you have completed a total of 3 cables. This completes row 5 (**fig. 20**). ✖

Smocking Plates

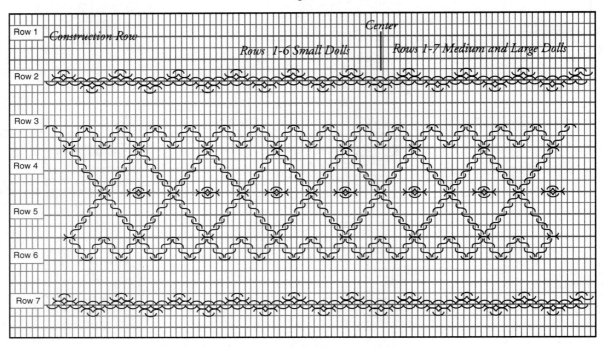

Sweet and Simple Doll Dress – page 56

Smocking Directions

Use three strands of DMC floss. Center the design. Row 1 will be used in construction. Small dolls pleat 7 rows - row 7 is a holding row. Medium and Large dolls pleat 8 rows - row 8 is a holding row.

Step 1. Smocking will begin on row 2 with a cable stitch. Place three cable stitches above and below the cable row. Refer to the graph for placement.

Step 2. Work two-step, half-space waves between rows 3 to $3^{1}/_{2}$.

Step 3. Work five-step, whole-space waves between rows $3^{1}/_{2}$ to $4^{1}/_{2}$ forming hearts.

Step 4. Repeat step 3 (five-step, whole-space waves) between rows $4^{1}/_{2}$ to $5^{1}/_{2}$ to form diamonds.

Step 5. Repeat step 2 (two-step, half-space waves) between rows $5^{1}/_{2}$ to 6 to form up-side-down hearts.

Step 6. In the center of the diamonds, on row $4^{1}/_{2}$, work six-step flowerettes. This will complete the smocking on the small doll dress.

Step 7. Medium and Large Dolls - Repeat Step 1 on row 7. ✳

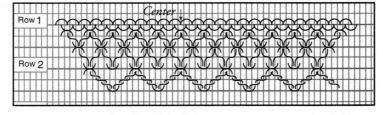

Shadow Embroidery Gown – page 127

Smocking Plate Directions

Use 3 stands of DMC floss. Center the design. Pleat 4 rows. Rows 1 and 4 are holding rows.

Step 1. Work cables across row 1, with a <u>down</u> cable at center front.

Step 2. Between rows 1 and $1^{1}/_{2}$ work baby waves, beginning with an <u>up</u> cable at center front.

Step 3. Between rows $1^{1}/_{2}$ and 2, work baby waves, beginning with a <u>down</u> cable at center front.

Step 4. Between rows 2 and $2^{1}/_{2}$, work three-step trellises, beginning with an <u>up</u> cable at center front. ✳

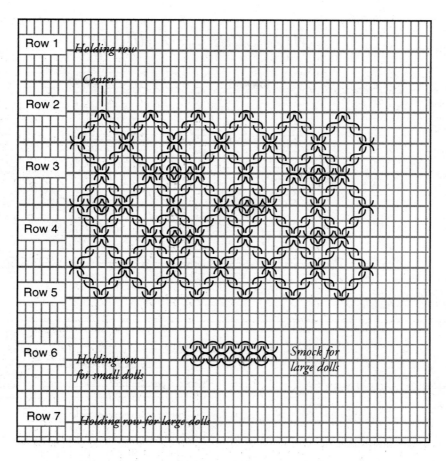

Printed Smocked Doll Dress – page 59

Smocking Directions

Use 3 strands of DMC floss. Center the design.

Row 1 will be used in construction. Small dolls pleat 6 rows - row 6 is a holding row. Medium and Large dolls pleat 7 rows - row 7 is a holding row.

Step 1. Work two-step, half space waves between rows 2 to $2^1/_2$, beginning with an up cable at center.

Step 2. Repeat two-step, half space waves forming diamonds between the following rows : $2^1/_2$ to 3, 3 to $3^1/_2$, $3^1/_2$ to 4, 4 to $4^1/_2$ and $4^1/_2$ to 5.

Step 3. Work six-step flowerettes in the center of the diamonds. Refer to the graph for placement. This completes the smocking for the small dolls.

Step 4. Medium and large dolls only - Row 6 - Work one row of cables. On top of this row work a second row of cables. Refer to graph. ❈

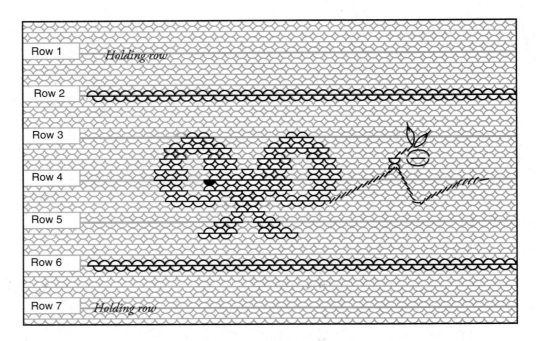

Row 1	*Holding row*
Row 2	
Row 3	
Row 4	
Row 5	
Row 6	
Row 7	*Holding row*

Smocked Bow Doll Dress – page 67

Smocking Directions

Use 3 strands of DMC floss for cables and vines, 4 strands for bow, 1 strand for bullions.

Pleat 7 rows. Row 1 will be used in construction. Row 7 is a holding row. Backsmock rows 3, 4 and 5.

Step 1. Smocking will begin on row 2 with cables across.

Step 2. Bow Center - Begin eight pleats to the left of center on row 4 with a down cable (black on graph). Cable across 15. Turn work upside down and cable across 15.

Step 3. Refer to the graph and continue stacking the left side of the bow.

Step 4. Refer to the graph and stack the right side of the bow.

Step 5. Work one single stitch in the center of the bow to complete the bow knot.

Step 6. Center of Bow Streamers - Starting three pleats to the left of center on row $4^1/2$, work five cable stitches starting with an up cable.

Step 7. Left Streamer - Refer to graph. Work two cable stitches (down and up). Work four cables below the two cables and then six cables to complete the left streamer.

Step 8. Right Streamer - Refer to graph. Work two cable stitches(up and down). Work four cables below the two cables and then six cables to complete the right streamer.

Step 9. Vine - Starting on row $4^1/2$, work 12 steps up to row $3^3/4$, work an up cable, work six steps down to row $4^1/2$, work a down cable, with the thread underneath the cable stitch work 11 steps up to row 4. Refer to graph for placement. Repeat for other side. At the top point of the vine on the right side and the lower point on the left side work a cable, three steps and two lazy daisy leaves.

Step 10. Beside the leaves work a bullion rose (three bullion stitches with 11 wraps on the outer stitches and 9 wraps on the inside stitch).

Step 12. Cable across row 6. ▨

Knickers Bibs

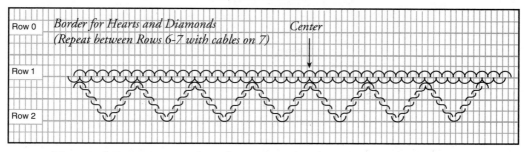

Top and Bottom Borders for Hearts and Diamonds – page 142

Pleat 8 rows. Smock the top and bottom holding rows on the right side with a stem or outline stitch (this replaces backsmocking). Use 3 strands of DMC floss for borders, 4 strands for hearts and diamonds.

Step 1. On row 1, work a row of cables, beginning at center front with an up cable.

Step 2. Beginning at center front with an up cable just under Row 1, work four-step trellises between Rows 1 and 2.

Repeat this pattern on the bottom two rows of smocking, with the cables on the bottom row and beginning with down cables at center front on row 7, working the trellises up to row 6 and back down again.

The hearts, diamonds and flowerettes will be worked from the graph. ❈

Simple Hearts

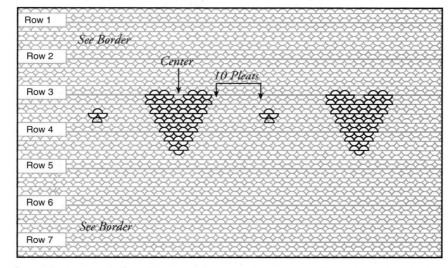

Simple Diamonds

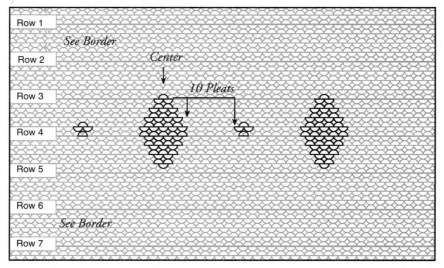

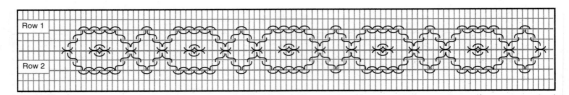

Border

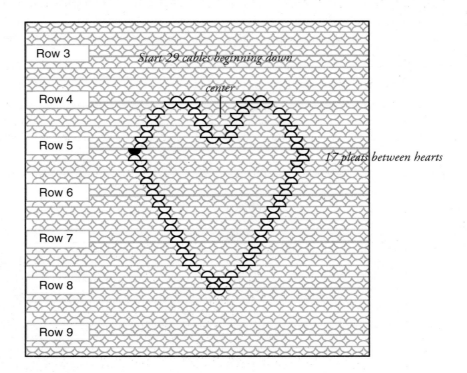

Start 29 cables beginning down

center

17 pleats between hearts

Quilt Square Eleven-Picture Smocking – page 163

Smocking Directions

Use 3 strands of DMC floss for borders, 4 strands for heart. Pleat 12 rows. The top and bottom rows are construction rows. Backsmock rows 3-8.

Step 1. Between rows 1 and $1^1/_2$, beginning on row $1^1/_2$ - work a two-step $^1/_2$-space wave up to row 1, seven cables, two-step $^1/_2$-space wave down to row $1^1/_2$, bottom cable, two-step $^1/_2$-space wave up to row 1, top cable, and two-step wave down to row $1^1/_2$. Continue across the row.

Step 2. Work a mirror image of step 1, between rows $1^1/_2$ and 2.

Step 3. Stack the hearts between rows 4 and 7. Start the heart on row 5 with a down cable (shaded on the graph), work 29 cables. Continue following the graph to complete the heart. There are 17 pleats between the hearts.

Step 4. Repeat steps 1 and 2 between rows 9 and 10. �

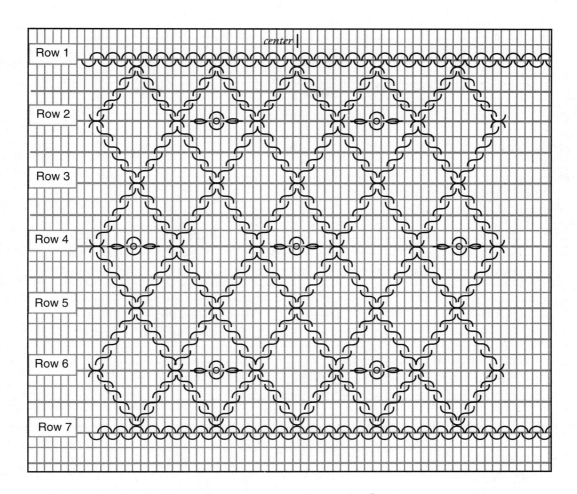

Row 1
Row 2
Row 3
Row 4
Row 5
Row 6
Row 7

center

Quilt Square Four–Geometric Smocking – page 159

Smocking Directions

Pleat 9 rows. The top and bottom rows are construction rows. Use 3 stands of DMC floss.

Step 1. Cable on rows 1 and 7. Begin row 1 with a down cable at center. Begin row 7 with an up cable at center.

Step 2. Between rows 1 and 2, 2 and 3, 3 and 4, 4 and 5, 5 and 6, 6 and 7, work four-step whole space waves forming diamonds.

Step 3. Work bullion roses (2 bullion stitches, 12 wraps each) with French knot centers in every other diamond space of row 4. Alternate roses in the diamond spaces of rows 2 and 6. ✷

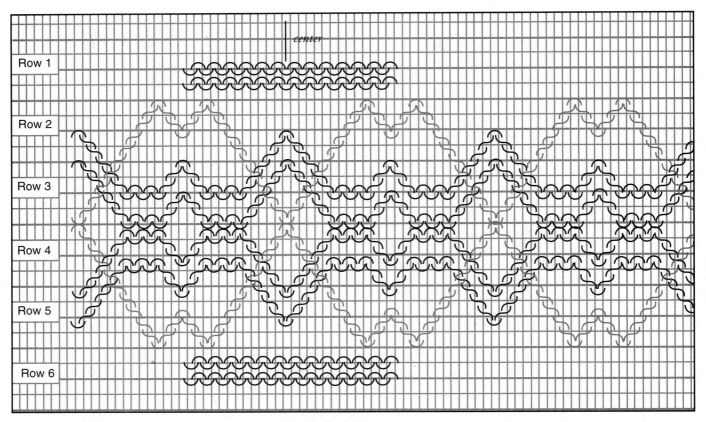

Ribbon and Smocking Pillow – page 15

Smocking Directions

Use three strands of DMC floss. The design will be centered.

Pleat 8 rows. The top and bottom rows are stablizer rows and will not be numbered on the graph.

Step 1. On Row 1, begin at the center with a down cable; cable the entire row, using the light rose floss.

Step 2. Just below Row 1, begin at the center with a down cable; cable the entire row, using the dark rose floss.

Step 3. On Row 2, begin at the center with an up cable, using the light rose floss. Work down to Row 3 with a 5-step trellis, then work 5 cables on Row 3. Work a 2-step trellis up to Row 2^1/$_2$, cable 1, work a 2-step trellis down to Row 3. Work 5 cables on Row 3, then work a 5-step trellis back up to Row 2. Repeat until the entire row is smocked.

Step 4. On Row 2^1/$_2$, begin at the center with an up cable, using the dark rose floss. Work down to Row 3^1/$_2$ with a 5-step trellis, then work 5 cables on Row 3^1/$_2$. Work a 2-step trellis up to Row 3, cable 1, work a 2-step trellis down to Row 3^1/$_2$. Work 5 cables on Row 3^1/$_2$, then work a 5-step trellis back up to Row 2^1/$_2$. Repeat until the entire row is smocked.

Step 5. On Row 3^1/$_2$, begin at the center with a down cable, using the teal floss. Work a 9-step trellis up to Row 1^1/$_2$. Work a cable, then a 2-step trellis down to Row 2, work a cable, then work a 2-step trellis back up to Row 1^1/$_2$ and work a cable. Work a 9-step trellis back down to Row 3^1/$_2$. Repeat until the entire row is smocked.

Step 6. On Row 4^1/$_2$, begin at the center with a down cable, using the dark rose floss. Work a 5-step trellis up to Row 3^1/$_2$, then work 5 cables on Row 3^1/$_2$. Work a 2-step trellis down to Row 4, cable 1, work a 2-step trellis up to Row 3^1/$_2$. Work 5 cables on Row 3^1/$_2$, then work a 5-step trellis back down to Row 4^1/$_2$. Repeat until the entire row is smocked.

Step 7. On Row 5, begin at the center with a down cable, using the light rose floss. Work a 5-step trellis up to Row 4, then work 5 cables on Row 4. Work a 2-step trellis down to Row 4^1/$_2$, cable 1, work a 2-step trellis up to Row 4. Work 5 cables on Row 4, then work a 5-step trellis back down to Row 5. Repeat until the entire row is smocked.

Step 8. On Row 3^1/$_2$, begin at the center with an up cable, using the teal floss. Work a 9-step trellis down to Row 5^1/$_2$. Work a cable, then a 2-step trellis up to Row 5, work a cable, then work a 2-step trellis back down to Row 5^1/$_2$ and work a cable. Work a 9-step trellis back up to Row 3^1/$_2$. Repeat until the entire row is smocked.

Step 9. On Row 6, begin at the center with an up cable; cable the entire row, using the light rose floss.

Step 10. Just above Row 6, begin at the center with an up cable; cable the entire row, using the dark rose floss. ⌗

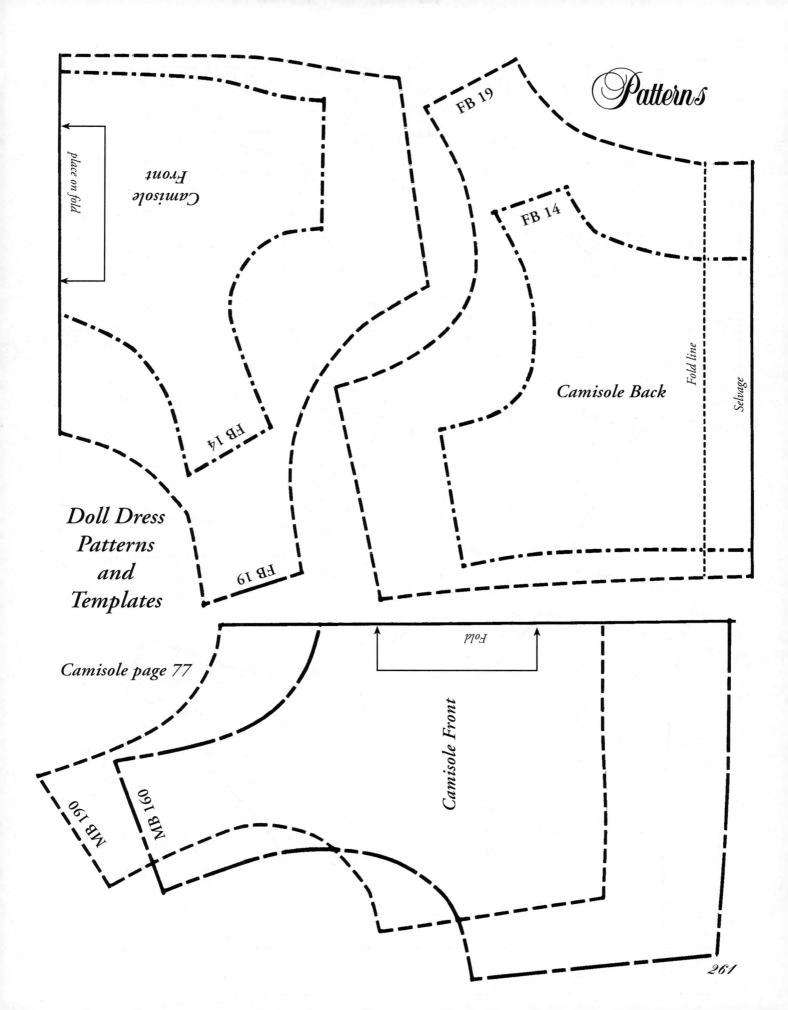

Patterns

FB 19

FB 14

place on fold

Camisole Front

Camisole Back

Fold line

Selvage

FB 14

FB 19

Doll Dress
Patterns
and
Templates

Camisole page 77

Fold

Camisole Front

MB 190

MB 160

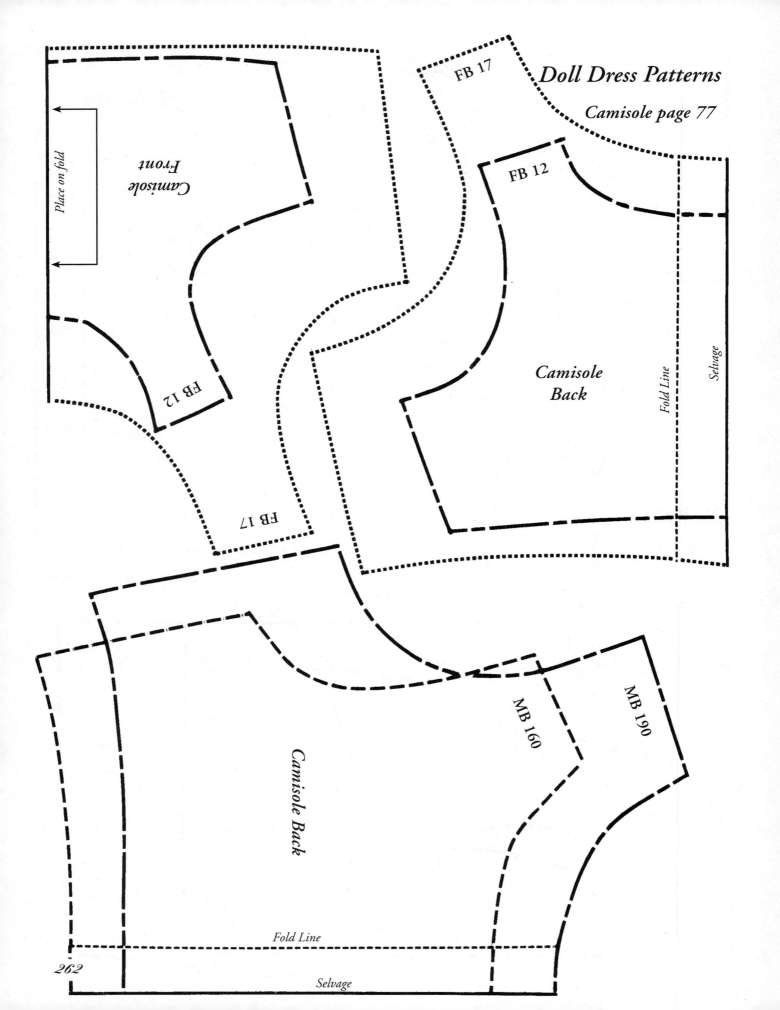

Doll Dress Patterns

Camisole page 77

Camisole Front

Place on fold

FB 17

FB 12

FB 12

FB 17

Camisole Back

Fold Line

Selvage

Camisole Back

MB 160

MB 190

Fold Line

Selvage

262

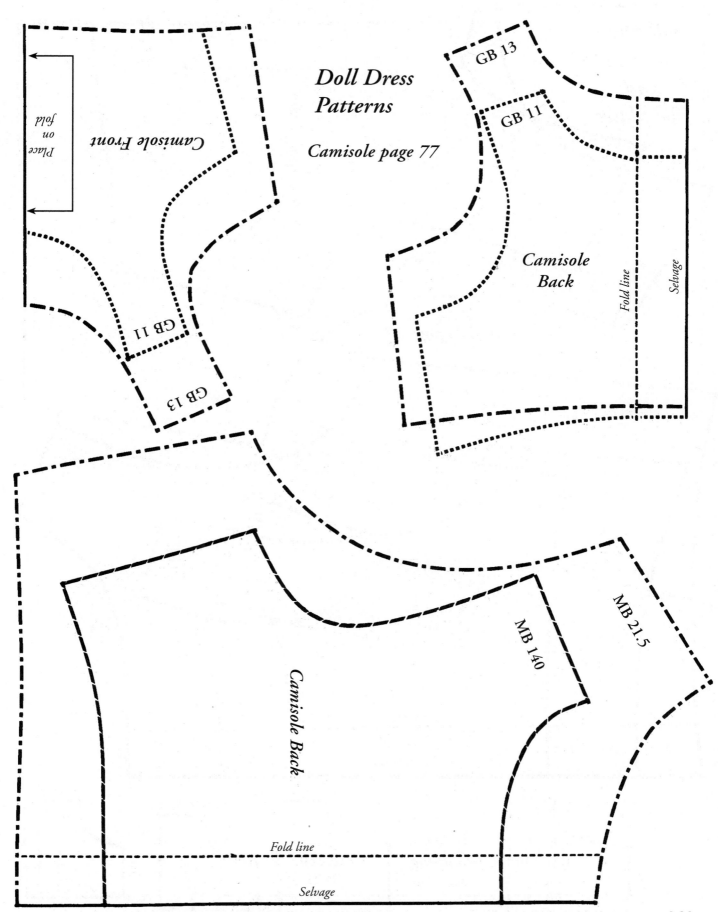

Doll Dress
Patterns

Camisole page 77

Place on fold

Camisole Front

GB 11

GB 13

GB 13

GB 11

Camisole Back

Fold line

Selvage

Camisole Back

MB 140

MB 21.5

Fold line

Selvage

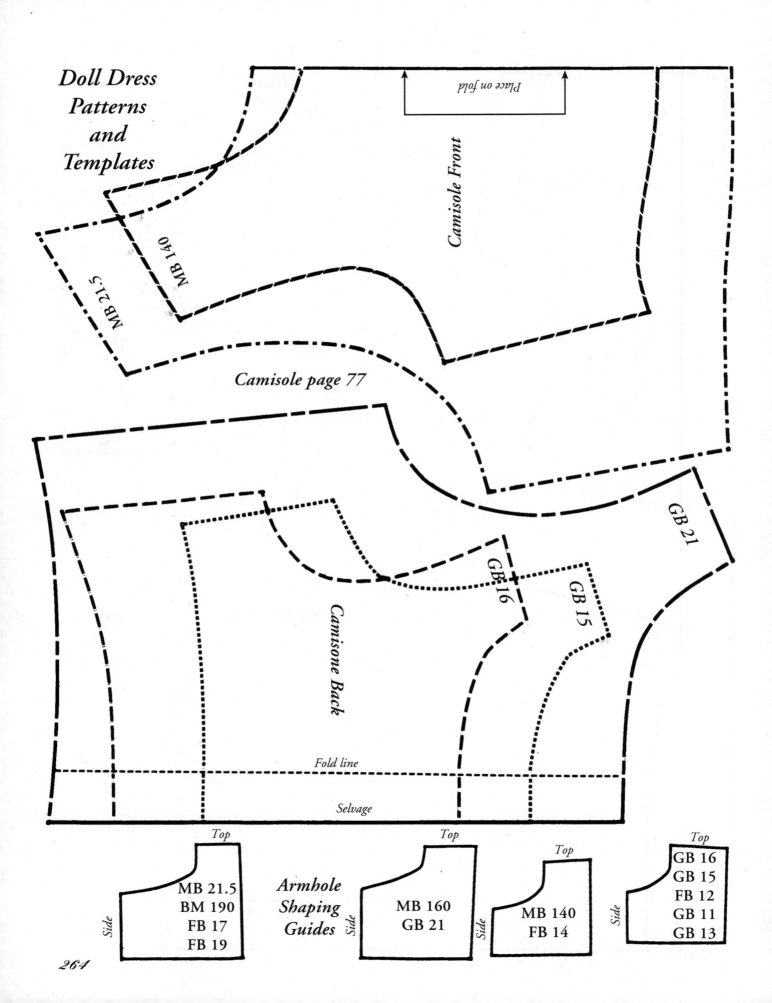

Doll Dress Patterns and Templates

Place on fold

Camisole Front

MB 140

MB 21.5

Camisole page 77

GB 21

GB 16

GB 15

Camisone Back

Fold line

Selvage

Top

Side

MB 21.5
BM 190
FB 17
FB 19

Armhole Shaping Guides

Top

Side

MB 160
GB 21

Top

Side

MB 140
FB 14

Top

Side

GB 16
GB 15
FB 12
GB 11
GB 13

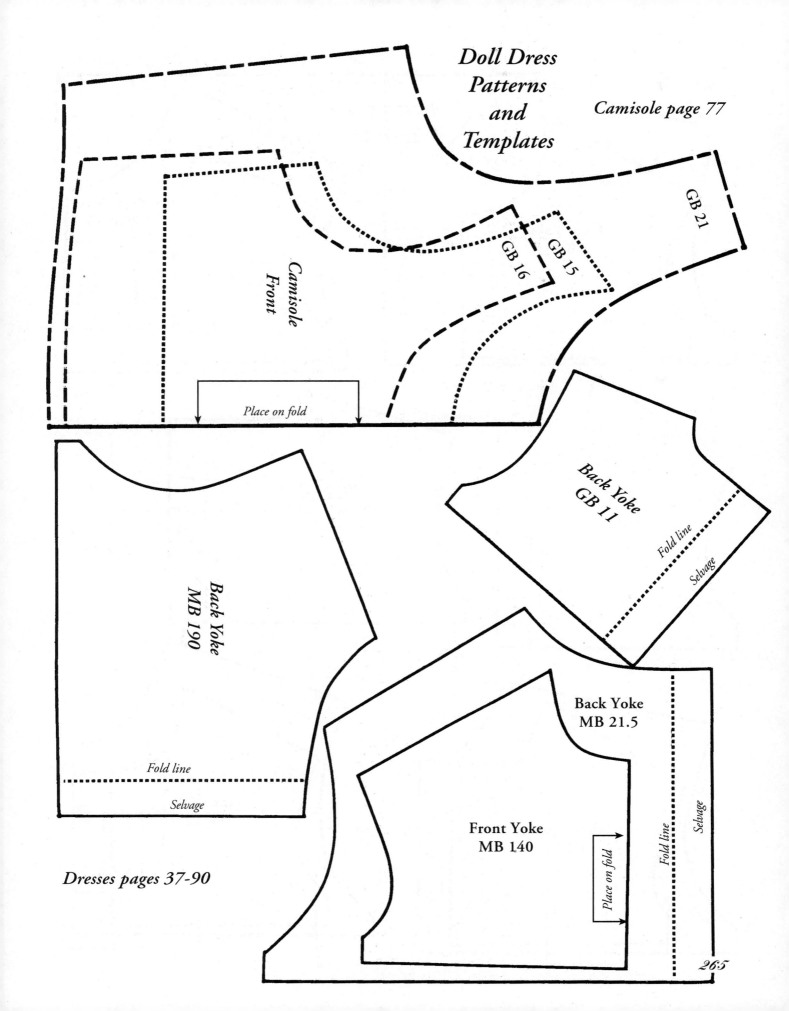

Doll Dress Patterns and Templates

Camisole page 77

GB 21

GB 16

GB 15

Camisole Front

Place on fold

Back Yoke GB 11

Fold line

Selvage

Back Yoke MB 190

Fold line

Selvage

Back Yoke MB 21.5

Front Yoke MB 140

Place on fold

Fold line

Selvage

Dresses pages 37-90

265

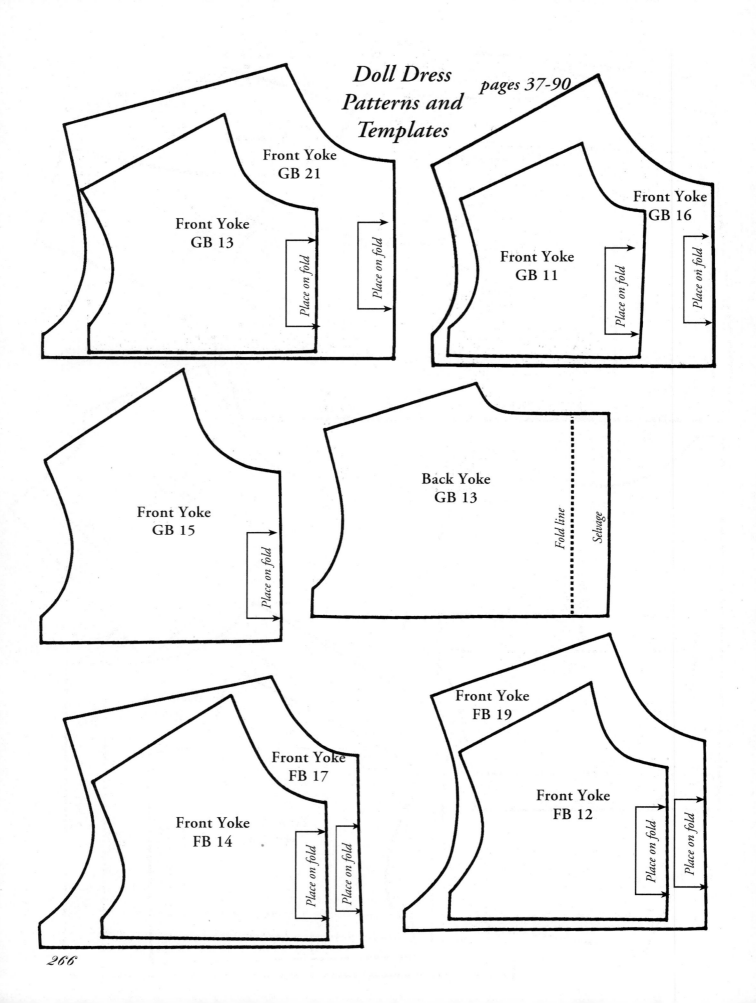

Doll Dress
Patterns and
Templates
pages 37-90

Front Yoke
GB 21

Front Yoke
GB 13

Place on fold

Place on fold

Front Yoke
GB 16

Front Yoke
GB 11

Place on fold

Place on fold

Front Yoke
GB 15

Place on fold

Back Yoke
GB 13

Fold line

Selvage

Front Yoke
FB 17

Front Yoke
FB 14

Place on fold

Place on fold

Front Yoke
FB 19

Front Yoke
FB 12

Place on fold

Place on fold

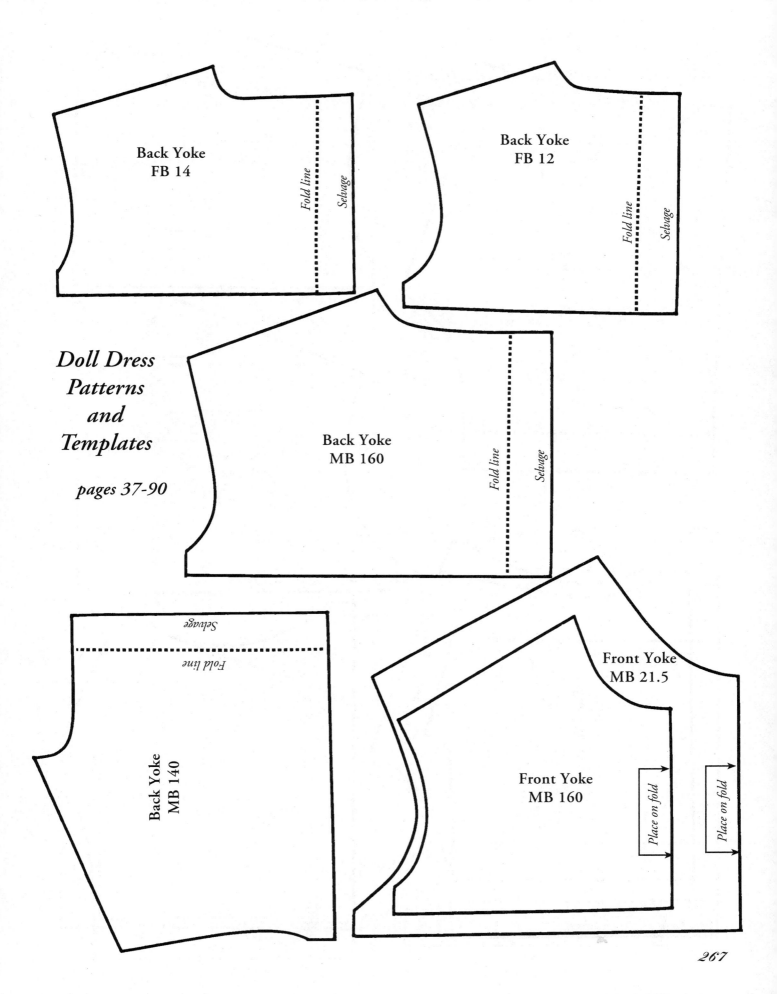

Back Yoke
FB 14

Back Yoke
FB 12

Fold line

Selvage

*Doll Dress
Patterns
and
Templates*

pages 37-90

Back Yoke
MB 160

Fold line

Selvage

Selvage

Fold line

Back Yoke
MB 140

Front Yoke
MB 21.5

Front Yoke
MB 160

Place on fold

Place on fold

267

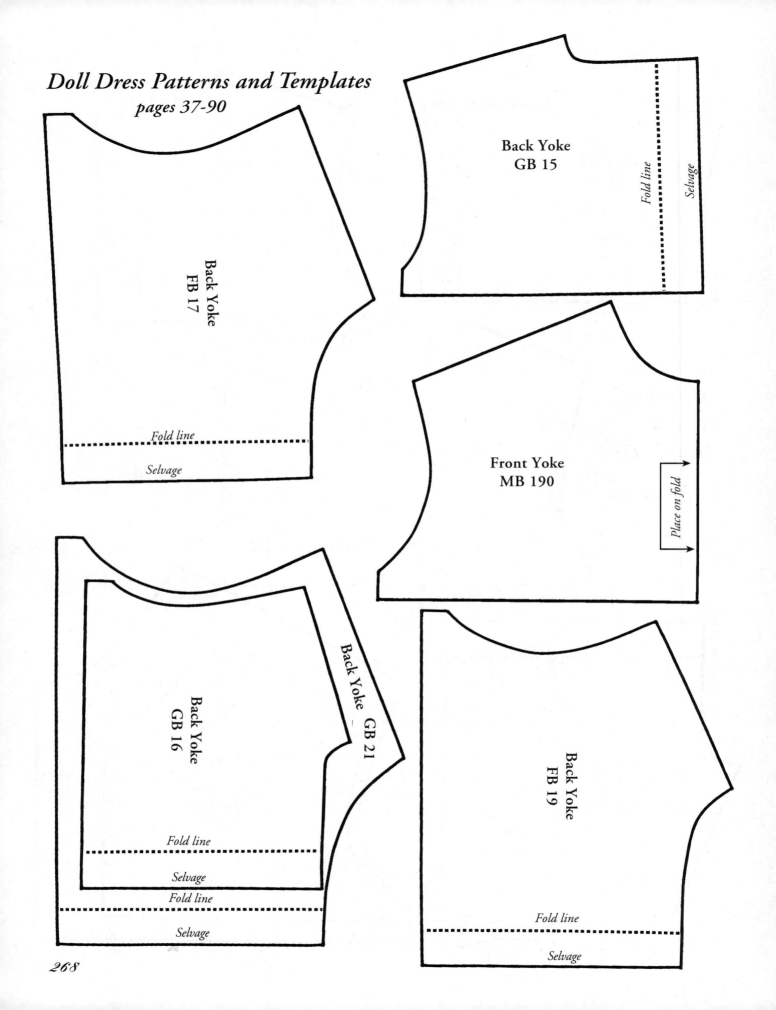

Doll Dress Patterns and Templates
pages 37-90

Back Yoke
FB 17

Fold line

Selvage

Back Yoke
GB 15

Fold line

Selvage

Front Yoke
MB 190

Place on fold

Back Yoke
GB 16

Back Yoke GB 21

Fold line

Selvage

Fold line

Selvage

Back Yoke
FB 19

Fold line

Selvage

Doll Dress Patterns and
Templates

pages 37-90

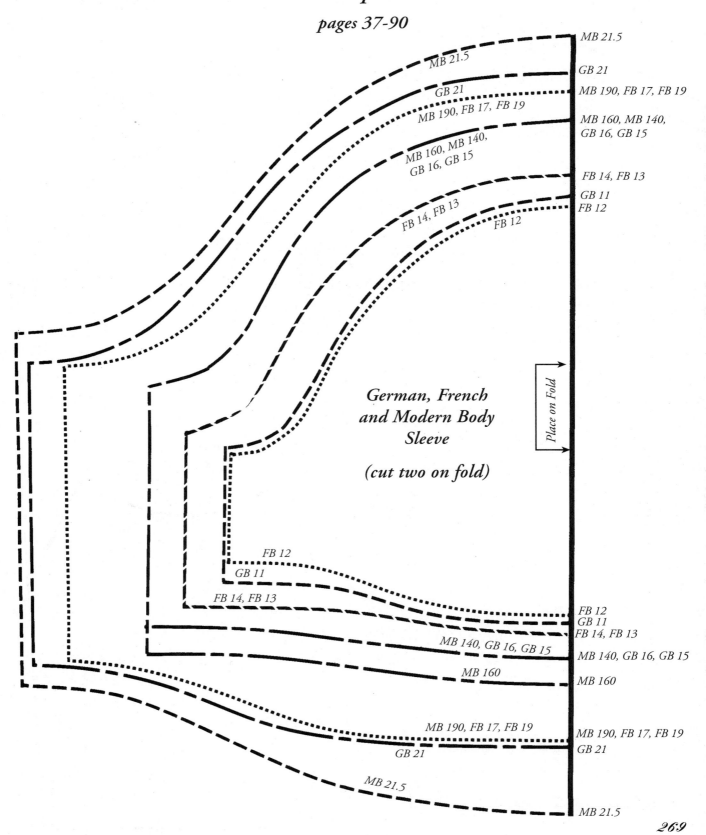

MB 21.5

MB 21.5

GB 21

GB 21

MB 190, FB 17, FB 19

MB 190, FB 17, FB 19

MB 160, MB 140,
GB 16, GB 15

MB 160, MB 140,
GB 16, GB 15

FB 14, FB 13

FB 14, FB 13

GB 11

GB 11

FB 12

FB 12

*German, French
and Modern Body
Sleeve*

(cut two on fold)

Place on Fold

FB 12

FB 12

GB 11

GB 11

FB 14, FB 13

FB 14, FB 13

MB 140, GB 16, GB 15

MB 140, GB 16, GB 15

MB 160

MB 160

MB 190, FB 17, FB 19

MB 190, FB 17, FB 19

GB 21

GB 21

MB 21.5

MB 21.5

Overlap dotted lines of front collar and
back collar for one piece collar.

Adjust neck if needed

Crazy Patch Collar Front

Craft Show 13

All seams ¹/₄"

page 112

Cut on fold

Adjust neck if needed

Crazy Patch Collar Back

Craft Show 13

All seams $^1/_4"$

page 112

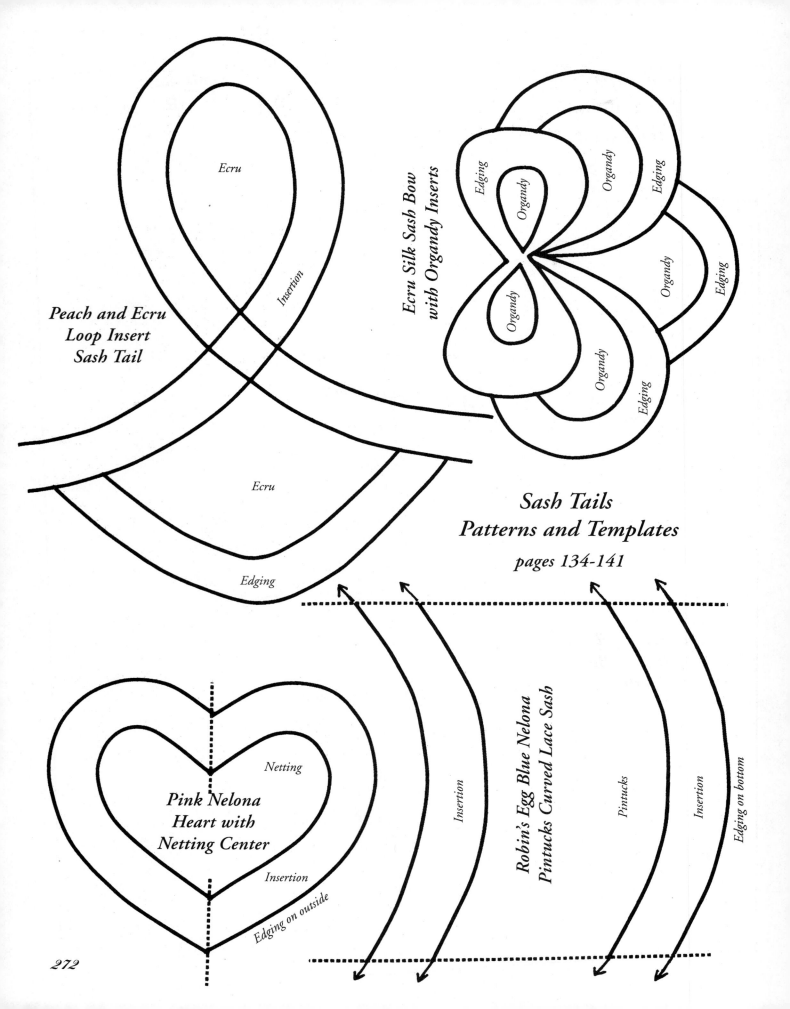

Peach and Ecru
Loop Insert
Sash Tail

Ecru

Insertion

Ecru

Edging

Ecru Silk Sash Bow
with Organdy Inserts

Edging

Organdy

Organdy

Organdy

Edging

Organdy

Edging

Organdy

Edging

Organdy

Edging

Sash Tails
Patterns and Templates
pages 134-141

Pink Nelona
Heart with
Netting Center

Netting

Insertion

Edging on outside

Robin's Egg Blue Nelona
Pintucks Curved Lace Sash

Insertion

Pintucks

Insertion

Edging on bottom

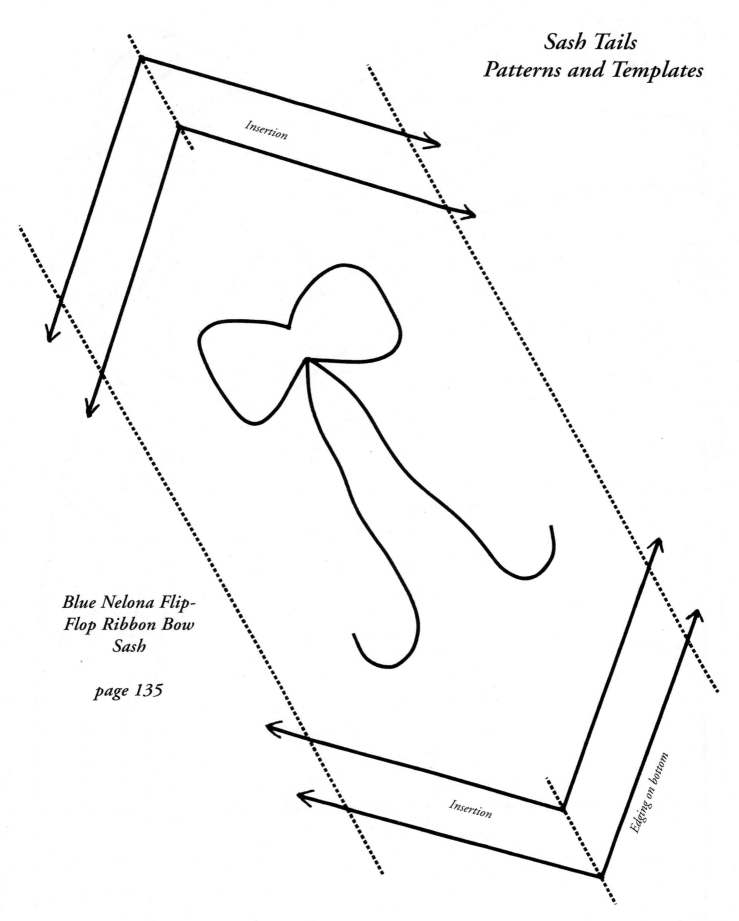

Insertion

Insertion

Edging on bottom

*Blue Nelona Flip-
Flop Ribbon Bow
Sash*

page 135

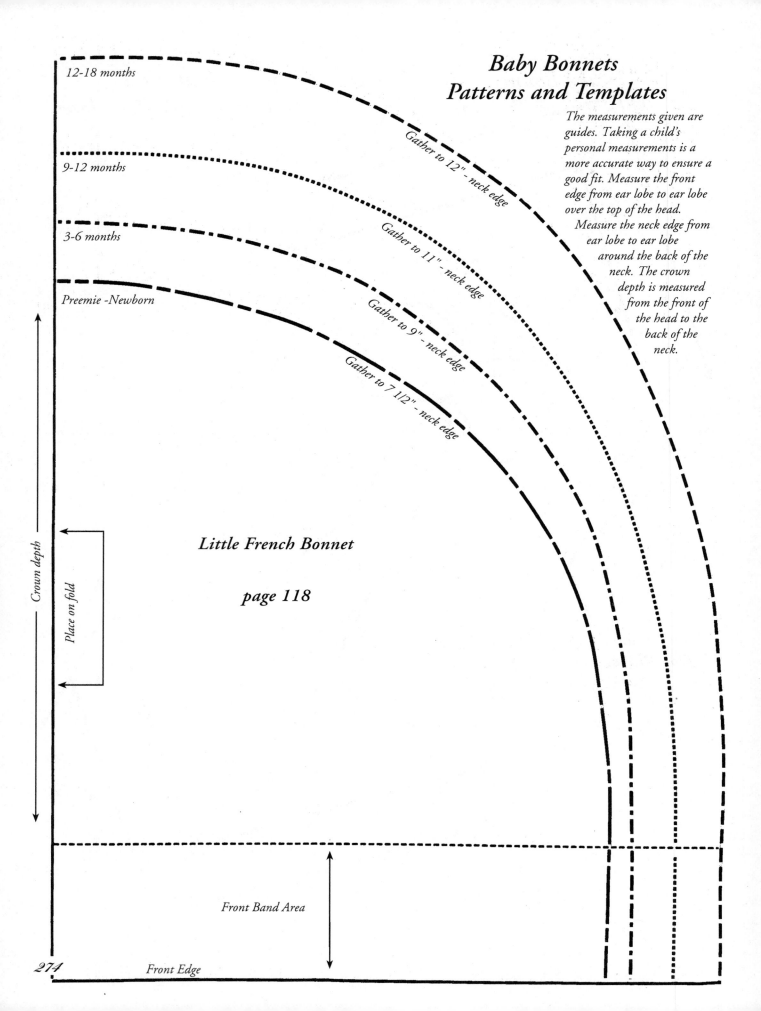

Baby Bonnets
Patterns and Templates

The measurements given are guides. Taking a child's personal measurements is a more accurate way to ensure a good fit. Measure the front edge from ear lobe to ear lobe over the top of the head. Measure the neck edge from ear lobe to ear lobe around the back of the neck. The crown depth is measured from the front of the head to the back of the neck.

12-18 months

9-12 months

3-6 months

Preemie -Newborn

Gather to 12" - neck edge

Gather to 11" - neck edge

Gather to 9" - neck edge

Gather to 7 1/2" - neck edge

Crown depth

Place on fold

Little French Bonnet

page 118

Front Band Area

274

Front Edge

Baby Bonnets
Patterns and Templates

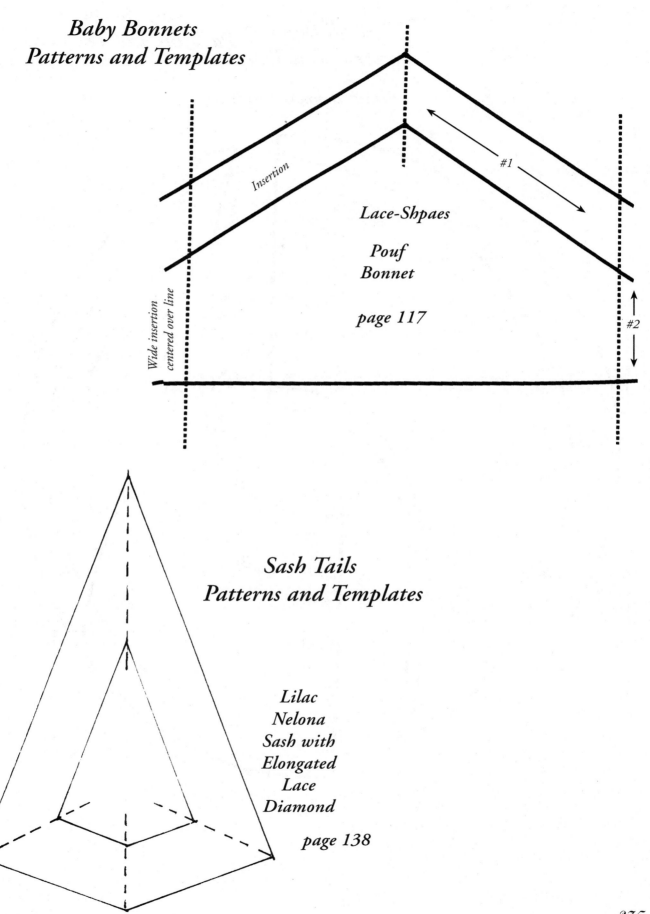

Insertion

Wide insertion centered over line

Lace-Shpaes

Pouf
Bonnet

page 117

#1

#2

Sash Tails
Patterns and Templates

Lilac
Nelona
Sash with
Elongated
Lace
Diamond

page 138

Doll Bonnets
Patterns and Templates

French Bonnets – page 83

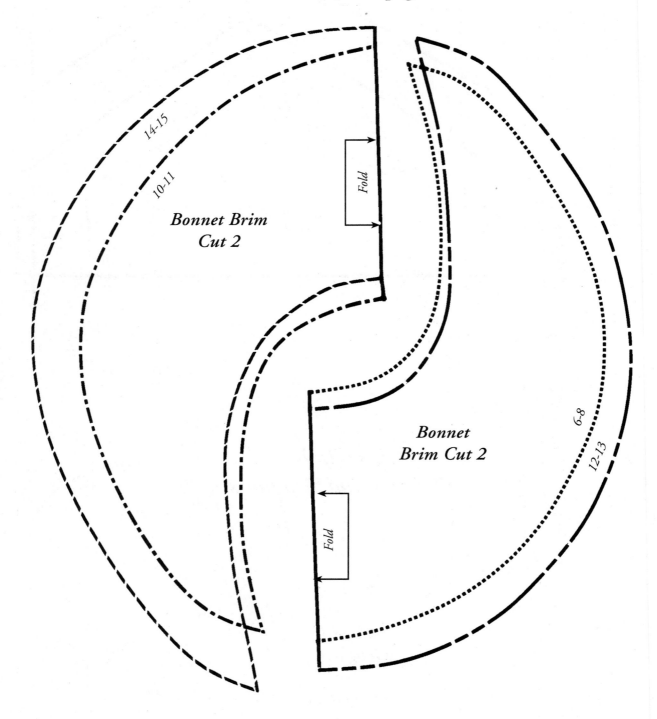

14-15

10-11

Bonnet Brim
Cut 2

Fold

Fold

Bonnet
Brim Cut 2

6-8

12-13

Doll Bonnets
Patterns and Templates   page 83

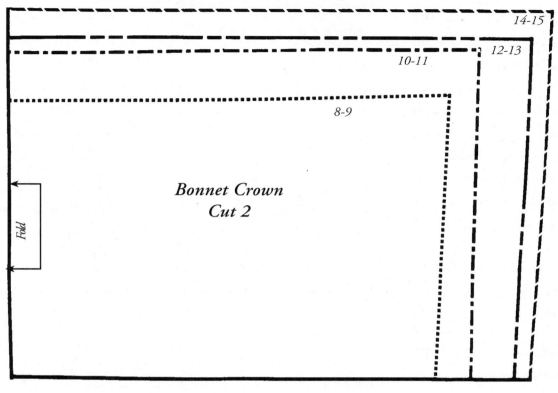

Bonnet Crown
Cut 2

14-15

12-13

10-11

8-9

Fold

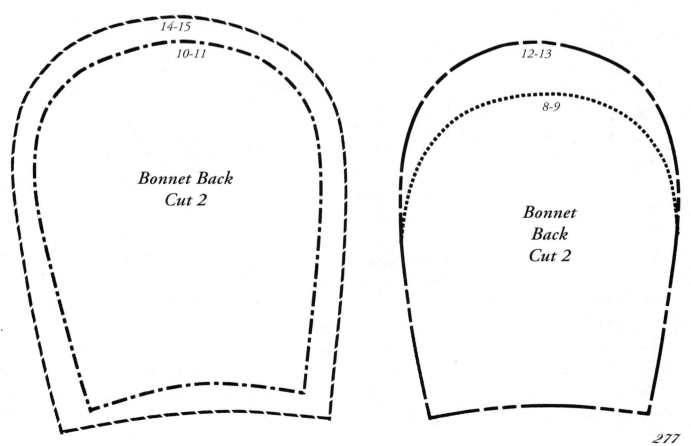

14-15

10-11

Bonnet Back
Cut 2

12-13

8-9

Bonnet
Back
Cut 2

Index

About The Author

$\mathcal{M}$artha Campbell Pullen, a native of Scottsboro, Alabama, is an internationally-known lecturer and author in the heirloom sewing field. After graduating with a degree in speech and English from the University of Alabama, she taught those subjects at almost every level of middle school and high school. Later, her studies led to receiving a Ph.D. in educational administration and management from the University of Alabama.

Her love of sewing and children's clothing encouraged the opening of Martha Pullen's Heirloom Shop in Huntsville, Alabama, August 1, 1981. Two months later, she opened Martha Pullen Company, Inc., the wholesale division. She has served on the board of directors of the Smocking Arts Guild of America and has presented workshops on French sewing by machine throughout the United States, Australia, England, and New Zealand. Books she has written and published include *French Hand Sewing by Machine, A Beginner's Guide; Heirloom Doll Clothes; Bearly Beginning Smocking; Shadow Work Embroidery; French Sewing by Machine: The Second Book; Antique Clothing: French Sewing by Machine; Grandmother's Hope Chest; Applique, Martha's Favorites; Heirloom Sewing For Women; Joy of Smocking; Martha's Sewing Room, Victorian Sewing And Crafts* and *Martha's Heirloom Magic.*

Martha is also the founder and publisher of a best-selling magazine, *Sew Beautiful,* which is dedicated to heirloom sewing. The publication charms more than 80,000 readers worldwide. She has just completed a television series for public television entitled, *"Martha's Sewing Room."*

She is the wife of Joseph Ross Pullen, an implant dentist, mother of five of the most wonderful children in the world, and grandmother of the six most beautiful, intelligent, precious and most adorable grandchildren in the world. She participates in many civic activities and is an active member of her church. She also volunteers with the Southern Baptist Foreign Mission Board.